Cases in American Foreign Policy

DONALD M. **SNOW**

University of Alabama

PEARSON

Boston   Columbus   Indianapolis   New York   San Francisco   Upper Saddle River
Amsterdam   Cape Town   Dubai   London   Madrid   Milan   Munich   Paris   Montreal   Toronto
Delhi   Mexico City   São Paulo   Sydney   Hong Kong   Seoul   Singapore   Taipei   Tokyo

Senior Acquisition Editor: Vik Mukhija
Editorial Assistants: Isabel Schwab,
Beverly Fong
Marketing Managers: Wendy Gordon,
Lindsey Prudhomme
Production Manager: Meghan DeMaio
Creative Director: Jayne Conte

Cover Designer: Karen Noferi
Cover Art: © Corbis
Project Coordination, Text Design, and
Electronic Page Makeup: Chitra Ganesan
PreMediaGlobal
Printer/Binder/Cover Printer: Courier
Companies

Library of Congress Cataloging-in-Publication Data
Snow, Donald M.,
   Cases in American foreign policy / Donald M. Snow.
      p. cm.
   Includes index.
   ISBN-13: 978-0-205-56793-5
   ISBN-10: 0-205-56793-2
   1. United States—Foreign relations—21st century—Case studies.   I. Title.
   JZ1480.S547 2012
   327.73—dc23
                                                           2011049943

ISBN 10: 0-205-56793-2
ISBN 13: 978-0-205-56793-5

BRIEF CONTENTS

CONTENTS

PREFACE

INTRODUCTION

During the third full week of May 2011, the "unsustainable" met the "indefensible" in Washington, DC. The forum was a fascinating and important international event that played itself out in Washington and Tel Aviv between the president of the United States, Barack Obama, and the prime minister of Israel, Benjamin Netanyahu. The context of the event was the state visit of Netanyahu to the United States. Given the frequency of high-level Israeli interaction with the United States government (it was Netanyahu's third trip to the American capital since Obama took office), there was nothing terribly unusual about the fact that the head of state of Israel would visit his American counterpart. What underlay the agenda between the two leaders and how those dynamics were enacted, however, represents a more fascinating, in-depth view of the operation of foreign policy in the modern international system.

The heart of the foreign policy question between the two states was the status of the moribund peace negotiations between Israel and the Palestinians, the central focus of which is, and has for some time been, the creation of a sovereign Palestinian state on territory occupied by Israel after the Six Days War of 1967—notably the Gaza Strip and the West Bank of the Jordan River. There is disagreement within both countries about the proper approach to those problems, and because Obama represents one position on the Palestinian question and Netanyahu represents its opposite, the internal debates become a foreign policy disagreement between the two countries as well. To Obama, the failure to make progress toward a Palestinian state represents an "unsustainable" situation (for reasons discussed in Chapter 11), and for Netanyahu, progress toward that goal according to the blueprint proposed by Obama is "indefensible" (for reasons also discussed in Chapter 11). Both leaders have their supporters and detractors in both countries; much of the purpose of the Netanyahu visit was to reinforce American supporters of *his* position and in the process to discourage Obama from active pursuit of his vision based in that opposition. The most open and public manifestations of this attempt by the leader of a foreign country to influence the policy of the United States government by effectively bypassing the president and appealing directly to American public opinion were Netanyahu's invited address to a joint session of the United States Congress on May 24 and his address to the most powerful pro-Israeli interest group in the United States, the American–Israeli Public Affairs Committee (AIPAC) on May 23. Obama explained his position in a televised address at the U.S. State Department on May 19 (before Netanyahu's arrival) and defended it before AIPAC after Netanyahu had spoken to them.

States seeking to influence one another is, of course, nothing unusual; doing so is much of the gist of foreign policy. The manner in which Netanyahu sought to influence the U.S. government was, however, different. In essence, he overtly sought to convince Americans, and their elected leaders, to reject the position of the president of the United States and to support the position of his government. Effectively, he did so by bypassing the traditional diplomatic forums in which such persuasion takes place in the interplay of governments. Instead, he sought to employ a form of public diplomacy to demonstrate to the president that his (Netanyahu's) position was more popular in the United States than Obama's and that he could mobilize that opinion to force the American leader to change policies. Had virtually any other head of state attempted a similar ploy, that leader would have been widely condemned for an improper intrusion by a foreign leader into the affairs of the United States. Because Israel occupies a special relationship with the United States, there was hardly a public murmur of dissent.

This episode is but one example of how the foreign policy landscape is changing. Much of the heart of foreign policy remains the formal relations of sovereign states with one another, but increasingly new actors and new forms and forums of interactions are becoming part of the equation and must be incorporated into discussions and understandings of foreign policy. The idea that a foreign leader could come to the United States and publicly disagree with a sitting American president would have been unthinkable a generation ago; with a changed international climate and domestic context, it was part of the new business as usual, what is now discussed within foreign policy analysis circles as a form of public diplomacy (appealing directly to national publics as a way to influence foreign policy).

Foreign policy remains a complex business operating at the intersection between domestic and international politics and evincing characteristics and dynamics of each environment. Much of the contemporary literature on and thought about how those influences are changing are highlighted in contemporary analyses of foreign affairs, including matters such as group dynamics in perceiving and making foreign policy decisions, the impact of private citizens and nongovernmental organizations (NGOs) in the interplay between states, and some decline in the general notion of a state-centric international environment employing the traditional tools of statecraft to achieve policy ends.

All of these new influences, and others, are certainly important additions to thinking about foreign policy and understanding it at a broad, systemic level. At the same time, the day-to-day conduct of foreign policy remains largely the province of state governments interacting with one another in idiosyncratic ways that are defined in terms of the individual characteristics of those states and the history and pattern of interactions between them. These interactions are not the totality of foreign policy, but they are an important source of the raw data on which any inquiry must be based. Moreover, it is specific situations and contexts that shape and must be consulted to understand the vagaries in how the United States deals with other states and how other states deal with it. That a world leader like Netanyahu could come to the United States and act in an official role in the manner that he did in May 2011 requires understanding discrete factors such as the American historic relationship with the state of Israel and the impact of Jewish and non-Jewish supporters of Israel within the United States. The "science" of foreign policy analysis is not so advanced that it can provide definitive, scientifically sound explanations of important parts of its subject without reference to these discrete factors.

Foreign policy and its analysis is, of course, more than the relations between the United States and individual countries, which is the topic of this book. While such an observation is clearly true and acknowledged by the author, it is equally true that part of the core of U.S. (or any other country's) foreign policy is indeed the pattern of its interactions with the world other individual countries. A study of foreign policy that ignores nontraditional sources of foreign policy will necessarily be incomplete, but an approach that ignores or does not take those relations into account will likewise be incomplete.

FEATURES

The chapters in this study attempt to address part of the equation involved in studying foreign policy by presenting descriptive studies of American foreign policy toward 12 individual countries. The country studies are paired into six parts of the manuscript based on the author's perception of how they best relate to one another and thus how they illustrate important underlying themes and interrelationships as they exist in American foreign policy in the world.

The ordering and combination of cases is suggestive, not restrictive. The organization as presented is a backbone of sorts for the internal organization of the text, but it by no means is intended to suggest what studies in what order should be assigned in any particular foreign policy course. Indeed, the internal organization of each individual chapter supports independence in case selection and ordering by adopting a common organization for each study, facilitating combining any of the individual studies with one another.

All of the chapters have several common features. Each pair of chapters begins with an introduction of the pair of studies within it. These introductions are intended both to introduce what American policies toward the two paired countries have in common and what dynamics may be shared. Thus, for instance, the introduction to Part II contains a brief discussion of the general dynamics of the nuclear proliferation problem (the major commonality between the two cases), thereby covering materials that would otherwise have to be repeated in each of the studies. Even if, for instance, an instructor were to assign the case on Iran but not North Korea (or vice versa), there would still be some intellectual virtue in assigning the introduction and telling students to pay less attention to the material on the case not assigned.

Each case study follows a common format intended to facilitate comparison across all cases or any two or more individual cases; indeed, one of the principal reasons for an original, single-authored text was to provide a uniformity of coverage impossible to achieve in compendia of published articles or even of papers commissioned to different experts expressly for a comparable volume. Each chapter begins with a preview that briefly suggests the major points and direction of the case. The preview is followed by brief introductory remarks about the country under study intended to create context for the lay reader and to introduce whatever pattern of historic relations with the United States may exist. The discussion then turns to a sketch of the country, divided into sections about its place in the world, general and specific statistical and comparative data about the country, and unique factors about that country in the contemporary world environment and as a problem for American foreign policy.

The major emphasis of the chapter is captured in the next and major section, U.S. relation with the particular country, emphasizing and organized around existing sources of dispute and contention between the two countries. The chapter then turns to a section that examines U.S. options for dealing with the particular country, followed by a concluding statement. Each chapter ends with a series of study and discussion questions covering the chapter's content and a list of reading and research materials that contains both studies cited directly in the body of the chapter and references for further examination of the country and its relations with the United States.

The actual text is divided into six pairs of country studies. The part structure acts as a kind of fish's backbone that provides an organizational rationale, but the consumer may wish to "de-bone" the fish before eating it (i.e., the structure does not dictate how it may be used). Part I examines how the United States has adjusted its relations with its two primary Cold War adversaries, the Soviet Union (now Russia) and China. Chapter 1 emphasizes the difficult adjustments Russia has made to its post–Cold War status and how the United States is affected by and seeks to affect that process of adjustment. Chapter 2 examines Sino–American relations, primarily through the lens of the growing economic interconnection between the two countries, the ongoing dynamics of that interrelationship, and the implications of those relations in a more uncertain future.

Part II examines both the nature of the problem of the spread of nuclear weapons to countries that do not currently possess them (nuclear proliferation) and the particular challenges that the two most frequently alleged nuclear proliferators, Iran and North Korea, pose to the international system and the United States. The emphases are different. Iran is a regional power currently without nuclear weapons and one whose policies are at odds with other countries in the area and the United States, to which the potential possession of nuclear weapons only adds complications and dangers. North Korea already possesses a small number of nuclear devices that serve as its major source of leverage on the regional and global scenes, and the major problem is how to persuade Pyongyang to abandon its arsenal.

Part III concentrates on the content and interplay of American relations with the two major rivals of the Asian subcontinent, India and Pakistan. India is by far the larger country, is the world's most populous political democracy, and stands poised to enter the ranks of the world's most important economic powers. Pakistan, on the other hand, is a clearly struggling, unstable state whose primary current interests to the United States lie in its participation in the American military effort in Afghanistan and the contest with global terrorism. Their mutual antagonism and history of conflict make relations with each difficult.

Part IV deals with the foreign relations involved in America's two wars of the twenty-first century, Iraq and Afghanistan. Both situations have some common elements (geographic location, for instance) but are otherwise discrete. The war against Iraq and the long occupation after it was almost entirely an American initiative, and the United States is now attempting to make the transition away from the occupation to dealing with Iraq as a normal sovereign state, with Iranian influence in postoccupation Iraq a major influence. The war in Afghanistan, on the other hand, was a direct response to the terrorist attacks of 9/11 and the sanctuary provided to Al Qaeda, although the war has continued since the Al Qaeda presence has virtually disappeared. The core of the ongoing problem is how the United States can end its involvement in what has become America's longest war.

Part V looks at American relations with two of its closest neighbors, Mexico and Cuba. The relations with each have a long and rich history but have been markedly different over the past half century. American foreign policy with Mexico has come to be focused on the issue of the two countries' long shared border, although the border veneer arguably provides a curtain behind which more profound concerns such as the nature of immigration, drugs, and even national security lurk. Relations with Cuba have been essentially nonexistent for the 50 years since Fidel Castro consolidated his communist revolution on the island, and Cuban exiles have helped shape a highly negative U.S. stance toward Cuba intended to force Castro and his policies off the island. Current concerns center on whether or how relations can be improved.

Part VI analyzes American relations with two of the most critical countries involved in Middle East politics, Israel and Egypt. The U.S.–Israeli relationship has been close since the declaration of the Israeli state in 1948, and the United States has served as the principal foreign guarantor of Israeli security since. Relations are strained, however, by disagreement about the peace process between Israel and its Arab neighbors (including Egypt), as illustrated by the May 2011 episode by which this preface was introduced. Egypt has been one of the major focal points of the so-called Arab Spring of 2011, and a major aspect of U.S. relations with Egypt is how the United States can make the transition from support for deposed Egyptian strongman Hosni Mubarak to a new and more popularly based Egyptian leadership.

SUPPLEMENTS

Pearson is pleased to offer several resources to qualified adopters of *Cases in American Foreign Policy* and their students that will make teaching and learning from this book even more effective and enjoyable.

Passport

Choose the resources you want from MyPoliSciLab and put links to them into your course management system. If there is assessment associated with those resources, it also can be uploaded, allowing the results to feed directly into your course management system's gradebook. With MyPoliSciLab assets like videos, mapping exercises, *Financial Times* newsfeeds, current events quizzes, politics blog, and much more, Passport is available for any Pearson political science book. To order Passport with the print text, use ISBN 0-205-20846-0.

MySearchLab

For over 10 years, instructors and students have reported achieving better results and better grades when a Pearson MyLab has been integrated into the course. MySearchLab provides engaging experiences that personalize learning and comes from a trusted partner with educational expertise and a deep commitment to helping students and instructors achieve their goals. A wide range of writing, grammar, and research tools and access to a variety of academic journals, census data, Associated Press newsfeeds, and discipline-specific readings help you hone your writing and research skills. To order MySearchLab with the print text, use ISBN 0-205-20845-2.

Longman Atlas of World Issues (0-205-78020-2)

From population and political systems to energy use and women's rights, the *Longman Atlas of World Issues* features full-color thematic maps that examine the forces shaping the world. Featuring maps from the latest edition of *The Penguin State of the World Atlas*, this excerpt includes critical thinking exercises to promote a deeper understanding of how geography affects many global issues.

Goode's World Atlas (0-321-65200-2)

First published by Rand McNally in 1923, *Goode's World Atlas* has set the standard for college reference atlases. It features hundreds of physical, political, and thematic maps as well as graphs, tables, and a pronouncing index.

ACKNOWLEDGMENTS

I would like to thank my colleagues at Pearson for their work on this book, including Vikram Mukhija, Beverly Fong, Lindsey Prudhomme, and Denise Phillip.

I would also like to thank the reviewers who made useful comments on this first edition, including John Ambacher, Framingham State College; Spencer

Bakich, Sweet Briar College; David Clinton, Baylor University; Andrew Essig, DeSales University; Katharine Floros, University of Missouri; Bryan-Paul Frost, University of Louisiana at Lafayette; Joseph Gaziano, Lewis University; Patrick Haney, Miami University; Eric Hines, University of Montana; Claus Hofhansel, Rhode Island College; Debra Holzhauer, Southeast Missouri State University; Christopher Jones, Northern Illinois University; Michael Kanner, University of Colorado–Boulder; Richard Krupa, Harper College; Peter Loedel, West Chester University; Lucas McMillan, Lander University; Jeffrey Mozier, Johns Hopkins University; Ellen Pirro, Iowa State University; Jungkun Seo, University of North Carolina–Wilmington; Jonathan Strand, University of Nevada–Las Vegas; Jon Western, Mount Holyoke College; David Yamanishi, Cornell College; and Adam Yeeles, University of Texas-Dallas.

Old Adversaries
and New Realities

During most of the second half of the twentieth century, the major focus of American foreign policy was on the international competition between the anticommunist coalition of states it led and the communist world—the Cold War. The two major pillars in the communist alignment of countries were also the world's two largest countries: the Soviet Union as the world's largest country in physical area and the People's Republic of China as the world's most populous state. This period effectively ended with the collapse of the Soviet Union and its Eastern European allies in 1991. The Soviet Union has been succeeded by a reduced Russian Federation that struggled throughout the 1990s to reestablish itself and that has only emerged in the 2000s as a viable player in the international realm, whereas China has steadily progressed to major power status on the back of its vibrant, capitalist-infused economic expansion. During the Cold War, the Soviet Union was the major concern of American foreign policy, with China occupying a somewhat lesser role; in the contemporary world order, those priorities are arguably reversed.

In the process of this transformation, the basic nature of relations between the United States and its principal Cold War enemies has changed in different ways with each country. What were relationships expressed almost exclusively in adversarial, military terms have become less confrontational, more congenial, and less easily represented primarily (or even largely) in military terms. The United States, Russia, and China are former adversaries, and much of the content of their relationships with one another is over the content and essence of post–Cold War relationships.

The process of change has not been easy for decision makers and especially for senior leaders who were either educated in the Cold War years or served in positions of authority or influence and whose frame of reference in the world was shaped by the mental constructs of Cold War thinking. This distinction may seem academic, even foreign, to the reader who was either not alive or cognizant of the foreign policy environment of the late twentieth century and to whom these distinctions are little more than abstractions on thinking about the Russians or the Chinese, but they are quite real and influential to those who lived through the Cold War.

The Cold War affected decision makers' perceptual framework in two distinct ways. First, the Cold War was a pervasive, compelling confrontation between the so-called "free world" bloc of countries led by the United States and the communist bloc led and controlled by Russia (as the Soviet Union) and, to a lesser extent, China. Managing that competition short of war was the first priority of foreign (and much domestic) policy before which all other priorities paled, and the United States developed an overall strategy for the competition—containment—that dictated U.S. policy toward other countries, international organizations like the United Nations, and even subnational groups like political parties or revolutionary movements within countries. When the communist threat collapsed, the overarching framework was rendered largely irrelevant, and American policy makers have struggled with little success to find a successor principle around which to anchor general foreign policy.

Second, a prime element of the Cold War environment was that it featured a competition between adversaries who thought of themselves as one another's enemies. This coloration of the relationship created the presumption of adversarial enmity in all relations between the principal contestants. That mutual perception has been difficult to overcome and has left a legacy of suspicion among Americans, Russians, and Chinese that is part of the perceptual environment in which policy is crafted.

Relations with the two countries have evolved in different ways. Post–Cold War Russia has struggled internally and externally in trying to adjust to a new political and economic reality and a new place in the world. Central to the foreign policy element of that adjustment has been the attempt to reinvigorate Russian power and prestige, largely through economic means, to reassert Russian status as a great power. The bulk of American power has been used both to try to help shape Russian internal development in democratic, pro-Western ways and to try to ensure that Russia becomes a fully "normal" state internationally. It has only been partially successful, primarily because the Russian leadership clings tenaciously to visions of returning Russia to the ranks of the great powers, an aspiration that raises fears of a return to a more aggressive Soviet past.

Relations with China have been dramatically different. During the early Cold War period, between 1949 and 1972, the two countries did not acknowledge one another's existence at the official level, and they have gone, in the period since, to becoming two of the world's premier trading and economic partners. Much of this change reflects the priorities of the Chinese in the economic realm, particularly as the Chinese fashioned themselves into the world's largest producer of consumer manufactured goods and unleashed their productivity on the world's most gluttonous consumer, the United States. In the process, China has emerged as an economic superpower challenging American preeminence in ways that some find troubling.

The nature of relations with these two countries is evolving differently as a result. Relations with Russia remain proper but cool and still have significant national security content over matters such as nuclear arms control (the New START) and the Russian invasion of Georgia in 2009. While some observers worry about a national security conflict with China, the primary concern is with the evolving economic relationship, and especially the growing indebtedness of the United States to the Chinese government and China's projected status as the world's largest economy.

Russia: Negotiating and Shaping Relations with a Former Adversary

PREVIEW

Russian–American relations were the central feature of U.S. foreign policy from the end of World War II until the implosion of the Soviet Union formally in 1991. Russia endured a serious decline by virtually all measures during the 1990s but has experienced a rebirth and resurgence internally and internationally during the 2000s. In the process, Russia first declined and later resumed a major place in American foreign policy as Russia's own circumstance has fluctuated. In the current context, a series of issues continue to divide the two countries, including maintenance of the nuclear balance between them, relations between Russia and its successor republics in Eurasia, and the continuing nature of the evolution of Russia as a political and economic entity. All this occurs within an American foreign policy debate over the direction of U.S. policy, of which Russian–American relations is a showcase example.

O n October 1, 1939, Sir Winston Churchill, in a broadcast in Great Britain on the same day that Nazi German armies entered the Polish capital of Warsaw, described Russia (then the Soviet Union) as "a riddle wrapped in a mystery inside an enigma." The statement, intended to capture the inscrutability of Russia and the difficulty of dealing with the Russians, was issued in the context of the German occupation of Poland, which had been at least partially endorsed by an agreement between the Soviets and the Germans on August 23, 1939—the so-called Nazi-Soviet or Molotov-Ribbentrop (named after the Soviet and Nazi foreign ministers who had negotiated it) Non-Aggression Treaty, one of the provisions of which divided Poland between them. In his radio address, Churchill, who would lead Great Britain through the war that had begun when the Germans initially crossed into Poland on September 1, 1939, said of the Soviets that they had "pursued a policy of cold self-interest in Poland." The Soviet Union, of course, later became an ally of the West in the war, playing a crucial role in the eventual overthrow of the Axis regimes.

The 1939 incident and description of Russia at the time rings nearly as true today as it did then in terms of describing the evolution of Russia and American relations with the world's physically largest country. Through history, there has always been a dynamic tension between the United States and Russia that goes back to the founding of the American republic. Russia was, for instance, a member of the Armed Neutrality of European states that opposed the British during the American Revolution and that at least implicitly provided assistance to the fledgling American colonies. San Franciscans, on the other hand, will tell you that the real purpose of issuing the Monroe Doctrine of 1823 was to warn the Russians, who were at the time establishing a fur-trading colony in San Francisco Bay (presumably including on Russian Hill) to desist in their colonization of what would become part of the expanding United States. Collaboration between the two countries during World War II quickly turned into the encompassing, potentially civilization-threatening Cold War that dominated international relations and their bilateral relations between the late 1940s and 1991, when the Soviet Union imploded and ceased to exist.

The Russian Federation, the main successor to the Soviet state, has been struggling to develop an identity and new place in the world ever since, including a tumultuous, even torturous evolution away from communism during the balance of the 1990s to a petroleum-propelled resurgence in the 2000s. The United States has cheered the positive side of this evolution, including the semblance of market economics and at least the traces of political democratization, and has viewed more cautiously the recent centralization of less democratically inspired politics within Russia. For many purposes, that development remains behind the veil of Western, and specifically American, full understanding: Russia indeed remains the multilayered complex of riddle, mystery, and enigma that Churchill described over 70 years ago.

American foreign policy toward Russia has reflected both the changing circumstances of Russia, its place in the world, and disagreement about how to deal with the Russians. Russia itself has been on a political roller coaster ride, both internally and in its foreign relations. The Russian Empire was part of the classic European balance of power that was shattered by World War I, and during the interwar years, the communist Soviet state that replaced the empire struggled to establish itself and to achieve acceptance as a major power in the international order, a historic goal of Russian affairs that continues to this day. The final decimation of the old international order in the flames of World War II left the Soviets, along with the United States, as the sole remaining global powers of the postwar period, and their Cold War confrontation dominated the international order for 40 or more years. The Soviets' status as an unquestioned superpower was shattered by the death of the Soviet state of which Russia was the center, and the Russians have been attempting to reestablish their importance in the global order ever since, a prospect that Americans view with divided enthusiasm.

Russia was, and still remains, one of the most economically and politically undeveloped of major powers. Dating back to the tsarist days, Russia has vacillated between periods of embrace of or isolation from the West and its political and economic ideas, choosing to assimilate in some ways at different times and eschewing Western forms or influences at others, and that pattern remains today. One of the critical flaws that helped lead to the collapse of operational communism was its inability to compete with the West, and strategies going back to Tsar Peter the Great in the early eighteenth century have attempted to incorporate parts of the West (most notably technology, as described later in the chapter) while retaining the distinctiveness of Russia in the process. Some aspects of the West, notably political democratization, have historically been alien to Russian development as a state, and the debate within Russia about how much of what the West calls development to adopt remains central.

Westerners, including Americans, have witnessed this vast Eurasian power with alternating levels of hope and suspicion. Europeans, with a longer and more intimate relationship with Russia than the Americans, have tended to treat Russia with more suspicion and caution. Americans, on the other hand, have applauded more enthusiastically when Russia has shown more active signs of westernization such as the apparent democratization that emerged in the 1990s under Boris Yeltsin, and they have consequently been more disappointed when such efforts seem not to achieve a broad-based emulation of Western democracy, as they appear not to have under the tandem leadership of Vladimir Putin and Dmitry Medvedev. Partly as a result, the domestic politics of U.S.–Russian relations are based in a schism between those optimists who see and hope to achieve a movement of Russia more intimately into the Euro-Atlantic order (the apparent goal of the Obama administration) and skeptics who reject the idea of Russian change and believe the relationship must remain largely framed in adversarial terms (the basic position of many within the George W. Bush administration).

These observations set the context within which to frame the discussion of U.S.–Russian relations. They are, as the subtitle suggests, historically enigmatic, fluctuating from periods of apparently greater comity and cooperation to periods of equally great despair about their present and future direction. It has become commonplace to describe the relationship as being at a critical "crossroads," but that description has been used so often as to border on being hackneyed. It is a complex relationship, as is probably fitting for two large and complex countries, each of which spans a continent physically and each of which has been and, at least in some respects remains, central to international relations.

Current Russian relations with the United States are somewhere between the poles of basic comity and conflict. The major theme of those relations currently hinges on the resurgence of Russia as a major power and how the

United States should deal with and attempt to influence that growth in Russia's place around the table of countries within a framework of less encompassing ties between the two countries because, as Shleifer and Treisman put it, "Today, Russia and the United States share few interests and even fewer priorities." The major engine of Russian reassertion of its place has been its emergence as a major energy supplier to the world, but everyone, including its leadership, basically understands that the energy stimulus cannot long endure and that Russia must diversify to compete. In its quest for development, it has been led by two leaders in the twenty-first century, Putin and Medvedev. Putin is an emblematic incarnation of the Churchillian vision of Russia, a powerful yet inscrutable figure originally plucked from obscurity within the Russian intelligence community by Boris Yeltsin but clearly obsessed with a return to Russian greatness and displaying a lesser commitment to democratization than westerners would prefer. Medvedev seems a more pliant, positive individual, but it is unclear how independent his power base is from Putin's and whether optimistic depictions of him are soundly grounded or the result of not-atypical Western wishful thinking. The 2012 Russian presidential elections shed some light on this subject; the one clear outcome is that Putin remains the senior partner in the relationship. In the meantime, Russia and the West remain tentative, and partially suspicious, partners.

RUSSIA: A SKETCH

Russia is a difficult, if not impossible, place to typify in simple, broad-brush terms. The Russian Federation that emerged from the rubble of the disintegrated USSR is physically the world's largest country, with a land area that spans the Eurasian area; as the Union of Soviet Socialist Republics, its physical area was over 8.5 million square miles (by contrast, the land area of the United States is 3.8 million square miles), and even after the splintering of the USSR into 15 independent states, the Federation retains 6.6 million square miles (approximately 1.8 times the size of the United States). Despite this physical vastness, however, Russia has historically had trouble feeding itself, with only 7 percent of its land considered arable; the rest is either too cold or too dry to sustain agricultural production.

The Russian enigma runs throughout any description one may draw of the country. Russia has existed as an entity since the thirteenth century, but much of it was under Mongol rule for two centuries, and the Russian Empire did not emerge as a major world actor until the eighteenth century. Although formally a part of the European balance of power during the eighteenth and nineteenth centuries, the Russian Empire was always considered something of an outsider among the royal courts of Europe, part Asian as well as part European, and the poorest, most backward member of the system. One of the consequences of World War I (in which Russia performed poorly and eventually sued for peace) was the overthrow of the imperial government and its replacement by the Bolshevik communists under V. I. Lenin; after the war, the other countries of Europe sought to isolate and exclude Russia in a "quarantine" they hoped would result in curing Russia from the "disease" of communism. The treatment, of course, did not succeed, and the Soviet Union (as the USSR was known in shorthand terms) emerged alongside the United States as one of the two major participants in the Cold War competition that dominated world politics from the late 1940s until the collapse of the Soviet Union in 1991.

The implosion of the Soviet Union is one of the most remarkable political events of the twentieth century and is a unique event in world politics. While Russia has endured for nearly 800 years, the Soviet experiment lasted less than 75 years from the beginning of the Bolshevik Revolution in 1917 until December 26, 1991, when its dissolution was formally announced by the government of Mikhail S. Gorbachev. What is remarkable is not that the Soviet state dissolved or that a regime and form of government was replaced; both have happened in the international realm. What *was* remarkable is that the process of dissolution of the Soviet Union occurred peacefully, with scarcely a hint or threat of violence. The result was that the Soviet Union—the inheritor of the Russian Empire that included most of the lands the empire had conquered and annexed—reverted to 15 independent states, of which Russia is the largest and most prominent.

The Russian reaction to this dissolution has been ambivalent. The Communist Party that had ruled for the duration of the Soviet experience has drastically declined (although some of its members have resurfaced in other guises), and residual longing for a return to the Soviet system is minimal. At the same time, the breakup has meant that physical Russia is diminished as a world actor, a situation about which there is considerable regret among many Russians. Vladimir Putin, who has characterized the demise of the Soviet Union as the most tragic world event of the twentieth century, is the strong symbol of this nostalgia.

The long-term impact of the breakup of the Soviet Union has been to leave Russia as a lesser state on the world stage than it was during its most glorious run as a Cold War superpower, and it has been the major theme of Russian foreign policy to find ways to reassert Russian influence and power in the world. How this can be accomplished, and how its pursuit should be viewed and aided or impeded, has been a major part of evolving American foreign policy toward its former major adversary in the world.

Russia in the World

The major dynamic of Russia as a part of the international system over the past half century has been akin to a pendulum swing, where one extremity of the swing is toward greater power and prestige and the other is a decline in both power and prestige. A half-century ago, the Soviet Union was one of the two great powers in the Cold War, and it was a state that seemed to many people around the world to be on the ascendancy in its competition with the capitalist world led by the United States. The peak of Soviet power, it now appears in retrospect, probably occurred somewhere around 1970, when by measures like nuclear weapons explosive power the Soviet Union surpassed the United States. By the early 1970s, however, tiny fissures began to appear in the façade of Soviet power, primarily in the form of the beginnings of economic decline that would ultimately contribute mightily to its decline and collapse. These problems were largely unnoticed or unappreciated either within or outside the Soviet Union, contributing to the utter surprise with which the implosion was received at the end of the 1980s. After the Soviet Union voted itself out of existence in 1991, the Russian Federation witnessed the continuing decline of former Soviet power, reaching its nadir at the end of the decade. The 2000s have seen the pendulum swing back to a larger role for Russia in the world.

All this change was both unprecedented and unanticipated. Seeing Russia adorned with vast nuclear and conventional military power, few in the West considered the possibility that the Soviet Union was really a Potemkin village—a false front—behind which the bases of Soviet power were slowly but inexorably crumbling. As is now known (but was not then), Soviet decline was well underway by the early 1970s in the form of economic decline, what Soviet economists later called "the era of stagnation." What that meant was that the socialist economy of the world's largest country simply quit growing and, by most measures, fell into decline in the early 1970s, progressively affecting the ability of the Soviet Union to compete across the board. The conditions that would undermine the Soviet state were exacerbated by the disastrous Soviet invasion and occupation of Afghanistan between 1979 and 1989 and, along with the increasingly visible nonperformance of the Soviet economy, convinced Communist Party general secretary Gorbachev that the Soviets could no longer afford to compete with the West but rather needed to end the competition and join more actively the world system.

These decisions, collectively known as *glasnost* (openness) and *perestroika* (restructuring), included democratization and a nonconfrontational foreign policy known as "new thinking" and were intended to fine-tune and improve, not to destroy, the Soviet socialist system, as Gorbachev explained in his 1987 book *Perestroika*. Their effect, however, was to open dissent, criticism, and ultimately demands for dismantling the structure of the Soviet Union. The process became public and ineluctable in 1989, as the countries of the Soviet orbit in Eastern Europe overthrew communist regimes and renounced their affiliation with the Soviet Union. They were soon joined by member republics of the USSR, who declared their intentions to secede from the union. When Moscow did not respond to stop the process, it continued. With the last tick of the clock in 1991, the Soviet hammer-and-sickle flag came down from atop the Kremlin, replaced on New Year's Day, 1992, by the Russian tricolor.

Russia was sent reeling by the experience. The shaky Soviet economy went into a freefall as it attempted to adopt Western values and forms with essentially no preparation for the transformation. The Soviet Union, for instance, was largely a noncash economy, meaning it had neither an efficient banking system nor the means to handle capital or capital transfer. The country also had no central bank to regulate the economy, which meant there was no reliable mechanism through which outside economic assistance could be made available to the Russians, for instance. In these circumstances, the black market thrived, and the Russian mafia emerged as a major economic participant and source of lawlessness within a chaotic society. In these circumstances, living conditions worsened in the Federation, and about the only bright spot to which Russians and outsiders could turn was that the country was able to hold reasonably honest elections at the federal level.

This reduced situation was enormously embarrassing to the proud, status-conscious Russians, and returning their country to its place among the first ranks of world powers was a common aspiration of most Russians at the millennium's turn. The figure who seized upon this desire and rode it to political power was Putin, a former career KGB officer whose name has become synonymous in the West with Russian resurgence and even Russian resistance to the West. His rise has coincided with and been propelled by some erosion of political democracy as the Russian condition is improved and, as Laqueur puts it, "Putin's strength [is that] the Russian people prefer stability to democracy." The engine of Russian resurgence has been economic revival, and the fuel for that engine has been the emergence of Russia as a major energy exporting country, joining what *New York Times* political correspondent Thomas L. Friedman terms the ranks of "petrolist" countries—states whose economy is closely tied to energy exports and where energy revenues are used by the state effectively to buy political support from the population. Much of the problem that Russia poses for American foreign policy is how intricately tied the Russian future is to a form of economic development that is also not conducive to Russia's emergence as a modern democratic partner.

The Physical Setting

The Russian condition is at least partially defined by its geographic characteristics and by its demographics. The most notable geographic features include the physical size of Russia and the natural resources within its boundaries. The demographics include an ethnically diverse population, particularly along its extremities, and a declining population among citizens of the Russian Federation.

As noted, Russia has the world's largest land area (Canada is second, the United States third). It physically spans Eurasia from the Baltic Sea in the west to the Pacific Ocean in the east. The Arctic Ocean essentially defines its northern boundary. It also borders on 13 different states. Its longest boundaries are with four countries: Kazakhstan* (6,846 km), China (3,645 km), Mongolia (3,485 km), and Ukraine* (1,576 km). Other countries bordering on Russia are Azerbaijan*, Belarus*, Estonia*, Finland, Georgia*, Latvia*, Lithuania*, North Korea, and Norway. Most of these countries (those noted with an asterisk) are former republics of the Soviet Union, who were former parts of the Russian Empire or were otherwise forcefully added to the Soviet Union and are considered by the Russians as the "near abroad," which the Russians now like to claim are part of its "sphere of privileged interests" (a euphemism for sphere of influence). Others include other former or current communist countries not part of the Soviet Union, and two Scandinavian states. What these states share is some level of animosity toward Russia. It has been said that Russia is surrounded by richly earned enemies, and it is not a bad description. Being ringed by potential adversaries adds to the Russian compulsion with security matters.

The vast Russian territory provides both advantages and limitations. As already noted, climate leaves only a fraction of Russia arable, and the country struggles to become agriculturally self-sufficient (a priority of the Medvedev government). An additional burden of Russian geography and climate is that Russia has always lacked warm-weather ports (port facilities that are not blocked by ice for part of the year), and it has been a geopolitically necessary priority of historic Russian foreign policy to try to gain permanent access to warm-water ports both for naval and commercial purposes. At the same time, Russia is richly endowed with mineral and energy resources. The latter have provided the basis for considerable Russian economic revival, although they are also a double-edged sword.

Russia has emerged in the twenty-first century as the world's second largest exporter of petroleum and as the world's leading supplier of natural gas. According to 2009 figures, Russia exports almost five million barrels of oil per day (bbl/day), ranking it behind only Saudi Arabia as a world supplier. The overwhelming importance of oil and gas to the economy is demonstrated by Shleifer and Treisman's observation that "hydrocarbons fund about one-third of the Russian government's budget."

Russian demographics is a sword that hangs over the country's future. The population of Russia according to July 2010 estimates in the *CIA World Factbook* stood at 139,300,000, making Russia the ninth most populous country in the world. That gross number is down from even two years earlier (when it stood at a little over 140 million), and the demographic time lines are all negative. The population growth rate (birth rate minus death rate) is –.465 percent, and life expectancy in Russia is actually in decline at 66.16 years, which is 161st in the world. This decline exists despite a Russian medical system that is far better than most other countries that have short life expectancies, and the figures are in worse decline for ethnic Russians (who comprise 80 percent of the country's population) than it is for other groups. Moreover, the mortality rate is not compensated for by an increased fertility rate, as Eberstadt explains: "By 2025, Russia is projected to have just 6.4 million women in their twenties, 35 percent fewer than today." To maintain population at its current levels, women generally need to produce 2.1 offspring each—in the Russian demographic situation, this smaller cohort of women would have to have an average of four children each, when the fertility rate is currently 1.5 children per woman.

The result is that the population of Russia is becoming both smaller and less Russian, with potentially dire consequences. Eberstadt summarizes the short- to medium-term problem: "Russia today is in the grips of an eerie, far-reaching, and in some ways historically unprecedented population crisis. Since the end of the Soviet era, the population of the Russian Federation has fallen by nearly 7 million, [and] life expectancy at birth in Russia looks to be lower today than it was four decades ago." In the longer term, the problem could be even worse. Ukrainian anti-Russian politician Yuliya Tymoshenko, for instance, predicts that "Russia's population will shrink even more dramatically, perhaps to below 100 million by the middle of the twenty-first century." In a RAND study, DaVargo and Grammich concur, arguing the Russian population could shrink by one-third by 2050.

Thanks both to its size and historically low levels of development, the Russian Federation has an impressive array of natural resources, and especially energy resources, that it has been able to exploit to fuel the economic resurgence associated with the Putin years (notably his presidency from 2000 to 2008). Even the impressive expansion of the energy sector, however, has had costs that shadow the future of the Federation, in at least three ways.

The most obvious problem is that the rate of exploitation of energy resources is not indefinitely sustainable and must be augmented for overall economic growth to occur. As noted, Russia is the world's second largest exporter, but it has only the world's eighth largest known reserves of petroleum (at 79 billion barrels). Continuing exploitation at current rates means Russian reserves will be depleted more quickly than those of other petroleum exporters, meaning the "oil card" can only be played in the way it has been in the past decade for so long. The problem is not so severe with natural gas, a commodity of which Russia has the world's largest reserves by a comfortable margin.

The second problem, arising from the first, is that the Russian economy is particularly vulnerable to the vicissitudes of the world economy. As the countries of the world slipped into the grip of the economic downturn in 2009, for instance, the GDP growth rate for a Russian economy dependent on resource export was ranked at 206th in the world at a –7.9 percent level. The reason, for course, was that the slowdown of economic activity was accompanied by a concomitant decline in demand for raw resources, including energy resources, that provide the motor for things like manufacturing. The result is to accentuate the problems of the Russian economy. As Laqueur puts it, "the country's municipal infrastructure is very poor, and its dependence on the export of oil, gas, and other raw materials is undesirable and, in the long run, dangerous." This problem was most dramatically demonstrated during 1998, when world prices for petroleum fell to $9 a barrel and the Russian economy basically imploded.

The third, and derivative, problem is that this dependency suggests that, like many other countries whose economies are essentially like those of countries in the developing world, the Russians are not entirely the masters of their own economic fate and are structurally, and in terms of the quality of life, still far behind the other countries with which they want to be compared. The situation has improved greatly since the 1990s, but even with the growth of Russia to being the world's eighth largest economy, per capita GDP still stands at $15,100, about a third that of the United States and ranking only 79th in the world. Despite impressive growth, especially in the middle of the 2000s, Russia still remains economically outside the mainstream of world powers.

The Russian physical endowment thus both helps accelerate and impede Russian desires to reemerge among the world's great powers. Things like Russian rates of dependency upon and exploitation of natural resources and its demographic time bomb provides a frame around understanding and dealing with the Russians, as does the unique evolution of Russia as a political entity.

Russia as a Unique State

Dealing with Russia is indeed like unpeeling Churchill's onion because the Russian experience has been unique among world states. The history of the Russian experience has produced a culture that is distinctly Russian and that presents different challenges to the world than do other states.

The overwhelming theme of Russian history has been expansion. What is now Russia began as a political entity in the ninth century, and the predecessor to modern Russia began around Muscovy (Moscow) in the thirteenth century as part of the process of expelling the Mongols from Russian soil. In the centuries that followed, Russia became the Russian Empire, pushing outward from its base west of the Urals into Asia and south into the Caucasus region. Although the Russian Empire was a victim of the First World War, the Soviet state that rose from its ashes maintained control of the old empire and expanded its holdings into places like the Baltic states on the eve of World War II. As the Cold War congealed in the second half of the 1940s, Russia's sway was effectively extended into Eastern Europe in the form of communist satellite states that were coerced into the Warsaw Pact. In this period, Russian/ Soviet power reached its territorial apex, achieving the territorial control of its most ardent xenophobes. The physical dimensions of that Russian expansion remain part of the legacy of which Russians are most proud, and Russian resurgence has as a subtext the desire to reassert Russian domain, a fear that unsettles its relations with its neighbors and former vassals.

The wind of expansionistic change has blown in both directions for the Russians, as one consequence of the breakup of the Soviet Union (which many observers consider to have been an empire) meant the dismantling of imperial lands garnered, normally reluctantly, from the various peoples who escaped that domain. One of the results of that uneven change has been, in Laqueur's view, to influence the political character of the people. "Contemporary Russia," he maintains, "is a conservative country. The Russian people have witnessed too much negative change in the past 100 years."

In addition, the breakup of the empire has created unique problems for Russia and its relations with the rest of the world. One of the artifacts of the Empire and Soviet Union was "russification," the attempt to impose Russian language, culture, and thinking in the conquered territories, and one of the major instruments of that emphasis was to encourage the development and growth of ethnic Russian communities in the additions to Russia. Shleifer and Treisman report that 16 million ethnic Russians remain in the near abroad. The Russians tend to think of non-Russians within and outside the Federation (but who are part of the old Soviet state) in two categories. The former Soviet states that are now independent are known in Russia as the "near abroad," and they are the territories which Russia claims as a "sphere of special interests" that is partly aimed at protecting Russian minorities in these countries. Georgia, with whom Russia went briefly to war in 2008 and which is a continuing source of tension between Russia and the United States, is an example discussed in the next section. Within the Federation, areas with a large non-Russian, largely Muslim population, mostly in the North Caucasus, are referred to as the "internal abroad," according to King and Menon, and pose an internal terrorism threat that is one of Russia's major concerns in the world. Chechnya is a prime example of this problem, and the January 2011 suicide bombing in Moscow's major commercial airport is evidence of its continuing status as a problem.

Part of the legacy of expansionism has been Russia's on-again, off-again flirtation with the West. Russia is, after all, partly European and partly Asian, which is part of its unique heritage and a distinction many Russians view with pride. At the same time, the most powerful states over the last 300 years have been Western, and much of their power has derived from a distinctly Western view of the world, including technology and other causes of material advancement. Going back at least as far as Tsar Peter the Great, the Russians have flirted with westernization as a way to overcome the historic backwardness of the Russian society. These flirtations have alternated with Russian rejection of westernization as destructive of Russian uniqueness, resulting in a paradox for the Russians historically and today pointed out by Shevtsova: "Russia is trying to copy the West while remaining anti-western in essence." Shevtsova further asserts that this dynamic underlies efforts by Russian President Dmitry Medvedev toward the West, which she described as "a mere reiteration of the Russian tradition of using technological innovation from the West to strengthen the old state."

The conservative bias of Russian history is further exemplified by Russian attitudes toward politics at odds with those of the West. Before the demise of the Soviet state, Russia had essentially no experience with democracy except for a brief interlude between the fall of the Empire and the success of the Bolshevik Revolution. Prodemocratic sentiment has been restricted to the intelligentsia, much of which has been an exile community, and although there is support for a move toward democracy among many Russians, it is one of several competing values to which the Russians aspire. Their ambivalence and willingness to reject democracy in return for greater security, for instance, has been a major element in the success of Putin in gaining and maintaining influence despite his cavalier attitudes toward Western-style democracy, a concept he regularly dismisses as inappropriate for Russia, to the discomfort of Western observers who want to see Russia become a more "normal" (by which they mean politically democratic) state.

U.S.–RUSSIAN RELATIONS

The context within which U.S.–Russian relations develops is the old Cold War competition, a 40-plus-years relationship that both colors the nature of how the two countries view one another and conditions the hopes and expectations they have about future relations. The net effect of the Cold War experience was a legacy of distrust and suspicion about how Russia and the United States do and can interact that, when combined with inherent characteristics of Russia, make positive change in relations difficult to create and to maintain.

The Cold War was an extraordinarily intense, encompassing international experience. The United States and the Soviet Union emerged from World War II as the only major countries with significant residual power, although their conditions were quite different. The United States suffered some of the comparatively lightest casualties among major combatant countries (a little over 405,000), and its economy was revived by turning a Great Depression–era economic system into "the arsenal of democracy." If anything, the United States was actually strengthened by the war and emerged from it as the world's most powerful state by a degree probably unparalleled except in the immediate wake of the Cold War in the 1990s. By contrast, the Soviet Union suffered the war's heaviest human losses (estimated at nearly 20 million, more or less equally divided among military and civilian casualties), and the devastation of the Soviet countryside and economic infrastructure by marauding Nazi armies was enormous. What the Soviets had at the end of the war was a huge Red Army that it did not demobilize and that became the instrument of Soviet power in the postwar world.

The Cold War competition was about how the postwar world would be organized, and it had both political and military aspects. The traditional members of the European balance of power were either defeated (e.g., Germany, Italy) or were exhausted by the war (e.g., Britain, France) and could no longer become the focal points for arranging power. Instead, the world went from multipolar (several independent sources—or poles—of power and influence) to bipolar (only two major states), and the question was how the United States and the Soviet Union would organize the international order. The two possibilities were an international order on which they both agreed and could manage peaceably and cooperatively and a world in which they would disagree and which they could not manage cooperatively. The latter prospect prevailed in the form of the Cold War.

The political source of the divide between the two giants was their philosophical worldview, about which both were quite evangelical. The American model stressed political democracy and capitalist economics as its central values, whereas the Soviet Union adhered to a model of communist authoritarianism and socialist economics. In philosophy and practice, the two views were almost entirely antithetical and irreconcilable. It was impossible to construct a vision of world organization that cooperatively encompassed both. Since both were evangelical, they sought to spread their beliefs, particularly to countries in Africa, Asia, and part of Latin America that were emerging from colonial status to being independent states. At the political level, the competition came to be principally about how much of the world map could be turned "blue" (pro-Western) or "red" (communist). As the competition was carried out around the world, it was a contest between communism and anticommunism.

The most visible and dangerous part of the Cold War was its military aspect. For over 40 years, the United States and the Soviet Union faced off against one another with large, lethal armed forces in a state of perpetual readiness for the "balloon going up" (the onset of war). Both sides retained large forces (including the forces of allies) along either side of the Iron Curtain (as Churchill described the barbed-wire fence dividing communist and non-communist Europe) as "forces in being" to fight the initial battles of that war, should it come. Away from the central battle zone of Europe, both sides used various forms of mutual defense arrangements to arm surrogates in countries willing to pronounce some allegiance toward one or the other.

The pinnacle of this military confrontation, of course, was the existence of nuclear arsenals on either side that increased in lethal capacities as time went by. By the 1970s, when that competition arguably reached its zenith, both sides had over 10,000 strategic nuclear warheads (weapons aimed at one another's territory) atop ballistic missiles against which there was, and arguably still is, no effective defense (discussed below). While the employment of these nuclear arsenals could easily lead to the mutual disintegration of both states and thus made essentially no sense, the fear that somehow nuclear war could be the ending of the Cold War was a pall hanging over both and created a set of perceptions about the other that has proven extraordinarily difficult to modify.

Two other points about the atmosphere created by the Cold War are worth noting. First, the nuclear shadow created a sense of enormous fatalism, certainly in the American population, during the darkest days of the Cold War—especially the 1950s and 1960s. The perception became widespread that it was not a question of *whether* there would be a nuclear holocaust but *when*. Within the United States, Americans debated the question in terms of "better red than dead" (surrendering to avoid a nuclear war) or "better dead than red" (whether it was preferable to go down in a flaming war) as people flocked to see apocalyptic movies like *On the Beach* or *Dr. Strangelove*. Hidden within these debates was the implicit assumption that a thoroughly malevolent, even evil, Soviet leadership was behind all these concerns.

The second perception added to the fatalism: the idea that the competition was perpetual, a *protracted conflict* in the words of Yugoslav dissident Milovan Djilas. There were, in the popular and most informed public views, only two ways the Cold War could end: peacefully or through a nuclear hot war that would destroy both countries. The possibility of a peaceful ending was viewed as so far-fetched as to be hopelessly naïve and unrealistic, and that meant the only way to avoid nuclear war was to keep the Cold War alive. The Cold War, in other words, was viewed as perpetual.

Suddenly and unexpectedly, however, it ended. The Soviet Union ceased to exist, and the question was what that might mean for the United States and the rest of the world. Initial reactions were sometimes hysterical. Within the George H. W. Bush administration, for instance, one important faction argued that the United States should do everything it could to save its mortal enemy because the alternative of a world without the Soviets would be so much more dangerous and unpredictable as to offer a worse prospect than "saving" the Cold War opponent and structure. Once that process began, however, it proved inexorable. From the Soviet ashes, the Russian Federation appeared, and American policy has been trying to adapt to this changed reality without consensus for the 20 years since.

Old habits and old perceptions die hard. The Russians as Soviets were America's dire enemy for so long that it has been difficult to countenance the possibility that relations between them can be based on a footing other than one of basic enmity and competition. When Russia was prostrate in the 1990s, the question was less urgent than it is today facing a resurgent Russia. In the last decade of the twentieth century, the problem was how to avoid total Russian collapse. Since the turn of the millennium, the concern has turned back to the possible need to control a resurgent Russian foreign policy and methods for doing so.

The current debate over dealing with the Russians can be depicted in terms of three overlapping areas of policy interaction, which are presented in no particular order of importance or priority. All are influenced by the Cold War experience. From the American vantage point, the question is one of Russian sincerity and trustworthiness when mutually cooperative outcomes are sought. From a Russian viewpoint, each is affected by a basic distrust of the United States honed over a period of four decades and by the degree to which American motives are influenced by the desire to stunt the reassertion of what the Russians believe to be their proper place in the world.

The first concern is the nature of economic and political development in Russia, and pits an American first priority on democratization and making Russia a more "normal" state against a Russian emphasis on returning Russia to the ranks of world powers. The second is bilateral security between the two countries in a post–Cold War environment and centers on the remaining symbol of the confrontation, the nuclear arsenals and their control. The third is the direction of Russian behavior in its own region, a question largely of how it deals with the near and internal abroad, as well as Russia's evolving role in the global system, including Russia's potential association with European and Atlantic institutions like the European Union (EU) and the North Atlantic Treaty Organization (NATO).

The Future of Russian Development

The failure of the Soviet Union left its successor state, the Russian Federation, without either a political or economic framework from which to fashion itself. When President Gorbachev declared the end of the political monopoly of the Communist Party of the Soviet Union (CPSU) as part of his reforms, the longer-term victim was the authoritarian, even totalitarian, political system that had been part of the Leninist legacy. When the Russian Federation was declared and its new president, Boris Yeltsin, was elected, the path seemed set toward democratization, and at least presidential elections have been fairly held since then. The idea that the process would lead to an orderly movement to Western-style political democracy was, however, sidetracked somewhat under the rule of Putin (who argues, somewhat vaguely, for a distinctive, Russian-style democracy that is somehow different from Western forms). Moreover, Putin's background is in the old Soviet KGB and the Russian version of that intelligence organization, the FSB, hardly citadels of democratic activism. According to Soldatov and Borogan, "When Putin came to power, he offered current and former officers from Russia's security services the chance to move to the upper echelons of power." They argue this presents a barrier to the emergence of democratic practices because "the security services have concluded that their interests, and those of the state they are guarding, are above the rule of law." President Medvedev, who was elected in 2008 (with Putin as his prime minister), is a more public advocate of democratization, but optimism about his ability to cause a movement toward more open rule is tempered by how effective he may be and how closely his prospects are tied to Putin.

Socialist economics was the other victim of the demise of Soviet communism, and Russia has struggled, with only moderate success, to make the transition to a market-based economy. Part of the problem was the enormous inefficiency of the Soviet economy (one of the factors leading to its demise was its inability to compete globally or even to satisfy internal demands). The new government has been saddled with this legacy of ineffectiveness in the economic realm, and basically unregulated growth of the private sector has only added to the chaos of disorderly growth. The situation was dire during the 1990s and has improved with the infusion of "petro-dollars" into the economy. As noted, this impact is problematic in the long run and is of concern regarding future Russian development since, as Laqueur points out, "To a large extent, Russia's prospects still depend on the price of oil."

The result of this uneven internal development is what Charap calls "the 'values gap'—the contrast between the ideal that defines politics in the United States and Russia's controls on participation in public life and continued limitations on personal freedom." For Americans who actively seek to undo the entire structure of animosity and discord between the two countries, political democratization is viewed as a central tenet, and the slowness and unevenness of Russian movement in that direction is a problem (which is why many view Putin as an antagonist). Those more suspicious of Russia counter that the lack of movement toward democracy simply reflects Russian history and character, including the depiction captured by Shevtsova (2010) of Russia as entrapped by "the 'dilemma of the captive mind'," which "boils down to a desperate clinging to old stereotypes in mentality and behavior and an inability to comprehend a new reality."

Bi-Lateral Security: The Nuclear Legacy

One important aspect of the Russian difficulty in making the transition to more democratic forms is the continuing perception of rivalry and animosity with the United States and the belief that their relationship remains military competitive and potentially combative (an attitude shared by some American analysts). As noted, part of Putin's strength has been in convincing the Russian people that trading off some of their political freedom for added security is a good bargain, and it is based on the residue of historically antagonistic military relations with the United States. The clearest reminder of that relationship is in the area of nuclear weapons, both in terms of remaining arsenals and the prospects of missile defenses.

Nuclear weapons were a double-edged sword in U.S.–Soviet relations. Their destructive potential defined the parameters of how bad total deterioration in their relations could reach (nuclear war), but they also helped nurture a healthy realization on both sides that no matter how bad the relations were, that deterioration could not be allowed to degenerate to war. This realization first appeared in the wake of the Cuban Missile Crisis of 1962, when the superpowers came as close they ever were before or since to nuclear war and did not like the prospect they saw. From that crisis, a growing recognition that they had a mutual interest in avoiding their own nuclear evaporation provided the first spark for winding down the Cold War, a phenomenon I have elsewhere described (Snow, *Necessary Peace*) as a "necessary peace" (the absence of war born not of the desire for friendship but from fear of war).

Nuclear arms control became the vehicle and symbol of this recognition and played an important physical and symbolic role in undermining the rationale of the Cold War. Physically, it placed at least some limits on the burgeoning lethality of nuclear arsenals and set in motion a process that would transcend the Cold War and provide the precedent and venue for nuclear arms reduction since the end of the Cold War. Symbolically, cooperation in arms control eventually helped abet a movement toward cooperation in other areas and thus became an important symbol for those who favored a policy directed toward reducing animosities and conflict in the overall relationship.

The so-called New START represents the contemporary manifestation of an arms control process that began in 1963 with the signing of the Limited Test Ban Treaty (LTBT) of 1963. The three nuclear powers (the superpowers plus Britain) were all party to this historic agreement that banned nuclear testing in the atmosphere and was, among other things, an indirect way to try to limit horizontal nuclear proliferation (the spread of nuclear weapons to current nonpossessors), an emphasis that continues. During the balance of the Cold War, a number of other arms control agreements were reached that defined the nuclear relationship, and since the end of the Cold War, the continuation of these efforts has been directed primarily at reducing the size of existing arsenals and discouraging proliferation; these efforts are tied in that progress in one seems to encourage progress in the other.

New START, as the Obama administration nicknamed the current culmination of the Strategic Arms Reduction Talks (START), was negotiated and signed by Obama and Medvedev in April 2010. It was ratified by the U.S. Senate during its lame duck session in December 2010 and approved by the Russian parliament in January 2010, thereby bringing its provisions into force. The agreement has two basic thrusts. One is to reduce the total warhead numbers to 1,500 for each country on no more than 800 launchers; the pre–New START limits were 2,200 warheads and 1,600 launchers (see Charap). The other is to reinforce procedures by which each country can inspect and monitor compliance with its provisions by the other.

While New START is arguably substantively innocuous, it was both important and controversial for other reasons. Its importance, in the minds of its supporters, was that in its absence, the arms control process might be interrupted and cooperation between Russia and the United States damaged in related areas such as bringing pressure on Iran not to become a nuclear weapons state. It thus had traction beyond the reduction of nuclear arsenals by approximately one-third, which still left both powers with more weapons than anybody else and with the continuing capacity to do grievous harm to one another. At the same time, the Obama administration has agreed to spend $85 billion over 10 years to improve the infrastructure of American nuclear forces to ensure that remaining forces maintain maximum physical and thus deterrent value.

Controversy arose over two matters relating to New START, basically on partisan political grounds within the United States. Led by GOP Senator John Kyl of Arizona, a number of Republicans argued that there were inadequate assurances within inspection provisions to ensure that the Russians could not cheat on the limits to which they had agreed. To paraphrase President Reagan's famous rejoinder about such agreements, the United States under New START could "trust, but verify," but it could not verify (monitor) adequately. The second and related Republican objection came over the implications of the agreement for ballistic missile defenses (BMD). Also, some maintained that the impacts were asymmetrical: the United States was forced to undo real capabilities, whereas the Russians, in Shleifer and Treisman's words, "mostly ratified cuts in the Russian arsenal that were occurring anyway as the weapons aged."

Ballistic missile defense has long been a partisan issue between Democrats and Republicans, dating back to the 1960s when such systems were first physically proposed. Generally speaking, Republicans (and especially GOP administrations) have favored and encouraged such systems for the potential protection they could provide against a nuclear attack, while Democrats have been skeptical of the practicality of these systems and have generally opposed deployment of them. The Obama administration basically follows in the Democratic tradition on the issue, although it has come out in tepid support for a minimal European-based defense system intended to intercept a small attack with nuclear weapons by a rogue state like a nuclear Iran.

This issue becomes internationally important because Russia (like the Soviet Union before it) adamantly opposes missile defenses. Part of their reason is a skepticism shared with Democrats that such systems can provide a meaningful defense against a concerted nuclear missile attack (a capability that has yet to be demonstrated). Another aspect of their objection is their belief, honed during the Cold War, that such defenses are aimed at Russia in an attempt to render the Russian nuclear threat "impotent and obsolete," as claimed in Reagan's famous defense of his ambitious Strategic Defense Initiative (SDI) proposal of the 1980s. Their third fear is that the research spawned by work on BMD might lead to spin-off discoveries which could produce exploitable military advantages for the United States. Finally (and arguably most importantly), the Russians have been notably unsuccessful in developing such systems themselves and thus want to cancel an area of competition in which they are unable to prevail.

The Republican objections have a distinctive Cold War aura to them that reflects the extreme distrust and animosity that existed during that period. Although the end of the Cold War largely removed any rational basis for war between Russia and the United States, many Cold Warriors cling instinctively to images of the Soviet Union and its penchant for cheating on agreements and even hatching plans for a nuclear strike against which defenses are necessary, yet another demonstration of the domestic political restraints on policy toward Russia. In the end, the Obama administration won the support of enough Republican senators to gain the necessary two-thirds vote for ratification (the final vote was 71–26 in favor) by promising that approval of New START did not in any way preclude the deployment of a missile shield in Europe that it was able to convince the Russians was too "thin" and ineffectual to pose a threat to them.

Russian Regional Foreign Policy

One of the major symbols of great power status attained by the Soviet Union and remembered longingly within Russia is possession of an acknowledged "sphere of influence" in which its interests were accepted as supreme by other powers. Those Russians like Putin who desire a similar level of international recognition now phrase this as a claim for a "sphere of special interests," as already mentioned. The problem with this designation is that the major power may use its status as a carte blanche to interfere in the affairs of states within its sphere, as the Russians did, over American objection, most recently in 2008 in Georgia.

Russia's invasion of the former Soviet republic and independent state of Georgia on August 8, 2008, (in response to a Georgian invasion of its renegade province of South Ossetia on the frontier with Russia on August 7) has come to serve as a partisan lightning rod of international and domestic concern about Russian relations with the countries of its region, notably the former republics of the Soviet Union. To the Russians, primary interest and influence in these countries is a geopolitical necessity and a sphere-of-interest prerogative of their status as a great power. To outsiders, heavy-handed actions like the invasion of Georgia are evidence of the kind of brutishness that was a hallmark of the Soviet past and a clear indication that things have not changed much in Moscow. The invasion occurred during the 2008 American presidential election campaign, and Republicans seized powerfully the Georgian cause, both to show the Bush administration's support for its pro-Western regime and to try to create a source of differentiation between the candidates for president.

The basis of the war was the status of mountain enclaves within Georgia known as South Ossetia and Abkhazia; the former had an ongoing secessionist movement seeking either independence or union with North Ossetia, which is separated from South Ossetia by the Russian–Georgian border. The Ossetians themselves are an independent ethnic group within Georgia, and along with the natives of Abkhazia, have resisted rule emanating from the Georgian capital of Tbilisi. Any distinctions between Georgia and these renegades could formerly be ruthlessly suppressed by the Soviets, who also provided protection for ethnic Russians who had migrated to both areas. The breakup of the Soviet Union and the emergence of a Georgian state after 1991, however, created tensions between Georgia and the two rebellious areas; in 1992 and 1993, the Abkhazians rebelled and established themselves—with Russian help—as a semi-autonomous region within Georgia; the initial military action by the Georgians in 2008 was part of its campaign to prevent a similar outcome in South Ossetia.

The war itself was unremarkable, pitting the Russian armed forces against much smaller Georgian forces that had been trained by the Americans and Israelis. The Georgian resistance (or counterintervention in Russian eyes) was quickly brushed aside by the Russians, and within days, the Russians menaced the Georgian capital, bringing ringing pleas for assistance from the Georgian president, American-educated (as a lawyer) Mikheil Saakashvili. On August 15, Georgia accepted the terms of a Russian-proposed ceasefire, and on August 26, Russia recognized the independence of both South Ossetia and Abkhazia from Georgia, a de facto condition which continues to prevail.

The Georgian (or South Ossetian) war became a cause célèbre, particularly within the United States as an irritant in U.S.–Russian relations. On August 11, President Bush declared that the Russian action "substantially damaged Russian standing in the world," and Vice President Richard Cheney declared that "Russian aggression must not go unanswered." The war became a partisan issue as GOP presidential candidate John McCain condemned the Russian action and declared the war "a matter of moral and strategic importance" to the United States. The message was clear: the United States stood firmly behind what it deemed the freedom-loving Georgians and their valiant and charismatic president Saakashvili against the thuggish actions of the Russians. The message extended to other former Soviet republics like Ukraine, which, along with Georgia, had been flirting with the West, including preliminary explorations of becoming part of NATO—a possibility the Russians deeply opposed on the not-unreasonable grounds that "no state would welcome the extension of a historically hostile military alliance up to its borders, no matter how often that alliance said its intentions were peaceful," according to Shleifer and Treisman. Although the Georgian war had no visible impact on the 2008 U.S. election, the Obama administration felt the need to establish its support for Georgia, sending Vice President Joe Biden to Tbilisi in April 2009 to reiterate that bond.

Russian attempts to reestablish influence or control over the near abroad and efforts to suppress separatists and other dissenters in areas of the "internal abroad" like the North Caucasus (e.g. Chechnya, Dagestan) that have opposed Russian rule have created a wedge in U.S.–Russian relations and especially a partisan divide on how to deal with the Russians inside the United States. This division, which acts as a barrier to policy change toward a more congenial relationship, comes principally (but not solely) from the political right in the country, who voice the opinion that Russian actions are as brutish as their predecessors' and that Putin in particular is simply the most recent Russian expansionist despot. This construction certainly underlay much of the opposition to New START—the notion the Russians could not be trusted—and toward increased dealings with Russia. President Medvedev, in these interpretations, was little more than a puppet to the master Putin, and Russia is to be viewed with restraint and handled only with a strong element of military power. The return of terrorism from the North Caucasus at the Moscow airport in January 2011 has muted this criticism.

All these issues affect the final U.S. concern, which is with Russian foreign policy in the world generally, and especially toward Europe. Current Russian policy reflects classic patterns of ambivalence as expressed by Shevtsova (2010): "The Putin-Medvedev foreign policy doctrine justified simultaneous cooperation with and containment of the West." This balance between cooperation and conflict is demonstrated by its attitude toward NATO. On one hand, Russia adamantly opposes further eastward expansion of NATO into places like Ukraine and Georgia, but it simultaneously cooperates with the NATO-based effort in Afghanistan (allowing a supply corridor into that country) and has some limited and evolving relationship with the alliance. Some Westerners (see Kupchan) openly advocate bringing Russia into the alliance as a full member, which the Russians do not discourage entirely. The future relationship between Russia and the EU remains a work in progress as well, subject to further development of the Russian economy and democratization.

U.S. OPTIONS

While relations between the two former Cold War adversaries are warmer and less dangerous than they were before, the countries are still at odds with one another on important matters. The question is the degree to which the United States has the ability to move Russian policy in directions more congenial to American preferences and interests.

The contemporary consensus seems to be that U.S. leverage and thus options are very limited. With direct military confrontation removed from the table, the two countries have a limited level of interaction and thus of interests that can be translated into leverage. American investment in the Russian economy is minimal, particularly compared to that of Europe, and thus there is a limited ability to influence economic development; this limits the ability to affect movement toward political democratization. Moreover, Charap points out that there are important sources of tension between the two countries: conflicting approaches to international security issues like missile defense; the "values gap" regarding conceptions of internal governance; and conflict over whether Russia has a sphere of influence, and if does, how the United States should treat it (Georgia being the most recent lightning rod of concern).

It is against this dual backdrop of conflicting policy preferences and limited leverage that American policy proceeds. The Obama administration issued, through Biden, the intention to "reset" the relationship in February 2009, a catchphrase that remains intact. The heart of this new approach has been, in Charap's words, "to engage with Russia on shared threats and on issues where interests converged, while pushing back against Kremlin actions that contradicted US interests." In effect, this change represented a movement away from the more personalized, confrontational approach of the Bush administration: Bush declared in 2001 a personal affinity for Putin, while his administration pursued a more hard-line policy toward the Russians, chiding them on the slowness of democratization and opposing their harsh treatment of internal-abroad factions like Chechen separatists, whom the Russians think of and treat as terrorists. The large intent of the Obama policy is clearly toward improving relations with the Russians from the condition in which it inherited those relations.

U.S. options are also constrained by American domestic politics. As noted earlier, the political right in the United States, most heavily represented within the Republican Party, maintains a more guarded, even confrontational, view toward the current Russian regime, a position hardened by the Russian invasion of Georgia in 2008. That issue illuminates the difference in worldviews between the Russians and their GOP opponents. To the Russians, American adoption of Georgia after the so-called Rose Revolution brought Saakashvili to power represents an unwelcome and unwarranted intrusion on Russian primacy in the near abroad; to American opponents of Putin and Medvedev, American championing of the Georgians was an act of support for democratization and freedom in the face of renewed Russian imperial intent.

The opposition to the Russians is particularly loud and often couched in highly patriotic language that has made the effort to lower the rhetorical confrontation and to reestablish warmer relations more difficult as part of "resetting" the relationship. New START, whatever its substantive merits, has been a first step in that process, and even it drew loud, if ultimately unsuccessful, ire in the form of opposition to ratification in the U.S. Senate. Nonetheless, those who want to improve relations with Russia must rely on Russian "good behavior"—actions that do not openly inflame and activate its American domestic opponents and skeptics. Since the two countries are at odds on a number of basic issues, this further limits the extent to which their relations can be warmed, but that may simply be an honest reflection of the current state of their relationship, one where both sides must "recognize the limits of their shared interests" and proceed accordingly, in Shleifer and Treisman's view.

Disagreement and discord extends to foreign policy directed toward nontraditional actors. While the U.S.–Russian relationship within general international organizations like the United Nations have moved from broad-based enmity and opposition during the Cold War to frequent cooperation in matters before the Security Council, there remain selective matters of disagreement (UN responses to Georgia, for instance). At the same time, the role of Russia in Euro-centered international organizations like NATO and the European Community remain controversial in terms of future Russian participation. The same is true regarding subnational actors. While the Bush administration in particular was prone to accept the Russian depictions of Chechen separatists as terrorists, it chafed at similar descriptions of the Georgians in their actions toward the Ossetians and the Abkhazians, and the Obama administration has also been less willing to lump together all internal-abroad opponents as terrorists.

CONCLUSIONS

The relations between the United States and Russia have run the gamut of possibilities. During the first century and a half of the American experience, those relations were occasional (e.g., Russian participation in the Armed Neutrality against Britain during the American Revolution, rubbing against one another in San Francisco Bay) and not very prominent. During the first half of the twentieth century, the United States joined much of the European world in first decrying the rise of communism in the Bolshevik Revolution and then embracing the Soviets in the common mission of World War II. The second half of the century was consumed by the encompassing competition of the Cold War and then adjusting to the remarkable implosion of the Soviet state and the communist threat it presented.

Relations between the two countries in the early twenty-first century are influenced by that past. Many Americans remain wary of the Russians both because of their enigmatic status and their Soviet legacy, interpreting events and trends in Russia through the conceptual lens of the Cold War experience. Other Americans are hopeful, even optimistic, about the prospects of transforming Russia into a "normal" state, which is to say one that progressively resembles mature Western democracies. The Russians themselves share ties to their history, longing for the power and prestige of the old Soviet days and trying to chart a distinctly Russian place in the world.

Within this context, U.S.–Russian relations have lost some of their urgency, as the United States has turned its attention to other parts of the world, notably the Middle East and East Asia. Russia is still a formidable power, particularly as a nuclear weapons state, but its importance has been eclipsed by other parts of the world in the American list of priorities. If Russia as the Soviet Union was the primary American foreign policy concern of the second half of the last century, that focus has shifted eastward to the other major communist country of the last century, China. U.S.–Russian relations have cooled in intensity and priority as the two country's interests have diverged and been subsumed by competition for attention, but they have not disappeared altogether.

STUDY/DISCUSSION QUESTIONS

1. Why, in Churchill's terms, is Russia an enigma? How have its traumatic changes since the end of the Cold War contributed to its enigmatic status?
2. Discuss the Russian self-image of Russia's place in the world. How did its status as the Soviet Union and its post-Soviet decline affect that self-image and its contemporary view of its place in the world, especially the attractiveness of "resurgence"?

3. What are the notable physical characteristics of Russia discussed in the text? How does each contribute to its present and future status? Emphasize the role of energy in your answer.
4. Discuss the idea of Russia as an expansionist empire. How do the Soviet and post-Soviet experiences demonstrate the problem of Russian expansionism and status as a great power?
5. How does the Cold War experience color the way that Americans view Russia? Cite examples.
6. What are the three overlapping areas of U.S. foreign policy concerns with Russia identified in the text? Describe each, including how American domestic politics affects and is affected by each of them.
7. What are the principal sources of limitations on the American ability to influence Russia in ways contributing to the accomplishment of U.S. foreign policy goals? How do these limits constrain the United States in pursuing different options of foreign policy toward Russia?

READING/RESEARCH MATERIALS

Aslund, Anders. "The Unit for Russia's Riches." *Foreign Policy* (January/February 2006), 42–49.

Brzezinski, Zbigniew. "Putin's Choice." *Washington Quarterly* 31, 2 (Spring 2008), 95–116.

Charap, Samuel. "The Transformation of US-Russia Relations." *Current History* 109, 729 (October 2010), 281–287.

Colton, Timothy J. "New Uncertainties Enliven Russia's Election Season." *Current History* 110, 738 (October 2011), 159–265.

DaVargo, Julie, and Clifford A. Grammich. *Dire Demographics: Population Trends in the Russian Federation.* Santa Monica, CA: RAND Corporation Monograph, 2007.

Djilas, Milovan. *The New Class: An Analysis of the Communist System.* New York: Harcourt, Brace, Jovanovich, 1957.

Eberstadt, Nicholas. "The Enigma of Russian Mortality." *Current History* 109, 729 (October 2010), 288–294.

Friedman, Thomas L. "The First Law of Petropolitics." *Foreign Policy* (May/June 2006), 28–36.

Gaddis, John Lewis. *Strategies of Containment: A Critical Appraisal of American Security Policy during the Cold War* (revised and expanded edition). New York: Oxford University Press, 2005.

Gaddy, Clifford G., and Andrew C. Kuchens. "Putin's Plan." *Washington Quarterly* 31, 2 (Spring 2008), 117–129.

Goldman, Marshall I. "Russia and the West: Mutual Assured Distrust." *Current History* 106, 702 (October 2007), 314–320.

Gorbachev, Mikhail. *Perestroika: New Thinking for Our Country and the World.* New York: Harper and Row, 1987.

King, Charles, and Rajan Menon. "Prisoners of the Caucasus: Russia's Invisible Civil War." *Foreign Affairs* 89, 4 (July/August 2010), 20–34.

Krastev, Ivan. "What Russia Wants." *Foreign Policy* (May/June 2008), 48–51.

Kupchan, Charles. "NATO's Final Frontier: Why Russia Should Join the Atlantic Alliance." *Foreign Affairs* 89, 3 (May/June 2010), 100–112.

Lacayo, Richard. "The Architects of Authoritarianism." *Foreign Policy* (May/June 2008), 53–57.

Laqueur, Walter. "Moscow's Modernization Dilemma: Is Russia Charting a New Foreign Policy?" *Foreign Affairs* 89, 6 (November/December 2010), 153–160.

Mendelson, Sarah E., and Thomas P. Gerber. "Failing the Stalin Test." *Foreign Affairs* 85, 1 (January/February 2006), 2–8.

Sestanovich, Stephen. "What Has Moscow Done?" *Foreign Affairs* 87, 6 (November/December 2008), 12–28.

Shevtsova, Lilia. "Medvedev's Potemkin Modernization." *Current History* 109, 720 (October 2010), 276–280.

———. "Think Again: Vladimir Putin." *Foreign Policy* (January/February 2008), 34–40.

Simes, Dimitri. "Losing Russia." *Foreign Affairs* 86, 6 (November/December 2007), 36–52.

Shleifer, Andrei, and Daniel Treisman. "Why Moscow Says No: A Question of Russian Interests, Not Psychology." *Foreign Affairs* 90, 1 (January/February 2011), 122–138.

Snow, Donald M. *The Necessary Peace: Nuclear Weapons and Superpower Relations.* Lexington, MA: Lexington Books, 1987.

Soldatov, Andrei, and Irina Borogan. "Russia's New Nobility: The Rise of the Security Forces in Putin's Kremlin." *Foreign Affairs* 89, 5 (September/October 2010), 80–96.

Trenin, Dmitri. "The Legacy of Vladimir Putin." *Current History* 106, 702 (October 2007), 346–348.

Tymoshenko, Yuliya. "Contining Russia." *Foreign Affairs* 86, 3 (May/June 2007), 69–82.

China: Coping with a Dynamic Adversary Turned Ambiguous Partner

PREVIEW

Relations between the United States and the People's Republic of China (PRC) have changed enormously since the end of the Cold War. Throughout that 40-year period, the two were bitter enemies, but the emergence of China as a major industrial country has brought them close together as trading partners. While some worry about the growing American trade imbalance with China and the economic challenge posed by their relentless economic growth, the two countries' relations have grown closer across the board, from economic to political areas. The two countries are among the elite powers of the world, and their interaction spans the spectrum of economic, military, and political forms of interaction. A major question that faces both countries, and specifically American foreign policy, is how Chinese–American relations will evolve in the future.

The relationship between the United States and the People's Republic of China (PRC) is unique among American foreign relations with the countries of the world. This singular relationship is between two of the world's largest countries (China has the world's largest population and fourth largest land area, whereas the United States is third in the world on both measures) has been uneven and tumultuous, bred of very different historical experiences with the world and with one another. Much of their recent history of interaction, like that between the United States and Russia, was the product of the Cold War confrontation, and the legacy of antagonism that arose from that epoch is part of the legacy the two countries seek to overcome as they traverse the early twenty-first century as major powers with heavily intertwined economies but lingering suspicions about one another; the result is a level of partnership but one whose nature is not entirely defined and is the subject of controversy and disagreement within both countries—an ambiguous partnership.

China, of course, has the world's oldest continuous civilization, with a history with artifacts that date back 7,000 years or more, standing in stark contrast to the slightly more than 400 years since European settlers first colonized what is now the United States. The Han Chinese developed the world's first great civilization and turned inward, isolating themselves from the outside world for more than two millennia, a status and preference symbolized by the Great Wall separating China from its northern Asian cohabitants. This self-imposed isolation, surpassed only by that of Japan among modern powers, resulted in a remarkably homogeneous society that persists to the current day (current estimates are that 92 percent of the population is Han Chinese; 99 percent of Japan's population is ethnic Japanese), and allowed Chinese culture and civilization to develop and mature in ways distinct from developments in other parts of the world. For a long time, the result was the world's most advanced civilization; but this was a status that did not last. Isolation eventually bred conformity and stagnation, and the other civilizations of the world eventually caught up to and surpassed the proud, insular Chinese, a condition the Chinese seem determined to reverse.

Modern Chinese history to the present is, in many ways, a reaction to and an attempt to rectify the consequences of societal stagnation. The nineteenth century is remembered by the Chinese as the "Century of Humiliation," a period when foreigners invaded and effectively turned China into a vassal state where Chinese were forced to cede much of their autonomy and sovereignty to Europeans whom they considered their cultural inferiors. The turmoil created by the European intrusion led to the first Chinese Revolution of the twentieth century, the so-called Wuchang Uprising of 1912 led by Dr. Sun Yat-Sen that overthrew the monarchy and instituted republican rule. In subsequent decades, the communists under Mao Zedong rebelled against the Nationalists (the heirs of Sun Yat-Sen), eventually prevailing in a 30-year campaign interrupted by a Japanese intervention and resistance to it. In 1949, the communists won and declared the People's Republic of China, while the Nationalists under Kuomintang leader Chiang Kai-shek fled to the neighboring island of Taiwan (Formosa), where their Republic of China remains a rival and major foreign policy concern of the PRC.

The triumph of the Chinese Communist Party (CCP) in 1949 had two major impacts on China and the world. First, it ushered in an era that continues to the present, featuring China's attempt to modernize and recreate its glory and status as a great power. While the ideological zeal of Mao and his early supporters did not move China notably in that direction, the rise to power of Deng Xiaoping and his policy of the "four modernizations" began a process whereby China has indeed entered the ranks of the world's significant powers. Second, the victory of Chinese communists made them a part of the emerging

Cold War and an adversary of the United States, thereby requiring Americans to rethink and adjust historic beliefs about their relationship to China.

China has always had a special place in the American psyche that has probably not historically been shared by the Chinese but that goes back to the beginning of U.S. history. Columbus's discovery of North America was, after all, virtually an accident, as his quest when he left Spain was to find a transoceanic route to the riches of the Orient; the Western Hemisphere landmass, in a sense, simply got in the way of his voyage. The fascination with the Orient, and more specifically China, extended into the early years of the American Republic: the magnificent Yankee clipper sailing ships were designed largely to reach and exploit what was viewed as the boundless treasure to be found in the "China trade," and Chinese immigrant laborers played an important role in the development of the American west, providing much of the labor for building the transcontinental railway that linked California with the rest of the continental United States.

Although there is no particular evidence that the sentiment was mutual, Americans developed what they saw as a "special" relationship between themselves and the Chinese. American missionaries were among the more prominent foreigners attempting to Christianize the Chinese population during the early and middle decades of the twentieth century, and Americans became major supporters of the Kuomintang (Nationalist) Party and its leader, Chiang Kai-shek, in their efforts against the Japanese both prior to and during World War II (the Republic of China was a formal ally during the war, the reason China was given a permanent seat on the United Nations Security Council in 1945). After the war, Dr. Walter Judd's "Committee of Six Million" (named for the alleged size of its membership, which was in fact many multiples smaller than that) assumed leadership of the so-called "China lobby" and extolled the cause of the Nationalists in their ultimately unsuccessful conflict with the Chinese communists.

The "fall" of China to the communists was a major trauma in U.S.–Chinese relations. Despite American support, the government of Chiang Kai-Shek was forced to flee the mainland in 1949, having been decisively defeated by the forces of Mao. There was considerable sentiment among American "China watchers" that the United States had somehow "sold out" the Nationalists and allowed the Communists to triumph, although it was not clear at the time or now what the United States could have done to reverse the outcome. Combined with the new Chinese partisanship in the emerging Cold War, the image of China changed from that of a friend to that of an avowed enemy—virtually overnight.

China's transformation into adversarial status was cemented by the PRC's unofficial intervention in the Korean War during the winter of 1950 and 1951. As American and allied UN forces moved through North Korea toward the border that separated North Korea from the PRC, the new Chinese government repeatedly warned that it considered hostile forces on its borders unacceptable and would respond accordingly. These warnings were ignored, and in one of history's most successful surprise actions, the better part of a quarter million Chinese "volunteers" snuck across the border undetected and counterattacked against the American forces. Although the Chinese government did not claim these intervening forces as its own (to avoid the legal consequences of going to war with the United Nations, among other reasons), China and the United States were the major opposing combatants on the Korean peninsula for the remainder of the hostilities that ended in July 1953. This military confrontation completed the change in the American view of China and set the atmosphere and environment for a deeply suspicious and adversarial relationship that is only eroding today.

Chinese–American relations are clearly in a state of flux and change, the exact outcomes of which have yet to be determined. The two countries spent 40 years as military rivals preparing for and threatening each other with military conflict, and there is a residue of suspicion that permeates the thinking of some American analysts that is a clear extension of those "bad old days" of U.S.–China relations. At the same time, the United States and the PRC have become two of the world's major economic partners in the area of trade and finance, a relationship that is virtually unprecedented (e.g., the degree of American indebtedness to China and China's stake in American prosperity for its own prosperity) and is evolving. No one knows exactly where that relationship is going in the future, and speculation about and attempts to influence the nature and quality of the evolving relationship forms much of the subject matter of ongoing foreign policy between the two giants.

CHINA: A SKETCH

Through most of its history, much about China was unknown to outsiders, which is a large part of the historic lure that it had. Words used to describe China typically include *exotic* and *mysterious*. China, of course, nurtured that perception by enshrouding itself against the outside world for well over a millennium, leaving descriptions to a few adventurers and explorers like Marco Polo. One of the emerging elements about China is its adaptation to the modern world, a concession that Chinese leaders and people see as a necessary concession for China to reclaim what it views as its rightful place among world powers. At the same time, the Chinese leadership emphasizes that change must be within a uniquely Chinese perspective and context.

China stands politically as one of the most distinctive states in the world. It is one of only four states left from the Cold War that still clings to its Marxist legacy. The other members of the communist world are far less significant: North Korea, Cuba, and Vietnam, although the North Koreans and Cubans remain enough of a problem to warrant coverage as cases within this volume. One commonality that they all maintain is the Leninist/Stalinist model of authoritarian rule, and the CCP is the only political party allowed within China, its authority basically unchallenged domestically or internationally. At the same time, China has largely abandoned the socialist economics that are the other distinctive characteristic of communist societies. The Chinese did not so much renounce socialism as augment it through the 1979 implementation of Deng Xiaopeng's "four modernizations," one of which was to allow the emergence of a limited and controlled introduction of Western capitalism into the so-called "special economic zones" (SEZs) in four Chinese eastern provinces that now form the motor of the Chinese economic challenge to the rest of the world. "Socialism with a Chinese face" was the official term used to describe this transformation, and it has created an economic system that contains both highly competitive Western-style corporations with a remaining numerical preponderance of government-owned means of production, the so-called state-owned enterprises (SOEs), many of which are controlled by party or government entities like the Chinese military. To emphasize the private enterprise aspect of the mix, Deng was famously quoted as declaring, "It is glorious to be rich." A mixed economy also exists in Vietnam, and it is not coincidental that the only communist states that still allow essentially no private enterprise, Cuba and North Korea, are also two of the poorest states in the world.

The Chinese economic miracle is what makes China distinct in the world today. In particular, China's emergence as an industrial society specializing in consumer goods has propelled its ascent into the ranks of the world's most prominent states. "Made in China" is now a common characteristic of many of the goods the world—and especially America—consume. The result has been a high and sustained level of economic growth: according to data reported in the *CIA World Factbook*, for instance, China's GDP growth rate for 2009 was at 9.1 percent (the third highest in the world) based on an economy valued at a GDP of $8.8 trillion, the third largest in the world. Economically, China is "a lopsided giant, an export juggernaut with one huge financial arm," according to Miller.

It is the Chinese economy that is distinctive about its rise in the world, with both domestic and international implications that are worth mentioning as context for understanding the dynamics of Chinese–American relations. Domestically, the burgeoning economy has brought with it dramatic improvements in the lives of many (but by no means all) Chinese, with demographic (e.g., urbanization) and political consequences. Politically, the major effect has been to cement the relationship between the population and the CCP as the sole holder of political power. Walder summarizes the situation: "the government's economic reforms and its loosening of controls over nonpolitical activities, together with the country's opening to the outside world, allowed a degree of freedom into peoples' personal, economic, cultural, and intellectual lives." Prosperity has fueled support for the regime, and there is little on the horizon that suggests a return to the 1980s tumult that eventuated in the tragic confrontation at Tiananmen Square in 1989. In fact, Walder draws an analogy between the situation in the United States in the 1960s and 1980s and the situation in China in 1989 and today: "If China's alienated 1980s generation was in many ways America's '1960s generation,' China's current youth generation in many ways resembles the 'Reagan generation.'" The result of economic transformation has been political tranquility and, as Miller observes, "the CCP's hold on power is likely to remain secure as long as it can continue to develop China's economy and jobs." Because few envisage a reversal of China's economic trajectory in the near term, dramatic internal political change in the country thus seems unlikely for the foreseeable future.

Internationally, the major consequence of China's economic rise has been to carve a much more prominent role for itself than it had previously and than it could possibly attain without it. The engine of this prominence is the extraordinary level of Chinese exports of consumer goods to the world, and especially the United States. China surpassed the United States in the export of consumer goods in the world economy in 2009 (with a global share of 17 percent, compared to 16 percent for the United States). A consequence has been the accumulation of an enormous reserve of foreign exchange in China, reported by Miller at $2.4 trillion at the end of 2009. In a May 2011 projection, the International Monetary Fund (IMF) announced that at current growth rates, China's economy would surpass that of the United States in sheer size by the end of 2015 (China's total GDP at $15 trillion, the United States at $14.8 trillion).

These economic impacts, which are examined more fully later in the chapter, are both reassuring and unsettling. They are reassuring in the sense that they are far less ominous than were Chinese gains in the area of military power (although that is still a concern) and because they tie China to the global economy, making China a more "normal" state than it might otherwise be. From this perspective, it is possible to conjure a positive image of the future, a possibility that Lieberthal raises: "Will Beijing and Washington overcome their mutual distrust over long-term intentions and create the 'positive, cooperative, comprehensive' twenty-first century relationship touted by President Obama and Hu Jintao in their April 2009 meeting in London?"

At the same time, many observers worry that China's wealth could be translated into military assets that, if combined with the enormous manpower potential of China, could result in a menace of enormous, if unpredictable, proportions on the region and possibly beyond. Lieberthal also captures this possibility: "Many Americans with significant influence on policy making believe that, as China becomes wealthy and strong, Beijing will seek to marginalize the United States in East Asia. . . . Many Americans are troubled by China's annual double-digit military budget increases and the growing capabilities the Chinese military is acquiring." The amount of Chinese monetary reserves is also unsettling to many observers of China who believe that these reserves could be used to create enormous international economic mischief if, for instance, China were suddenly to flood world markets with its reserves, to call in the many loans in which it has invested (especially in the United States) with those reserves, or to decide to quit financing the American debt with those reserves. While almost any of those possibilities would have enormous negative potential consequences for China as well (see discussion below), it is also indicative of the underlying relationship between China and the rest of the world that these kinds of possibilities cause as much consternation as they do.

These dynamics help to frame the "ambiguous partnership" between the United States and China. The "new" China with which the United States must deal is a far different place than the China of the Cold War. During that earlier time frame, the major defining characteristic of U.S.–Chinese relations was military confrontation, with the Korean War and mutual nuclear saber-rattling as the primary manifestations of that relationship. With the thawing of relations begun in 1972 by an invited visit of the American table tennis team to China (so-called "ping pong diplomacy"), military bombast has dissipated, and the military content of differences has narrowed to one mostly of future Chinese intent. Politically, the economic revolution has resulted in the extension of considerable personal freedoms for the Chinese people, although these do not—and may well not, for the foreseeable future—extend to political democratization in a way that would please Americans. Economically, while the PRC remains a titular communist state, it has embraced most of the trappings of Western capitalist production, and the basis of competition is not the clash of economic philosophies so much as it is over the terms and efficiencies with which free market principles are applied by the two countries and the future that confrontation may produce. The real crunch question in the equation is whether political and economic freedom can exist independently of one another or whether they are inseparable in the long run.

China in the World

The trajectories of the two major powers of the Cold War communist world could hardly be more different, but there are similarities as well. During the Cold War, the Soviet Union was considered the senior, stronger pillar of world communism, yet the discontent against communism of the 1980s overwhelmed and overthrew Soviet communism and similar systems throughout Soviet-dominated Eastern Europe starting in 1989; China endured Tiananmen Square in 1989 and emerged stronger in some ways for the experience. Russia has seen its stature in the world decline and is now attempting resurgence to the first rank of countries; China has eclipsed the Soviet successor state of Russia and has steadily climbed to a position approaching that of the superpower Russia once was. No one talks of the twenty-first century as a "Russian century," but the possibilities that China will be a, if not the, dominant country of this century are widespread. As a result, China is now arguably considered a more important state in the world, and thus in American foreign policy, than is Russia. The Russian trajectory in the world is uncertain, dependent on economic developments not yet evident; the challenge of the Chinese economy to the world is far less ambiguous.

China and Russia have made similar bargains with their people, both of which are frustrating to Americans and others who believe that the democratization of both countries is pivotal to their emergence as positive, peaceful members of the international order. The "petrolist" economy created by Putin's use of petroleum revenues has created an arguably Faustian bargain between the state and the Russian people, effectively buying off the extension of their political rights with immediate economic gains. Deng Xiaopeng, the principal architect of the Chinese economic miracle, made a similar bargain between the CCP and the Chinese people, in effect a quid pro quo wherein the government agreed to make the Chinese people prosperous if they left the party's control unchallenged. The difference is that the Chinese economic promise is backed by a much firmer economy than is the Russian, and thus it may well prove more adaptable and resilient with time. Moreover, a generational change is about to occur in China, as students who were sent to the West for their educations reach and begin to exercise positions of authority; their attitudes have been shaped by their exposure to the outside world, although it remains to be seen how much they will seek to change the bargain between the people and the CCP.

The future prospects for the two former Cold War adversaries are also much different. The physical path for China is clearer and brighter because of China's firm stature in an international system in which economic measures increasingly define power, but it is uncertain in what direction the leadership and people wish to move. China's current major priorities are still internal: "economic growth and political stability," in Economy's December 2010 terms, and its foreign dealings gain value to the degree they contribute to that goal. As a result, Medeiros argues, "China does not yet see itself as a global power—even less as a global leader."

If the Chinese see interactions with the outside world primarily as a tool to promote their internal situation, Russians see the relationship in the opposite way. Russia's abiding concern, even fixation, is with returning to its "rightful" place as a major power, even a superpower. To the Russians, economic change and growth gains its greatest significance to the extent that it contributes to achieving its foreign policy goals. Which approach works best remains a question.

China emerges as a power in transition with an apparently very expansive future that creates great uncertainties for the United States and its relations with the world's most populous country. While the future for China, and thus the parameters of the challenges it may pose, are overwhelmingly positive from a Chinese perspective, they are bounded by physical limitations that may mitigate or shape the nature of that challenge.

The Physical Setting

By any physical measure, China is a formidable country. It is, as already noted, the world's most populous country, a distinction it will cede to India within the next decade, and it is the fourth largest country in area in the world. Its sheer size made it an important place even before it began its transformation to being a modern, competitive country economically and politically, and projections of current trends, particularly in the economic area, suggest strongly its potential to be a dominant member of the community of states.

China's size, however, also brings some liabilities that are not universally shared, particularly in comparison with the United States, whose size it approximates. The United States has land borders that potentially need defending with only two countries (Mexico and Canada), neither of which is a historic enemy. By contrast, as Medeiros points out, "China lives in a tough neighborhood. . . . China shares border with 14 nations [*sic*], some of which it has gone to war with." The countries it has fought—and with which it still has ongoing border disputes—include India (over disputed Kashmiri territory it occupies as discussed in Chapter 5) and Russia (with which it has considerable territorial disagreements over large parts of Siberia). In addition to international border frictions, China has its own equivalent of Russia's internal abroad, featuring potentially rebellious breakaway efforts in places like Tibet, Inner Mongolia, and Uighur-dominated Xinjiang Province (a Muslim majority province in western China). Further, its long-standing dispute over Taiwan is a major concern of the Chinese government. Historically, China dealt with the peoples on its border by reducing them to *suzerain* status (tribute-bearing entities demonstrating deference to China), and many in the region and beyond fear and suspect that a more powerful China will attempt to reassert this form of sphere-of-influence relationship as it grows in international stature.

Despite its vast size, China is also a resource-dependent country, particularly in the energy area. China does have sizable stores of a variety of mineral resources and various ores (mining is one of the largest forms of employment in the country), but the country is deficient in the energy resources necessary to sustain and nurture further economic development (energy consumption is the single most reliable indicator of economic activity in developed, industrial societies). This is particularly true of petroleum energy: China produces almost 4 million barrels of oil per day (fifth most in the world) but consumes 8.2 million barrels per day (third in the world). The gap is filled with importation, which is today the fourth largest among world countries. With only the world's 13th largest known oil reserves (20.35 billion barrels, slightly less than American reserves), China is thus an aggressive competitor in the world's oil market, which leads it to support oil rogues like Iran and even minor oil producers like Sudan. China's need for additional access to oil is underscored by its desire to continue growing as an industrial power and by its decision to produce as many as 15 million automobiles a year for domestic consumption.

China also faces a different, and less publicized, natural resource problem: potable water. In a ground-breaking article on China's place in the world in a 2005 *Foreign Affairs* article, Zheng Bijian pointed out that part of the motivation for China's "peaceful rise" as a world power comes from a shortage of water. Maintaining that China's current resources are "one-quarter of the world's average," this contributes to a major "shortage of resources" with which the government must come to grips. To dramatize the consequences of the problem, Pope and Lomberg explain that "water tables of major grain-producing areas in northern China are dropping at a rate of five feet per year," an ominous sign. Kurlantzick adds, "Much of northern China's breadbasket is in danger of going dry."

China's oil and other natural resources quandary create additional policy problems and limitations for the regime. One regards pollution and alternate energy sources. China, and especially its cities, have among the highest levels of pollution of anywhere in the world, a condition the Chinese government is committed to alleviating. China has, for instance, become a major advocate of the global warming movement's goals (a point of potential cooperation with the Obama administration). At the same time, energy needs propel China in opposite directions: one of the major energy sources China has in some abundance is coal, which opponents of global warming maintain is a major contributor to carbon dioxide pollution. This example, however, illustrates that natural resources are a particular concern. Robert Kaplan, a major critic of China, summarizes the concern: "China's foreign policy ambitions are as aggressive as those of the United States a century ago . . . and are propelled by its needs to secure energy, metals, and strategic minerals in order to support the rising standards of living of its immense population."

The Chinese also have a demographic problem with two prongs: an aging population and low birth rates, both of which contribute to a future with a shrinking population that has lower levels of productive labor. Improvements in medical care have reduced China's death rate, with the beneficial effect that life expectancy in China is now 74.5 years (compared to Russia's slightly over 66 years). At the same time, China's 30-year old "one child" policy (couples are officially allowed to have only a single child) has resulted in an average birth rate of 1.5 babies per female, meaning, according to Feng, "fertility has dropped to a level lower than that of many developed countries, including the United States, Britain, and France." The result, as Kurlantzick points out, will be at least 400 million elderly Chinese by 2040, for whom there is an inadequate social welfare system currently in place. The Chinese recognize this problem, and although they have not officially rescinded the one-child restriction, it has been relaxed in parts of the country, exceptions are granted in some categories (e.g., in cases where both parents are only children and for ethnic minorities), and increasingly, parents who want more than one child simply pay the fines levied for doing so. As noted in Chapter 1, a fertility rate of 2.1 is generally considered necessary to maintain population size, with the result that the overall Chinese population is likely to shrink by as much as 200 million by the middle of the century unless the policy changes.

Given China's enormous population, a reduction is not necessarily a bad thing, but it has consequences, especially when combined with an increasingly aged population that arises from longer life expectancy. For one thing, Feng states, "each future generation will be 25 percent smaller than the one preceding it," and this will mean "the abundance of young, inexpensive labor" that has been a primary reason for Chinese manufacturing competitiveness "is soon to be history." In addition, China will face the same consequences that other countries (including most dramatically its neighbor Japan) have had to confront: an increasing burden on a shrinking workforce to support parents and grandparents without a well-developed social welfare system to shoulder the burden. While too much can be made of these trends, Feng warns that "the aging of China's population represents a crisis because its ramifications are huge and long-standing, and because its effects will be hard to reverse."

An additional aspect of Chinese demographics concerns the uneven physical development of the country. Almost all of the growth and modernization associated with the Chinese economic miracle have occurred in the eastern part of the country, notably the four SEZs, whereas much of the western part of the country remains almost wholly undeveloped. This unevenness has led to increased demands for additional resources directed toward China's poorest regions, and one answer has been population migration and urbanization. As Economy points out in the November/December 2010 *Foreign Affairs* one result is that "half the world's new construction occurs in China, and, according to one estimate, the country will construct 20,000–50,000 new skyscrapers during the coming decades." Rapid urbanization creates a number of problems of its own (e.g., pollution, the need for government-funded sectors such as education) that divert the Chinese from other activities. China has, however, an impressive record of infrastructure development such as the unveiling of the world's fastest passenger trains in 2010, and an educational system that is world-class and has, by most measures, eclipsed the performance of American schools.

China's physical environment is thus a source of both opportunity and challenge for the country as it faces the world. China started its growth into being a major force in the world a little over 30 years ago, in 1979, and its transformation in the intervening years has clearly been impressive. The pace of change in China has been dizzying, and it remains one of the world's most dynamic societies, a stark contrast with the centuries that preceded this change and were marked by virtually no change in the Chinese situation. This contrast in both how China is developing and how the world can cope with a China so unlike the "mysterious" Oriental power of the past helps form the context of Chinese uniqueness in the world.

China as a Unique State

One major reason it is difficult to know how to deal with China is because of China's uniqueness within the community of states. The veil of Chinese "inscrutability" has been partly lifted since Deng Xiaoping opened the Chinese economy to the world, but it has not been removed altogether. The Chinese economy is among the most vibrant in the world, and yet it contains paradoxes that make future projections difficult.

While hardly anyone doubts the China will continue to grow as an economic giant, for instance, exactly what dimensions and consequences its growth will eventually take are far less certain. China has sustained economic growth partly at the expense of its own citizens; the levels of consumer activity by Chinese citizens is far lower than for the countries with which it trades, and the annual savings rate for Chinese citizens is among the highest in the world. Growth has also been uneven: there are far more prosperous Chinese in the eastern part of the country than in the less developed western areas, and even as the overall size of the economy challenges and threatens to surpass the rest of the world, China's huge population dilutes its impact on individual Chinese: at $6,700 in per capita GDP, China ranks no better than 130th in the world. How long the Chinese will sustain personal deprivation in the name of state economic growth is an open question, and the Chinese government's decision to vastly increase automobile production for the domestic market is at least indirect evidence that the government recognizes the problem as well. The shrinkage in numbers of entry-level workers due to demographics will eventually prejudice economic growth, and shrinking global natural resources (e.g., availability of energy) and problems specific to China (e.g., inadequate water supplies) pose additional imponderables.

China is also a militarily unique state. Historically, the emphasis of Chinese military forces has been defensive: China historically has been more concerned about keeping the "barbarians" out rather than in spreading its domain beyond its suzerain sphere of influence. The current force of modernization is certainly aimed at reinforcing China's ability to defend itself, but commentators worry that it will be extended outward, certainly to those areas, such as parts of the South Pacific, that have strategic resources that the Chinese need. Given its militant communist past, others worry that China could turn into a major military competitor to the United States both within the region and even globally. China has consistently maintained itself not to be an aggressive, expansionist power, but it is also sufficiently opaque to allow contrary images to be formed and sustained by outsiders.

China's political intentions are likewise cloudy. China is certainly a dominant player in the world economy and is one of the more aggressive proponents of the power shift in the economic realm from the predominance of the G8 (of which it is not a member) to the G20 (of which it is a member). At the broader level of influencing global politics, the Chinese intent is much more ambiguous, a trait attributed in no small measure by Economy to Chinese ambivalence about its role. "If the international community is in the dark about China's 21st-century trajectory," she argues in *Foreign Policy*, "it is likely because there is no real consensus among the Chinese themselves." It is within this setting that American foreign policy is debated.

U.S.–CHINESE RELATIONS

The relations between the United States and China are virtually unique among American foreign policy situations in the world. The two countries have very close relations on one level—primarily in the economic realm—but are warily related at other levels. There is some tension between them even at the economic level, as each views the other's economic trajectory as possibly dangerous to it. In addition, there are historically based suspicions on the part of the Americans, undoubtedly shared in some way by the Chinese, about the military intentions each has toward the other. These tensions, in turn, affect the relations between the two countries at the more purely political level, in matters as diverse as policy toward North Korea and Taiwan and global environmental and energy policies.

The result is a kind of dynamic tension between the two, something that Medeiros describes as the "'stakeholder paradox'. On one hand, Washington is encouraging China to define broadly its national interests. . . . On the other hand, many American and international strategists worry that this policy may broaden China's global ambitions while improving its capabilities to pursue them."

Chinese vibrancy, in other words, is valued because it can contribute to the prosperity of the United States and other countries of the world; given the historic animosity between communist China and the West, however, the enthusiasm is tempered by the fear that China may develop menacing muscles as it become more vibrant.

The Chinese have made efforts to ease these apprehensions. The "peaceful rise" thesis put forward by Zheng Bijian, for instance, carried at least implicit governmental backing, and enumerations of Chinese foreign policy goals are generally stated in nonthreatening terms. Medeiros, for instance, argues that there are five basic Chinese foreign policy goals: first, "a stable international environment to facilitate continued reform and development at home"; second, reassurances "that its growing capabilities will not undermine other states' economic and security interests"; third, reductions in "the ability of other nations to contain, constrain, or otherwise hinder China's revitalization"; fourth, a determination to "diversify its access to energy and other natural resources"; and fifth, reduction of "Taiwan's international space." The first two objectives are overtly reassuring to a wary West, and the other three priorities offer only mild or historically based antagonisms, notably regarding Taiwan.

The historic flash point in this relationship has been Taiwan. China considers the island Republic of China an integral part of the PRC, whereas some Taiwanese favor a formal declaration of independence from the mainland, a possibility vehemently opposed by the PRC government. The basic U.S. position has been the "one China" policy, which advocates the unification of the two entities through peaceful accession of Taiwan to the PRC on terms similar to those by which Hong Kong was incorporated into China.

Interactions between the United States and China begin within the context of the interaction between Chinese and American foreign policy goals and also with recognition that the realities of the evolving China place boundaries on those relations and the ability of the United States to influence Chinese policy. Shambaugh, for instance, suggests "six dimensions of today's China that the United States needs to recognize." These are: (1) acceptance of the likelihood that "Chinese economic growth is likely to continue apace indefinitely"; (2) political change that will occur "slowly and in its own fashion"; (3) a military capability that is "becoming a force to reckon with"; (4) emergence as "truly a global actor—but only a partial global power"; (5) continued Chinese ambivalence that makes it "confident abroad but insecure at home"; and (6) a determination that "the 'Taiwan issue' has essentially been resolved."

This is a complex and apparently contradictory list in some regards. It poses a China that is vibrant and growing, but one that is reluctant to be assertive, despite the development of capabilities that can allow it to be more assertive (military power). At the same time, it cautions against any romantic notions the United States (or at least some Americans) might have about somehow recasting the Chinese in the American political image. The various dimensions of the relationship that emerges from this backdrop can be viewed from three separate but interrelated vantage points: economic relations, military relations, and political relations. The more positive the relationship is on each dimension, the more likely that cooperation is likely on the other dimensions; the converse is also likely true.

The Economic Dimension

As anyone who has shopped for consumer goods recently can easily attest, the heart of economic relations between China and the United States arises from the lopsided trade in consumer goods between the two countries, a phenomenon that rests on what Miller refers to as the two pillars of Chinese financial foreign policy: "accumulating foreign exchange reserves and sending money abroad." The accumulation of reserves, of course, is the result of China's development of the capacity to produce consumer goods at prices that undersell its international competition because "Beijing continues to subsidize exports heavily" through preferential business loaning practices and exchange rates, according to Miller. The United States is the largest consumer of these products, creating an imbalance in trade between the two. Despite ongoing efforts to create some balance by increasing American exports to China, the gap remains wide. The result is that China has, as mentioned earlier, developed a huge surplus of American dollars, many of which it has invested back into the United States.

A major area of Chinese investment has been in subsidizing loans (through bonds and the like) floated by the American government to finance its deficit spending. This deficit has, in turn, been the object of great political concern in the United States for at least two reasons. The first is the assertion that China increasingly "owns" the United States because of the sheer volume of loans they have underwritten. The other is that the Chinese might choose at some politically or strategically vital time to quit buying American loans, causing a crisis of vulnerability in the United States economy and compromising America's ability to do its business. Although figures are not available regarding exact amounts, for instance, much of the American military efforts in Iraq and Afghanistan have been financed by Chinese-backed deficit spending; what would happen to either of those efforts if suddenly the Chinese announced they would buy no more American securities?

It may provide cold comfort, but there are mitigating factors, the most prominent of which arise from the mutual dependence of the two countries upon one another. One source of this is the high interconnectedness between American purchase of Chinese goods and the internal Chinese economy. Lieberthal explains: "high American personal consumption and high Chinese personal savings are directly linked, each enabling the other. Effectively, the United States has borrowed China's savings to finance personal consumption. At the same time, China has accumulated the money to maintain high savings and make loans to the United States by producing goods that Americans buy with consumer dollars." China, in other words, can only harm the American economy by taking actions that would harm China as well.

This logic extends to the worrisome accumulation of American dollars by the Chinese. This phenomenon has quite rightly been the subject of concern within the United States, particularly by figures such as Donald Trump because, among other things, it may signify negative trends about American economic competitiveness in the world. That this accumulation also affords China useful leverage against the United States, however, is not as obvious as it may seem.

Holding a great deal of American dollars creates a paradox of sorts for China. Some Chinese economists join their American counterparts in decrying this phenomenon, but because it creates a dependency for China regarding the strength of the American economy. Lieberthal describes this in terms of what he calls a "dollar trap. It [China] holds so many dollars that if it tries to sell enough of them to make a serious impact on its exposure, the sale will weaken the dollar and increase the value of the currencies China is purchasing instead." The result is an anomaly of mutual dependence that Miller captures: "In truth, the United States and China are holding each other hostage. The United States needs China to buy its obligations, and for the foreseeable future, China will have few other places than the U.S. dollar to store the foreign currency it has accumulated."

For the time being, China and the United States are thus in an economic embrace, if one that is conceptually uncomfortable for both countries. This balance is also probably stable for the time being, and shrill cries of concern about the Chinese resultant ability to hold an economic hammer are probably overstated since economic actions by China to hurt the United States would also be harmful to China, possibly with negative domestic political ramifications (an economic downturn in China might make Chinese wonder if their political bargain with the government is such a good deal, for instance).

At the same time, no one would argue that it is in the long-term interest of the United States to be in the dependent status it is in with China. The root of China's current advantage is that it has seized a comparative competitive advantage with the United States in the area of consumer industrial production, and the danger is that this advantage could spread to other areas, including those with military, strategic applications. Almost no one disagrees with the proposition that future economic advantage will be tied intimately to technological domination. Technological innovation has long been an American strong suit, but that advantage is narrowing, at least in part because China is investing its resources (many derived from its relationship with the United States) into areas that can improve its relative position, notably infrastructure and education. Standardized test scores, for instance, indicate the Chinese have erased in the gap in some areas like science and mathematics education, and that unless the United States adopts *domestic* policies that will make it more competitive in these areas, there could be significant *foreign policy* ramifications with China (a topic discussed in the next major section).

The Military Dimension

Military modernization is the "fourth modernization" prescribed by Deng Xiaoping in 1979 (the other three are agriculture, science and technology, and industry), and it has been the most controversial. The reason is simple: although China's program of military modernization has been justified publicly as largely defensive in nature, it has produced military capabilities that may be usable in the future for more adventurous, even aggressive purposes. As Godwin puts it, "When viewed from the perspective of China's neighbors and the United States, however, Beijing's defense modernization programs appear too extensive to be designed for a military capability limited to the defense of continental China and its territorial and maritime claims."

How troubling these prospects are depends on the overall view different people have about China. To the devout Cold Warriors (those whose experience and orientation remains within a Cold War perspective), the prospects are threatening, long-standing, and particularly foreboding to the so-called neoconservatives who were highly influential in the George W. Bush administration. Kagan and Kristol, writing in *Present Dangers* (a kind of neoconservative bible), argued in 2000 that "The past decade also saw the rise of an increasingly hostile and belligerent China." Legro, an advisor to then Vice President Richard Cheney, argued in 2007, "Virtually every strategic thinker in the United States agrees that China, if present trends continue, represents a greater potential threat in the long run than any other nation in the world." Kaplan, a vocal protagonist of the Chinese regime, agrees, warning "There is an arms race going on in Asia, and the United States will have to face this reality when it substantially reduces its forces in Iraq and Afghanistan."

Those who see China primarily as a threat favor a policy of containment of the PRC. In Kagan's words, "A successful containment strategy will require increasing, not decreasing, overall [U.S.] defense capabilities. . . . Containment would seek to compel Beijing to choose political liberalization as the best way to safeguard their economic gains and win acceptance in the international community." This preference, which formed the basis for the Bush administration's policy toward the Chinese militarily, is known as strategic hedging, or "Asia-first," according to Shambaugh. Operationally, the policy translated into an attempt to encircle China with American-initiated defense arrangements. Shambaugh adds that "for most Asian governments, the US effort effectively to encircle China with a ring of security relationships creates unease and places those governments in an uneasy position vis-à-vis Beijing."

Not everyone agrees with this interpretation of Chinese intent. No one denies that the Chinese military is growing in size and capability, but they do disagree on how ominous these developments are, particularly for the United States. Part of the disagreement arises from the exact dimensions of Chinese defense expenditures, which, according to Thompson, "vary considerably, ranging from $69.5 billion to $150 billion." Even if one accepts the higher end of this range, it still represents no more than one-fifth to one-fourth of the amount the United States spends on defense (because the United States routinely places defense-related spending in budgets other than those for defense, such as nuclear weapons in the Department of Energy budget, there is similar disagreement over how much the United States spends as well), and despite robust, double-digit increases on the Chinese budget, it would be a long time before the physical expenditure gap is narrowed appreciably.

Analysts of diverse orientations are forced to admit that China does not yet pose a military threat to the United States. Thompson states the position bluntly: "China simply does not have the capability to challenge the United States in the Pacific, although its modernization program has increased its ability to engage the United States close to its [China's] shores." Kaplan maintains that to the Chinese, "Central Asia, Mongolia, the Russian Far East, and Southeast Asia are natural zones of Chinese influence" and that there is a military aspect to that influence. These are also areas in which the United States has relatively minor interests (i.e., interests with little or no military implications), so that Kaplan admits that "the chances of a war between China and the United States is remote; the Chinese military threat to the United States is only indirect."

The larger concern with Chinese military expansion has been in its power projection capabilities, notably naval and air assets that can be projected to the island chains off the China coast where, among other things, the rich Spratly Island oil reserves are located. This increase in capability is generally assigned to Chinese interests in the two island chains off its coast. Economy (December 2010) explains that Chinese naval strategy has "three stages: first, to a navy that can cover the 'first island chain,' which includes islands from Japan to Taiwan and the Philippines; then to a regional navy with capabilities extending to Guam, Indonesia, and Australia [the second chain]; and finally, to a global force by 2050." The first stage of this progression is dangerous to the United States only to the extent it could bring China and the United States into direct military conflict over Taiwan, to which the United States has traditionally offered its physical protection. The second could pose a problem for keeping open the sea lanes in important naval "choke points" like the Straits of Malacca; only the third, and distinctly most distant, goal offers any real challenge to American naval supremacy in the world.

How much of a military problem China poses to the United States is an ideologically influenced case of "glass half full, glass half empty." A positive spin on Chinese military growth suggests this is only a natural development for a very prosperous trading country seeking to reestablish itself within the ranks of the world's powers; as such, it is a process to be watched but not over which to sound the alarm. China's military growth is part of a larger "glass half full" that can be made fuller by improved relations across the board that are not affected overly negatively by the military expansion. The other side views a historically antagonistic China as a present and potentially future enemy (a "glass half empty"), meaning the buildup is a foreboding of unpleasant relations to come; the implication of this interpretation, of course, is to raise warning flags about, and to proceed with caution on, other foreign policy matters.

The Political Dimension

Hosting the 2008 Summer Olympics was China's "coming out party" as a major international actor, intended to demonstrate that China was a modern, normal state rather than a Maoist totalitarian outsider, the ghost of which has long haunted China's international image. It was, in Zheng Biajin's words in his 2005 article, a chance to demonstrate that "China advocates a new international political and economic order. China's development depends on world peace—a peace that its development will in turn reinforce." The Olympics had the major task of replacing the image of tanks rumbling in Tiananmen Square with the smiling, joyous faces of the world's finest athletes and their supporters enjoying the People's Republic of China.

China is indeed a very different place than it was in 1989, when the suppression in Tiananmen Square took place, and this change presents opportunities for political collaboration, but within limits. Walder describes how the atmosphere has changed: "China's gradual approach to economic reform has worked. . . . China's overall political trajectory now looks quite favorable. . . . Chinese youth and educated public now display a strong sense of national pride. . . . China's party leaders are fundamentally united in their views about the directions the country should take." For the United States, this is both good and not so good news. Positively, it means a more confident and apparently less paranoid, militaristic China that is less a threat to world peace. Not so positively, China has developed its consensus on the basis of a nondemocratic political bargain that places limits on how closely it and the United States can become allied in the international sphere. A major source of limitation comes, according to Lieberthal, from the fact that "neither side, even today, trusts the long-term intentions of the other toward itself."

China and the United States share concerns in a number of policy areas, although their differing perspectives mean they do not (and likely will not) always see these problems and their solutions in exactly the same light. Finding a common ground on issues will thus be possible but difficult, as a brief examination of three points of policy intersection may suggest.

The first is the problem of North Korea. The Democratic Republic of Korea (DPRK) has been a major provocateur in the region, largely because of its nuclear weapons program (see Chapter 4), and its aggressive behavior (as seen in the 2010 confrontation with South Korea) is a major source of regional, and even global, concern. China has traditionally been the DPRK's closest ally and as close to a "friend" as it has in the world, although both sides view one another with some suspicion—China because of the nature of the North Korean regime, and the North Koreans because they are not quite sure the Chinese do not entertain predatory feelings toward them.

The United States and China share an interest in controlling, and even defusing, tensions on the Korean peninsula, which means, at a minimum, convincing the North Koreans to abandon their nuclear program. The longer-term solution to the tensions on the peninsula, however, requires political change in North Korea itself toward a more stable, responsible regime. The two giants are not in close accord on exactly how to achieve that goal and what the future might be.

The question is the future of the DPRK. The United States (and its South Korean allies) clearly prefer a gradual liberalization of the North, which includes moves toward economic modernization and democratization as the necessities for creating a stable regime. The ultimate logic of such change leads to a reunification of the peninsula into one Korea, and this is a prospect that China does not so readily embrace, even if it would stabilize the peninsula.

China, quite simply, prefers a divided Korea because it means that there is no hostile or potentially hostile regime on its borders. It was the prospect of forceful reunification by the United States in late 1950 that caused Chinese informal intervention in the Korean War, and there is little reason to believe the Chinese are any more amenable to having a united Korea aligned with the United States directly on its border today than it was 60 years ago. As a result, China "would prefer to see a far more modern, authoritarian state develop in North Korea— such a state would create a buffer between China and South Korea" in Kaplan's view. Americans, and particularly those who view the region in negative, military terms, should doubt the viability or peacefulness of such a North Korea. Thus, while both China and the United States want a less troublesome North Korea, they disagree about the shape of that country, and this disagreement is partly fueled by their mutual uncertainty of the other's intention: Does the United States see its preferred solution as a kind of Trojan horse to present China with an enemy on its borders? Or is China motivated by wanting to maintain a hostile vassal state as a buffer state in the ongoing Asian competition?

The perpetual Taiwanese question is similar. Ever since the triumphant Chinese communists forced the Nationalist Chinese of Chiang Kai-Shek off the mainland and onto Taiwan in 1949, there has been a dispute over that island's status. The Nationalists on the island view it as the base of the Republic of China (the mainland's name before the communist takeover), and the PRC considers it a renegade, hostile province of China. Both the mainland and most Nationalist Chinese in principle agree that China and Taiwan are part of the same country; their difference is over the process and eventual status of Taiwan as part of China.

The United States has been involved since the beginning of this rift as the chief protector of Taiwan, and over the years has heavily armed the island's armed forces and helped develop a vibrant, prosperous economy there. Moreover, the United States has been the chief military protector of Taiwan, with an American Sixth Fleet that has the security of the Strait of Taiwan separating the island from the mainland as a major priority. China can only forcefully occupy and annex Taiwan by forcibly confronting the United States, raising a prospect of war between them, and this reality has both helped deter any such visions that Beijing holds and hindered relations between Washington and the PRC.

Once again, both China and the United States accept in principle the long-term accession of Taiwan to union with the mainland, which is the heart of the "one China" policy. Because Taiwan is both very wealthy and possesses considerable technological know-how, a Taiwan that is part of China would greatly increase the clout of the Chinese economy, and in fact, Taiwanese investors represent the single largest source of foreign private capital going into China. The question which continues to befuddle progress toward unification centers on the terms of accession, which translates into how "special" a status Taiwan will have after union. The precedents of Hong Kong and Macao, formerly independent entities now incorporated into China, are often offered as a model, but the outcome of those experiments is not yet complete. Until it is, the countries on the two sides of the Taiwanese Strait arm themselves against one another suspiciously, with arsenals bristling, and a United States that is not quite certain of Chinese intent stands on the sidelines, prepared physically to come to Taiwan's aid. The most dangerously combustible situation is what might happen if Taiwanese separatists gain control of the island and issue a declaration of independence. Such an act could produce a PRC military threat or action that could produce a confrontation with the United States.

Limited, suspicious cooperation between China and the United States extends to other, nonterritorial concerns. The current issue of global warming is an example of this concern. During the Bush administration, the issue was a matter of major contention between the two states. Bush vigorously opposed international control efforts such as those included in the Kyoto Protocols on the grounds that they placed an especially heavy, unfair burden on the United States since the costs of emissions control would fall heavily on private American polluters, who would have the costs added to their products, making them less competitive. In addition, the Bush administration argued that important competitors—and rising polluters—like China and India were exempted from the Kyoto regulations, despite their increasing contribution to the global carbon dioxide problem. China largely ignored the controversy, believing carbon-based pollution was simply the cost of development.

Those positions have changed, and the United States and China emerged from the Copenhagen follow-on meetings to the Kyoto process (see a discussion in Snow, Chapter 13) having cosponsored one of the few positive recommendations that arose from the conference. Lieberthal cites three principal reasons for this coincidence of interests: "First, President Obama's view on the issue is the opposite of President Bush's. . . . Second, the Chinese government has greatly increased its own attention to climate change in the past two years. . . . Third, the scientific community's understanding of the speed, scope and consequences of climate change is improving rapidly." Even in this coincidence of interests, however, there is the seed of rivalry. Part of Obama's advocacy of tackling global warming has been a challenge to make the United States the leader in discovering and commercializing "green" industries to lower pollution, and the Chinese have announced a similar intent. In the area of global warming, China and the United States will both cooperate and compete.

U.S. OPTIONS

What emerges from an analysis of contemporary U.S.–Chinese foreign relations is a sort of ambivalence—a relationship that combines cooperation and competition and that is conditioned by a legacy of antagonism and misunderstanding of one another. At the economic level, the two countries are bound together almost like Siamese twins: they cannot be separated nor can either take actions harmful to the other without injuring themselves. At the same time, each retains some residual distrust of the other: Will China use its store of American dollars to damage the United States? Will the United States attempt somehow to renege on its financial obligations to China? Militarily, China poses little real threat to the United States, and the United States has little reason to menace China militarily, yet there remain mutual suspicions of one another that keep them at arm's length. Politically, there are points of convergent interests, but always tinged by at least a latent divergence as well.

It is within this context that American options in relations with China must be cast. Two things are abundantly clear about the future. One is that China is determined to continue its ascent to the ranks of major powers in the world. As Godwin states the case, "Beijing's primary strategic objective is to foster a security environment that allows the country to sustain the national development so crucial to China's future and to its ambitions to become a global power." There is apparently some disagreement about exactly what the destination of this path to great power should be, as Economy (in *Foreign Policy*) notes: "A great debate has arisen among China's intelligentsia over the country's role in the world." That debate, of course, is about *what* role China will play, not *whether* China should adopt a leadership role.

The other reality confronting American policy makers is that there is not a great deal the United States can do to shape the Chinese future. As Shambaugh points out, American policy during the Bush years rested on four "pillars." The first was *shaping*: the use of interchanges at the people-to-people level to impress the Chinese with the desire of Americans to have a healthy relationship, and it was a strategy "aimed largely at Chinese society instead of government." The second pillar was *engagement*, attempts to "build a sound institutional infrastructure that would anchor the relationship, buffer it from inevitable disruptions, and establish bases for cooperation." Most of this effort has been focused on the economic level. Third was *integration*, efforts to integrate China into the international system as a normal state, featured such efforts as sponsoring Chinese membership in the World Trade Organization. The fourth, and most controversial, pillar was *strategic hedging*. This "Asia-first" element of strategy, as discussed earlier, has been a staple of the neoconservatives and was manifested in the attempt of the United States to develop security relationships with countries on China's periphery, a practice the Chinese understandably have found offensive.

How much of the Bush legacy should the Obama administration have adopted as policy? The first three pillars are positive and not objectionable to the Chinese because they do not offer direct assaults on China's development but only help shape its international direction. If the United States wishes to increase its effectiveness in these areas, it may be that the answer is not so much in direct dealing with the Chinese but in the reinvigoration of its competitive base with the Chinese. Shambaugh suggests, for instance, that the United States should "develop its own domestic strategy for dealing with China," which includes elements such as reforming American education to competitive levels with China and other countries in areas such as mathematics and science education as a way to reestablish competitiveness or supremacy in areas of technological prominence (e.g., so-called green technologies) that are likely to dominate the future. China has a much greater incentive to pay heed to a vigorously competitive United States than a quiescent, even declining, country whose most distinguishing domestic economic characteristic is its chronic overconsumption. The Obama administration is cognizant of this strategic need, although it is being resisted by a Congress much more driven by other priorities such as deficit reduction.

The fourth pillar of Bush policy, strategic hedging, is the most vulnerable to change. This policy connotes a basic wariness of China's intentions that does not sit well with the Chinese and may actually lend credibility to those in China arguing for more robust military modernization as a hedge against the Americans. Moreover, it is not at all clear how much leverage the United States gains by implementing parts of this strategy, such as basing agreements with Central Asian former Soviet republics that are proximate to western China. Moreover, reminders of the American commitment to defend Taiwan may be unnecessarily provocative given the recognition by the United States, China, and most Taiwanese that the integration of the island is a matter of timing and the form of association, not a question of long-term Taiwanese independence.

These kinds of policy options arise from a situation in which the United States is in no position to force more fundamental change on China, a country which has become, by many measures, a peer of the United States. Rather than, for example, beating the Chinese over the head with demands for political liberalization (the jailing of Chinese dissident and Nobel Peace Prize recipient Liu Xiaobo, for instance), it may be wiser and more productive to adopt a more modest role and set of expectations. Economy (November/December 2010) proposes such a set of policy options: "The White House needs to consider a policy on three different planes. First, the Obama administration should continue to work with others to help influence Beijing. . . . The White House must also continue to make clear that it believes certain core values should underpin the international system. . . . The third plane of U.S. policy should concern the United States' domestic interests and objectives." One can quibble with this list, but what is striking is its modesty, a realization that the United States is in no position to dictate to one of the world's largest (in population) and most powerful members anymore, if it ever had such a capability.

CONCLUSIONS

Relations between the United States and China have gone from bitter antagonism in the wake of their opposition in the Korean War of 1950–1953 to a broad, if tentative, level of cooperative interaction in contemporary terms. The evolution of that change has been stimulated by the rise of China as a major manufacturing power that is now the United States' major external supplier of consumer goods, and that relationship has effectively intertwined the economies of the two sides in ways that are intimate but not entirely comfortable to either. China needs a healthy America to buy its goods and for investing its profits from those sales, while Americans worry about the possibly compromising vulnerability that this situation creates for the United States. The two countries have become partners, but the exact nature and direction of that partnership is ambiguous and the subject of real disagreement.

Much of the concern about China in the United States stems from invidious comparisons between the trajectories of the two powers. Many Americans (and others) see the United States either in decline or at least static, while Chinese dynamism and growth may signal that it will surpass the United States as the world's most significant country. As noted earlier, projections already show that the sheer size of the Chinese economy will surpass that of the United States as soon as 2015, even if the crushing size of the Chinese population and the uneven development of the country will mean that there will be great pressures on the use of that wealth. Chinese military power is growing, and even if it is not, as most observers agree, a current threat to the United States, it certainly could become so in the not-so-distant future. Likewise, China remains politically unassertive in the international realm, but will that condition remain as well?

The extent to which Chinese growth is a major concern for the United States depends, to a large degree, on the way China develops in the future, and like all change, that direction is not entirely predictable. For years, China has been considered a rising power, and it has, to a remarkable extent, risen to the rank of a world major power. The future, however, remains clouded. As leading China observer Minxin Pei (2006) puts it, "China may be rising, but no one knows whether it can fly."

STUDY/DISCUSSION QUESTIONS

1. How are U.S. relations with the People's Republic of China unique? How has Chinese history over the past two centuries contributed to China's evolution and the nature of the U.S.–PRC relationship? How does that historic relationship affect current American attitudes toward China?
2. What were the "four modernizations" in China? How have the implementation of these contributed to the Chinese "economic miracle"? How does this phenomenon help explain differences in Chinese and Russian development since the end of the Cold War?
3. What sources of Chinese vulnerability emerge from an analysis of the physical setting of modern China? Elaborate.
4. Typify the general nature of U.S.–Chinese ongoing relations. Apply your distinctions to the economic, military, and political dimensions. What economic constraints does the relationship impose on both countries? Is Chinese military modernization menacing to the United States? What are the possibilities and limits on political cooperation?
5. What options are available to the United States to influence Chinese behavior in ways favorable to United States interests? What are the opportunities and limitations to successful interactions?

READING/RESEARCH MATERIALS

Biajin, Zheng. "China's 'Peaceful Rise' to Great-Power Status." *Foreign Affairs* 84, 5 (September/October 2005), 18–24.
Bush, Richard C., and Michael O'Hanlon. *A War Like No Other: The Truth about China's Challenge to America.* New York: John Wiley and Sons, 2007.

Deng, Yong, and Thomas G. Moore. "China Views Globalization: Toward a New Great Power Politics?" *Washington Quarterly* 27, 3 (Summer 2004), 117–136.

Economy, Elizabeth. "The End of the 'Peaceful Rise'?" *Foreign Policy* (December 2010), 77–78.

———. "The Game Changer: Coping with China's Foreign Policy Revolution." *Foreign Affairs* 89, 6 (November/December 2010), 142–152.

Feng, Wang. "China's Population Destiny: The Looming Crisis." *Current History* 109, 728 (September 2010), 244–251.

Fravel, M. Taylor. "China's Search for Military Power." *Washington Quarterly* 31, 3 (Summer 2008), 125–141.

Gilboy, George J., and Benjamin J. Read. "Political and Social Reforms in China: Alive and Walking." *Washington Quarterly* 31, 3 (Summer 2008), 143–164.

Godwin, Paul. "Asia's Dangerous Security Dilemma." *Current History* 109, 728 (September 2010), 264–266.

Hale, David, and Lyric Hughes Hale. "China Takes Off." *Foreign Affairs* 82, 6 (November/December 2003), 36–53.

Kagan, Robert. "What China Knows That We Don't: The Case for a New Strategy of Containment." *The Weekly Standard*, January 20, 1997.

———, and William Kristol (eds.). *Present Dangers: Crisis and Opportunity in American Foreign and Defense Policy*. San Fransciso, CA: Encounter Books, 2000.

Kaplan, Robert. "The Geography of Chinese Power: How Far Can Beijing Reach on Land and At Sea?" *Foreign Affairs* 89, 3 (May/June 2010), 22–41.

Kurlantzick, Joshua. "The Asian Century: Not Quite Yet." *Current History* 110, 732 (January 2011), 26–31.

Legro, Jeffrey W. "What China Will Want: The Future Implications of a Rising Power." *Perspectives on Politics* 5, 3 (September 2007), 515–533.

Lierberthal, Kenneth. "The China-US Relationship Goes Global." *Current History* 108, 719 (September 2009), 243–249.

McGregor, Richard. "5 Myths about the Chinese Communist Party." *Foreign Policy* (January/February 2011), 38–40.

Medeiros, Evan S. "Is Beijing Ready for Global Leadership?" *Current History* 108, 719 (September 2009), 250–256.

Menon, Rajan. "Pax Americana and the Rising Powers." *Current History* 108, 721 (November 2009), 353–360.

Miller, Ken. "Coping with China's Financial Power: Beijing's Financial Foreign Policy." *Foreign Affairs* 89, 4 (July/August 2010), 96–109.

Naughton, Barry. "In China's Economy, the State's Hand Grows Heavier." *Current History* 108, 719 (September 2009), 277–283.

Pei, Minxin. "Dangerous Denials." *Foreign Policy* (January/February 2005), 54–56.

———. "The Dark Side of China's Rise." *Foreign Policy* (March/April 2006), 32–40.

Pope, Carl, and Bjorn Lomberg. "The State of Nature: The *Foreign Policy* Debate." *Foreign Policy* (July/August 2005), 66–74.

Shambaugh, David. "A New China Requires a New US Strategy." *Current History* 109, 728 (September 2010), 219–226.

Snow, Donald M. *Cases in International Relations* (5th edition). New York: Pearson Longman, 2012.

Thompson, Drew. "Think Again: China's Military." *Foreign Policy* (March/April 2010), 86–90.

Walder, Andrew G. "Unruly Stability: China's Regime Has Stating Power." *Current History* 108, 719 (September 2009), 257–263.

Nuclear Proliferation Residues

Nuclear weapons have been a major concern of American foreign policy since before 1945. Prior to World War II, research had commenced in a number of countries that would be part of that war on the weapons potential of nuclear energy; the United States entered that competition largely at the urging of Albert Einstein, who warned ominously of the possibility that Nazi Germany would obtain "the bomb." The United States succeeded in testing the world's first nuclear device on July 16, 1945, at White Sands, New Mexico, and three week later it employed these weapons for the first, and to date the only, time they have been used in anger against human populations in the bombings of Nagasaki and Hiroshima, Japan, on August 6 and 9 to hasten the end of the war in the Pacific.

Nuclear weapons have had a prominent if changing role in American policy ever since. When the then Soviet Union exploded its own nuclear fission device in 1949, it began a nuclear arms race between the two superpowers that was the most visible and deadly symbol of the Cold War competition. The fear of an all-out, civilization-threatening, nuclear third world war was the dominant underlying dynamic of international relations for over 40 years, eased only by the peaceful implosion of the Soviet Union in 1991, as discussed in Chapter 1. The nuclear arms race has retreated from the front burner of American concern as Russia and the United States have negotiated a series of arms control treaties aimed at reducing their arsenals to lower levels of weaponry, thereby attenuating the problem of so-called "vertical nuclear proliferation" (the accumulation of larger and larger nuclear arsenals by countries already possessing them).

American concern with nuclear weapons has shifted from the Cold War nuclear arms race to the other face of nuclear weapons concern: horizontal nuclear proliferation (the spread of nuclear weapons to countries that previously did not possess them). Nuclear weapons possession has spread slowly among the states of the world. The United States and the Soviet Union entered the nuclear "club" in the 1940s, Great Britain in the 1950s, and France, China, and Israel in the 1960s. South Africa was briefly a member but destroyed its arsenal when it democratized in the early 1990s, and India and Pakistan joined the ranks of nuclear powers in 1998.

The spread of nuclear weapons has also been emotional and controversial. Generally speaking, those countries that have the weapons deplore the idea of additional countries getting them on the grounds that such acquisition will destabilize the situation and increase the prospects of their usage by putting additional "fingers on the nuclear button." States contemplating such acquisition tend to view such concerns as ungrounded and imputations that their possession would somehow be more destabilizing than possession by current nuclear states as baseless and condescending. The irony is that when these states do gain nuclear capability, they also tend to join the ranks of those advocating against further horizontal proliferation. This problem, known as the N+1 problem (where "N" is the number of states in current possession and "+1" represents the problems posed by new members) applies to the current situation within the international community.

Current concerns surround the impact of two states, Iran and North Korea (technically the Democratic People's Republic of Korea, or DPRK). As the case studies in this part show, each case is somewhat different. North Korea already has a small number of nuclear weapons and declared itself to be the ninth nuclear state after successfully testing a device in 2006. The foreign policy problem of dealing with North Korea thus centers on how to convince them to dismantle their arsenal or how to ensure that they do not employ those weapons, a concern magnified by the 2010 crisis between the two Koreas. The Iranian case, with which the part begins, is a more classic proliferation exercise since the Iranians have not, as of this writing, achieved or publicly admitted the actual fabrication of a bomb. The differences between the two instances are accentuated by the relatively different importance of the two countries in their regions and the world. Iran is the largest and potentially most powerful and influential state in the Middle East, but it is also the most prominent non-Arab state in the Islamic Middle East. North Korea, by contrast, is a minor player in a Far East balance of which China, Japan, Russia, the United States, and South Korea are the major powers, and nuclear weapons represent virtually the only claim that North Korea has to important status in the region. Iran is a major actor in its region regardless of whether it has nuclear weapons; a North Korea without these weapons is not. As common ground, the United States has a long-standing antagonistic relationship with each country, dating to 1979 and the fall of the shah in Iran and to the 1950–1953 Korean War with North Korea.

Dealing with each of these problems has been very difficult and frustrating for the United States. Domestic political considerations within the United States are not part of the difficulty. There is domestic consensus in opposition to nuclear weapons possession by either Iran or North Korea, and there is no "pro-Iran" or "pro-DPRK" domestic political constituency to oppose harsh American policy; the only relevant domestic political pressure comes from the

Israeli lobby (see Chapter 11), which favors particularly draconian measures toward Iran.

The United States has attempted to bring international pressure against both regimes through the United Nations and elsewhere. These efforts have been especially intense toward Iran, but their effectiveness has been limited. Iranian oil resources provide leverage with energy-deficient countries like China, and the lure of lucrative nuclear power contracts makes countries like Russia somewhat reluctant to antagonize the Iranians. Six-power negotiations with the North Koreans have attempted to harness or reverse their nuclear program, but concerns like those discussed in Chapter 2 create some ambivalence in China's posture toward the North Koreans.

Each case is thus distinct and represents a different context for coping with the problem of proliferation. At this writing, Iranian proliferation remains a prospect rather than an accomplished reality, but should it occur, Iran's place in the world makes it a major source of international concern. North Korea has already crossed the nuclear threshold, making the problem one of reversing rather than preventing weapons spread. The volatile politics of the Korean peninsula, however, make it an important concern for the region and the United States as well.

Iran: Facing Down Regional Aspirations and Nuclear Weapons

PREVIEW

Relations between the United States and Iran have been universally negative since the Iranian Revolution in 1979, an event with a strong anti-American overtone after over three decades of close collaboration between the two countries. This chapter looks at the nature of that relationship historically and in terms of the context of Iran and its place as the largest power in the region with aspirations to be the regional kingpin. It examines the current state of U.S.–Iranian enmity, focusing on three major issues: the Iranian nuclear weapons program; the particular threat that Israel feels a hostile, nuclear-armed Iran poses to it; and the prospect of U.S.–Iranian cooperation in achieving settlements to the wars in Iraq and Afghanistan. After looking at preferred American outcomes to aspects of these disagreements, the chapter critically examines U.S. options for achieving its policy ends: military actions, sanctions, negotiations, or continuation of the status quo.

The extremely negative, confrontational relations between the United States and Iran are, in a sense, enigmatic. The two countries have vastly different historical experiences: the United States is one of the two oldest continuous political democracies in the world (Switzerland is the only country with a longer unbroken democratic reign), but Iran is the second oldest country (mostly as Persia) in the world, after China. The United States is currently the most powerful and consequential state in the world, whereas Iran/Persia has, at various historical times, been one of the world's most powerful states, and it clearly has aspirations to reassert its position, at least in the Middle East. Neither country formally recognized the other until the middle of the nineteenth century, and their history of significant relations only began

55

as part of Allied efforts to deny Middle Eastern oil resources to the Germans in World War II.

The relationship between the two countries since World War II has been intimate but schizophrenic. In the period between the end of World War II and 1979, the United States was the prime partner of the Iranian regime of Shah Reza Pahlevi, and the relationship between the two countries at both the intergovernmental and personal levels was very close. That relationship included the significant westernization of Shiite Iran, a dubious proposition that was encouraged by the shah as part of his attempt to reassert Iranian domain in the world, and it was a policy in which America enthusiastically and controversially participated. One result was to create a sizable minority in Iran who were highly westernized and sympathetic to the United States; it also, however, created a seething hatred among other Iranians, including the most conservative, religious Shiites in Iran, whose religious convictions, codes, and ways of doing things rejected the westernization the shah sought to institute and which the Americans helped create.

The result was a schizophrenia that bubbled over in 1979, when the shah was overthrown and replaced by a radical Shiite theocracy, of which the Ayatollah Ruhollah Khomeini was the most visible symbol until his death in 1989, and which remains in power to this day. The basic grievance of the religious majority of Iranian Shiites was that the process of westernization desecrated their Islamic belief system and that the state must be returned to a Muslim model based on Islamic precepts, including religious (*sharia*) law and a theocratic hierarchy of governance. The result has been over 30 years of harsh, autocratic rule by a religious majority that has included a strident anti-American and anti-Israeli foreign policy that has put the United States at considerable odds with the government of Iran, with which it has not had formal diplomatic relations since April 7, 1980 (days after an abortive raid to free American hostages held by Iranian "students" in the American embassy in Tehran).

The current pivot of American–Iranian relations is the question of Iranian acquisition of nuclear weapons, a process it has been pursuing for a number of years. There are various and conflicting arguments about the Iranian nuclear program, including its intent (the Iranians have long denied the purpose of their program is to produce nuclear weapons) and at whom it is aimed. The likely antagonist for Iran in nuclear terms is nuclear-armed Israel, and a possible confrontation between these two states, both possessing nuclear weapons, results in a regional "horror scenario" most would like to avoid. The prospect that Iran will be able to obtain nuclear weapons capability in a short period of time, in turn, creates visible political palpitations in Israel, which has threatened to attack and try to destroy or damage the program, a course with unknown but potentially dire consequences. The United States, meanwhile, seeks to restrain both sides—discouraging Iranian weapons development and Israeli military action—but in an international atmosphere of restrained ability to influence events and of domestic suspicion on both sides about its intentions and will to impose terms of settlement.

U.S.–Iranian relations are both very complex and contentious. The heart of the bilateral relationship between the two countries is whether or on what terms some form of relationship between the two can be restored, a question that is complicated by the schizophrenic experience they share with one another. At the same time, those relations are made more difficult because of foreign and domestic policy issues that impinge upon their purely diplomatic relationship. One of these, explored both in this chapter and the case study on Israel, deals with how or whether the United States can intervene in and moderate the extremely volatile Iranian–Israeli relationship; this issue is prejudiced in the United States by the American embrace of Israel's position on the conflict. The other surrounds conflicting and complimentary American and Iranian interests in the Middle East: the United States has, after all, significantly involved itself in Iran's backyard, with major combat operations in countries bordering Iran on the west (Iraq) and east (Afghanistan) during most of the 2000s and serving as the major obstacle to the spread of Iranian influence in the small, oil-rich, largely Sunni countries along the Persian (or Arabian) Gulf.

Two points of caution, each of which affects the ability to discuss the issues surrounding U.S.–Iranian relations in a calm and analytic manner, should be made before turning to that discussion. Both arise from the politicization and rise of partisanship evident in the current American political debate. They are connected. The first is the emotional content of the relationship: many in the American policy elite view the relationship with Iran, at least implicitly, through the lens of the humiliating Iranian hostage crisis of 1979–1981 and thus favor a harsh foreign policy stance with which to confront the Iranians. Anti-Iranian sentiment has a more military content as a result. As Barry Posen puts it, "tensions between cool analysis and saber rattling suggest less about the problem posed by Iran than about the difficulty of having a reasoned strategic discussion in Washington today; hawkishness is now the ticket for admission." This emotional, "macho" tenor is particularly pronounced because of the connection between U.S. relations with Iran and Israel and is especially pronounced because of suspicions among more militant Israelis and their American supporters about the Obama administration's commitment to Israel. As Barry Rubin asks, "Will Israel entrust its security to a U.S. administration that is arguably the least friendly to Israel in history?" Since preventing Iranian nuclear weapons acquisition is the linchpin of Israeli foreign policy, Rubin's reply to his own question is "the answer likely is no." As a result, American initiatives toward Iran must be conditioned by the likely interpretations that will be placed on them in U.S.–Iranian–Israeli terms, a significant source of restraint on American policy options.

IRAN: A SKETCH

By many measures, Iran is the most important single state in the Middle East, and certainly in the Islamic Middle East. It is the largest country in the region in physical terms, it is strategically located at the top of the Persian Gulf and in the middle of the transit routes between Europe and Asia, and it has some of the world's largest known reserves of crucial energy resources. Moreover, it has the second largest population of all Middle Eastern states (after Egypt). It has long been one of the pivotal societies of the Middle East region, with a history dating back to early biblical times and a spotted history of dominance and importance in the geopolitics of the region.

Despite all this, the Iranians suffer from an inferiority complex of sorts, believing that their status and stature are underappreciated regionally and globally. The Iranians believe that they are the premier civilization of the region and should be accorded the status of a major regional player in the international politics of their part of the world. Their desire for "respect, dignity, and a restoration of lost pride," in the words of Kinzer in a recent study of Iran and Turkey, is a major driver of Iranian policy toward the world, including the sometimes strident, xenophobic bombast that accompanies their pronouncements about international affairs. When the shah was in power, the United States stood in league with Iran's quest for global reassertion; since the shah's overthrow, the same United States—the "Great Satan"—stands as the principal impediment to Iran realizing its self-proclaimed place in the global sun.

By any objective measure, Iran should clearly be the dominant actor along the oil-rich Persian Gulf littoral, but it is a status that is denied to it because Iran is also unlike its neighbors in two important ways. First, the majority of the other countries along the Gulf are, or consider themselves to be, Arab (meaning they can claim their beginnings occurred on the Arabian Peninsula), whereas the Iranians trace their beginnings to immigration from the east, and their ethnicity is closer to the Aryans of ancient India. They are thus ethnically distinct from their neighbors. At the same time, the Iranians have the largest Shiite Muslim population in the region, whereas their neighbors, except Iraq and Bahrain, have Sunni Muslim majorities. They are thus also distinct from their neighbors in sectarian terms.

Iran as a regional and global actor can only be understood in terms of its unique characteristics, and so the discussion of U.S.–Iranian relations must begin by placing Iran in context. The discussion will begin with a brief excursion on Iranian history, concentrating on the period since World War II. It will then look at the demographics of the country and thus why it is both so pivotal and such a difficult place with which to deal. It will conclude by looking at the implications of Iran's unique status in its region.

Iran in the World

As noted, present-day Iran is the inheritor of one of the world's oldest political histories. The formation of what is now Iran is normally dated to the consolidation of the Persian Empire in 549 BCE by Cyrus the Great, and Iranians still enlist that past as part of their claim to a place in the world. (Of some irony in the current context, among Cyrus' famous acts was restoring Jerusalem to Jewish rule. When U.S. President Harry S Truman formally recognized Israeli independence in 1948, he symbolically declared, "I am Cyrus.") Although the Iranians/Persians have, like most of the countries and peoples of the region, had a mixed experience of hegemony and subjugation through the ages, they remain committed to an allegiance to one of the world's longest-standing traditions. The restoration of Persian glory was the major goal of the shah of Iran during his quarter-century of rule in the country, and it remains a principal desire of the contemporary regime as well.

Modern Iranian history can be dated to the 1920s when Reza Khan, the father of Reza Pahlevi, asserted himself as the new shah (king) of Persia. The country's name was changed to Iran in 1935, and after the war the allies (principally the United States and Great Britain) provided the central backing for the shah's rise to and maintenance in power. When the British were forced to retreat from empire in the latter 1940s and early 1950s, the United States became the dominant outside influence in the country, supporting both the shah's militant rejection of and resistance to the Soviet Union and the process of modernization and westernization on which the shah launched the country.

The shah's program of modernization was intended to restore the "Peacock Empire" of Persia to something like its historical place in the world. To accomplish this, Iran used its petroleum wealth to develop a modern state and a state-of-the-art military capability with the willing assistance of the Americans. In return for considerable technical support and military hardware from the United States, the Iranians acted as the major police force in the region for the United States, a capable surrogate that made sure the oil kept flowing at acceptable prices and that also meant the United States did not need a major physical presence in the region.

This arrangement worked well into the 1970s, when it began to disintegrate. There were several causes. The major problem was that the White Revolution, as the shah's modernization program was known, had very mixed impacts on Iran itself. Westernization promoted great economic growth and prosperity for some (mainly a developing middle class that remains a problematical force in the country) but was dislocating for others. Many rural peasants, for instance, were forced to move to cities, the infrastructure of which was unprepared to absorb them, in order to find jobs, and modernization included the expropriation of lands from the Shiite clergy, thus creating two interrelated disaffected groups within society. At the same time, modernization also entailed secularization of an extremely conservative Shiite country, thereby creating the seeds of religious discontent and opposition to the shah's regime. It has been argued that had the United States chosen any country in the world most likely to resist the kind of Western modernization at which it excels, it could not have done better than choosing heavily Shiite Iran.

Opposition to the shah—and his American allies—congealed in the mid-1970s. It was aided by two additional factors. One was the incumbency of Jimmy Carter in the White House. The signature theme of Carter's foreign policy was the enforcement of human rights, and Iran's secret police, known as SAVAK, were among the world's most notorious violators. Carter insisted that the shah's government rein in SAVAK, and when it complied, the government lost a critical ability to infiltrate and monitor the growing opposition to the shah's continuing reign. Second, the shah personally began to feel the debilitating effects of the cancer that would eventually kill him, and when the opposition to his rule took to the streets in mass protests in 1978, he was apparently too sick to make effective decisions for dealing with the protests.

These dynamics came to a head in January 1979, when the shah left the country on an advertised vacation that everyone knew was an effective abdication of power. The Iranian Revolution was joined. Within days, Khomeini returned triumphantly to the country from exile in Paris. After a period of jostling between the militant mullahs (religious teachers) and their peasant allies and the middle class descendants of Muhammad Mossadeqh (the democratically elected president of Iran who was overthrown—with assistance from the CIA—in 1953, thereby allowing the rise of the shah to power), the religious elements were triumphant; the theocratic Islamic Republic of Iran was declared and began its purge of any remaining vestiges of the shah's regime. One of those vestiges was the United States, and the symbolic attack on the United States took the form of the occupation of the American embassy in Tehran by Iranian militants and the holding captive of the American personnel in it from November 4, 1979 to January 1981, when the siege ended on the eve of Ronald Reagan's inauguration as the 40th president of the United States.

This brief discussion illustrates two aspects of the Iranian–American experience relevant to understanding the current situation. One is the theme of Iran's demand to be treated as a major regional power, a status to which it believes itself to be entitled by virtue of history. This theme is Iranian and exists quite apart from whoever may be in power in Iran at any point in time. The second theme surrounds the relationship between the United States and Iran. It has indeed been schizophrenic: under the shah, the United States was Iran's greatest supporter (to the dismay, one might add, of many of Iran's Sunni Arab neighbors); after the Iranian Revolution, the United States became Iran's central enemy. The year 1979 is the stark dividing point, certainly for the Iranians, but also because it marked the overthrow of the pro-American Iranians at the hands of the anti-American Iranians. Put this way, it is more understandable why turmoil in Iran always has an American tinge to it since resistance to the anti-American theocracy is presumed to be associated with pro-American elements who are essentially the inheritors of the pre-1979 traditions. The most recent manifestation of this presumption was the rise of the so-called Green Movement of opponents to Iranian President Mahmoud Ahmadinejad in 2009 and hopeful interpretations of what that movement meant. As Aslan puts it, "For most of us, the Green Movement was an empty vessel to be filled with our dreams."

The Physical Setting

Many of the discussions about Iran and American options there seem to progress from an implicit assumption that Iran is "just" another Middle Eastern state. Such an assumption, presumably not shared by policy makers who know better (or should), is incorrect. As even a cursory examination reveals, Iran is a large, well-endowed, and thus important country on several dimensions.

First, Iran is a physically large country. It has a land area of 631,659 square miles, which is roughly the same size as Alaska, making it the 18th largest country in the world in land area. It is by some measures the largest country in the Middle East, and it is the second largest country in the world with a majority Muslim population (Indonesia is the largest in area). Iran has a population estimated in the *CIA World Factbook* at 76,429,284 in July 2010, ranking it as the 19th most populous country in the world, the most populous country in the Asian Middle East, and the third most populous Muslim-majority country (after Indonesia and Egypt). It is also only one of two major countries (along with Iraq) that has a Shiite majority; roughly 89 percent of Iran's population is Shiite, as opposed to around 60 percent of Iraqis. Virtually all of Iraq's other regional neighbors have Sunni majorities, tiny Bahrain being an exception.

Much of Iran's contemporary claim to international status arises from its resource riches. Like most of the Persian Gulf littoral, Iran's rise to importance is the direct result of the dependency of world societies on fossil-fuel, carbon-based energy, notably petroleum and natural gas. Iran, with a 2010 export rate of 2.21 million barrels per day, is the world's eighth leading petroleum exporter, a ranking that is depressed by the major international economic sanctions against the regime. It does, however, possess the world's third largest known reserves of petroleum (after Saudi Arabia and Canada) with 137 billion barrels. Its natural gas reserves are the world's second largest (behind Russia's), estimated at 29.61 *trillion* cubic meters.

As long as the world remains dependent on fossil fuels for energy, Iran will thus remain a pivotal place, both because of the size of its reserves and the fact that among countries with major reserves, Iran is by far the largest and most powerful state: most of the other major reserves are in very small countries like Kuwait or underpopulated countries like Saudi Arabia—Iraq is a partial exception. The Iranian economy, despite efforts by the shah to broaden its base, remains highly dependent on taxes from oil revenues, which comprise over 80 percent of Iranian government budgetary sources. The possession of large reserves, however, also has major geopolitical importance. As Baktiari points out, "China and Russia . . . are wrapped up in Iran's energy sector. China is aggressively pinning down future sources around the world, and Russia is assisting Iran in the construction of a civilian nuclear reactor in Bushehr." Energy resources thus provide the Iranians with a major source of leverage that makes it difficult to form an effective world front in opposition to Iranian policies.

The Iranian economy is, and has for sometime been, the country's Achilles heel. Despite the vast energy wealth the country possesses, its gross domestic product (GDP) per capita—the standard measure of comparative economic performance—stood at about $12,500 in 2010, ranking a country in the top 10 percent of countries in area and population in 91st place by this measure, right in the middle of world countries. This ranking reflects the underachievement of the economy on a variety of measures and is generally attributed to government mismanagement of the economy (particularly by Ahmadinejad, whose economic stewardship has been typified as "hare brained") and the impact of international economic sanctions against the regime. Indeed, analysts like Chadar argue that it is economic suffering that may eventually become the pivot of potential economic instability and thus pressure to change the regime.

The physical position of Iran should not be ignored, particularly in regional terms. As a glance at the map of the Middle Eastern region quickly shows, the country sits astride the Persian or Arabian Gulf (Persian Gulf to Iranians, Arabian Gulf to Arabs) through which so much of the world's oil supply flows, and the waters of the region's major naval choke point, the Straits of Hormuz, wash against Iranian soil and could conceivably become the basis for interrupting that supply. Moreover, as noted, Iran has major borders with the two countries with which the United States has been at war during the 2000s. An Iran in league with the United States could have been a significant source of assistance in the conduct of those conflicts; a hostile Iran could only make those operations more difficult. This same geographical factor also extends to the development and enforcement of stable postconflict conditions in both Iraq and Afghanistan.

Iran as a Unique State

If Iran were a Sunni Arab rather than a Shiite Persian state, its position in the Middle East and the problems it poses for the region and the world would be entirely different. In all likelihood, Iran would be viewed as the regional hegemonic power, a status it clearly yearns to possess, and it would be looked to by other countries in the region for leadership and direction. Moreover, the pathway to the world's petroleum energy would clearly and unambiguously lead through Tehran.

That is not, of course, the situation, and so Iran's place in the region and the world is much more problematical and ambivalent. Within the geographic and geopolitical Islamic Middle East, Iran is, in many respects, an outsider, part of the region and its dynamics by virtue of location and adherence to Islam, but apart by virtue of ethnicity and the form of Islam that its inhabitants practice.

Iran's resulting unique status makes it simultaneously easier and more difficult to deal with. Because Iran is an outsider, it is not clearly part of any pan-Arabic solutions or approaches to regional problems, such as Israel. Some of the bombast that is associated with Iran's very public opposition to Israel reflects its outsider status and its felt need to establish its anti-Israeli bona fides more strongly because it is not an Arab state coming to the aid of fellow Arabs (the Palestinians). At the same time, the rivalry between Iran and its Arab neighbors also means that there is less of a united front from the region on any issue, including Israel.

Iranian exceptionalism in the region makes the approach to some of the problems dividing the Middle East from the rest of the world triangular rather than bilateral. When the United States, for instance, seeks to craft policy toward Iran, one concern is how such positions will be received in other Islamic capitals, and the calculation is almost always a matter of disagreement. The Israeli–Iranian nuclear relationship is, for instance, complicated by uncertainty about what regional Arab states would *really* think about some form of Israeli military action against the Iranian nuclear facilities. On one hand, other Muslims would have no choice but to condemn such an action on anti-Islamic bases, but there is the undercurrent always present that some of them would not feel terribly bad about seeing the Shiite Persians attacked and weakened (the Israelis argue that many Arabs would privately applaud an attack, according to Goldberg, "Point of No Return").

Iran's status as a unique state thus simply adds to the complication of dealing with the largest country in a complex and contentious region, and it is made more difficult by the additional fact that Iran has, among the major Islamic states, the most Islamist, militant government. Like everything else about Iran, the effects of Iran's fundamentalist militancy tend to cut both ways. The Iranian theocracy—partly because it is a Shiite theocracy and partly because the resulting militancy it demonstrates stands in contrast with the comparatively religiously moderate regimes in many Arab countries—is another wedge between Iran and its neighbors. One of the characteristics of militant Shiism is its evangelical character, and many of the Sunni government are fearful of Islamist sentiments that arise from and are encouraged by the Tehran regime. At the same time, Iran clearly wants to assert leadership in this part of the world, and one of the ways it apparently believes it is possible to do so is by presenting itself as the most anti-American and anti-Israeli member of the Muslim world. The clearest indication of this thread of Iranian behavior is Iran's support for Hamas and Hezbollah in their opposition to Israel.

U.S.–IRANIAN RELATIONS

As already indicated, the relations between Iran and the United States have run the gamut of possibilities. For over 30 years after World War II, the United States was Iran's closest ally among the major powers, and cooperation between the shah's regime and administrations in Washington was very high. For this closeness, Iran received considerable American assistance in the White Revolution and had its military adorned with the finest first-line American equipment. In return, the shah's military acted as a surrogate for American power in the region, ensuring that there were no major threats to the flow of petroleum to the West.

This close relationship had within it the seeds of the contemporary antagonism. Arab regimes in the region seethed at the favoritism shown by the Americans toward the Shiite Persians and found common ground in militant opposition to Israel (which the shah supported with things like oil exports, making matters worse). More importantly, the process of political, social, and economic change that the White Revolution sought to institute and with which the United States was so intimately associated had the negative effect of alienating great parts of Iranian society, notably the large, highly religious urban peasantry and the Shiite religious hierarchy (unlike Sunni Islam, Shiism has a loose hierarchical organization with the ayatollahs at the top and the mullahs—or teachers—at the bottom), both of which were displaced by White Revolution policies and offended by the secularization of Iranian society. The harsh repression of Iranian dissidence by SAVAK, which was associated in the popular mind with the Americans as well, only added to the resentment many Iranians felt against not only the shah's regime but also against the Americans.

The depth of the rupture in Iranian–American relations and the hopefulness many Americans have toward repairing that breach can only be understood by recognizing the sources of anti-Americanism in Iran. Collaboration with the shah's programs helped to create a highly westernized, Americanized political elite and to some degree a middle class who had, and presumably among the survivors still has, some positive feelings toward the United States and Americans. That very Americanism, however, was and still is deeply resented by those who were displaced and abused by the shah's regime, and that resentment exists against both those Iranians who supported the shah *and* against the United States. And it is the coalition of those peasants and religious figures that seized power in 1979 and continues to rule.

Two events provide the signature for the current antipathy between the two regimes. One of those was the Iranian Revolution of 1979 itself, an act by which fundamentalist Iranian Shiites and their followers overturned the shah's regime with a breathtaking rigor and ruthlessness that effectively deprived Iran of most of its highly educated, wealthy, and professional groups, who were either purged (and in many cases killed) or fled into exile. That revolution, however, must also be seen as a profoundly *anti-American* revolution because of the complicity that Iranian supporters saw between the corrupt, apostate shah's regime and the "Great Satan" in the United States. This element of the revolution is absolutely critical to understand because it continues to fuel and resonate within parts of Iranian society in ways that most Americans cannot comprehend. As Milani puts it, "For decades, the Iranian regime has used anti-Americanism to crush its opponents and expand its power abroad."

The other event symbolizes why the United States reciprocates the animosity toward it by Iranians. After the shah fled from Iran, he came to the United States (at the reluctant invitation of President Carter) for treatment for his terminal cancer. As the militants consolidated control in Tehran, they demanded that the U.S. government return the shah to Iran to face the religious justice system they had created. Knowing that compliance would be tantamount to a death sentence for their erstwhile ally, the American government refused these demands.

In retaliation for the American refusal, Iranian "students" seized the American embassy and its personnel in Tehran on November 4, 1979. The result was the so-called Iranian hostage crisis, an event that played itself out on national television in the United States daily for 444 days until the hostages were released on January 20, 1981. The imagery of this indignity was vivid: major electronic news organizations began their nightly telecasts with a visual depiction of a blindfolded American hostage and a banner noting how many days the crisis had lasted. The image of animosity that was seared into the American mind has far outlasted the event itself and helps explain why opposition to the Iranian regime retains the resonance that it clearly does for many Americans.

These two events also affected American views on Iran. During most of the shah's reign, Iran was depicted as a staunch U.S. ally with a heroic, dashing shah at the helm, and Iranian students and military personnel were frequent sights in the United States. The fall of the shah, and especially the humiliating hostage crisis, radically transformed the positive image to a negative view captured and symbolized by the scowling visage of Khomeini staring down from huge billboards across Iran. America's view of Iran turned decisively negative in 1979 and has never recovered from that change.

Both of these events were very emotional and give the continuing relationship a hard, ideological edge of antagonism that probably makes matters worse than they otherwise would be. The Americans become a convenient displacement object—a whipping boy—for the Iranians. As Lindsay and Takeyh put it, "To satisfy their revolutionary impulses, Iran's leaders have turned anti-Americanism and a strident opposition to Israel into pillars of the state." On the other side, the hostage crisis feeds into xenophobic opposition to Iran that becomes arguably excessive and further divisive when observers like Rubin assert that "Iran's regime is the farthest thing from a rational state that the United States has confronted since Nazi Germany."

Given the depths of their mutual antagonism, a minimal U.S.–Iranian relationship would seem the likeliest course, and in some ways it is: the two countries have had no regular diplomatic relations since the twin events depicted above, and official discussions between them, such as they are, use the Iranian "interest section" in New York (the base for its United Nations delegation) as its venue. This separation allows each side officially to maintain it has nothing to do with the infamous other, and despite President Obama's apparent offer of willingness to open dialogue between the two countries in 2009, relations remain frozen.

Aloofness might be the preferable relationship between the two countries, but circumstances will not allow that to occur. As the world's major global power, the United States has what it considers important interests in the Middle East, where Iran views itself as the pivotal state. Moreover, both Iran's physical location and its importance in the world's energy supply make it impossible for the United States to ignore. The world would indeed likely be a simpler, more tranquil place if the United States and Iran could simply leave one another alone, but that is not possible.

In the current environment, the United States and Iran find themselves involved in three separate but interconnected disputes. The first and most internationally volatile source of contention is the Iranian nuclear program and more specifically whether or when Iran plans to attempt to become a nuclear-weapons state. The second dispute is more triangular, centering on the relationship between Israel and Iran and the role of the United States in seeking to keep that relationship nonviolent. This facet is connected to the Iranian nuclear program by virtue of Israeli fear that nuclear capability will be threatened or used against them. The third dispute is the policy of Iran in the two violent conflicts on Iran's border in which the United States has been engaged over the last decade. This facet of the relationship tends to center on whether Iran will act as a facilitator of peaceful outcomes in Afghanistan and Iraq or as a further, continuing source of difficulties for the United States.

The Iranian Nuclear Program

Whether Iran will become the world's 10th actual nuclear weapons state (depending on how the Israeli arsenal is described) is the current major point of contention between the United States and Iran and between Iran and much of the rest of the world. As of 2010, there were eight countries that publicly admit possessing nuclear weapons (the United States, Russia, Britain, France, China, India, Pakistan, and North Korea, in the order they obtained the capability) and a ninth, Israel, which neither admits nor denies that it has these weapons (the consensus is that Israel has an arsenal of over 200 nuclear bombs). The question is whether Iran should be admitted to the nuclear club, and assuming a negative answer, what (if anything) can be done to stop it.

Outside of Iran itself, hardly anyone wants to see the Iranians transform their nuclear research and power program into a nuclear weapons–producing industry. Some of the motivation for this opposition is general and arises from the belief that the proliferation of nuclear weapons to countries that do not currently possess them is a destabilizing influence in the world since it increases the number of "fingers" on the nuclear "button": the number of states that have the capability to start a nuclear war. The generalized belief that the further spread of nuclear weapons should be prevented is particularly strongly felt by the countries that already possess them; these countries in general believe their possession is *not* harmful to international tranquility but that adding new weapons states presents new, partially unforeseeable, and potentially dangerous problems (the so-called N+1 problem in proliferation circles).

In the particular case of Iran, however, this unease and opposition is magnified because of the nature of the Iranian regime and its apparent aspirations in the world. Among Israelis in particular there is alarm that the Ahmadinejad regime, if in possession of nuclear weapons, might use them to destroy Israel, regardless of the probable consequences of doing so (i.e., the probable retaliatory destruction of Iran). While no state has ever used these weapons when facing a nuclear-armed opponent, the Israelis nonetheless face what they consider an "existential threat" (physical threat to their existence) and have responded with robust plans to attack and try to destroy the Iranian program, a policy alternative discussed in some detail by Goldberg ("Point of No Return") in the next section.

There are also more general objections to the Iranian program that tend to reflect regional effects that Iranian nuclearization could have. Lindsay and Takeyh, for instance, provide a representative catalogue of possible destabilizing influences. They argue nuclear weapons would make Iran more aggressive in the region (a concern to Arab Sunni states); encourage terrorism against the United States; create the risk of greater nuclear escalation in the Middle East by causing other states to seek these weapons to deter Iran; upset the geopolitical balance in the region; and undercut nonproliferation generally by offering another instance of successful nuclear weapons spread. More specifically, they maintain "Iran's nuclearization would make the Middle East a more dangerous place, it would heighten tensions, reduce the margin for error, and raise the prospect of mass catastrophe."

The Iranians respond to these concerns with feigned disbelief. The government of Iran has consistently and steadfastly maintained it has every right to maintain a peaceful nuclear research and power program and that, as Kodmani argues, "Iranians are almost unanimous in believing that their country has a sovereign right to enrich uranium. They want international acknowledgement of their country's importance in the region." The United States acknowledges Iran's right to a peaceful program, but the physical activity within Iran—principally the construction of multiple centrifuges capable of producing weapons-grade nuclear material—seems to belie this peaceful intent.

The Iranians can (and still may) defuse this crisis with the United States and the rest of the world by decelerating their program (e.g., reducing the number of centrifuges under construction), allowing unfettered examination of all facilities by International Atomic Energy Agency (IAEA) inspectors, and renewing their commitments under the Nuclear Non-Proliferation Treaty (NPT) of 1970. Periodically, they suggest a willingness to do all of these things, but the world remains suspicious both of their actions and intentions. It has been clear that the Iranians are not yet willing to reduce their nuclear program to the point that it is no longer capable of being transformed into a weapons-producing industry. This observation in turn raises the question of why Iran wants to maintain the nuclear option in the face of great international opposition.

Two major reasons stand out for Iranian intransigence in renouncing the possibility of their exercising the nuclear option. The first is the matter of prestige. The Iranians, as noted earlier, want to be treated as a major power, and one of the residues of the Cold War period is the perception that nuclear weapons possession is the standard for great power status and as an acknowledgement that Iran is indeed a great power, both assertions with domestic political appeal. As Baktiari puts it, "Iranians tend to support the nuclear program as a matter of national pride. The conservatives in Iran's government are successfully using the nuclear issue as a means to cement their own power through nationalist fervor." In addition, the nuclear card places them on a more level plane with the hated Americans, whom they believe have treated them in a condescending fashion with a carrot-and-stick approach that, as Kinzer summarizes, "may be appropriate for donkeys, but not for dealing with a nation ten times older than" the United States.

There is also a geopolitical side to the nuclear issue. Another reason that Iran may seek to keep the nuclear option open is for *deterrence*. To some observers, a primary reason the Iranians may want to maintain the nuclear option is to deter an attack against them by the United States. Pollack, for instance, argues, "From an Iranian perspective, possession of nuclear weapons makes sense for purely defensive reasons. If you have nuclear weapons, the

United States will not dare use force against you, but if you do not, you are vulnerable." McFaul, Milani, and Diamond agree, suggesting "Iran's leaders seek nuclear weapons to deter a U.S. attack." Kinzer adds that the deterrent effect is one of the few regional certainties of an Iranian nuclear breakout: "the possible consequences of an Iranian nuclear capability are largely conjectural (*save for one: nobody would think of invading Iran*)." (Emphasis added.) Riedel concurs, stating "a nuclear deterrent means that their country will never again be invaded by an enemy" (as it was in 1980 by Iraq), thereby guaranteeing "a future free from the fear of outside attack."

This line of argumentation, of course, can also be extended to the Iranian relationship with Israel, although the Israelis deny the connection. The Israelis believe there is a third motivation for the Iranian program: the destruction of Israel. Given the depth of conviction that prominent Israelis feel about this prospect and the closeness of the United States and Israel, this becomes essentially an independent factor in the calculation of relations between the United States and Iran.

The United States and Israeli–Iranian Relations

Possibly the most volatile and uncertain aspect of the Iranian nuclear program is Israeli assessment of it and plans toward it. Beyond the general sense of opposition to Iran's acquisition of nuclear weapons as systemically destabilizing, the Israelis have the vivid fear that the main reason the Iranians want these weapons is to carry out the total destruction of Israel. Israel is a small state with the bulk of its population concentrated in a handful of urban areas (e.g., Tel Aviv, Jerusalem), meaning the country could be effectively obliterated with a relative handful of nuclear weapons (this is a problem shared by several regional states). Moreover, the schizophrenic nature of relations between the Persians/Iranians and the Israelis is at an absolute nadir, with the Ahmadinejad regime regularly threatening the Israelis with inflammatory rhetoric (e.g., the denial of the Holocaust) that has many Israelis convinced the regime will stop at nothing short of eliminating Israel from the planet. Given the likely response to an Iranian attack against Israel (Iran's destruction) and the fact that real power in Iran resides with the religious hierarchy and not the president, others question whether much of this rhetoric is little more than baseless bombast for domestic consumption, parallel to regular Iranian denunciations of the United States.

The threats to Israel and the United States from Iran are not, of course, symmetrical. A nuclear-armed Iran poses a physical existential threat to Israel that it does not and will not pose to the United States. As a result, the Israelis are understandably more fixated on the possibility that Iran will gain this life-threatening capability, and they have publicly stated their willingness to entertain more robust responses to the prospects than the United States is willing to consider. Chief among these possibilities, as chronicled in some detail by Goldberg ("Point of No Return"), is the plan to launch a preemptive attack against the Iranian program's physical facilities before they become fully operational in order to retard the success of Iran's nuclearization. Many in

Israel believe that the danger is so real and threatening that they must entertain a unilateral attack on Iran regardless of American support. This assessment also reflects the division between Israel and the Obama administration, as noted earlier. The other side of the coin, as stated by Riedel, is that a preemptive attack would make Iran "likely to become even more determined to get the bomb" and "more inclined to use it."

This proposal and its possible consequences clearly demonstrate the division between the United States and Israel on the Iranian nuclear program. The success of an attack against Iran's facilities is problematical since Iran has taken considerable measures to harden and disperse elements of the program in order to reduce the kind of vulnerability that allowed Israel to take preemptive action against Iraqi and Syrian facilities in the past. Attacking Iranian facilities would likely set the program back three to five years but would not derail it altogether. Given the unknown consequences of such an attack—such as a broader war in the region—the question is whether such a result is worth the broader risk. As Goldberg ("Point of No Return") summarizes the division between the allies, "The Americans consider a temporary postponement of Iran's nuclear program to be of dubious value. The Israelis don't."

The Iranians, of course, are well aware of these deliberations and also likely are susceptible to the counterargument that such Israeli planning simply makes going nuclear more attractive to Iran as a way to extend deterrence to Israel as well as the United States. An attempt to destroy Iran's nuclear program might, in other words, have the undesirable effect of stimulating the Iranian acquisition of nuclear weapons rather than retarding it, a self-fulfilling prophecy opposed by all.

The United States is caught in the middle of this aspect of the Middle East confrontation. The United States is at the forefront of those opposing Iranian nuclear weapons as a matter of nonproliferation principle and also because of opposition to this development both by Israel and Iran's neighbors, who join Israel in the fear of being blackmailed by a nuclear Iran (although they do not fear so much the possibility of a nuclear attack from Iran). The Americans also oppose an Israeli attack on the grounds that such an action would have unpredictable and possibly catastrophic regional effects, including galvanizing anti-Israeli sentiment in both Sunni and Shiite Muslim countries. At the same time, "Washington . . . is Israel's only meaningful ally," as Goldberg ("Point of No Return") puts it, meaning the United States cannot appear to abandon Israel strategically. Solidarity on the issue is, however, controversial within the Arab world, because a United States that roundly condemns the Iranian nuclear program has been quite content with an Israeli de facto nuclear monopoly in the region for nearly half a century, which some Muslim states see as hypocritical on the Americans' part.

Regional Considerations

While the nuclear question casts a shadow over the entirety of U.S.–Iranian relations, there is a regional dimension to the relationship as well. Part of this regional concern is how the United States balances its multiple and sometimes contradictory interests in the region. The goal of American policy in this part of the Middle East is clearly best served by regional tranquility, which is a commodity in short supply but which allows the United States to pursue interests in Israeli security, access to petroleum energy, and the transformation of the region into a stable and hopefully democratic bastion. To even approach these goals, the United States must attempt to confront and neutralize both Israeli–Arab–Iranian antagonisms and rivalries within the Muslim world between the Iranians and the Arabs. This combination is no small order, of course, and one at which the United States has not been overly successful. The roiled waters of the region are, of course, made even choppier by ongoing confrontations such as that between Iran and Israel over nuclear weapons and by American military presence in two wars in countries bordering Iran.

Like so many of the issues, the question of Iranian actions toward the wars in Afghanistan and Iraq is schizophrenic. The Iranians have clear interests in what goes on in both countries. Both countries border Iran, and both have long historic and other ties to Tehran: Iraq shares Iran's distinction of having a Shiite majority, and one of the official languages of Afghanistan is Dari, also known as Afghan Persian. Moreover, both are within what Iran thinks of as its legitimate sphere of influence as a major regional power.

The schizophrenia arises over how the Iranians should respond to the American occupation of both countries, including the diminishing residual presence of the Americans in Iraq. In one sense, the American presence has posed a threat to be opposed: it puts the Great Satan near the Iranian frontier, and American and Iranian interests in the outcome of each are not identical. Symbolically, the American military presence so close to Iranian territory is further evidence of Iranian inadequacy as a major power. In another sense, both countries, for different reasons, prefer settlements in the countries that would stabilize the situations for both, and outcomes that restore peace within both countries would facilitate the withdrawal of American military presence from the region in which Iran hopes to reign as the regional power.

The ability of the United States and Iran even to discuss mutual interests and forms of cooperation to end the two wars and turmoil in Iraq and Afghanistan is greatly impeded by the lack of relations between them. Since they have no diplomatic relations, it is difficult for them to interact to discuss the possibilities of even limited cooperation because they lack a venue within which to conduct the necessary discussions. Since they do not recognize one another, for instance, the only way they can talk face to face is in secret, and the requirement of secrecy is difficult to maintain and dictates talks that involve small groups of not very high-level, high-profile negotiators (people whose numbers and identities could be obscured from the media). At the same time, there are political elements in both countries that view any interaction with the other as being in league with the devil and would respond with considerable political vitriol to even the hint of interchanges between the two enemies.

The result is an ironic standoff. The exploration and implementation of mutually reinforcing and beneficial initiatives by the Americans and Iranians in Afghanistan and Iraq could provide a diplomatic wedge behind which the tension between the two could be reduced, as well as calming the situations in Iraq and Afghanistan and thus reducing tensions between the United States and Iran and regional tensions generally. Neither side, however, has been able to take the initiative to begin such a process because of the very animosity such deliberations would seek to relieve. The result is that neither party is willing—or politically able—to take the bold initiative to enter a path that would lead to improved relations. The reason is that such an initiative would result in bitter denunciation of the instigators of talks as being "soft" in the face of a hated and distrusted enemy.

U.S. OPTIONS

The question of what the United States seeks to accomplish in its relations with the Islamic Republic of Iran can be divided into two subquestions. The first deals with how the United States desires the current impasses in which it finds itself enmeshed with Iran to be resolved: the Iranian nuclear weapons program, the related confrontation between Iran and Israel, and the potential for Iranian–American cooperation in the world, and especially in ending the conflicts in Iraq and Afghanistan (both of whose situations are discussed in separate chapters). The second question is about the longer-term nature of U.S.–Iranian relations: can they be changed from the dismal state in which they have existed since 1979?

Stating these preferences is complicated by the fact that there is very basic disagreement on how or whether the United States should deal with Iran, and these disagreements clearly reflect basic levels of distrust and animosity. These disagreements include the veracity of the Iranian regime and its moral character (concerns no doubt mirrored in Tehran about the United States). Moreover, there is the question of the extent to which the United States is capable of achieving its desired preferences, a matter of the amount of leverage the United States possesses to influence Iranian behavior.

This debate is prejudiced domestically in the United States by strong anti-Iranian sentiment that could become quite loud and vitriolic if improvements in relations between the two countries were proposed. The shadow of the hostage crisis is a wraith that could easily be reasserted, and Ahmadinejad's intemperate rhetoric would be a lightning rod for negative sentiments. Pro-Israeli elements would add fuel to the fire of opposition. As a result, even suggesting improved relations—such as simply talking to Tehran—is politically risky, as the Obama administration learned early in its tenure.

What the United States would prefer in the short run from the three basic sources of tensions already described is straightforward enough, even if the means to achieve those preferences is not. Clearly, the United States seeks to have Tehran abandon its nuclear weapons program and to place its nuclear industry under the kinds of international monitoring that will reassure all who need such reassurances that Iran cannot and will not attempt to "break out" and restart its efforts to become the 10th nuclear weapons state. Hardly anyone outside of Iran disagrees with this outcome; how to accomplish it is much more difficult. A cessation of the Iranian nuclear weapons program would, of course, also reduce the Israeli incentives to take the risky action of attacking and trying to destroy Iranian facilities. It would not solve all the bases of Israeli–Iranian animosity, however, since it would leave Iranian support for anti-Israeli groups like Hamas and Hezbollah intact and the subject of separate discussions. Whether or to what extent the United States and Iran could come together to influence movement toward peaceful solutions in Afghanistan and Iraq is more problematical, given the degree of distrust between the two countries and the residual political opposition to any cooperation between them this animosity entails.

There is also disagreement about what the long-term nature of American–Iranian relations can or should be. For Americans, the ideal outcome would be the transformation of Iran from theocratic authoritarianism to some form of responsible political democracy with which it would naturally be in agreement and with which it could have normal, productive relations. Unfortunately, the Iranian government rejects this kind of future as a threat. As Vaki observes, "Washington's democracy promotion program . . . is received in Tehran as an unmistakable attempt at regime change" (i.e., the overthrow of the existing regime). Moreover, this is the kind of outcome that many Iranians associate with American collaboration with the shah, a process and outcome the Iranian Revolution rejected. Proponents of improved relations over the longer term argue that only the transformation of Iranian society to something like a modern democratic basis will allow Iran to become a normal member of the international system and enjoy friendly relations with the United States, but they admit the transformation will be long and difficult because of the nature of Iranian society and the current regime. Those advocating change are likely to attach themselves to apparent prodemocratic signs like the Green Movement. Opponents of improved relations argue the intractability and disruptive nature of the regime and believe that it can only be changed by violent upheaval, either internally or externally generated.

Leverage is the clear problem that the United States has in trying to move the Iranians in the direction of American preferred outcomes on the issues dividing the two countries: what positive or negative actions the United States can take or threaten to move the Iranians closer to positions the United States occupies. The general consensus has been that the United States does not have great leverage over Iran short of severe actions, especially military, that the United States is unlikely to exercise against the Iranians. The nature and probable effectiveness of American options, however, are different for different aspects of the disagreements the country has with Iran, as a review of those options reveal.

Analytically, one can lay out four policy options the United States can entertain, with varying levels of effort, appropriateness, and likelihood of success attaching to each. The four, in descending order of severity, are military actions, economic and other sanctions against the regime in Tehran, negotiations between the American and Iranian regime, and doing essentially nothing.

The first option, military action, often is articulated under the robust-sounding rubric of "taking no option off the table" since the most extreme option and thus the one first to be removed from active policy consideration (taken off the table) is likely to be the use of military force against the Tehran regime. Enthusiasm for the military option generally arises among those segments of the American policy community prone to act "tough" in dealing with other countries and in the Iranian case gains some momentum as a form of reprisal for the embarrassment of the hostage crisis a third of a century ago.

There are several objections to serious consideration of the military option against Iran. The first and most obvious is where the military force would come from since virtually all American military assets are already committed to Iraq and Afghanistan, and although the military occupation of Iraq essentially ended at the end of 2011, there is virtually no enthusiasm in the United States about transferring that commitment elsewhere. The second is that effective military action against Iran would be very difficult. Iran is, after all, a large, populous country that would put up a spirited resistance to the introduction of American forces on its soil: it is not a "walkover" like Iraq, which had American forces effectively tied down for eight years, was. Third, there would likely be very little international support for any proposed American-led military attack against Iran; the Iranians have too many countries dependent on their energy supplies to expect them to oppose Tehran vigorously. Fourth, the only American objective for which U.S. military force might be appropriate is the destruction of the Iranian nuclear program. Given the nature of that program, it is unlikely that measured, non-manpower-intensive efforts like aerial bombardment would do much more than setting the Iranian program back; the only truly effective military action would be almost have to be a full-scale invasion and occupation that the United States currently could not launch or support and which would be universally opposed by the world. This combination of admonitions leads Takeyh to conclude, "the United States has no military option in Iran."

Not everyone agrees with this assessment. Most analysts agree that a full-scale war against Iran would be unsustainable and probably excessive to the issue (Iranian proliferation) it seeks to redress, but some would maintain that limited, surgical applications of American airpower (possibly in conjunction with Israeli strikes) could be useful in retarding Iran's ability to build a nuclear bomb and might help persuade the Iranians of the futility of reactivating the program once it was damaged or destroyed. Lindsay and Takeyh, however, offer an example of how limited and available American force could be used to assuage Israeli fears: "Washington should also be prepared," they argue, "to deploy U.S. troops on Israeli soil as a tripwire" to an Iranian attack should they gain nuclear weapons status since launching such an attack would automatically entail killing Americans and make an American nuclear response virtually certain.

Whether a military option is at all attractive depends largely on how much of a problem a nuclear-armed Iran presents. Opinion is divided on this subject. At one extreme is the Israeli belief that a nuclear Iran would be a military loose cannon providing an existential threat that must be prevented at all costs. Others disagree. Riedel, for instance, expects that a nuclear Iran "will not be a crazy or suicidal state" but "will behave like a normal nuclear state," and that even if Iran obtains nuclear arms, "the region will not face the apocalypse."

The second, slightly less robust, American option is the continued, even accelerated, use of economic and other *sanctions* (the threat or use of negative or positive actions to bring compliance with a policy) against the regime in Tehran. Such actions against the Tehran regime are by no means new; some forms of this kind of punishment against the Iranians was part of the response to the hostage crisis of 1979, and new forms of unilateral sanctions by the United States and international sanctions against Iranian misdeeds have been common since. As a current policy response, the recourse to sanctions means finding new forms of restriction to place on the Iranians.

The use of sanctions in general and in particular against Iran raises four objections. The first is that they do not work, or at least do not work in the ways intended. The appeal of sanctions as a foreign policy tool is that they impose deprivation on the target but that they require generally much less sacrifice on the part of the country imposing the sanctions than more robust forms of response like military actions. This asymmetry of effects, of course, makes sanctions politically popular in the sanctioning state(s) because they represent actions without personal pain, but that advantage is countermanded by the fact that sanctions do not always cause the governments against which they are imposed to change the behavior for which they were imposed in the first place. The classic negative example (examined more fully in Chapter 10) is Cuba, against which the United States has had strict economic sanctions for over a half century but which have proven absolutely ineffective in forcing the Cubans to abandon their communist regime. Proponents of sanctions rightly point out that sanctions do not always fail, especially to the degree that critics suggest.

The second objection to sanctions is that they generally hurt the wrong people in the target country; they "punish the innocent" rather than those in control. Economic sanctions (the most common form) generally restrict things like trade, which means banning commodities historically imported from the sanctioning country and consumed by rank-and-file citizens of the country against which the sanctions are aimed. These average citizens tend to bear the brunt of whatever effect sanctions may have, while members of the elite who make and perpetuate whatever conditions caused the sanctions to be imposed can often find ways around whatever is being generally denied. The purpose of sanctions in Iran, for instance, is to cause the religious hierarchy that rules the country to change course; most of these individuals are quite ascetic, however, and so it is hard to deprive them with sanctions, whereas more normal consumers are deprived because of the sanctions. Moreover, the more deprivation the sanctions impose across time, the more likely they are to boomerang: people may come to associate their suffering not with their own government (one intention of sanctions) but with the sanctioning state.

Third, there is the question of what sanctions can be imposed that may be effective. The normal progression of sanctions is that they begin with a limited list of prohibited actions, and when these fail, more commodities or services are added to the list. Presumably, the first items on the sanction list are those that supposedly would have the greatest effect, while additions represent lesser concerns. At some point, the list of sanctions reaches an effective end, and the sanctioning country is left with nothing meaningful left to restrict. As 2010 progressed, for instance, the Obama administration suggested that it might extend the Iranian sanctions, but it was not at all clear what there was left that the Americans could meaningfully add to the list.

Finally, sanctions are only effective if they are universally applied. If there is an incentive for some state or states to ignore or violate sanctions and to provide states against which sanctions exist with items on the sanction list, then sanctions lose their punitive value and effectiveness. This is clearly the case with Iran, where countries desirous of gaining access to Iranian resources like China and Russia have a strong incentive to break ranks on sanctions in order to gain preferential access to the energy wealth that Iran possesses.

The first two policy options are essentially negative (the "stick" of a "carrot and stick" approach), imposing harm on Iran for failing to comply with American preferences. The third option, however, is more neutral in these terms. The use of negotiation with the Iranians suggests that if the two countries were to sit down at some level and discuss their mutual interests, they might find enough common cause to allow them to relax the enormous enmity they have toward one another and even to move toward something like the normalization of relations ruptured for so long.

President Obama suggested this approach in his 2008 election campaign, to the derision of opponents who believe the Iranian regime is so obdurate in its opposition to the United States and so bizarre in its general behavior that it cannot be seriously negotiated with. Certainly, the depiction of President Ahmadinejad and his extremist positions on issues like the Holocaust lends credence to critical interpretations and raises the question of who the United States could negotiate with and about what. At the same time, there is precedent for using even very narrow negotiations as a wedge that can produce broader understanding and reduced tension. The process that led to the end of the Cold War, for instance, arguably began with narrowly tracked negotiations about nuclear arms control with a Soviet government believed to be as evil and intractable as the Iranian regime is considered today, and the Chinese invitation to the U.S. table tennis team to play in China in 1971 ("ping pong diplomacy") was a critical wedge in opening U.S.–China relations.

While the Obama administration has quietly pursued discussions with the Iranians, it has been impeded by three barriers. The first is that a negotiation requires two (or more) negotiating partners, and the Iranians have not shown a willingness to engage the Americans in even preliminary talks. Both sides instead engage in rhetorical sparring that only makes it more difficult for them to come to the table. The second problem is about what they can negotiate. What, in other words, is the parallel opening to nuclear arms control with the Soviets in the U.S.–Iranian relationship? The best candidate would appear to be the exploration of common interests in forging postwar conditions in Iraq and Afghanistan. In neither of the cases are American and Iranian interests identical, but both have a core interest in at least minimal stability in both countries.

For the United States, stability offers a symbol of the achievement of at least some of their objectives and provides cover for disengagement. For Iran, stability reduces tensions on its borders and probably facilitates its efforts to establish influence on the postwar regimes in the two countries. The third barrier is domestic. Segments of the political right in the United States, bolstered by pro-Israeli elements, are adamantly opposed to any interaction with the Iranian theocracy under any circumstances short of the renunciation of religious rule.

The final American policy option, and the path of least resistance, is to do essentially what has been done in the past—the status quo of hostile non-relations with an unresponsive, maverick Iranian regime. This solution avoids the charge, in essence, of consorting with the devil (for both sides) and leaves each with the other as a convenient political whipping boy on whom to blame whatever ills in the region confront them. The path of inertia, however, means that none of the basic divisions between the two states—nuclear weapons, Israel, and regional instabilities—are directly addressed by the two states in concert, an outcome that may be intolerable enough to each of them individually and both of them collectively to avoid.

What an examination of the options the United States has for influencing Iran reveals is that none of the options are obviously or overwhelmingly attractive. Military threats against Iran that are believable (the United States could actually carry them out) are unlikely to be effective in changing Iranian behavior, and threats (like invasion) that might be effective probably are not credible since they would too greatly tax or exceed American capabilities for outcomes arguably not worth the level of effort expended. Sanctions have been in place for over 30 years, have been progressively more robust, and have been less than totally effective. What more can be done? Diplomatic initiatives have not borne fruit to this point, and that leaves the basically unattractive option of continuing a status quo that no one finds satisfying. The problem boils down to a lack of meaningful leverage on the United States' part to accomplish the ambitious preferences it has toward a recalcitrant Iran and demonstrates the dynamics of interaction between a global power and an assertive regional power in the regional state's backyard.

CONCLUSIONS

The relationship between the United States and Iran is complex, emotional, and frustrating. The two countries have been the closest of friends in the Middle East but are now adversaries of the first order and view one another with the greatest of suspicion and disregard. Both countries have demonized the other for different reasons, and the images of a "crazy" Iran and a "Great Satan" Uncle Sam do not facilitate the emergence of reason in their relations.

The American preference is for Iran to shuck what the United States considers the sectarian tyranny of theocratic rule in Iran because it presumes that this is what Iranians also want and that a more democratic Iran would be friendlier to the United States than the current regime. Thus, Americans probably overemphasize signs of political turmoil in that country and believe that, as

Kinzer argues, "the flame of freedom still burns in Iran—although, unlike Turkey, it is not allowed to burn in public." The presumption that a freer Iran would be to American advantage may be more problematical than the United States wishes it might be. For many Iranians, after all, the United States is both the symbol of the hated shah and of the destruction of Iran's only experience with real democracy in the 1950s under Mossadeqh. It is not at all clear that a democratic Iran would throw itself into the waiting arms of the Americans.

The emergence of a post-theocratic regime is also not a very strong short-term likelihood. The current regime is ensconced in power, and although it faces opposition and great economic difficulties, its hold on power does not appear to be in significant danger. Thus, the United States must, for the foreseeable future, face an enigmatic and difficult opponent, the nature of which is captured well by Lindsay and Takeyh: "Tehran is an adversary that speaks in ideological terms, wants to be a dominant regional power, and is capable of acting recklessly. But it is also an adversary that recognizes its limitations, wants to preserve its hold on power, and operates among wary neighbors."

STUDY/DISCUSSION QUESTIONS

1. How have U.S.–Iranian relations been schizophrenic? Discuss, using 1979 as the division point in those relations. How does this history imbue the relationship with a particularly emotional character on both sides?
2. Describe Iran. How does Iran feel it fits into the world and its geographic region? Include a discussion of the White and Iranian Revolutions in your answer, and how these events color American and Iranian perceptions of the other.
3. Describe Iran physically and demographically. How is Iran a unique state?
4. What are the three major sources of foreign policy contention between the United States and Iran? Describe each.
5. What are the preferred outcomes to U.S.–Iranian disputes from an American viewpoint? What options does the United States have to pursue its interests? Describe and assess each option in terms of its feasibility and likelihood of success.
6. If *you* were in charge of crafting U.S policy toward Iran, what kind of policy would you pursue? Defend your position.

READING/RESEARCH MATERIALS

Aslan, Reza. "What We Got Wrong." *Foreign Policy* July/August 2010, 109–110.

Baktiari, Bahman. "Iran's Conservative Revival." *Current History* 106, 696 (January 2007), 11–16.

Chadar, Fariborz. "Behind Iran's Crackdown, an Economic Gap." *Current History* 108, 722 (December 2009), 424–428.

Donovan, Michael. "Iran, Israel, and Nuclear Weapons in the Middle East." *CDI Terrorism Project* (online), February 14, 2002.

Dreyfuss, Robert. "Is Iran Winning the Iraq War?" *Nation* 286, 9 (March 10, 2008), 22–28.

Ehteshami, Anoushiravan. "The Middle East's New Power Dynamic." *Current History* 108, 722 (December 2009), 395–401.

Elliot, Hen-Tov. "Understanding Iran's New Authoritarianism." *Washington Quarterly* 30, 1 (Winter 2006/2007), 163–180.

Goldberg, Jeffrey. "How Iran Could Save the Middle East." *The Atlantic* 304, 1 (July/August 2009), 66–68.

———. "The Point of No Return." *The Atlantic* 306, 2 (September 2010), 56–69.

Gonzalez, Nathan. *Engaging Iran: The Rise of a Middle East Power and America's Strategic Choice.* Westport, CT: Praeger Security International, 2007.

Jervis, Robert. *Why Intelligence Fails: Lessons from the Iranian Revolution and the Iraq War.* Ithaca, NY: Cornell University Press, 2010.

Kaplan, Robert D. "Living with a Nuclear Iran." *The Atlantic* 306, 2 (September 2010), 70–72.

Kinzer, Stephen. *Iran, Turkey, and America's Future.* New York: Times Books, 2010.

Kodmani, Bassma. "Clearing the Air in the Middle East." *Current History* 107, 709 (May 2008), 21–26.

Lindsay, James M., and Roy Takeyh. "After Iran Gets the Bomb: Containment and Its Complications." *Foreign Affairs* 89, 2 (March/April 2010), 33–42.

McFaul, Michael, Abbas Milani, and Larry Diamond. "A Win-Win Strategy for Dealing with Iran." *Washington Quarterly* 30, 1 (Winter 2006/2007), 121–135.

Milani, Mohsen. "Tehran's Take: Understanding Iran's U.S. Policy." *Foreign Affairs* 88, 4 (July/August 2009), 46–62.

Nasr, Vali, and Roy Takeyh. "The Costs of Containing Iran." *Foreign Affairs* 87, 1 (January/February 2008), 85–94.

Pollack, Kenneth M. "Bringing Iran to the Bargaining Table." *Current History* 105, 694 (November 2006), 365–370.

Posen, Barry. "Overkill." *Foreign Affairs* 89, 4 (July/August 2010), 160–163.

Riedel, Bruce. "The Mideast after Iran Gets the Bomb." *Current History* 109, 731 (December 2010), 370–375.

Rubin, Barry. "The Right Kind of Containment." *Foreign Affairs* 89, 4 (July/August 2010), 163–166.

Sick, Gary G. *All Fall Down: America's Tragic Encounter with Iran.* New York: Random House, 1985.

Takeyh, Roy. "Time for Détente with Iran." *Foreign Affairs* 86, 2 (March/April 2007), 17–32.

Vaki, Sanam. "Tehran Gambles to Survive." *Current History* 106, 704 (December 2007), 153–168.

North Korea:
Balancing Recognition
and the Nuclear Card

PREVIEW

Relations between the United States and the Democratic Republic of Korea (DPRK, or North Korea) have been uniformly negative since that country was established as a result of the division of the Korean Peninsula at the end of World War II. In 1950, the two countries fought one another as principal combatants in the Korean War, a conflict that has yet to be formally ended. The United States has served as a major supporter of North Korea's major rival, the Republic of Korea (ROK, or South Korea), since then. As South Korea has entered the first rank of world powers, the North has lagged behind, and only its nuclear weapons program provides it with a sense of national importance. The DPRK nuclear program is the main point of contention between the two countries, and one that periodically becomes potentially combustible. How the United States and the DPRK can navigate their way through the tangle of nuclear weapons and proliferation concerns, along with other issues, is the major thrust of this analysis.

In November 2010, the Democratic Republic of Korea (DPRK) announced that it had developed the capacity to engage in large-scale nuclear fuel reprocessing, a capability that had heretofore eluded it and which the international community—headed by the United States—had sought to prevent it from achieving. Thanks to initiatives announced in 2006, North Korea had become the ninth nuclear weapons power, and the best estimates of its nuclear weapons status suggested it probably possesses 6 to 8 reasonably primitive, low-yield nuclear warheads. Gaining the modern reprocessing capability that it had constructed could provide the springboard for enlargement of that arsenal, both in terms of the number of weapons and the potency of the arsenal.

The result has been a concerted effort to try to reengage with the hermitic North Koreans in an effort to slow the North Korean nuclear weapons program or to persuade them to abandon it altogether. This effort is but the latest in a series of negotiations between the DPRK, the United States, and the other countries of East Asia to bring under control the potential destabilization that a nuclear North Korea could pose.

Within little more than a week after the reprocessing announcement, and almost certainly related to it, the strained relations between the two Koreas turned violent, a sporadic occurrence on the peninsula. In this case, North Korean artillery attacked civilian facilities on Yeonpyeong Island, off the western coast of the two countries, killing four South Koreans: two military personnel and two civilians. The South Koreans accused the North Koreans of a naked, unprovoked act of aggression, mobilized, and threatened an "overwhelming" military response. The DPRK countered that the attack was a response to provocative South Korean military exercises near its territory and also threatened further military actions. The United States, South Korea's closest military ally, issued stern warnings and moved the aircraft carrier *U.S.S. George Washington* into position off the Korean coast. Behind the scenes, the United States pleaded with China, the North Koreans' closest partners, to bring pressure on the regime of DPRK strongman Kim Jong Il to back away from an escalation that could send the peninsula into a bloody reprise of the Korean War 60 years ago. In December 2010, an informal U.S. delegation headed by outgoing New Mexico Governor Bill Richardson visited Pyongyang to try to reduce tensions.

In some ways, the crisis had a familiar aura. The North Koreans were faced with two other difficulties at the time the crisis arose—or was precipitated by Pyongyang, depending on one's view of it. One of these was a succession crisis, as an apparently failing North Korean leader, Kim Jong Il, announced that one of his sons, Kim Jong Un, was his chosen successor. Like his father, the 26-year-old successor was basically unknown before his selection, and questions inevitably emerged about how smoothly the process would go. At the same time, the extremely poor DPRK was in the throes of one of its periodic food shortages and in desperate need of outside assistance to avoid another round of suffering for its population. As had occurred in the early 1990s, this situation had led to North Korean militancy that resulted in an agreement with the United States and others to come to the country's rescue. Some saw a familiar pattern in the 2010 confrontation.

The November 2010 confrontation, of course, was resolved short of fullscale violence, as similar incidents have been and as part of an apparent pattern in North Korea's relations with the outside world discussed more fully later in the chapter. The flare-up did, however, symbolize the deep and abiding problems of a politically divided Korean peninsula and the problems that it creates for a United States with deep interests in the area dating back to its successful intervention on behalf of South Korea in 1950. The North Korean nuclear program, which loomed in the background of the 2010 incident and casts a shadow over the ongoing status of the peninsula and the region generally, was at the heart of the need to diffuse the crisis, but it must be seen in the context of a broader set of interests in the future of the Koreas that begins with the hermitic North Koreans.

North Korea is, like its sibling in the south, a basically artificial state. Prior to the end of World War II, the Korean peninsula was one unified and generally independent Korea, although it had suffered the humiliation of occupation and colonization by Japan between 1910 and 1945. The Japanese surrender opened the way for a reestablished Korean independence, but the nature of wartime politics dictated that an immediate postwar occupation to reestablish order be a joint venture between the two principal victorious allies in the Pacific, the United States and the Soviet Union. The line of demarcation between the two zones was roughly along the 38th Parallel, which became the de facto international border that remains in place to this day.

Although this occupation was supposed to be a temporary event to pave the way for the independence of the entire peninsula as one country, the developing vagaries of the impending Cold War caused the United States to install and nurture an anticommunist regime that eventually became democratic in its southern zone, while the Soviets installed a communist regime in its northern occupation zone. Scheduled reunification elections were not held in 1948, with both sides arguing (probably validly by both) that elections in the other zone would be rigged, and the temporary division into a North and South Korea began to emerge as the de facto permanent solution.

In June 1950, the North Koreans attacked and invaded South Korea in what became the first major violent Cold War confrontation. The United States immediately announced its intention to come to the aid of the South Koreans, who on their own stood little chance against the much better armed North Koreans (the post–World War II occupation agreement limited armament to defensive arms only, an admonition the Soviets ignored to a greater degree than did the Americans). Americans troops poured out of Japan onto the Korean Peninsula, eventually stopping the North Korean advance outside the port city of Pusan (the so-called Pusan Perimeter). A series of attacks and counterattacks ensued in the following months, and in January 1951 the battle lines stopped along the 38th Parallel, which remains the armistice line and de facto international border between the two Koreas to the present. Fighting continued until 1953, when the negotiators arranged what has become a durable but occasionally combustible cease fire, as the November 2010 incident demonstrated.

There has never been a peace agreement ending the hostilities, meaning that a technical state of war remains between the ROK and the DPRK, in which the United States is a major partner by virtue of its defense of South Korea during the war and since. Although the response to the 1950 North Korean invasion was technically a United Nations operation, the leading role among intervening powers was and continues to be played by the United States. In addition to providing massive amounts of developmental assistance that has helped propel South Korea into the ranks of Asian economic powers, the United States has maintained military forces in South Korea as a deterrent to a renewed effort by the North at forceful reunification. The current number of American military personnel in South Korea is about 28,000.

These events serve as the backdrop for considering contemporary U.S.–North Korean relations. North Korea, unlike the South, is one of the poorest, least developed countries in the world, and it is among the most authoritarian and isolated states as well. It is not unfair to say that its nuclear weapons program is its virtual sole claim to importance in the world, and that it would be essentially inconsequential without those weapons and the possibilities for mischief those weapons represent. The world does not want North Korea to become a full-blown nuclear power because it is viewed as a rogue, potentially unpredictable state whose possession of weapons of mass destruction can only serve as a destabilizing influence on the region and the world more generally. The North Koreans appear to understand this apprehension and act to exploit it. For them, nuclear weapons serve both as the basis of their claim to be recognized and dealt with as equals in an environment where only their possession of these weapons validates such a claim, and as a trump card in negotiations with the rest of the world. The question that lies not far below the surface is how to deal with this dilemma, and it is an issue that creates great disagreement, particularly in the United States.

While the nuclear question is at the heart of U.S. relations with the DPRK, there are other, related influences as well. Currently, the question of regime succession is a matter of importance, as the North Koreans approach the turnover of power for only the third time in the country's over 60-year history. Who rules North Korea and how they rule also influence other related issues that include efforts to develop the country and bring it more fully into the international system. At the same time, the desire among the populations of both Koreas to move toward reunification remains an important long-term goal among the populaces of both countries.

NORTH KOREA: A SKETCH

North Korea is one of the least inviting places on the face of the earth. Other than for the vagaries of the outcome of World War II, there is no reason for a divided Korea to exist. For most of its history, Korea was an independent kingdom on the peninsula. The bookends of its independence were domination by China that ended in the 300 CE period and the Japanese occupation between 1910 and 1945. Between those times, Korea had existed as a single entity, and once World War II ended, most Koreans had the expectation that their country would be reunified and achieve independence.

Postwar geopolitics intervened to upset those expectations. As the United States fought its way toward the Japanese home islands during the latter parts of the conflict in the Pacific, it confronted the presumed necessity of a massive invasion of those islands and a spirited and bloody resistance to that invasion (estimates of a million killed were common, compared to overall American casualties—killed and wounded—of 405,000 in the war). In order to dilute the possible bloodletting, the United States turned to its Soviet ally to aid in an invasion, presumably anticipating that the Soviets would absorb some of the casualties. Soviet leader Josef Stalin, who was aware of the American development of nuclear weapons that might end the war short of an invasion, agreed. His price for doing so included an occupation zone in Korea after the war ended. The Americans agreed, and although the invasion's necessity was cancelled by the Japanese surrender after the nuclear bombing of Hiroshima and Nagasaki on August 6 and 9, 1945, the division of Korea into American-dominated and Soviet-dominated zones was implemented in accord with the wartime agreement. Entirely without their own participation in the decision process, the Koreans were divided into what became two quite separate states.

The Korean War represented the only serious effort to unify the country since 1945, and thanks to American intervention under the banner of the United Nations, the North Korean attempt at forceful unification failed. After that war concluded, the boundary between the two Koreas—the 38th Parallel—became the world's most heavily armed and fortified frontier, and behind it, two quite distinctive countries have developed, each influenced by the wartime experience.

While South Korea has developed as a very prosperous, democratizing country that is one of the economic miracles of Asia, it is the North Korean experience that is of most relevance here. The DPRK was a clear loser in the Korean conflict, its own armed forces virtually decimated by the Americans and their UN allies and their continued independence only guaranteed by a massive, if unofficial, intervention on their behalf by the Chinese in late 1950 that kept the Americans from unifying the country under anticommunist rulers. (The Americans reached the Chinese–North Korean border in late 1950, and UN commanding general Douglas MacArthur argued, among other things, that the allies should have used nuclear weapons to end the war on its own terms.) The Americans stayed after the war as occupiers and guarantors of South Korean independence, and part of the basis of their defense was nuclear weapons, the centerpiece of current disputes between the Americans and the North Koreans. As Norris explains, "The fact that North Korea was threatened by nuclear weapons during the Korean War, and that for decades thereafter U.S. weapons were deployed in the South, may have helped motivate former President Kim Il Sung to launch a nuclear weapons program of his own." While the motivations of the North Koreans both to launch their nuclear program in the late 1950s and to continue it may be more complex than that, nonetheless the experience in the war undoubtedly posed part of their reason and is certainly an ongoing part of antagonistic relations between the United States and the DPRK.

The so-called Hermit Kingdom has developed in a state of virtual isolation from most of the influences of the outside world ever since. Much of this isolation has been self-imposed by the North Koreans for reasons that are debated outside the country. The standard reason given is the extremely austere, authoritarian, and Stalinist worldview of the regime, which seeks to maintain its iron grip by denying its citizens a vision of the better living conditions elsewhere (notably in South Korea, which has a per capita GDP well in excess of 10 times that in the DPRK). Thus, a reclusive condition that does not allow knowledge of the outside world provides the protection the regime needs from invidious comparisons by its own citizenry. At some odds with this interpretation, Myers adds the rejoinder that the regime is also deeply racist, asserting "North Korea is not Stalinist—it's simply racist." Regardless of the reasons for its isolation, remaining immune from outside influences is an important part of the DPRK's ongoing existence and is a major part of the difficulty of dealing with and particularly of trying to bring about change that would facilitate better relations.

The Physical Setting

The combination of its geopolitical situation as part of the divided nation of Koreans, its isolation from the rest of the world, and its belligerence as a member of the international community help frame an understanding of North Korea and its place both in the world and as an irritant for American foreign policy. The physical setting of the country only adds to its problems and its interface with the world at large.

North Korea is not a physically imposing place. Its location on the Korean peninsula (sometimes known colorfully as a "dagger aimed at the heart of Japan") is sandwiched between a vibrant, prosperous ROK on the south and the People's Republic of China and Russia in the north, as examining a map of the region demonstrates. It is a relatively small country, with a land area of over 75,000 square miles (figures from the *CIA World Factbook*), making it the 98th largest country in the world and slightly smaller than the state of Mississippi. By comparison, South Korea is physically slightly smaller, with an area of 62,325 square miles (108th in the world). North Korea also has a relatively poor natural endowment, including no known sources of petroleum or natural gas, to form a natural basis for development.

What is physically most notable about the DPRK is its extreme poverty, particularly in comparison to the more prosperous south. North Korea's 22.7 million citizens (2010 estimate) exist on the basis of $1,800 GDP per capita (2009 estimate), which ranks 193rd in the world—virtually the bottom. By contrast, the roughly 48.6 million South Koreans enjoy a per capita GDP of $28,100, which ranks 48th worldwide. The stark figures for the DPRK are no better illustrated than in the inability of the country to feed itself. According to the BBC News background note on the country, "Aid agencies have estimated that up to two million people have died since the mid-1990s because of acute food shortages caused by natural disasters and economic mismanagement." The result is that North Korea is a perpetual beggar country that literally relies for its very existence on outside assistance that it often haughtily disdains, helping to explain its apparently erratic behavior toward the outside world. In a nutshell, the DPRK depends to a critical degree on foreign sources that it rejects and seeks to exclude.

The condition of North Korea, and particularly the comparison with its other half south of the 38th Parallel, also points to the political dilemma of reunification, an underlying theme of peninsular politics. The artificial division of the country in 1948 separated many Koreans from family members on one side of the 38th parallel or the other, and there has been very limited contact between South and North Koreans since. Because the division is arbitrary and represents no historical reality other than the geopolitics of ending World War II, there has been a basic grassroots desire to see the two halves reunited—a sentiment that has probably receded somewhat as successive generation have been deprived of access to one another. There is, however, some reluctance among elites in both countries to entertain such possibilities, for reasons rooted in the physical contrasts between the two and parallels with what happened when divided Germany reunited starting in 1991.

There are in fact two very distinct Koreas today, and the integration of those halves into one whole would be a monumental task, the precedent of which in Germany suggests the difficulties involved. The most obvious contrasts are economic: a comparatively rich, expanding capitalist economy in the south and a highly stagnated, underdeveloped economy in the socialist north. Integration of the two economies would involve the massive infusion of capital from the south into the DPRK, as well as the training of the population of the north to function and contribute to the postindustrial southern economy. While some outside assistance would likely be available to assist in this process, the German precedent suggests that most of it would have to come from the south, and the fear is that such a transfer would dampen the vitality of the southern economy—a phenomenon that has antecedents in the post–Cold War German experience. Twenty years after the fact, former East and West Germany have not fully integrated economically (as well as socially), and it would almost certainly take at least that long for the same process to work out in the Koreas.

It is the political dimension that is most difficult. South Koreans are both more affluent and more numerous than their North Korean counterparts, and the South Korean political elite expects it would dominate a unified Korean state, in much the same way that West German political parties and politicians have dominated the politics of a unified Germany. The communist leaders of North Korea represent a small and privileged group within the current state, and it is questionable how much popular support they would have even in the north should unification occur. Once again, the German precedent suggests they would almost certainly be shunted aside at best and criminalized and prosecuted at worst, neither of which are attractive alternatives. By their willingness to inflict suffering—at the most extreme, starvation—on segments of their own population, the North Korean leadership has demonstrated its basic resistance and insensitivity to popular demands, and it has every reason to believe this emotion would be reciprocated if the population of the DPRK was no longer under its iron thumb. At the same time, it is also not entirely clear how enthusiastically the South Korean population would embrace the reductions in their economic status that sacrifice in the name of successful integration of the two halves would entail. The physical circumstances of the Korean peninsula thus serve as a powerful backdrop against fundamental changes in what almost everyone agrees in the abstract is an unfortunate status quo.

North Korea as a Unique State

By any standard measure, North Korea should not be a terribly important member of the international community. Its size, population, and lack of economic development suggest a very marginal player in the world, one on a par with other very underdeveloped countries in the Afro-Asian world. Even the facts that it is an authoritarian regime and that it remains one of the only two states in the world that actively proclaims itself to be a communist state (the other is Cuba) do not provide enough reason for the United States to take the level of notice it did in the November 2010 crisis.

North Korea becomes a consequential place because of several unique factors about the DPRK that cumulatively make it a matter of U.S. foreign policy concern. These factors include its physical location in East Asia, its unique governance form, the difficulty of influencing its regime, and its possession of nuclear weapons. These factors are, of course, interactive and cumulative in their impact. Together, they make North Korea a much more important place than it would otherwise be, a fact of which the North Koreans are abundantly aware. They also make it a difficult antagonist with which to deal.

North Korea's location is strategic in East Asia. It sits in the middle of the most powerful members of the Asian balance: China and Russia to its north, the ROK to its south, and Japan basically to its east. This relationship is important because it gives a relatively small and marginal DPRK a stake in and ability to influence how those greater sources of power treat it, and particularly in current circumstances, the degree to which other countries intrude upon or provide aid to it. Because North Korea is physically smaller than any of these neighbors (with the marginal exception that it is physically slightly larger than the ROK) and far less powerful by any standard measure, this makes North Korean military power critical to its ability to act as a more than a minor factor in the region. Simply put, a North Korea without nuclear weapons is basically a powerless pawn in the region; a DPRK with those weapons is a state with which the others must reckon. Over time, the North Koreans have demonstrated what many in the West have described as a virtually paranoid need to be recognized and treated as an equal; geography helps explain why.

The unique nature of governance contributes to this complex of unique factors. One of the ways in which the DPRK is truly unique is in the extreme continuity of its political leadership. Ever since Kim Il Sung (the designated "Great Leader" of the country) was installed as the leader of the country by the Soviets in 1948, power has rested in the hands of his family in control of the communist party. When Kim Il Sung died in 1994, he was followed into power by his son and designated successor, Kim Jong Il (the self-proclaimed "Dear Leader"), who has served since. Because of health problems, Kim Jong Il began a process of anointing a successor in 2009, and in late 2010 (at about the time of the November crisis with the ROK) announced that one of his sons, Kim Jong Un, would in turn become North Korea's leader when his father died, thus ensuring that patrimonial nepotism would survive into a third generation.

The foundation of this remarkable continuity has been the authoritarian rule of the regime and its close collaboration with the North Korean military.

The DPRK remains one of the most closed societies in the world (there is no legal access to the Internet, for instance, and only a small and highly controlled "Intranet" within the country), and one ruled within an iron hand. Thus, there is never public discussion of dissent with the regime or its succession, although some reports in 2010 suggested that one reason for the November 2010 crisis was to paper over discontent with the anointment of Kim Jong Un. This relationship is tenable because the regime is in close union with the powerful North Korean military (the DPRK maintains over a million-man army, extremely large for a country its size). In a desperately poor, resource-deprived society, the North Korean military has first access to what is available, and the bargain for that priority includes ongoing support for the patriarchy.

The result of this pattern of governance is an extremely isolated North Korean regime that has proven particularly resistant to outside influence. Part of the reason for this isolation is pragmatic, to keep the North Korean population ignorant of the paucity of their existence and particularly of invidious comparison with the South. Some of that isolation, however, reflects an attitude of North Koreans toward the outside world, what Myers describes as "a paranoid nationalism that has informed the regime's actions since the late 1940s." This extreme sense of nationalism is partially based on what Myers calls "the celebration of racial purity and homogeneity" that suggests the inferiority and corrupting influence of all outsiders, which is to be fiercely resisted. Isolation from the rest of the world is thus based on a desire to avoid racial mongrelization by intermingling with others, an influence sometimes attributed to the Japanese occupation of the peninsula. Its effect is certainly to make relations between North Korea and others—including, possibly even especially, Americans—more difficult and the common bonds between the North Koreans and others more difficult to identify and nurture.

All of these unique factors come into focus because of North Korea's nuclear weapons program. Location, governance, and isolation may make North Korea distinctive, but it is nuclear weapons that make the DPRK important and a problem that cannot be ignored. Without nuclear weapons, the DPRK is, in Lankov's 2009 words, a country "on a par with Mozambique or Uganda" and one of essentially little relevance in its region. With nuclear weapons, however, North Korea represents a potential threat to its neighbors and even beyond—if it obtains long-range missile delivery capability, for instance, or in the nightmare scenario that it supplies such weaponry to terrorists. The North Koreans are well aware of the importance of their nuclear weapons and thus wield the nuclear option like a sword. North Korea without nuclear weapons may be inconsequential, but a DPRK either with them or with the option to produce them is quite another matter.

The physical setting and unique properties of North Korea define it as a player on the international scene and as a problem with which the United States must deal. American attitudes and posture toward the Hermit Kingdom have vacillated over time, and advocacies of various courses of action remain matters of public debate, particularly when there are spikes—almost always negative—in the tone and tenor of that relationship.

U.S.–NORTH KOREAN RELATIONS

Although the relations between the United States and the DPRK have been uniformly negative since the Korean War, the exact nature and extent of those relations has varied within a fairly narrow band. Two variables, one emanating from each side, seem to be emblematic of those relations at different points. From the American side, the key difference tends to be how or whether to deal with North Korea directly or at all. When relations are at their least antagonistic, the United States has normally been willing to deal directly with the North Koreans bilaterally, symbolizing recognition of status for the heavily isolated North Koreans that the regime in the North clearly covets. The United States government took this comparatively positive posture toward the North Korean regime in the early 1990s as a way to retard the DPRK's nuclear weapons program, and the result was the 1994 Framework Agreement. Among its emphases, according to Norris, was that "political and economic relations would be normalized, and both countries would work toward a nuclear weapons-free Korean peninsula." In addition, the United States guaranteed the supply of nuclear fuel for DPRK power reactors (fuel that cannot be converted for weapons purposes) and of badly needed grain supplies. Of key importance to the North Koreans, these negotiations were largely one-on-one with the Americans. These conditions extended to relations between the Koreas, including limited access to family members across the border and the extension of ROK unconditional aid to the DPRK as part of the so-called "sunshine policy."

The Bush administration reversed this relationship, demonstrating the other extreme American approach, which is to isolate and ignore North Korea. The primary advocate of this approach was John Bolton, Bush's ambassador to the UN at the end of his tenure, who has particularly harsh views of the DPRK. Bush cut off the assistance connected to the Framework Agreement and refused to carry on bilateral talks with the North Koreans, instead insisting on multilateral forums for interchange, notably the six-party talks (the United States, China, Russia, Japan, and North and South Korea) to deal with nuclear issues. The Obama administration had partially reversed this approach before the November 2010 confrontation; the use of former President Bill Clinton as the envoy to achieve the release of two American journalists in August 2009 was a symbol of this approach.

The North Koreans' behavior is also variable. At one extreme is the belligerence, even bellicosity, which was evident in the November 2010 crisis, when the DPRK repeatedly threatened "all-out war" against South Korea. At other times, the North Koreans display a much more flexible, conciliatory stance that suggests their willingness to negotiate something like a return to the conditions created in 1994. Unfortunately, such initiatives appear to be part of a broader North Korean approach to its relations with the West that is captured by Lankov (2010): "North Korea's leader have deftly stuck to a single strategy: start negotiations, squeeze aid out of the international community by making incremental concessions (while trying to cheat), and then walk away from the talks and stage a provocation or two—only to return in exchange for more payoffs."

These two variables, of course, are interactive. The United States is more likely to respond to the North Koreans on a conciliatory basis when the DPRK is holding out the olive branch than when it is talking and acting in a more warlike manner. Likewise, North Korean intransigence, especially on the nuclear weapons issue, seems to be at its highest levels when the United States is ignoring it, and one can even argue that it is such American behavior that triggers increased levels of DPRK intransigence.

There is, of course, an "800-pound gorilla" that shadows the relationships on the Korean peninsula, and that is the prospect of a renewed Korean War, as was threatened most recently in 2010. At a strictly rational level, the prospect makes virtually no sense. The more populous, heavily armed South Koreans would almost certainly defeat the DPRK, especially with expected American help. This rational analysis is countermanded by the apparent instability, fragility, and even potential irrationality of the North Korean leadership, and leaders like Bolton essentially argue that nothing is beyond their range of possible behaviors. It is not entirely clear that North Korea does not recognize and manipulate these fears when it is soliciting aid from the West. One thing, however, is certain. Such a war would certainly be breathtakingly destructive, likely destroying much of the bases of South Korean prosperity in which so much effort has been expended. Its impact could also spread beyond the peninsula. As Lankov (in *Foreign Policy* online) puts it, "a 21st century war on the Korean peninsula would have disastrous consequence, not only for Korea, but for a world economy that is still emerging from recession." As one grim note, the South Korean capital of Seoul is within artillery range of North Korea, and the DPRK has literally thousands of long-range artillery pieces aimed at that largest ROK population center.

This dour description forms the backdrop against which U.S.–DPRK relations are played out. It is a basically frustrating relationship for the United States because, as Lankov (2010) points out, "the United States and its allies have no efficient methods of coercion at their disposal. The regime is remarkably immune to outside pressure." In this atmosphere, the Obama administration has followed a low-key policy that it calls "strategic patience" as a means slowly to make relations less dangerous and confrontational. The interplay of policies can be seen in two current, ongoing sources of concern. The first and most prominent of these is the nuclear weapons question, centering on American efforts to cause the North Koreans to back away from their movement toward becoming a full-fledged member of the nuclear weapons "club." The other is the question of political stability in North Korea, centering currently on the succession crisis and ultimately on the question of future reunification.

North Korean Nuclear Proliferation

The problem of North Korean nuclear weapons is, in a sense, almost as old as U.S.–DPRK relations dating back to the Korean War. Aside from creating a general atmosphere of enmity and tension, nuclear weapons were in the background of the war and its aftermath: American commander General Douglas MacArthur suggested their possible usage to end the war, and after the hostilities continued, the United States stationed nuclear weapons on South Korean soil as part of its deterrent against a second North Korean invasion. This nuclear shadow may have been a major factor in motivating the beginnings of a nuclear program by Kim Il Sung sometime during the latter 1950s, as mentioned earlier. Within the secretive North, very little is known about how decisions are reached, but it is difficult to imagine that living under the nuclear gun for decades does not influence the North Koreans.

Regardless of the motivating factors, a nuclear program has been ongoing in the DPRK for at least a half century. To allay concerns that its intent was to build nuclear weapons, the North Koreans signed the Nuclear Non-Proliferation Treaty (NPT) in 1984 but later threatened to withdraw its membership, precipitating the negotiations that led to the Framework Agreement of 1994. That agreement held until 2002, when President George W. Bush included the DPRK in his "axis of evil" designation and, at the behest of hard-line advisors like Bolton, terminated the agreement in December 2002 and suspended direct negotiations with the northerners, preferring the six-power talks as an alternative that was disdained by the DPRK. The DPRK responded to this shift in American policy by announcing its intention to withdraw from the NPT on January 10, 2003. Relations to restrain the North Korean nuclear program have spiraled downward since. In 2006, North Korea announced it was prepared "to declare itself formally as a nuclear weapons state" (a declaration it followed through on in December 2006) and the six-power talks were suspended by the end of that year. On-again, off-again negotiations were held in 2007 and 2008 and were punctuated in April and May 2009. At that time, North Korea announced indefinite suspension of the six-power talks, expelled International Atomic Energy Agency (IAEA) inspectors from its nuclear facilities, conducted a series of missile tests, and reportedly exploded a nuclear device underground. This process of self-assertion was accentuated in late 2010, just before the November crisis, when selected American scientists were allowed to see the state-of-the-art nuclear facilities the DPRK had developed. Because these facilities were far more advanced than it had been believed the North Koreans could construct, they have added to the alarm the outside world—and especially the United States—has about the nuclear weapons program. The reason is simple: these advanced-design facilities can produce weapons-grade plutonium at a much higher rate than older designs the DPRK possessed, thus providing the country the ability to fabricate more bombs faster than otherwise assumed.

The North Koreans have been very protective of their program and have shown great reluctance to bargain it away, as the United States wants them to do. Lankov (2009) offers a cogent, three-part explanation for this reticence on their part: "Pyongyang cannot do away with these programs. That would mean losing a powerful deterrent and a time-tested tool of extortion. It would also relegate North Korea to being a third-rate country."

The first factor, also present in Iranian motivations discussed in Chapter 3, is as a deterrent to predatory enemies. Even with its bloated armed forces,

North Korea is a military midget squeezed among major East Asian competitors except for their knowledge that the DPRK has nuclear weapons. The northerners have learned the deterrent value of nuclear weapons from the Americans across the 38th Parallel and undoubtedly see their program as a rejoinder against what they would term American aggression. The North Koreans may feel especially vulnerable to outside interference in the period of leadership transition currently underway.

The second reason to maintain these weapons is as a means to help implement its strategy of alternating threats with promises of compliance in order to gain aid from the West. Part of that strategy is a tit-for-tat in which the DPRK gains badly needed outside assistance in return for promising repayment in terms of something that other countries want from it. Since there is very little else that the DPRK has that others want, promises of good behavior in the nuclear weapons area is one of the few incentives they can offer. The 2010 crisis is an example: it occurred in the midst of one of North Korea's periodic food crises, when the regime badly needed outside assistance to feed its population.

The third factor is prestige. As noted, the North Koreans are an exceptionally proud, even aloof, people, and it has been a virtual fixation of their leadership to be treated as coequals in the community of states. Since the DPRK is at best a third-rate country by every other measure, its elevation to being the ninth member of the exclusive nuclear weapons club offers it a source of status that it could not otherwise even hope to achieve. The haughty North Koreans must be taken seriously because of their nuclear attainment and ambitions, and the removal of that source of national pride would be a sharp embarrassment for them in the world.

Controlling or eliminating the North Korean nuclear weapons program stands clearly at the top of the list of U.S. issues with the DPRK. It is probably not unfair to say that were the Hermit Kingdom not a presumptive member of the nuclear weapons club, it would occupy a very low priority in American foreign policy. The North Koreans know this is true and extends to how much of the world views them. As a result, they cling much more tenaciously to their program than they might otherwise. From an American perspective, this creates an ongoing source of annoyance and a policy debate that extends to the other major area of U.S.–DPRK relations.

Evolution of the North Korean State

Much of the American concern about the DPRK's erratic behavior arises from the nature of the regime and the future of the DPRK on the Korean peninsula. From an American vantage point widely shared by its neighbors, North Korea will likely remain a source of instability and concern as long as it remains a reclusive, backward dictatorship desperate to assert its status within the community of states and willing to engage in risky international behavior to achieve its goals. In order for this situation to change for the better, political and economic change are both necessary. Unfortunately, the prospects for either kind of improvement are not great, at least in the short or medium future.

Political change is clearly tied to the process of governmental succession in the DPRK. Like most authoritarian (including communist) systems, the North Koreans have never developed a legitimate form (one based in public assent) for changing governments, instead relying on a nepotistic handover of power from generation to generation of the family of which Kim Il Sung was the original political patriarch. The support of the North Korean military, whose loyalty is rewarded by a preferential place in society, has been critical to what stability the succession process has evinced, but it has also meant a strong preference for the status quo of an antagonistic, militarized demeanor toward the outside world and an antiquated, inefficient economic system occasionally incapable of meeting even the more meager requirements of the population. Any dissent against the system is ruthlessly suppressed by the regime, and knowledge of the contrast between the conditions of DPRK and the outside world is carefully filtered from public view. The result is that there is no known internal dissident movement active trying to induce internal change that might modify the North Korean stance toward the world.

The process of succession from the second to the third generation of family rule is underway in North Korea, and, according to most observers, it is following familiar patterns. Like his father, anointed successor Kim Jong Un was a virtual unknown prior to his elevation to leader-in-waiting. With no prior military service, the 26-year-old was appointed to the rank of four-star general in 2010 (making him the youngest person in the world holding that rank). His role in the November 2010 crisis is basically unknown, but his appointment indicates the continuity of synergism between the Kim family and the North Korean military. There is very little public evidence that his accession to power will change the North Korean position in the world in a positive way.

An improvement in the North Korean economy is also probably necessary before any other positive change can occur. Since a keystone of DPRK foreign policy behavior has been to precipitate crises that can be negotiated into economic—especially food—assistance whenever periodic shortages emerge such as the food crisis that accompanied the 2010 crisis, economic assistance could provide a wedge to begin improving relations. Some movement toward an institutionalized process of aid provision was part of the agenda when the two Koreas met and began a dialog in 2000 that did result in limited rights of visitation for families divided by the border and cooperation in athletic events like the World Cup, but that process was interrupted in 2002 and 2003 by worsening of DPRK relations with the United States such as the Bush renunciation of the Framework Agreement. Any incremental improvements have been sharply curtailed by the course of hostilities begun publicly in 2010, but their resumption remains a possibility.

It has historically been commonplace to assume that the ultimate solution to peninsular instability is the reunification of the two Koreas. Certainly that was the underlying hope of talks between the two countries in 2000, but it has become a forlorn hope at best more recently. Part of the reason lies in the highly divisive, bitter, and long aftermath of the Korean War and habits of confrontation across the 38th Parallel frontier that now span nearly 60 years. North and

South Koreans have come to distrust and dislike one another politically, and the stark differences in their societies have undoubtedly created cultural differences and animosities that undercut the national unity they once felt.

The memory of a united Korea is less poignant as well. Any Korean who lives in either country and is not at least 65 years old has no personal recollection of one Korea, and families divided by the division of the country have now been separated for at least three generations; there are very few living Korean who personally know relatives living in the other country. In the abstract, the desire to reunify remains strong and a distant aspiration, but it increasingly lacks a perceived immediacy.

The absence of popular pressures makes the inertial drag of negative factors surrounding reunification stronger. At best, the process of reunification would be traumatic for the political and economic elites of each country. There is thus a reluctance to proceed toward that goal within elites, and the position is made easier to sustain in the absence of great public pressure to change courses. Germany is the parallel experience here, but the dynamics of reunification there were stimulated by the virtual collapse of the communist regime of East Germany as the Cold War ended. The prospects for a similar collapse of North Korea seem unlikely for the time being, meaning the basic status quo is likely to endure.

U.S. OPTIONS

North Korea has been a source of frustration for successive American administrations. The basis of this frustration has been both what the United States would like to see North Korea do that it currently is not doing and also what the United States can do to bring about changes in DPRK behavior more in line with American interests. An examination of each of these interrelated dimensions helps define the limitations of American leverage in its bilateral relations with the Hermit Kingdom.

American basic interests arise from two sources: the geopolitics of the post–Korean War balance on the peninsula and American opposition to nuclear proliferation as applied to East Asia and specifically to North Korea. The preferred outcome for the United States in both cases stems from a desire to see military tensions on the peninsula relaxed, thereby contributing to peninsular stability and removing some of the DPRK's perceived need to continue to pursue a nuclear weapons future.

Over 60 years after the beginning of the Korean War, the United States retains a military presence in South Korea at a current level of about 28,000 personnel for two basic reasons. The first is to provide a deterrent to North Korean aggression in the form of an old-fashioned "trip wire" similar to the stationing of American troops on the front lines in Europe for over 40 years (a DPRK invasion would necessarily involve an initial attack on American troops, guaranteeing American casualties and thus an American response), a reminder that traditional geopolitical reasoning has not disappeared from the foreign policy equation on the peninsula. The second reason is to bolster the defense of South Korea as part of the ROK's efforts to thwart and reverse North Korean military adventurism. A relaxation of tensions between the two, especially along the 38th Parallel, could mean a reduced need for an American presence and the removal of some, or even eventually all, American troops from the peninsula—arguably the true end of the Korean War.

The second basic interest of the United States is in reversing the process of North Korean nuclear proliferation, a goal that also has two underlying motivations. The first of these is opposition to proliferation, and particularly the spread of nuclear weapons to what are viewed as potentially unreliable, even irrational, possessors. This policy goal, of course, transcends North Korea, but it is nonetheless applicable to the DPRK, as Bush accentuated by including the North Koreans in his designation of the "axis of evil." The second motivation is to avoid further proliferation in the East Asian region should North Korea emerge as a major nuclear weapons possessor. A DPRK with a large arsenal could pose an existential threat to its southern neighbor and a deadly threat to Japan, forcing both to make the reluctant decision that they must become nuclear weapons producers to deter the North Koreans from using those weapons against them or in engaging in coercive diplomacy against its neighbors based on the nuclear threat. The further spread of these weapons in a region where all the other major players represented in the six-power talks (Russia, China, and the United States) are already nuclear powers could increase the possibilities of instability in ways difficulty exactly to predict but certainly to be avoided if possible.

These two thrusts are, of course, related. A heavily militarized North–South confrontation on the peninsula provides the fuel both for needing to retain American forces in place near the frontier and for the North Koreans not to abandon their nuclear program. The DPRK is, of course, well aware that it is not a major influence on the regional or global scene by any measure save its military, including nuclear, status. A reduction of the military confrontation that involves reducing North Korea's military machine might free resources for other forms of development, but it also runs the risk of relegating the North Koreans to the status of being an insignificant regional pawn whose protection in a hostile environment relies on the sometimes fickle patronage of a Chinese regime that is known to be growing weary of protecting their Pyongyang partners. Given the potential risks involved, North Korea has chosen to maintain a tense atmosphere in the region.

There is an ironic horror scenario that lies behind these concerns. It is the possibility of a new war between the Koreas, and it is a fear enlivened whenever a serious confrontation between them occurs. The irony lies in the general agreement—particularly by outsiders—that such a war would be an unmitigated disaster for all involved in which neither side could claim anything resembling victory. The common assumption is that such a conflict would begin with a North Korean invasion of the South preceded by a massive artillery attack that would destroy most of urban, northern South Korea, notably Seoul and its environs. If such an attack were to include nuclear weapons, its destructive impact would be especially dire. While this attack and its resulting devastation would be difficult to prevent initially, it is further agreed that once the initial thrust was stopped, South Korea would overwhelm the DPRK, in the process deposing its leadership. The result would be the destruction of the South Korean economy, the overthrow of the North Korean regime, and a peninsula in tatters.

Given this scenario, which the North Koreans presumably also understand, starting a new war would be totally irrational and self-defeating for the DPRK. Enigmatically, although the North Koreans undoubtedly realize this, they cannot publicly rule out the possibility because it is only the assertion of the threat represented by their military might that gives them any leverage in the area. To admit that an attack is unthinkable would be tantamount to surrendering whatever leverage the DPRK has in dealing with the United States and the South Koreans. As a result, they must periodically threaten an "all-out war" that they must know would be certainly suicidal and would likely destroy both countries. This rationale makes it necessary for the North Korean regime to maintain the image of being at least slightly "crazy" to keep its adversaries slightly off guard in dealing with it.

The ability of North Korea to continue its obstinate ways has been at least partially aided by the inability of the United States to develop an agreed-on, effective manner for dealing with the DPRK. For the most part, there have been two alternative options that have been tried at one time or another, and neither has been stunningly effective.

Lankov (2009) provides a description of the two sides to the American internal debate between what he calls the optimists and the pessimists. As he puts it, "The optimists believe that negotiating with Pyongyang will set North Korea on the path of Chinese-style political and economic reforms, help it become a 'normal state,' and thus convince it to abandon its nuclear ambition." In other words, if the DPRK is treated civilly, it will return the favor. The Obama administration, following on the lead of the Clinton administration, essentially adheres to this model, although its policy of "strategic patience" reflects recognition that the success of this approach will not be immediate but will take time. The logic of this position also underlies the formulation of the Framework Agreement, which essentially rewards the North Koreans for moderate behavior, especially on the nuclear weapons issue.

The alternative view, put forward by the so-called pessimists, is that all such efforts are hopeless because the North Korean regime is irredeemable. As a classic rogue regime, the only sensible approach flowing from this position is to isolate the regime, convince others to adopt a policy of opposition, and even work behind the scene to help induce regime change (i.e., an overthrow of the regime) or even popular pressure (e.g., a Libyan-style revolt) to induce a change of regime from within the country. People like Bolton, who is the chief champion of the regime-changing approach, "prefer coercive sanctions" to rewarding favorable behavior, according to Lankov (2009).

Both of these approaches have been attempted—the optimistic approach by Clinton and Obama, the pessimistic approach by Bush—and neither has been particularly successful. One can argue (as champions of a more positive approach do) that the policy of engagement ushered in by the Clinton-inspired Framework Agreement might have been successful had it not been overturned by the Bush administration (in which Bolton was a major influence on North Korean policy) and that a return to a positive approach by Obama is hamstrung by the DPRK's recollection of how such an approach was offered and then withdrawn before. The antagonistic actions of the North Koreans in the 2010 crisis adds some fuel to the argument that the regime in Pyongyang is irredeemably hostile and can only be confronted successfully with the threat or use of force.

One way in which these differences are most dramatically demonstrated is in varying approaches to talking to the North Koreans. The United States and the DPRK do not have formal diplomatic relations with one another, and most direct contacts between them come through the North Korean diplomatic mission to the United Nations in New York. On the question of negotiating on matters such as the nuclear weapons question, there have been two alternative methods for conducting these talks (in addition to refusing to talk to the North Koreans at all). One approach has been direct, bilateral talks between the two, such as the 1994 negotiations that produced the Framework Agreement. The status-hungry North Koreans very much prefer this forum because it symbolically raises their status to that of coequal with the Americans. The other approach is through the six-power talks that include the South Koreans, Russians, Chinese, and Japanese in addition to the Americans and North Koreans. Those who find direct one-on-one talks distasteful or too rewarding of DPRK behavior prefer these multilateral talks because they relegate the North Koreans to the status of one among several states in regional talks (Americans also like this method because it helps present a united regional face toward North Korean intransigence on the weapons issue). Offering to talk in one or another forum is a major way in which the United States signals its willingness to accommodate North Korean demands and sensibilities.

Advocacy of a more or less conciliatory approach to the North Koreans has domestic political bases in the United States that constrain how those relations are conducted. So-called "hard-liners" like Bolton oppose any attempts to negotiate with the DPRK, especially on a bilateral basis, arguing that doing so rewards North Korean bad behavior and is generally ineffective, particularly given what they see as the North Korean penchant for violating any agreements they may reach. In areas such as nuclear promises, this position, which is expressed in a preference for military confrontation and political isolation, is not without merit. Any advocacy of a willingness to negotiate with rather than to confront the North Koreans is predictably met with vociferous criticism by generally conservative advocates of a harder-line approach.

Those who prefer a return to something more like the atmosphere that resulted in the Framework Agreement argue that the hard-line approach has not yielded positive results in changing North Korean behavior and that isolation simply drives the North Koreans further into the paranoid shell that fuels their militancy. The so-called "soft-liners" who argue for dealing directly with the North Koreans bilaterally or in multilateral settings (e.g., the six-power talks) maintain that eventually the DPRK is going to have to be brought positively into the community of states and that "carrots" may provide better incentives than the "sticks" of confrontation and isolation. This position also has some merit, as suggested by the apparent success of the Framework Agreement until it was voided by the Bush administration. The soft-liners consider the position of the hard-liners unsophisticated, even crude, while the hard-liners find the soft-liners' position excessively idealistic and ineffectual. The strength of each acts as a block against the implementation of the total preference of either.

The major trump card in how to approach North Korea may be held by the Chinese. The People's Republic of China is as close to an ally as the DPRK has, although it is a guarded relationship. The two countries remain two of only four in the world that even nominally adhere to a communist ideology— giving them some form of similarity—but the Chinese have strayed noticeably from Marxist economics. The PRC was the country that came to the aid of the North Koreans in 1950, helping them avoid the imposition of an American-backed regime throughout the country, but China is also a historic enemy whose potential predatory intensions toward the peninsula the DPRK regime recognizes, forming part of its reluctance to embrace Beijing more fully. Because China is closer to North Korea than any other state, however, efforts to contain North Korean intransigence are often directed toward the Chinese for their assistance. This was certainly the case in 2010.

The Chinese remain ambivalent and thus unhelpful in dealing with the North Koreans. On one hand, they are reportedly increasingly annoyed with the more aggressive behavior of the rulers in Pyongyang and would prefer that they act in ways that are less regionally upsetting: the DPRK is a source of frustration for them as well as for others. At the same time, they are unwilling to embrace policies of change that might lead to fundamental change within North Korea since the outcome could lead to a unified Korean peninsula under a regime that is not friendly to the Chinese and not controllable by them, and possibly to the emergence of an antagonist on its frontiers that the Chinese "volunteers" swept across the Chinese–Korean border to prevent in the frigid winter of 1950.

The role of the other major regional partner, Japan, is also mixed. By self-choice, Japan is the only major state in the region (other than South Korea) that does not possess nuclear weapons. South Korean abstinence is based on a reluctance to antagonize the North Koreans and thus further roil tensions on the peninsula, whereas the Japanese have a long, historically based aversion to anything nuclear and especially to nuclear weapons. Their nuclear "allergy" has been reinforced by the nuclear power meltdown accompanying the 2011 tsunami in northern Japan.

Japan and South Korea do not want to "go nuclear," although either could do so physically in a short period of time. A positive nuclear weapons decision would be very unpopular politically in either country *unless* the cause was North Korean provocation arising from its nuclear weapons status. DPRK nuclear militancy is thus the major reason that Japan or South Korea might feel forced to make an otherwise unpopular decision both would prefer to avoid, and so both very actively favor denuclearization of the DPRK both as a matter of nonproliferation principle and as a reflection of the geopolitical cloud the North Korean nuclear force casts over the area.

Progress in resolving American–North Korean differences on these issues has not been overwhelmingly successful. Neither the optimists nor the pessimists have provided a formula that produces DPRK compliance with American policy preferences, indicative of the lack of fundamental leverage that the United States has over the Pyongyang regime. The United States cannot, as it does in some places, implicitly or explicitly threaten military action against the regime because the delicate military situation there makes any American threats that might escalate to a general peninsular conflict appear hollow threats indeed. The United States is fundamentally displeased with North Korea, but there is relatively little it can realistically do about it.

CONCLUSIONS

The relations between the United States and North Korea have been uniformly difficult, negative, and even bizarre since the end of World War II. The two countries introduced themselves to one another in the three years of bloodshed of the Korean War that began in 1950, a war that technically continues to this day and is punctuated by the two countries' faceoff along the world's most heavily fortified frontier, the 38th Parallel that divides North and South Korea. Minor antagonistic incidents between the Americans and their South Korean allies and the northerners are routine; serious sporadic clashes such as occurred in November 2010 are periodic manifestations of the underlying animosities on the peninsula.

The situation is ironic and arguably tragic. The irony is that the fundamental objective is the American desire to prevent the DPRK from restarting the Korean War, an ironic possibility given the likelihood that such a conflict would virtually destroy the peninsula and almost certainly lead to the extinction of the DPRK regime, prospects the North Koreans must understand. The tragedy lies in the extreme impoverishment of the North Korean people, particularly in comparison to their kin south of the border. Life is miserable in North Korea, and most of the blame lies with the regime.

At a purely abstract, rational level, the solution to the Korean peninsula and American relations with it is simple: the reunification of the peninsula as a democratic state. Unfortunately, such an outcome faces currently insurmountable barriers. The major roadblock is on the peninsula itself, where political elites on both sides of the frontier cannot bring themselves to embrace an outcome historically favored by the vast majority of Koreans. South Koreans fear the enormous German-style impact of reunion on their own prosperity, and the North Koreans recognize that they, like the East Germans, would almost certainly lose power and face relegation to political inferiority. The United States has not been an active advocate of this solution because there is such division politically about how to deal with the peninsula and more recently because American economic distress leaves it incapable of playing a very positive role in peninsular integration. China, the regional country with the greatest interests and deepest pockets, retains great reservations about the prospects of a potentially antagonistic Korea on its borders (a fear which, after all, helped motivate its intervention in the Korean War).

Unable to break the logjam that could lead to an enduring peace and tranquility on the peninsula, U.S.–North Korean relations remain heavily antagonistic and militarized. The very sharp point of that confrontation is the existence and evolution of the North Korean nuclear arsenal, a problem the United States desperately wants to obviate and make go away but which it has yet to find the wherewithal completely to accomplish. As Bluth puts it, until there is fundamental change on the peninsula, "an unending cycle of confrontation and accommodation is inevitable as long as this (North Korean) regime endures."

STUDY/DISCUSSION QUESTIONS

1. Discuss the 2010 confrontation between the United States and the DPRK. What factors served to precipitate it? How was it resolved? In what ways did it represent a familiar pattern in U.S.–North Korean dealings with one another?
2. Discuss the emergence and development of North Korea since the partition of the Korean Peninsula at the end of World War II. Contrast the evolution of the DPRK to that of South Korea (the ROK).
3. What makes North Korea a unique state? What is the role of nuclear weapons in defining its uniqueness and importance in the world? Elaborate.
4. What has been the nature of U.S.–DPRK relations? What have the prevailing views in the United States been on how to deal with the North Koreans? Apply your distinctions to the two major contemporary issues in U.S.–DPRK relations identified in the text.
5. What are the basic American interests toward the DPRK? How do these interests come together over the possibility of renewed war in Korea?
6. What have the two basic approaches to U.S.–North Korean relations been in the American political arena. What are the political bases of each, and how do they limit one another?
7. The irony of dealing with North Korea is preventing the DPRK from launching a war that would destroy it and South Korea, according to the text. Assess that assertion. What kind of policies do you think best lead to minimizing that danger and reducing the extremely negative relationship between the two countries?

READING/RESEARCH MATERIALS

BBC News. "North Korea Country Profile." *BBC News Online*, November 11, 2010.

Bluth, Christoph. "North Korea: How Will It End?" *Current History* 109, 728 (September 2010), 237–243.

Cha, Victor D., and David C. Kang. *Nuclear North Korea: A Debate on Engagement Strategies*. New York: Columbia University Press, 2005.

Cumings, Bruce. "The North Korea Problem: Dealing with Irrationality." *Current History* 108, 719 (September 2009), 284–290.

Demick, Barbara. *Nothing to Envy: Ordinary Lives in North Korea*. New York: Spiegel & Grau, 2010.

Fackler, Martin. "Obama Speech Marks Shift on North Korea." *New York Times* (online), November 11, 2010.

———. "Obama Warns North Korea in Speech." *New York Times* (online), November 10, 2010.

Lankov, Andrei. "Changing North Korea: An Information Campaign Can Beat the Regime." *Foreign Affairs* 88, 6 (November/December 2009). 95–105.

———. "How to Stop the Next Korean War." *Foreign Policy* (online), December 16, 2010.

Lieber, Kier A., and David G. Press. "The Rise of U.S. Nuclear Supremacy." *Foreign Affairs* 85, 2 (March/April 2006), 42–54.

McEachern, Patrick. *Inside the Red Box: North Korea's Post-Totalitarian Politics.* New York: Columbia University Press, 2010.

Mendelsohn, Jack. "The New Threats: Nuclear Amnesia, Nuclear Legitimacy." *Current History* 105, 694 (November 2006), 385–390.

Myers, B. R. "North Korea's Race Problem." *Foreign Policy* (March/April 2010), 100–101.

Norris, Robert S. "North Korea's Nuclear Program, 2003." *Bulletin of the Atomic Scientists* 59, 2 (March/April 2003), 74–77.

Perkowich, George. "The End of the Proliferation Regime." *Current History* 105, 694 (November 2006), 355–362.

Pilat, Joseph F. "Reassessing Security Assurances in a Unipolar World." *Washington Quarterly* 28, 2 (Spring 2005), 59–70.

Sigal, Leon V. "The Lessons of North Korea's Test." *Current History* 105, 694 (November 2006), 364–365.

Specter, Arnold, and Christopher Walsh. "Dialogue with Adversaries." *Washington Quarterly* 30, 1 (Winter 2006/2007), 9–26.

Changing Interests with Regional Rivals

Relations between the United States and the two major powers of the Asian subcontinent, India and Pakistan, bear some of the strongest stamp of the Cold War past of America's foreign relations with any countries in the world. Those relations were born of the partition of the former British Empire's hold on the area in 1947, which unleashed a wave of activity and instability, including three wars, as the subcontinent split into Hindu and Islamic states. The wounds that accompanied dissection of the region two-thirds of a century ago remain prominent in the international politics of a volatile region with the added complication of admitted nuclear weapons possession on both sides since 1998.

The relationships between the United States and these two countries have, in a sense, been enigmatic. During the Cold War period that encompassed nearly two-thirds of the period of the subcontinent's independence, the United States found itself more closely associated with the military dictatorship of the Pakistanis against the democratic government of India, a direct result of Pakistan's willingness to enlist in the anticommunist crusade while India remained neutral in that contest. Only with the end of the Cold War and the emergence of India on the world stage as a major economic force beginning in 1991 have those relations shifted somewhat more toward American friendship with the world's largest political democracy and away from a fragile Pakistani state that is often listed among the failed or failing states of the world.

American foreign policy toward this region and its major entities is evolving. The last three presidential administrations in Washington have moved toward warmer relations with India as the two countries recognize their underlying interests in political democracy and the global economy. That relationship remains partially geopolitical in terms of an American balance of power in the southern and eastern Asian regions between India and neighbors China and Pakistan. The relationship with Islamabad, on the other hand, is currently more closely associated with the extent and quality of Pakistan's participation in the American military effort in adjacent Afghanistan, including actions that the Americans believe would help achieve their goals but that might come at the expense of political stability within Pakistan. Both sets of relations are in some state of transition and change.

The contest with international religious terrorism, a nonstate actor, has become a central part of the regional calculus and U.S. relations between the two countries. The focus has most clearly been on Pakistan, parts of the government of which have semiclandestinely nurtured what the Pakistanis call freedom fighters and the Indians call terrorists to operate in Kashmir and arguably elsewhere in India. Pakistan has been used as a sanctuary for terrorists—as the elimination of Usama bin Laden on Pakistani soil demonstrated—and thus brings the United States and India, both terrorist objects, into close collaboration.

The relationship between the United States and the two historical rivals demonstrates clearly that traditional state-centered geopolitics is highly relevant in analyzing at least this part of the world. India and Pakistan are quintessentially military rivals, and the politics of Pakistan can only be understood in terms of Pakistan's absolute obsession with security based on what it views as the Indian threat to its existence. The United States has no inherent interest in the military competition beyond a strong desire to avoid the escalation of tensions to all-out war between nuclear-armed contestants. America's current interest in Pakistan is almost entirely geopolitical (in the broad sense of that term), centering on Pakistan's contributions to the war in Afghanistan and the fight against Al Qaeda. Indo–American relations, on the other hand, tend to center on evolving, competitive economic relations. While other considerations are present in American relations with both countries (Al Qaeda in Pakistan, global warming as a result of Indian industrialization, for instance), it is traditional considerations largely framed in geopolitical terms of reference that are the most prominent both in those relations and in understanding them.

American relations with the each of the two countries are different, based on differences between them that help frame American regional and country-specific interests. India will become the most populous country in the world somewhere around 2030, and its nuclear relationship with Pakistan—the world's sixth most populous country—combine to imbue American relations with the Asian subcontinent with an importance that they did not have when American attention was much more closely riveted on the worldwide struggle of the Cold War. Whether the United States can achieve its goal of greater tranquility in the area and congenial relations with both India and Pakistan are the major challenges for America's relations with these regional rivals.

India: Befriending and Redefining Relations with a Rising Democracy

PREVIEW

Relations between the United States and India, the world's two largest political democracies, have, until recently, never been close. India received its independence from the British Empire in 1947 in a process that left residual conflict with Pakistan, also created by the same partition, which has been a major aspect of Indian foreign policy since and which has only marginally affected or been affected by the United States. During the Cold War, India refused to become part of the anticommunist alliance that confronted Soviet-led communism, creating some breach between the two states. Since the end of the Cold War and India's economic movement toward great power status, relations have improved steadily, and the two countries have reached the point of generally amicable relations. There are, however, several points of contention between the two countries, although none with likely explosive consequences. The United States has a limited ability to influence the future of Indo-American relations in ways beneficial to American interests.

India is one of the world's oldest civilizations, along with those of China and Persia. The earliest signs of Indian civilization have been traced back to the Indus River Valley, where the world's oldest irrigation system was constructed nearly 3,500 years ago. With the influx of Aryan peoples into what is now the Asian subcontinent, the first signs of a continuous Indian civilization have been traced to about 1,500 BCE.

India has been a ripe prize for invading conquerors over the ages. India was the ultimate destination of Alexander the Great and his armies, and although his quest fell short of subduing the subcontinent, others would follow. The evangelical Arabs and their new Muslim religion arrived in the western part of the country in the eighth century CE, and they were followed in the twelfth century by the invading Turks in the northern part of the subcontinent. Rule in India was consolidated under the Turkish Moguls (or Mughals) between 1526 and 1857, a time of notable progress that produced such lasting artifacts as the Taj Mahal. The Portuguese arrived in coastal enclaves such as Goa in the fifteenth century; they were followed closely by the British East India Company, and Britain eventually established reign over the whole subcontinent, which they referred to as the British Raj. India only achieved its independence in 1947, when the British, exhausted by the effort in World War II and facing restive populations in the subcontinent and elsewhere, granted independence to the area.

The vehicle for independence was the partition of the Raj into Hindu and Muslim states through negotiations led by British war hero Lord Louis Mountbatten. Influenced both by assurances from the two major independence movements in the region—one Hindu, one Muslim—that they could cooperate in a postcolonial environment and by a British desire to shed colonial responsibilities as quickly and painlessly as possible, the result was a highly imperfect division that remains a source of considerable controversy and difficulty.

The movement toward the independence of the Asian subcontinent had its roots in the early 1900s, but blossomed during the period between the world wars. It consisted of two separate major groups. The Hindu majority was led by Mohandas Gandhi (known among his followers as "Mahatma," the "Great Soul") and the Indian Congress. Muhammad Ali Jinnah led the Muslim League, which represented the Muslim minority scattered about parts of the subcontinent. The Muslims, who had arrived on the subcontinent in several invading waves, had never fully assimilated with the native Indians, and it was the goal of all sides to divide them into separate political entities at independence.

The negotiations led by Mountbatten had the major purpose of dividing, or partitioning, the subcontinent into a Hindu state, India, and a Muslim state, Pakistan. The negotiators desired to divide the two political jurisdictions so that Hindus would be in one state and Muslims in the other, but they were faced with three separate but thorny problems that made a totally satisfactory partition impossible. The first of these was that the two populations were in fact intermingled, meaning that no boundary could entire separate one from the other. This problem continues to this day: there are, for instance, approximately 150 million Muslims in India who, according to Kronstadt and colleagues, are "relatively poor, undereducated, and underrepresented in the professions." The second was that any boundary that came close to ethnic division was geographically challenged. In the west, for instance, the boundary chosen cut across portions of the Indus River irrigation system, leaving waters absolutely necessary for Pakistani agriculture vulnerable to interception by the Indians. Since Muslims were concentrated in both the western and eastern parts of the subcontinent, the result was a two-part Pakistan: western Pakistan (the Punjab) and eastern Pakistan (Bengal) separated from one another by 1,000 miles of Indian territory, an arrangement that ultimately proved untenable, leading to the secession of the eastern part of the country to form the state of Bangladesh in 1971. Third, there were a number of parts of the subcontinent, generically known as the "princely states," for which accession to one country or another was not obvious and for which independence might have been an attractive alternative.

Each of these problems created an explosive difficulty that has inflamed the entire subcontinent ever since and that has played a major part in how India has evolved as a state (as well as the development of Pakistan, discussed in Chapter 6). The inability to create a neat and discriminating boundary meant that the border chosen left many Hindus in what became Pakistan and many Muslims in India, where both sides feared violent retribution. The result was a massive, panicky migration in both directions; almost all of this occurred along the border between West Pakistan and India and involved upwards of 12 million people, the largest population migration in human history. The result was to begin the relationship between the two states in a particularly poisonous tenor that erased any memories of the cooperation they had promised while the partition was being negotiated and to establish Indo-Pakistani conflict as the leading, and most internationally concerning, aspect of Indian and Pakistani foreign relations. As evidence, the two countries fought wars in 1948 (over partition), again in 1965 (over a disputed territory known as the Rann of Kutch that spread over into Kashmir), and again in 1971 (what became known as the Bangladesh War). In 1999, nuclear-armed India and Pakistan faced off briefly once again (the so-called Kargil War of 1999); the world held its collective breath at the prospect that the fighting could possibly escalate to a nuclear war. In 2001, an attack by Pakistan-based terrorists on the Indian parliament again brought the two by-then nuclear-armed protagonists to the brink of war.

The second problem centered on the geography of partition, and especially water. West Pakistan and much of Indian territories that abut it are very arid (12–15 inches of rain a year), and agricultural activity necessary to sustain the Pakistani population depends critically on irrigation waters from the Indus irrigation system. The six Indus Valley rivers that provide the water to sustain both areas rise in the mountainous Himalayas, and they all flow either through parts of what became India or through Kashmir before getting to Pakistan. When the new borders were erected, they cut through the system: three rivers flowed first through India, where they were subject to interdiction by India, and the others flowed through Indian-controlled Kashmir. In 1948, India cut off the flow of the rivers flowing through their territory briefly (during the Pakistani harvesting season), creating panic and great animosity. Although the water flow was reinstated, it left a bitter legacy that inflamed relations. The problem was formally resolved by the World Bank, which led the negotiation of the Indus Waters Treaty of 1960, but the issue of water continues to be a sticking point in Indo–Pakistan relations.

The third major problem was the disposition of those territories that were not clearly or unambiguously parts of either India or Pakistan. The most prominent of these was and continues to be Kashmir (technically Jammu and Kashmir), a state in the northern extremity of the subcontinent with a Muslim-majority population but traditionally ruled by an Indian maharajah.

The problem was the result of the terms of the partition as it affected these ambiguous areas. Under the terms established, states like Kashmir were given two choices: accession to Indian or joining Pakistan. A third possible option, independence, was not available, as negotiators feared the result would be excessive balkanization of the subcontinent. Accession to one or the other state was supposed to be by plebiscite. The Indians, however, realized the result would be that the Kashmiris, roughly three-quarters of whom were Muslim, would choose to become a part of Pakistan, an outcome they deemed unacceptable because Kashmir sits on the border with China, commanding historic invasion routes between India and China (who are long-time rivals as well). As a result, the Indians negotiated the accession of Kashmir to India by an intergovernmental agreement with the maharajah, and Kashmir became the only Indian state with a Muslim majority, a settlement to which Lord Mountbatten apparently acceded. The Pakistanis were infuriated because the process was a clear violation of the principle of self-determination and, more geopolitically, because it meant the headwaters of the major Indus Rivers flowing from Kashmir to Pakistan were under Indian control. The legacy of Kashmir remains the thorniest issue of the subcontinent to this day.

This turmoil at birth helped define India as it evolved after independence. The subcontinent attained its independence as the Cold War was beginning, and the two new states adopted different approaches to the competition. Pakistan became a partisan, joining pro-Western organizations and having close relations with the United States—as well as China. India, on the other hand, concluded that its interests were not well served by taking sides and became, instead, a leader of the nonaligned countries. This decision, as will be discussed, had a negative impact on the U.S.–Indian relations, particularly during the height of Cold War tensions when there was an assumption that states either had to be "for" or "against" communism and that those who chose not to be part of the anticommunist crusade were thought to be procommunist—which many states like India in fact were not.

As a result, U.S.–Indian relations during the Cold War were at best cool and occasionally adversarial. In some cases, this was a matter of personalities: Richard Nixon and his trusted foreign policy advisor Henry Kissinger had a strong dislike for India's Prime Minister Indira Gandhi during the 1970s, adding to difficulties arising from India's signing of a treaty of "friendship" with the Soviet Union in 1971, an agreement which "struck many in the United States as tantamount to alignment with the Soviet Union," according to Feigenbaum.

The year 1991 was a watershed for India and its relations with the United States, in two ways. First, it signaled the end of the Cold War, leaving irrelevant much of the rhetorical animosity toward India that resulted in its unwillingness to join the American coalition in opposition to a Soviet Union that disappeared in the process. Second, the Indian government adopted a series of economic reforms similar to those that had already been put in place in the West and that opened the Indian economy to a much greater emphasis on private enterprise. India began to become part of the globalization system that arose during that decade, and the result was to begin to catapult India into a leadership role and prominence in the early twenty-first century.

INDIA: A SKETCH

India is a country of enormous contrasts and complexities viewed from any direction. Menon describes India by analogy: "A sprawling latter-day Austro-Hungarian Empire, with a dizzying array of languages, castes, and religions . . . modern India has defied pessimists who were drafting its obituary not long after its birth." These contrasts and complexities affect not only how one describes India, but how it deals and is dealt with in the world.

The contrasts are everywhere, and can be illustrated by examples. Jaguar, one of the world's most prestigious makes of automobiles, is owned by an Indian corporation (the Tata Moor Group), but "India is home to some 500–600 million people living in poverty" (Kronstadt et al.) for whom Jaguar ownership is an impossible dream. The prestigious Indian Institute of Technology (IIT) is one of the world's most highly regarding centers of education in science and technology, whose graduates are sought worldwide; at the same time, the overall literacy rate in the country is only 61 percent, tying India with Sudan for 172nd place among the world's countries. At an estimated 300 million, India claims to have the largest middle class in the world, yet it is universally considered to have the world's largest impoverished population as well. Many of these same problems have been or are shared with India's neighboring giant, China, although the Chinese have been in the development process for over a decade longer than the Indians and are consequently further ahead than the Indians.

India's enormity and diversity add to its situation. India is the world's seventh largest state physically, with an area approximately one-third that of the United States, but that area must support the world's second largest population (which will surpass China's and become the largest somewhere around 2030). That population, in turn, is nearly four times that of the United States, meaning a gross concentration of people per unit of territory between 10 and 12 times that of the United States. This population is also remarkably diverse: India has, for instance, 14 official languages, with the most used, Hindi, being the first language of only a little over two of five Indians; English is the language of most major official business in the country.

The dynamism of rising India is tempered by its past and its physical and historical legacy. Parts of the Indian "miracle" chronicled by enthusiasts like *New York Times* correspondent Thomas L. Friedman emphasize the extremely dynamic, forward-looking pockets of India, of which the high-tech citadel of Bangalore serves a mecca of advancement paralleling the Silicon

Valley phenomenon in the United States and the cause of questions of whether Indian technology may somehow surpass that of the United States in a world where Indian ascendancy somehow crosses American descent from its position of preeminence. Such images, however, are conditioned by the extreme contrasts of an India of grinding poverty for many of its people that can only be changed through massive efforts that go well beyond the current and even near-future capability of an Indian political and social system that has not historically shown much regard or concern for its destitute masses and its historically defined lower castes. Indian advances must be counterbalanced by these sobering legacies. Of some symbolic importance, India is one of the few countries in the world where a revolutionary insurgent group espousing a Maoist political philosophy (the Naxalites, discussed below) is still active. This movement poses no major threat to the political system, although the rebels "have destabilized much of the country's east by attacking large landholders and other members of the upper classes," according to Kurlantzick. Its sheer existence and persistence is a reminder that India provides hope and progress for some but not all of its citizens.

India in the World

India is impossible to ignore because of its size and location. According to 2010 data from the U.S. Census Bureau, approximately 17 percent—over one in six—of the world's population of 6.853 billion people currently live in India, and that proportion is unlikely to shrink in the next two decades or so. Historically, that bulk was noteworthy but not a matter of enormous geopolitical concern because India was geographically isolated from the world's geopolitical mainstream in a part of the world that most of the world's major powers could either ignore or treat as marginally important. This was particularly true in the convulsive, European-dominated nineteenth and twentieth centuries. The twenty-first century, on the other hand, is often described as an "Asian century," and India is one of the two anchors of the Asian continent, along with China.

Until recently, China has caught the attention of most of the West, and certainly the United States, because of the enormous growth of the Chinese economy, particularly in the highly visible area of consumer goods on American retail shelves. Popular images of China are no longer dominated by stereotypes of backwardness and quaint practices; instead the rapidly rising skyscrapers of Shanghai (see 2) or the 2008 Beijing Olympics are what westerners think of when their images of China are stirred.

Parallel shifts in attitude toward India have not caught up with those of China, despite reasons to believe that the developmental trajectories of both countries are similar, even if India is currently still a decade or so behind. Regarding the Indians, one is as likely to think of the "black hole of Calcutta" as one is to conjure the shining modernity of Bangalore. China has its vibrant, wealthy entrepreneurs; India is the land of annoying telemarketers and electronic service personnel with difficult-to-understand English over the telephone. "Outsourcing" is a frequent negative associated with India, even if more American jobs have been sent to China than to the subcontinent.

A quiescent and backward India has been easy to ignore because what happened on the subcontinent as a whole was largely ignorable, with the possible exception of violent conflicts between India and Pakistan—but that is changing. As India grows and develops, it is becoming a commercial and technological power, and one that is increasingly difficult not to take into account. While the Indian rise has been overshadowed by China, this rising importance has extended to relations between the United States and India. As Menon points out, for instance, "The United States is the leading investor in India, and trade between the two nations has nearly quadrupled, making the United States India's largest trading partner."

Geopolitically, the Indian position is becoming more important as well. The enormous amount of the world's energy production in the Persian (Arabian) Gulf transits to its destinations via the Indian Ocean around the Cape of Good Hope in Africa to the west and eastward through the Straits of Malacca to Japan and other eastern destinations. As commerce with Asia increases worldwide, the IO, as it is known, is becoming a strategically more important and contested body of water. One of the most potentially important aspects of this competition is between India, whose territory projects prominently into the IO, and China, with the United States serving as a potential arbiter and balancer of naval power in the region—a role that was beyond most imagination not long ago.

What makes an assessment of India and its place in the world difficult, however, is that India is very much a country in transition, and the question "transition to what?" has not been entirely answered, nor is an answer completely foreseeable. Nandan Nilekani, an Indian entrepreneur and the founder of InfoSys (India's second largest high-tech firm) summarizes this ambivalent status in his influential 2009 book *Imagining India*: "India now stands evenly balanced, between reluctance to change in the face of immense challenges and the possibilities we have if we do tackle these issues head-on. . . . In the long term we will either be a country that greatly disappoints when compared with our potential or one that beats all expectations."

The Physical Setting

Geography has provided India with a very mixed setting. The country, as noted, is physically very large: only China among world countries entirely located in Asia (thereby excluding Russia) is bigger physically, and the Indian landmass is a land of contrast, from some of the world's highest peaks in the Himalayas to the broad and swampy coastal plain as it nears parts of the Indian Ocean. The population of India will surpass that of China in 2032, according to Luce, and by 2050 there will be more English speakers in India than in any other country. Almost half the land is arable, but India suffers from a shortage of water more severe than that of China, according to Menon. India borders on six other countries (Bangladesh, Bhutan, Burma/Myanmar, China, Nepal, and Pakistan), with long-standing and occasionally violent border disputes with two of them (China and Pakistan). India is blessed with a rich variety of natural resources, but petroleum is not among them. Indian oil production in 2009 was 878,000 barrels a day (24th in the world) compared to a consumption of nearly three million barrels a day (fifth globally); Indian known oil reserves stand at about 5.8 billion barrels, 23rd in the world.

The demographics of India are as rich and diverse as the land itself. Ethnically, the majority of the Indian population is Indo-Aryan (72 percent); Dravidians compose an additional 25 percent, and the remaining 3 percent are spread among a number of smaller groups. India is also a land of religious diversity. Although four-fifths of the population are Hindu, an additional 13.4 percent are Muslim, another 2.3 percent Christian, and 1.9 percent are Sikhs. As already noted, there are 14 official languages spoken in different parts of the country: Hindi, the language with the largest number of speakers, is spoken by about two-fifths of Indians. All of this diversity is divided politically among 28 states and seven union territories.

Much of the contemporary interest surrounding India comes from its economic growth since 1991. The Indian economy, with a GDP of $3.68 trillion, is now the fifth largest of any country in the world, and it is projected to become the world's third largest economy in gross terms. At 7.4 percent in 2009, India's GDP growth rate was 10th in the world. Fueled largely by advances in the technological sector, India is clearly becoming a world-class economic power.

Indian growth has a leavening side, however, that is the product of its enormous population and the burdens it places on the country. While gross economic figures have exploded onto the world scene, India shares with China the problem of supporting a vast population, and it is over a decade behind the Chinese both in growth and expansion and in facing this difficulty. India's GDP *per capita* is much less impressive than the size of its economy, standing at $3,200 (165th among the world's countries), and, as already noted, that wealth is not uniformly distributed. As Mukherji puts it, "India has more poverty than any other nation in the world."

Finding a way to uplift those very large portions of the Indian population who have not entered the economic boom is a central problem facing India's political leadership, and it is one that the Indians have not truly addressed in any comprehensive way (which is one of Nilekani's critiques of the current system). For most Indians, life remains primitive and difficult. As evidence, Menon cites UN statistics on quality of life as measured by the UN Development Program's Human Development Index, "a composite of basic quality of life indicators," on which India rated 132nd of 179 countries in 2009, leading him to the conclusion that "the rural poor, who number about 500 million, have seen little improvement."

There is a good news–bad news dynamic to this situation. On the positive side, India has a basically youthful population, and the part of that population aged 25 or younger (thus candidates to enter the workforce) is favorable for Indians, in sharp contrast with the aging of populations in most of the more developed countries, including China. As a result, India is not in any short-term danger of facing an increasing burden of having to divert energy and resources to the elderly, although development will change that somewhat: Indians currently have an average life expectancy of 66.5 years (160th in the world), and spreading modernization will certainly lengthen average life expectancy in the process. The result will be a generation of what Bloom calls "baby boomers," Indians of the age to be a part of the productive work force but for whom a comprehensive role in the evolving economic system has not yet been devised.

The problem for India is that the economic revolution has not been widespread enough to mobilize large parts of the population. As Mukherji puts it, "economic reform has not yet benefited enough young Indians for the country to harness the potential of its youthful workforce." There are several reasons that are regularly cited for this shortfall, but at the heart of the problem is the Indian educational system. Feigenbaum points to the stark contrast used at the beginning of this section. As he states it, "Although the country has world-class talent in some areas . . . it still faces daunting challenges in its labor market and in its educational system. . . . Demands for education, especially among the growing middle class, vastly outstrips supply, and 160 million Indian children are out of school."

The consequence, of course, is underutilization of the existing workforce, thereby slowing the velocity of overall growth and improvements in quality of life. "Economic reforms have not yet benefited enough Indians to harness the potential of its youthful workforce," Mukherji writes. Moreover, he lays the blame directly at the feet of the Indian political system: "The government's inattention to areas such as literacy promotion and employment generation has helped produce unacceptable levels of absolute poverty. . . . the major challenge facing literacy promotion is the low quality of government schools." There are varying explanations of why the Indian political system has not been more effective in addressing the problems faced by the country, but a ponderous, inefficient, and often corrupt bureaucracy is an often-cited shortcoming, along with a class-based political worldview that has traditionally paid little attention to the vast peasantry to which so much of India's economic potential is tied.

Education is only one of the economic challenges that face Indian development. A 2010 Congressional Research Service (CRS) study headed by Kronstadt lists five underlying economic problems facing the country. Three of these are structural problems associated with the performance of the economy itself: "inflation approaching double digits," "unemployment and underemployment" in areas not directly a part of the expanding sectors of the economy, and "pressure on monetary policy" in areas such as taxation and investment strategies. The other two are more basic to the country itself: an "inadequate and inefficient" infrastructure and a "very complex" bureaucracy, a diplomatic way of saying a corrupt and inefficient political support system.

While the demographic and developmental tasks facing India are enormous, there is very little sense that that they will not somehow be surmounted because, to its enormous credit, the country is undergoing its transformation from third-world, developing status to the first rank of powers while maintaining the devotion to political democracy that it has had since its inception. Periods of rapid development are very often accompanied by restrictions on the democratic process (or delaying the onset of democratization in previously authoritarian political systems), but India has essentially bucked the odds. As Menon puts it, "India confounds conventional theories of democracy, which identify as prerequisites a high level of literacy, a substantial middle class, and the absence of sharp inequalities." This is but one of the ways in which India stands out as a unique place in the world.

India as a Unique State

As the preceding section should indicate, the Indian experiment of the rapid modernization of a very large country within a democratic political context makes it unique in the contemporary world, but it also accentuates the difficult route that faces India as it attempts to enter the ranks of the world's great powers. What may set India apart more than any other single factor is that Indian change is occurring within the context of instability and even violence within its borders. India has its own equivalent of the Russian "internal abroad" that manifests itself in two particularly important and anomalous ways. The first of these surrounds the situation of Kashmir that both poses an internal concern and is a source of the major tensions with neighboring Pakistan; the other is the persistently nagging continued existence of a Marxist insurgency in rural Indian states led by the so-called Naxalites.

Tensions over Kashmir, as noted, go back to the partition of the subcontinent, when India annexed the state at the request of the local maharajah and in defiance of public support from its majority Muslim population. Much of that population was, and still is, unhappy with its inclusion within the Indian polity. Part of their displeasure in the beginning stemmed from the disruption of traditional patterns of commerce between Kashmir and what became Pakistan, and, according to Lamb, "its best communication with the outside world lay through Pakistan." Part of it was associated with the armed occupation of Kashmir by Indian armed forces to ensure the integrity of the new province and the acquiescence of the Kashmiris in the process. At the same time, many were unhappy both with the range of options presented to them at the time of partition and at the eventual outcome of the process.

As noted earlier, one of the major options not available to the residents of Kashmir in 1948 was independence from either India or Pakistan. At the time, most Kashmiris almost certainly preferred union with their Muslim brethren in Pakistan to separatism, but the passage of time and lack of resolution of the Kashmir problem has led to the emergence of an illegal secessionist movement in the area. At the same time, sizable portions of the indigenous population support union with Pakistan (so-called Azad, or Free, Kashmir), thus creating an ongoing source of internal unrest and the need to expend resources on both internal and external security of the region.

The current situation reflects the inability of the parties to reach either an internal or international accord over Kashmir. The fate of Kashmir was a major issue in the 1971 war between India and Pakistan that eventuated in the establishment of Bangladesh, and the truce reinforced and legitimized a semipermanent frontier in Kashmir separating parts of the area controlled by Pakistan and parts under effective Indian jurisdiction that has been a de facto frontier since 1948. This "line of control" is a barbed-wire fence reminiscent of the iron curtain in Europe that separates Azad Kashmir from the state of Jammu and Kashmir. It does nothing to resolve the internal Indian controversy over political self-determination in Kashmir (a matter the Indians are understandably somewhat reluctant to have resolved), but it does leave Pakistan—as the sponsor of Azad Kashmir—in control of the headwaters of the Indus Rivers and India in control of the strategic passes along the Chinese frontier. At the same time, ongoing frictions, including the dispute with China and purported Pakistani support for terrorists operating out of camps in Kashmir, remain part of the agenda affecting Indo–American relations.

The other, anomalous phenomenon in democratic, developing India is the existence of an ongoing Maoist insurgency in the country. The Naxalites (named after the West Bengal village of Naxalbari in which they originated) are a rural-based group that operates, according to Menon, in "one-third of the country." The estimated strength of the insurgents is in the low thousands of fighters, but the underdeveloped infrastructure of India provides them adequate remote, inaccessible sanctuaries to remain outside the effective jurisdiction of the Indian armed forces. While no one would suggest that the Naxalites present any fundamental threat to India's viability, "India's security is challenged not only by the threat of terrorism . . . but also by the domestic insurgency of the leftist Naxalites," as Feigenbaum points out.

The existence of these two movements accentuates how India is different from other developing countries. There are at least two Indias that are part of the equation. One of these is the extremely vibrant, modernizing sector of Indian society, symbolized by places like Bangalore that are leading symbols of Indian ascent in the world of major powers. The other, however, is the backward, rural India of enormous deprivation and discontent that harbors separatists and insurgents. In fully modernized societies, both of these kinds of groups and the threats they pose either never existed or have been resolved, but in India they remain part of the tapestry of Indian existence. One way to solve Kashmiri secessionist sentiment, for instance, might be to "buy them off" with developmental favors in much the same way the Turks have done with their Kurdish minority in the Anatolian eastern part of Turkey. It is also hard to imagine that the sources of succor and support for the Naxalites would long subsist in conditions of obviously growing prosperity in the areas where the Maoists currently operate.

That political democracy and eye-popping development exist alongside grinding poverty that breeds insurrection is part of the uniqueness and anomaly of modern India. In what direction does India focus its attentions: to further development and entrance onto the global center stage? Or to alleviation of the conditions which breed opposition? India's resources are large and growing, but it is not clear that it can simultaneously attack one set of problems without harming the other. For the time being, India seems committed to becoming a world power and thus to deferring its internal problems (or at least giving them less emphasis). This trajectory accentuates the real tension within India and affects the way Indians interact with the rest of the world, including the United States.

U.S.–INDIAN RELATIONS

As the preceding discussion should indicate, American relations with India have undergone two distinct phases. The first phase was the Cold War, during which Indian unwillingness to become a partisan actor in that competition left relations strained between them. During this period, the United States tended to "tilt" toward Pakistan in disputes in southern Asia, in part because Pakistan was willing to commit to the anticommunist cause and later because Pakistan provided a conduit through which the United States could pursue rapprochement with China. This bias toward Pakistan became especially evident in the 1971 Bangladesh War, where the United States backed Pakistan in its attempt to prevent the secession of East Pakistan and opposed Indian efforts favoring the secessionists such as providing sanctuary for East Bengali refugees. The outcome of this exercise was partially to solidify Pakistan's support in opening China, but it also resulted in India's signing of its friendship treaty with the Soviet Union and a legacy of interpersonal and international tension between the two democracies.

Relations have improved markedly since India's 1991 decisions to enter the globalizing economy. One of the lingering sources of contention between the two countries had been socialist leanings such as central planning—even including Soviet-sounding five-year plans—that alienated the Indians from the American private sector and its supporters, and these were quietly jettisoned in the move toward free market economics. As India has increasingly moved to become more like the developed West, American attitudes and relations with the subcontinent's giant have also warmed. India was the destination of President Bill Clinton's last foreign trip while in office, and the administration of George W. Bush built upon that foundation, instituting its Strategic Dialogue with the Indians. India's prime minister, Manmohan Singh, was the first dignitary invited to the White House by President Obama in 2009, a further symbol of the close relations built, in the words of the Kronstadt CRS study, "on shared values such as democracy, pluralism, and rule of law."

Strategic Interests and Relations

American relations with India have also become more extensive and intimate because of increased American interest and involvement in the complex international politics of the south Asian region from the Persian Gulf to the Pacific. At the risk of some simplification, the complex of strategic concerns that involve both countries is depicted in Figure 5.1.

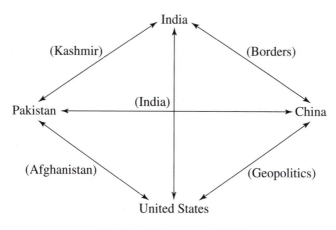

(Nuclear Weapons and War)

FIGURE 5.1
U.S.–Indian Strategic Relations

The figure requires some explanation. It is organized as a four-party model, with each of the parties connected to one another in one primary way or another. Thus, viewed primarily from an Indian perspective, India and Pakistan are primarily connected by their mutually exclusive interests over Kashmir, India and China face one another across common and contested borders, and Pakistan and China share a common interest in opposition to and limiting the influence of India. The United States enters the equation because it also has interests with each of the others, although those interests are disparate and sometimes conflicting. The primary current American interest with Pakistan, for instance, is over Pakistan's relationship with terrorism and Afghanistan and the American conduct of the war there, and since India also has interests in Afghanistan, there is an American interest in Indian policy toward the conflict as well. American strategic relations with China at the geopolitical level tend to center on making sure China does not become overwhelmingly dominant in the region, a factor that gives it common cause with the Indians in places like the Indian Ocean, where a naval competition is looming and is, according to Joshi, an increasing concern of the Indians.

Overshadowing all these relationships is the nuclear balance. All four of the countries depicted in the figure are nuclear weapons possessors, of course, since India and Pakistan entered the nuclear "club" officially in 1998, and nuclear weapons affect all their relationships in one way or another. The primary concern that overwhelmingly influences the United States surrounds the historically volatile Indo–Pakistani relationship and the possibility that a future conflict between them could escalate to a nuclear war that could, in the worst case, spread and affect other countries. The United States shares with India a fear that Pakistani nuclear weapons might somehow find their way into the hands of terrorists, who might use them against either country. Chinese development of nuclear weapons, demonstrated in 1964, is generally conceded to have been the major impetus to India's decision to acquire "the bomb," which in turn spurred the Pakistani effort. In turn, the fear of nuclear war has been an underlying characteristic of Sino–American relations for nearly a half century.

American strategic interactions with India are the dominant concern of this chapter (the Pakistan factor is examined in Chapter 6). The United States and India share some interests and diverge on others, but it is important to note that most of these concerns are of greater importance to India than they are to the United States. Four of these are worth noting: Indian–American relations over China, Pakistan, nuclear weapons, and the Afghanistan War.

India and China are the two most powerful countries in the region by any measure: population, demographics and geography, or military power. According to Globalfirepower.com's analysis that aggregates CIA and Library of Congress sources to produce comparable figures not readily available in the same usable form in other sources, China has the world's second most powerful armed forces, whereas India's are ranked fourth. They are also emerging powers, each of which seeks dominant influence in the south Asian region but who share a long history of some level of animosity toward one another. The United States, on the other hand, does not want either to become strong enough to pose an existential threat to the other or to be so dominating as to be capable of excluding American commercial interests from the region. The American interest is in a Chinese–Indian balance of power; India and China each would prefer to be the dominant power of the region.

The primary venue of Chinese–Indian animosity has been their shared border in the northern and eastern parts of India. Part of this conflict involves strategic areas (the invasion routes) between the two in Kashmir, and China occupies a part of what India considers Kashmir in the Aksai Chin area. In retaliation, the Indians claim parts of the Chinese state of Tibet as Indian territories. Part of their competition is also geopolitical in a broader sense. Some analysts (such as Robert Kaplan) argue that much of the coming geopolitical competition in the world will center on the Indian Ocean and eastern Asia, where the Indians and Chinese can collide. This is, as Kaplan (2010) explains, a major concern of the Indians: "India fears being encircled by China unless it expands its own sphere of influence. The two countries' overlapping commercial and political interests are fostering competition, and even more so in the naval realm than on land." China thus stands in the way of a larger Indian regional role. Kaplan concludes, "As India extends its influence east and west, on land and at sea, it is bumping into China." The American interests in this competition are to keep it below the level of war and for a balance between the two that the United States can help broker and that does not preclude the pursuit of American political and commercial interests in Asia.

The Indian relationship with Pakistan has long been combustible and is one in which the United States took sides during the Cold War. The flashpoint of the Indo-Pakistani contention, of course, has always been Kashmir (although it has other foci as well, as Cohen points out), and the two sides are not much closer to reaching a mutually acceptable accommodation beyond the de facto line of control established in fact in 1948 after accession to India and legitimized after the 1971 war. Kashmir has been a major consideration in all of the eruptions of war between the two countries and continues to be the issue most likely to bring them to violence in the future. To make matters worse in the current context, there have been well-documented indications that Pakistani support for Taliban militants has been intermingled with their clandestine training of Azad Kashmir fighters and that training camps in Pakistani-occupied Kashmir may also contain the training grounds for terrorists who have attacked India—for instance, the 2008 Mumbai attack.

American objectives in this dispute have been to try to calm passions and to try to move toward a negotiated peace, positions which do not satisfy either party since any agreement would likely entail sacrifice by both. When partition occurred, the United States favored a plebiscite in Kashmir and joined many other states in condemning the annexation of the area by India, positions that did not please the Indians. At the same time, the United States has maintained close military ties with Pakistan that are only now being nourished with India, and so there was an implicit assumption in India that this country favored Pakistan in those clashes (especially in 1971). On the other hand, the United States put pressure on Pakistan to desist in its efforts to train militants to send into Afghanistan, and this entreaty has included training for Azad Kashmir recruits, an emphasis the Pakistanis see as pro-Indian and as acquiescence in India's continuing control of Kashmir.

American motives center on seeking a more commodious relationship between India and Pakistan. One aspect is the nuclear equation: what could happen to cause a deterioration of relations to war, and possibly nuclear war. Ganguly cites one not implausible example, arguing that another Mumbai-type terrorist attack in which the Pakistanis could arguably be implicated could ignite an Indian retaliation because "an Indian failure to respond decisively would virtually guarantee future terrorist attacks." Ganguly does not believe such a response would be initially nuclear, but once on the "slippery slope," the escalatory process is unknown. The other reason for an American strategic concern with Indo-Pakistani peace is that it would relieve pressures on the Pakistani armed forces, most of which are trained and deployed near the Indian border for a future war with India. Figures aggregated by Global Firepower, for instance, indicate the Pakistani armed forces are only about half those of the Indians in total manpower, ranked 15th in the world compared to India's fourth in strength. A lessening of Indo-Pakistani tensions could relieve pressure on the Pakistani military, allowing it to reconfigure and redeploy to help more in the suppression of pro-Afghan forces in the mountainous border areas along the Pakistani–Afghan frontier, thereby assisting American efforts in Afghanistan.

Nuclear Weapons and Afghanistan

The United States also has interests in nuclear developments in the region. The Indians and the Americans have disagreed on whether India should have become a nuclear power to the point that, Feigenbaum concludes, "The thorniest obstacle to U.S.-Indian cooperation was India's nuclear program." At the same time, India has been a reasonably responsible member of the nuclear weapons club. As Menon points out, "India has not deliberately helped or encouraged other nations with their nuclear ambitions." Because of this positive Indian record, the United States and India have entered into an agreement to improve India's civilian nuclear program with American assistance. The Pakistani record, as discussed in the next chapter, is not so pristine (e.g., the efforts of Pakistani nuclear scientist A. Q. Khan), and there are fears in Washington that one or more of Pakistan's nuclear weapons might fall into the hands of terrorists. If denuclearization of the Indian subcontinent is no longer a feasible goal, defusing tension that might lead to activation of those weapons is still a clear American interest.

The Indians and the Americans also interact over the outcome of the conflict in Afghanistan, a country over which India and Pakistan have a long-standing contest for influence. Afghanistan, of course, stands between Russia and India, and its strategic location has long made it the subject of conflict, as in the century-long Great Game between Great Britain (as the colonial power in India) and Russia for paramount interest. In a different form, that competition continues between the Indians and the Pakistanis. The Pakistanis favor a weak, pro-Pakistani, Muslim government in Kabul that will not create the need for them to divert resources to the Afghan frontier, and it was in pursuit of that goal that it originally encouraged (or created) the formation of the Taliban. India, on the other hand, prefers a stronger Afghanistan with a central government less rooted in control by the Pashtuns, and one that favors their goals: "Indian leaders wish to limit Islamabad's influence in post-war Afghanistan," according to the Kronstadt CRS study. The American position does not fully embrace either the preference of India or Pakistan, but the need to secure the frontier between Afghanistan and Pakistan has brought the United States into closer collaboration with Pakistan on the war, a situation the Indians do not embrace but which they nonetheless understand. Ongoing tensions between the Americans and the Pakistanis over the nature of their border cooperation, of course, work to India's benefit.

Beyond the more or less pure geopolitics of the subcontinent, the United States and India have significant interactions with one another on a number of other issues, three of which will be mentioned here. They are the question of global climate change and what to do about it; India's desire for greater global recognition, captured in its desire for permanent membership on the UN Security Council; and the impacts of Indian development on the United States.

Other Issues

The first issue is global climate change and dates back to the enunciation of the Kyoto Protocols of 1997, the first international regime to address this contentious topic. Negotiated with the full support of the Clinton administration in the United States, the protocol contained two distinct provisions that became matters of contention between the United States and India. One was the assignment of responsibility for the problem and its resolution. Because it was (and is) the world's largest emitter of carbon dioxide (the major contributor to global warning), the United States was assessed the greatest responsibility for reducing its emissions as part of the solution. At the same time, the protocol excluded historically developing countries whose industrial sectors had not been major contributors. Included in this category were India and China, both of which were becoming major polluters as their economies developed.

These two provisions created a major point of contention when George W. Bush became president in 2001. The Kyoto Protocol had been signed by Clinton before leaving office, but as an international treaty, it required Senate advice and consent, which had not occurred, and Bush, much of whose support was grounded in the U.S. energy industry that opposed the protocol (and questioned the existence of global warming) refused to transmit the treaty to the Senate for its consideration. His grounds for doing so were that the treaty imposed onerous burdens on the United States that would harm American economic competitiveness because compliance would add costs to American industries not shared equally by others. His position also condemned the exclusion of countries like India and China, both of which have become, according to Menon, "among the top five" emitters of carbon dioxide. India joined other developing economies that were not covered by Kyoto in the position that "the West bears primary responsibility for the problem and so should carry the main burdens of cutting emissions," again in Menon's words.

Because of its scheduled expiration date in 2012, countries involved in the Kyoto process met in Copenhagen, Denmark, in December 2009 to try to conclude a follow-on agreement. Major points of contention included the extent of American responsibility for ameliorating the problem, measures and guidelines for determining progress, and the role of new polluters like India and China previously excluded from the restrictions. The conference failed to produce anything resembling even a draft or comprehensive statement of principles on the subject, but India did join China and the United States in issuing a final, unofficial statement exhorting countries to continue to work toward a new agreement. Indian–Chinese mutual interests in this area, however, remain one of the few areas where they still find common ground on which they can agree.

Chinese–Indian cooperation does not, however, extend to promoting India's elevation to a permanent seat on the UN Security Council. As a leader of the developing countries through the Cold War–era nonaligned movement (which for some purposes continues to exist), India has always been a strong supporter of the world body, despite its disagreements with New York over specific issues like Kashmir. The Indians, as part of their desire for greater international prominence (as well as to promote the prominence of the developing world generally), have been historic proponents of expanding permanent membership beyond the current five members (the so-called P-5) to a broader base. The United States is generally supportive of the idea of expansion and the inclusion of India in an expanded council, but the entire issue has two sources of contention that have precluded implementation to this point.

The first disagreement is over who should be invited to become permanent members. As Menon suggests, the Indians favor a group known as "P-4": Brazil, Germany, India, and Japan, all of which "are wannabes that hope to join" the permanent members, but there are countries that also seek that status, such as Argentina, Egypt, Indonesia, Italy, Mexico, Nigeria, Pakistan, and South Africa. There is thus divergence about how much the council can be expanded and to whom the invitation will be made. As Yardley points out, "China is now the only permanent member that has not explicitly endorsed" Indian inclusion on the council, and Stewart adds that "China and Russia oppose any new permanent members." Since the veto that the permanent members hold would extend to expanding the council and specifying who is allowed to join, this is a major stumbling block.

There is also disagreement about the powers and privileges that any new permanent members would enjoy. The current distinctions between permanent and nonpermanent members are whether members are elected for specific terms or indefinitely and whether they have a veto. In the current enlargement debate, this also involves two possible concerns. Expanding permanent membership would answer the first concern since, by definition, new permanent members would be on the council in perpetuity. The question of expanding the veto is, however, more controversial. Stewart, for instance, maintains that "none of the council's permanent five members will countenance either limiting its veto power or extending that power to others." This position is rarely stated publicly or bluntly, but it arises from the increased difficulty of getting nine (or more members) to agree to resolutions given how hard it is to get agreement among the five present members. The compromise solution, of course, would be a kind of hybrid new membership that created permanence or tenure but without the veto. India and other aspirants reject this alternative as creating an unacceptable "second-class citizenship" for new members and as a limitation on their ability to affect world affairs conducted through the world body.

Finally, there are some relatively minor frictions between the two countries, particularly evident in the economic area. There are, for instance, "obstacles to bilateral trade and investment, including in the high-technology sector," according to Kronstadt and colleagues, that are largely carry-overs from the pre-1991 period of Indian protectionism and that are in the process of being addressed by the two countries. Outsourcing, the practice of moving American jobs out of the United States to cheaper providers in foreign countries, has been a matter of some domestic American public irritation, largely associated with the use of telemarketers and technical support functions provided by Indians to American consumers. At the same time, there are concerns in such areas as the "reverse brain drain," where Indian students trained at American universities who have historically stayed in the United States to pursue careers are instead going back to the new, rich technological environment in Bangalore.

What this overview portrays is a picture of gradual improvement in U.S.–Indian relations from a period of estrangement during the Cold War to gradual expansion and warming of those relations in the contemporary environment since 1991. There are, of course, sources of disagreement and friction between these two huge democracies, but they are not deep or fundamental enough to create unbridgeable, irreconcilable situations. The question remains, however, the extent to which the United States can influence better and closer relations between the two countries.

U.S. OPTIONS

While current relations between the United States and India arise from a backdrop of some level of historical animosity, they do not have the domestic political baggage in the United States that creates opposition and limits toward dealing with the problems that linger in the same way that affects U.S. relations with, for instance, Russia or China. When President Obama declared in 2009 that the Indian people "should know they have no better friend and partner than the people of the United States," his assertion could reasonably be criticized as overstated, but it did reflect a gradual political consensus that has arisen in the United States since 1991 and that has been embraced and nurtured by his predecessors. As noted, both Presidents Clinton and Bush were strong supporters of more intimate ties with India; Obama was merely reflecting the domestic political consensus in the United States.

At the interpersonal level, relations between Indians and Americans have always been close. As the Kronstadt study points out, for instance, "Influence of a geographically dispersed and relatively wealthy Indian-American community of some 2.7 million is reflected in Congress' largest country-specific caucus." The governors of two southern states, Louisiana's Bobby Jindal and South Carolina's Nikki Haley, are both Republicans of Indian descent. Roughly 100,000 Indian students study in American universities, more than study in any other foreign country, and Indians are prominent among those who receive advanced degrees in science, mathematics, and engineering from American institutions of higher education. Historically, most of these advanced students have become residents of the United States, playing a major part in American preeminence in high technology. Moreover, the Indian development model has been identified and widely publicized by people like Friedman as exemplary in the twenty-first century world.

American and Indian interests are not, of course, identical in the world, and there are points of disagreement and friction between them. Most of these, like the geopolitics of the South Asian area, are more directly concerns of India than they are concerns of the United States, whose core interests are largely confined to maintaining relative peace and stability and continued access to the region for American economic interests. Although the exact shape of a durable peace in the region may be somewhat different for the Indians than the Americans, there is no fundamental discord on the overall goal.

The United States has very limited tools it can employ to bring about Indian acquiescence to American policy goals, but that limitation is conditioned by the fact that the differences they have are not profound. While it may remain true, as Menon asserts, that "Indians remain ambivalent about US power and do not want the American military ensconced in South and Central Asia," the post-Afghanistan environment in the United States may be receptive to a lower American military profile in that part of the world anyway.

At the same time, there are important common goals favored by the two countries. As Feigenbaum says, "The United States and India share important interests: both seek to restore global growth, protect the global commons, enhance energy security, and ensure a balance of power in Asia." Given these commonalities, the fact that "New Delhi seeks a United States that will help facilitate India's rise as a major power" (Feigenbaum) may not be an unreasonable position for the United States to take toward the world's other largest political democracy.

CONCLUSIONS

Two somewhat contradictory things stand out about the relationship between the United States and India. The first is that they have much more in common than what divides them. Both, for instance, have strong commitments to political democracy that set them apart from many of the other largest countries in the world, and in both cases, the basis for that system is their common Anglo-Saxon colonial heritage. Granted, the Indians have a long way to go in developmental terms, but given their common political commitments, the United States can only applaud and seek to help the transformation of India into a full-scale democratic beacon in a part of the world where democracy is the exception, not the rule. An additional part of that Anglo-Saxon heritage is a common language, English, of which the two countries are the most numerous speakers.

Their commonalities go beyond a shared political ideology. Both countries have shared a commitment to education and global advancement of science and technology. It is not coincidental that there is a symbiosis between the extremely ambitious best-educated Indians and the world's best higher education system in the United States. The relationship is not perfectly symmetrical: Indian education for its elite is on the rise, whereas there is evidence of some decay in the American commitment, but the two countries are still at the forefront of the production of knowledge and its application, a common commitment that should continue into the future.

India and the United States also have no shared history of major animosities and certainly no tradition of violence between them. During the Cold War, the two countries disagreed geopolitically in a world where the United

States saw the containment of communism as its highest order of priority and India believed an emphasis on development best served its interests. Despite the tendency in the United States during the height of the Cold War to equate the absence of overt opposition to communism with support for the other side, there was never any explosive potential in this disagreement. Similarly, the American tilts toward Pakistan were annoying to the Indians and may have provided extra capability to their Pakistani opponents in those conflicts, but there was never any danger of American intervention on the side of the Pakistanis. Relations may have been cool, but they were not frigid.

The year 1991, in retrospect, was a pivotal year in the relationship. The collapse of the communist world ended that basis for Indo-American antagonism, and the decision of India to pursue Western-style economic development put the two countries on parallel tracks that have become more obvious in recent times. The basis of antagonism has dissipated, and the roots of friendship have been nurtured. How much the relationship will blossom may remain a matter of conjecture; that it will continue to improve in some way seems foreordained.

The other general observation is that, in important ways, the two countries remain far apart, a limit on how close they may become. Indian society writ large does not resemble American society, although there are pockets of similarity between the entrepreneurial elites in the two countries. It may not, for instance, be coincidental that Indian Americans are relatively affluent or that the most visible Indian American politicians, Governors Jindal and Haley, are both conservative Republicans. At the same time, there is certainly no American equivalent to the half billion or so Indians who live in the most abject of circumstances. Before India and America become mirrors of one another, India must go through a long and difficult transition period, the strains and requirements of which will almost certainly act as an anchor on the rapid development of the most advanced parts of Indian society. It is not yet clear that India's elite political classes have come entirely to grips with the burdens of development for the entire population, leaving some uncertainty about what will happen next in the relationship.

India is also geographically a world apart from the United States, anchoring a part of the world that has historically not been central to American attention or concerns. The United States has had, as noted in Chapter 2, a fascination with the "mysteries of the Orient" for a long time, but most of that interest has been directed toward China and the exotic areas of Southeast Asia, not toward India and the subcontinent. The two cultures remain largely alien to one another, and while so-called "Bollywood" (the Indian motion picture industry) may show some indications of a movement of India toward U.S. culture, there is little indication of a similar movement in the other direction.

This separation also limits the extent to which the United States has deep interests in the area. Strategic interests tend to be to the north (the Persian Gulf region, including Afghanistan) or to the east (China), not toward the subcontinent, and thus there is less between the two countries that can come into conflict than is true in some other areas. Economic and political ties are on the increase, and they occur and arguably can flourish in an atmosphere unpolluted by a long and unhappy tapestry of animosity or of long-term close association.

STUDY/DISCUSSION QUESTIONS

1. How has the experience of partition of the Indian subcontinent in 1947 affected subsequent development and problems in the region, and especially in India?
2. Why was India described as "a country of enormous contrasts and complexities" in the text? What challenges do these present to India? Elaborate. p 107
3. How does the nature of Indian development and demographics affect Indian development in the future? How do these help define Indian uniqueness and its relations with the United States?
4. Describe Indo-American security relations, using Figure 5.1 as an organizational tool. How do those interests differ and coincide?
5. Indo-American relations have other sources of disagreement beyond the geopolitical realm. Describe those areas of disagreement. How important and fundamental are they?
6. Why was 1991 a "watershed" year for India, its development, and relations between the United States and India?
7. Describe the likely future of U.S.–Indian relations. Are domestic American politics a major factor in those relations? Why are there reasons for cooperation between the two countries in the future?

READING/RESEARCH MATERIALS

Bajpai, Kenti P., and Amitabh Mattoo. *Engaged Democracies: India-U.S. Relations in the 21st Century.* New Delhi: Har Anand, 2007.

Bloom, David E. "India's Baby Boomers: Dividend or Disaster." *Current History* 110, 735 (April 2011), 136–142.

Castenada, Jorge G. "Not Ready for Prime Time: Why Including Emerging Powers at the Helm Would Hurt Global Governance." *Foreign Affairs* 89, 5 (September/October 2010), 109–122.

Cohen, Stephen P. "Shooting for a Century: The India-Pakistan Conundrum." *Current History* 110, 735 (April 2011), 162–164.

Feigenbaum, Evan A. "India's Rise, America's Interest: The Fate of the U.S.-India Partnership." *Foreign Affairs* 89, 2 (March/April 2010), 79–91.

Friedman, Thomas L. *The World Is Flat: A Brief History of the Twenty-First Century.* New York: Farrar, Straus, and Giroux, 2005.

Ganguly, Sumit. "What If Pakistanis Strike India Again?" *Current History* 109, 726 (April 2010), 170–172.

Global Firepower. "Indian Military Strength." Globalfirepower.com, January 11, 2011. http://www.globalfirepower.com/country-military-strength-detail. asp?Country_id=india.

Gould, Harold A. *The South Asia Story: The First Sixty Years of US Relations with India and Pakistan.* London: Sage Publications Pvt. Limited, 2010.

Joshi, Shashank. "Why India Is Becoming Warier of China." *Current History* 110, 735 (April 2011), 156–161.

Kronstadt, Alan, Paul K. Kerr, Michael F. Martin, and Bruce Vaughn. *India-U.S. Relations*. CRS Report for Congress. Washington, DC: Congressional Research Service, October 27, 2010.

Kaplan, Robert D. "Center Stage for the Twenty-First Century: Power Plays in the Indian Ocean." *Foreign Affairs* 88, 2 (March/April 2009), 16–32.

———. "India's New Face." *The Atlantic* 303, 3 (April 2009), 74–81.

———. *Monsoon: The Indian Ocean and the Future of American Power*. New York: Random House, 2010.

Kurlantzick, Joshua. "The Asian Century: Not Quite Yet." *Current History* 110, 732 (January 2011), 26–31.

Lamb, Alastair. *Kashmir: A Disputed Legacy, 1846–1990*. Herringtonfordbury, UK: Roxford Books, 1991.

Luce, Edward. *In Spite of the Gods: The Rise of Modern India*. New York: Doubleday, 2007.

Menon, Rajan. "Pax Americana and Rising Powers." *Current History* 108, 721 (November 2009), 353–360.

Metcalf, Barbara D., and Thomas R. Metcalf. *A Concise History of Modern India*. Cambridge, UK: Cambridge University Press, 2006.

Mukherji, Rahul. "A Tiger Despite the Chains: The State of Reform in India." *Current History* 109, 726 (April 2010), 144–150.

Nilekami, Nandan. *Imagining India: The Idea of a Renewed Nation*. New York: Penguin Books, 2009.

Stewart, Patrick. "Irresponsible Stakeholders: The Difficulty of Integrating Rising Powers." *Foreign Affairs* 89, 6 (November/December 2010), 44–53.

Talbot, Strobe. *Engaging India: Diplomacy, Democracy, and the Bomb*. Washington, DC: Brookings Institution Press, 2004.

Wolpert, Stanley. *India*, (4th ed.). Berkeley: University of California Press, 2009.

Yardley, Jim. "India Digs in Its Heels as China Flexes Its Muscles." *New York Times* (online), December 29, 2010.

Pakistan: Bolstering a Potential Failed State and Ally

PREVIEW

India and Pakistan share common geography and history, and thus relations with one are related to relations with the other. At the same time, there are significant differences between them, and thus the United States has different relations with Pakistan than it does with India. Part of the difference is the result of the 1947 partition of the Asian subcontinent, which left its Muslim and Hindu populations in very contrasting kinds of countries with varying circumstances, and part of the difference arises from the post-partition experience each has had. U.S.–Pakistani relations are governed both by Pakistan's internal difficulties and its relations in the region, and the two countries struggle to maintain close relations despite differences over matters as fundamental as the Pakistani nuclear arsenal and Pakistani relations with Kashmir, Afghanistan, and terrorists, all amidst fears of Pakistan's emergence as a "failed state." American influence in Pakistan has ebbed and flowed, making somewhat tenuous the American ability to influence Pakistan and its policies and arguably increasing the need for a more consistent, Pakistan-centered foreign policy toward the country. It is not clear how the American assassination of Usama bin Laden on Pakistani soil in May 2011 will affect overall U.S.–Pakistani relations in the long run.

Like its neighboring rival India, Pakistan is located on territory that produced some of the earliest civilizations in the world. As the Library of Congress (LOC) country study on Pakistan points out, "humans lived in what became Pakistan around 2.2 million years ago, and the first civilization in South Asia, the Harappan Civilization, is believed to have started around 3000 B.C. in the Indus River valley." These earliest human presences in the area were not directly related to the Muslim inhabitants of contemporary

Pakistan, of course. The Muslim intrusion onto the subcontinent, as described in Chapter 5, began with the first Arab invasion around 711 CE, when General Muhammad bin Qasim introduced the new religion in the Sindh area, and was continued by a number of other intrusions from the north, most notably those associated with the Turkic Mughals, who ruled much of the northern subcontinent—including modern Pakistan and much of northern India—until European rule was established in the nineteenth century.

British rule was established in the nineteenth century when the British government took over administration of the subcontinent from the British East India Company and established the Raj. While the British colonization had large effects throughout what became India and Pakistan, it was especially traumatic for the Muslim population, particularly the British response to the so-called Sepoy Rebellion of 1857. As the LOC study states, "Prior to 1857, Muslims were prominent in economics and administration. . . . The British responded [to the Sepoy revolt] by dropping Urdu and Persian as official languages and replaced them with English, thus rendering many Muslims illiterate and unemployable." Low levels of literacy and educational deficiencies continue as major contemporary millstones within Pakistan.

The 1947 partition that created India and Pakistan was particularly traumatic to the Muslims who became the citizens of Pakistan. They suffered from the same early effects as the Indians: the massive human migration across the newly established border, for instance, and the imperfections of the border when India shut off the flow of water from the eastern rivers of the Indus River system during harvest season in 1948. As Jones relates, however, this was hardly all or even the worst of the impacts: "Ever since its creation, Pakistan has been turbulent and chaotic," he writes. "The country has been under military rule for nearly half its existence. No elected government has ever completed its term in office. It has had three wars with India and has lost half its territory. Its economy has never flourished. Nearly half of its population is illiterate and 20 percent is undernourished."

Most of the ills portrayed in the quotation are internal, with the exception of Pakistan's dismemberment with the secession of East Pakistan to create Bangladesh in 1971—one outcome of the third war with India. The net effect of Pakistan's trauma is both internal and external, and it is interactive. The result of partition was to create a Pakistani state that felt, and still feels, that it is in a state of permanent siege. As Rubin and Rashid put it, "the perception among Pakistan's national security elite [is] that the country is surrounded by enemies determined to dismember it. . . . Until that sense of siege is gone, it will be difficult to strengthen civilian institutions in Pakistan." The major impact of Pakistani external paranoia has been to elevate the military to a disproportionate position of power within the political system, and it has generally acted as a drag on the development of a more open, democratic, and possibly competitive Pakistan.

This unique perception of being a country under what it believes to be an existential threat is not unique to Pakistan, of course—one can argue it is a fundamental condition within Israel. It is, however, pervasive in Pakistan and has been since the partition itself. As Jones puts it, "Immediately after independence many Indian leaders made no secret of their hope that Pakistan would collapse and that the subcontinent would subsequently be reunited."

Many Pakistanis, rightly or wrongly, believed the Indians, and notably Indian leader Indira Gandhi, moved to push for Pakistani collapse along with India's involvement in the 1971 war between the two countries. That war began, as most conflicts between the Indians and Pakistanis have, over Kashmir, but fighting also occurred in East Pakistan as the Bengali majority of that wing of Pakistan rebelled against what they considered underrepresentation and discrimination in Pakistani governance from the Punjabi elite of West Pakistan. When the government of Pakistan moved to suppress the rebellion on March 25, 1971, it became an open secessionist movement that was suppressed brutally by the Punjabi-led Pakistani forces. As many as one million people, mostly Bengalis, were victims of the bloodshed, and as many as 10 million Pakistani Bengalis fled across the border into Indian East Bengal, where they immediately posed a massive refugee problem for the Indians.

India responded by intervening in the civil strife in East Pakistan on December 3, 1971, and with their help, the Pakistani forces surrendered on December 16. The rebels were successful; they left the union with Pakistan on the next day and declared the establishment of the state of Bangladesh. What had always been a delicate political arrangement (the two parts of Pakistan were separated by 1,000 miles of Indian territory and were dominated by antagonistic ethnic groups—the Punjabis and Bengalis) thus collapsed, an outcome that Lord Louis Mountbatten, the British architect of the partition, had foreseen. Jones, for instance, maintains "Mountbatten predicted this arrangement could not last for more than twenty-five years." He was only off by a year in this prediction.

Indian motives in assisting the process of self-determination for Bangladesh have been controversial and are worth mentioning because they are part of the atmosphere of ongoing Pakistani–Indian relations, and they were viewed in a particularly jaundiced manner by President Richard M. Nixon and his national security advisor, Henry Kissinger, both of whom intensely disliked Gandhi personally. Gandhi and her government argued their actions were humanitarian and pragmatic: Indian troops were dispatched for the humanitarian purpose of alleviating the slaughter by the Pakistani forces, and India needed a way to relieve the refugee problem, which ending the fighting would facilitate. Some Americans (notably administration figures like Nixon and Kissinger) and many Pakistanis attributed a more sinister, geopolitical motive: championing Bangladesh statehood also reduced the Pakistani threat to India by one-half, as the population of the country was cut literally in half when Bangladesh achieved statehood. The result was a weaker and less threatening Muslim state confronting India.

Both arguments have merit. The Pakistani slaughter in East Pakistan was reprehensible, and the refugee flood did stretch Indian capacities to the limits. The secession did, at the same time, simplify the Indian and complicate the Pakistani strategic positions. A Pakistan that included both the current country and Bangladesh would be the world's third most populous country (displacing the United States) with a 2010 population of over 340 million, roughly one-third the population of India. With a population of a little over 184 million (sixth in the world), current Pakistan has a population base only a little over one-sixth that of India (Bangladesh's population of 156 million is seventh in the world). The numerical balance would favor India under any circumstances, but not by as much, and as former U.S. ambassador to Pakistan Ryan Crocker puts it, contributes to the perception that "Pakistan fears for its basic survival."

Pakistani foreign relations are also dominated currently by the situations in Kashmir and Afghanistan, each of which will be discussed more fully later in the chapter. By way of introduction, however, it is necessary to mention three other aspects of the Pakistan environment relevant to the current discussion. The first is that Pakistan regularly appears on the list of "failed states" in the world. The basis of the notion of state failure is the prospect that a state can become dysfunctional to the point it ceases effectively to exist as a governing entity. Somalia is the prototype. While no one actually classifies Pakistan as a state that *has* failed, it is a state that has the significant potential to unravel. Pakistan is normally ranked in the top 10 states in the world with this potential in *Foreign Policy* magazine's annual listing of state failure (it was 10th in the 2009 rankings, for instance). Cohen (2004) conditions this concern somewhat. "Each time Pakistan has been declared a 'failed state,'" he argues, "it has come back from the grave—albeit with a weakened economy, and disturbing demographic and educational trends."

While Pakistan's likelihood of collapsing as a state may be debatable, it is an indication that the Pakistani political condition is tentative and delicate, which is a matter of concern in light of the other two factors. The second aspect of the Pakistani government worth raising is the fact that Pakistan is a nuclear power, with what Allison argues is an arsenal of about 100 nuclear bombs, and as Haqqani (2007) points out, "Pakistan's economy is the smallest of any country that has tested nuclear weapons thus far." Pakistan is also the only nuclear weapons possessor to appear on the failed states list.

Pakistan as a potential nuclear failed state gains even greater significance because of the prominence of the country in the area of global terrorism. Pakistan is regularly accused by India of organizing and training terrorists for missions in Kashmir, and the Pakistani Inter-Service Intelligence (ISI) agency is generally credited with creating the Taliban to combat anti-Pakistani elements in Afghanistan. Suspicions that Pakistani officials had to have known that Usama bin Laden was "hiding in clear sight" in a palatial compound in Abbottabad for several years tend to center on the ISI as the repository of that knowledge. Associated with the Taliban development have been various terrorist groups, and some of these in turn have proven to be Frankenstein monsters who now view Pakistan as the enemy. Riedel summarizes the situation. "Pakistan is both a sponsor of terrorism . . . and a victim of jihadist terror," he writes. "Pakistan is the most important battlefield of the war against

Al Qaeda and the jihadist global terrorist menace." The combination of Pakistani political instability, nuclear weapons possession, and terrorist residence in the country that forms the greatest horror scenario, of course, is the possibility that a crisis or failure of governance in Pakistan could result in terrorists obtaining a Pakistani nuclear weapon.

Pakistan thus occupies a very important place in the contemporary world. Its rivalry with India has spanned almost two-thirds of a century, has erupted in violence on several occasions, and could, in a renewed violent confrontation, present the world with its first true nuclear war (a nuclear war where both sides possess the weapons). The geopolitics of its rivalry spill over into places like Afghanistan and make Pakistan a major factor in the global contest over terrorism, and many observers argue that much more U.S. attention should be directed toward the Pakistani terrorism connection than currently is. At the same time, Pakistan is domestically a volatile, potentially unstable place where foreign policy and domestic actions and proposals intermix in sometimes explosive ways. Pakistan is clearly a place to be concerned with in the formulation of U.S. foreign policy.

PAKISTAN: A SKETCH

Unlike its Indian antagonist on the subcontinent, "the idea of Pakistan," to borrow the title of Cohen's 2004 book, is of very recent vintage. According to Cohen, "the concept of a separate Indian Muslim political entity was first put forward by Choudhary Rahmat Ali" in 1933 and arose from the ruminations of a group of expatriate Muslim students at Cambridge University. Unlike the patriots who would argue for the formation of India, those who wanted an independent Muslim state did not have a long and coherent historical past on which to draw inspiration. Instead, they created a new concept, Pakistan, as an acronym with the letters in its name deriving from the various physical areas that constituted Muslim "homelands" (roughly, areas to which Pakistanis had migrated or were original inhabitants). These areas were: *Punjab, Afghania* (the Northwest Frontier Province), *Kashmir, Iran, Sindh, Turkharistan, Afghanistan,* and *Baluchistan.* The acronym means "land of the Paks," and it translates from Urdu as "pure (Pak) country (stan)." The rationale of this alignment was to draw together all of the Muslim peoples of the subcontinent.

The problem was that all schemes dreamed up by exiles from the region had little correspondence to historical reality. The regions that would become parts—provinces and the like—had no historical experience as a unified state or people and were, in some cases, historical rivals whose loyalty was to their particular region, not the center. Thus, the Balochs remain more loyal to Baluchistan than they are to Pakistan, and the loyalty of Pashtuns in the Northwest Frontier Province and the Federally Administered Tribal Area (FATA) is often more as Pashtuns than as Pakistanis. Parts of the territory—notably Kashmir and Afghanistan—were not even included in the Pakistani state, making the artificiality and completeness of the state even more questionable. These centrifugal dynamics were particularly evident in differences between East and West Pakistan, which were ethnically (Punjabi versus Bengali) and culturally distinct (the warrior culture of the Punjabi versus the more sedentary, pacific culture of the Bengalis). Above all that, these areas have had in common is their common adherence to Islam, and this has not always proven enough to create a coherent state or peaceful outcomes to the disputes they have had among themselves and with the outside world. It is, for instance, probably not coincidental at all that the two most roiling problems of Pakistani policy—other than the perpetual death grip with India—are over parts of Pakistan outside Pakistani jurisdiction: Kashmir and Afghanistan.

Man-made tensions and difficulties have, in recent years, been intermingled with natural disasters that helped shape the domestic environment and how Pakistan looks at the outside world. In 2005, for instance, a massive earthquake occurred in eastern Pakistan, including Pakistani-occupied areas of Kashmir—known by the Pakistanis as Azad (Free) Kashmir. The earthquake's effects killed an estimated 80,000 and left another three million homeless in its wake. In this circumstance, there was a massive international effort aimed at alleviating the disaster, including funds and foreign personnel. India cooperated with these authorities—for instance, allowing the breach of the Line of Control dividing Indian- and Pakistani-controlled parts of Kashmir—to allow relief efforts to get to remote locations, and the mutual effort even sparked some cooperative negotiations between the governments of India and Pakistan. In 2010, however, massive flooding in Pakistan proper resulted in the dislocation of millions of Pakistanis and the death of over 1,600, and international responses were tepid at best.

Pakistan in the World

Because of its circumstances, Pakistan feels it is a state very much isolated and on its own facing a hungry predator in India and uncertain friends elsewhere. Paramount among its international concerns is the ongoing competition with India, a confrontation in which Pakistan is severely disadvantaged: India's population, as noted, is much larger than Pakistan's, and so are its armed forces. The active duty Pakistani military stands at about 650,000, with reserves of 528,000 and active paramilitary forces of 302,000, according to 2008 figures compiled by GlobalFirepower.com from standard sources; the equivalent figures for India are active duty forces of 1.325 million, reserves of 1.155 million, and paramilitary forces of nearly 1.3 million. Convinced that the Indians will seize any opportunity to destroy them, the military places an inordinate level of demand on meager Pakistani monetary resources and demands power within the political process to support its mobilization along the border with India. This obsession affects the nature of those armed forces as well: because massive direct warfare between the two would occur in the relatively flat borderlands they share, the Pakistanis have a largely conventional, "heavy" armed force suited for those kinds of engagement (e.g., large numbers of tanks and artillery pieces) that are ill-suited for engagement with opponents in mountainous regions like Kashmir or against its own internal enemies, such as Pakistani Taliban operating in the Swat Valley north of Islamabad in 2009. Military preparedness presents itself to the world as Pakistani militarism, which is further reflected in the prominence of military personnel at the helm of the Pakistani state or lurking closely behind the throne of civilian regimes.

Pakistan's obsession with national survival and defense is further reflected in its neglect of other functions of government. One of the most notable areas of neglect has been in national development and especially education. The literacy rate in Pakistan is only 49 percent, and military demands for government revenues means little is left for the educational system. As a result, a "youth bulge" in the Pakistani population (a large cohort of relatively young Pakistanis) is not receiving the kind of education that will prepare it for any but the most meager jobs and particularly not for the kinds of jobs that will propel Pakistan upward among world economic powers. Instead, many parents are forced to send their children to the notorious *madrassas*, fundamentalist Islamic schools that feature literal memorization of the Koran and hatred of the West but often leave their graduates with little more than elementary arithmetic skills.

The conditions of modern Pakistan would be deplorable and regrettable under any circumstances, but they are poignant and relevant because of where and who Pakistan is in the world. Physically, the state of Pakistan, even reduced thanks to the 1971 secession of the east, borders on four states: India, China, Afghanistan, and Iran. All of these are important regional or international players, and Pakistan is part of all their intrigues and power politics. As the world's sixth most populous country and second most populous Muslim state (after Indonesia), Pakistan cannot be ignored, and its currently sole possession of the "Islamic bomb" only adds to its claim to attention from the world, including the United States.

The Physical Setting

Like almost all the countries in the region, Pakistan is a very diverse place. Its diversity ranges from the highest peaks of the Himalayas through a broad plain (in which most of the population resides and which is the country's "bread basket") that empties into the Indian Ocean through the Arabian Sea. It is not an imposingly large place, with an area of 307,374 square miles that makes it the 36th largest country in the world in area, slightly less than twice the size of California. It borders on four other countries, with its disputed border with Afghanistan (the so-called Durand Line, named after the nineteenth-century Briton who established it) and its long border with India being the most contentious in geopolitical terms and in importance in its foreign policy. It also has borders with generally friendly China and with Iran, over which it has a latent disagreement over Balochi irredentism.

Pakistan is demographically diverse: the largest ethnic group in the country is the Punjabi (44.7 percent in 2009 figures from the *CIA Factbook*), followed by the Pashtuns (or Pakhtuns, among other spellings) at 15.4 percent, Sindhis at 14.1 percent, Sariakis at 8.4 percent, Muhgjirs at 8.4 percent,

Balochis at 3.6 percent, and several others. Most of these ethnicities are regionally located within one or another of Pakistan's four provinces plus territories. Punjabi is the language spoken by the most people (about 48 percent), but Sindhi, Siriaki, Pashtu, and Urdu are also indigenous languages spoken by various ethnic groups. To further complicate the linguistic picture, the LOC study points out, "Urdu is the national language and the language of most print media. English has official status and is often regarded as the language of the elite and the upwardly mobile." To further highlight the ethnic and political differences and stratification of the population, Cohen (2004) adds, "Each of its provinces is associated with a single ethnolinguisitic group: Punjab with Punjabis, Sindh with Sindis, Baluchistan with Baluchs, and the Northwest Frontier Province (NWFP) with Pashtuns. Pashtuns and Punjabis are found throughout the country." As noted, the Pakistanis are united only by their religion: approximately 95 percent of Pakistanis are professed Muslims, with a strong Sunni majority (75 percent) and Shiite minority (20 percent).

By any economic measure, Pakistan is an underdeveloped country. Its 2010 GDP was estimated at $451.2 billion, which is 28th in the world. The economic growth rate, measured by GDP growth, stands at 2.7 percent, 135th in the world, and per capita GDP is near the bottom at $2,400, 182nd in the world. Although 24.4 percent of the land is listed as arable, much of Pakistani agriculture relies on irrigation from the Indus River system which, as the 2010 floods demonstrated dramatically (nearly half the delta country through which the rivers flow was inundated at one time or another), is fickle. The country has relatively meager natural resources for development. The *CIA Factbook* lists these assets as natural gas, "limited" petroleum reserves (at 436.2 million barrels of known reserves, 49th in the world), "poor quality" coal, iron ore, copper, and small amounts of other minerals.

Energy production and use, normally the bellwether of economic development in the industrialized world, also testifies to the paucity of Pakistan's natural and human endowment. In a part of the world that contains much of the globe's known petroleum reserves, Pakistan comes up noticeably short. The country does not consume much petroleum (at 373,000 barrels a day, its consumption was 34th in the world in 2007). The positive aspect of this consumption level is that it requires only about 319,500 barrels a day in oil imports (in 2007 figures, 33rd in the world); the negative aspect is that the low consumption figure suggests a low level of economic, and particularly industrial, activity in the country requiring energy. Pakistan also has relatively small known petroleum reserves, estimated in 2010 at 436.2 million barrels, 49th among the world's countries.

The picture that emerges of Pakistan is that of a poor, fractured, and fractious internal society whose major sources of adhesion are a shared religion—the rationale for creating the Pakistani state in the first place—and a shared concern, even obsession, with the threats from predators on its boundaries. The two factors are, indeed, interactive. The fear of outsiders, principally the Indians, may create cohesion, but it also imbues the Pakistani military with a sense of importance and influence that makes it a driving force internally in the country. That force, in turn, has dampened political—that is, democratic—and economic growth in the country, which adds to fractiousness internally and makes the external threat an even more necessary element in what cohesion the state possesses. The result is a delicate circularity in Pakistani life that needs to be broken if the country is to emerge as a more normal member of the international community—a highly desirable outcome given Pakistan's status as a nuclear weapons possessor. The question is how, or if, the circle can be broken and repaired without plunging Pakistan into a more treacherous and dangerous status. Dealing with these problems arises from the combination of factors that makes Pakistan a unique state.

Pakistan as a Unique State

Individual elements of Pakistan's distinctiveness in the world are not uniquely Pakistani. Pakistan is not by any means the only country in the developing world where the military has historically or is currently playing a leading role: modern Myanmar (Burma) is an obvious parallel in the region, although the unique symbiosis between the military and religion is distinctive to Pakistan. The retardation of political and economic development are also hardly unique to Pakistan, but Pakistan is the only country in the world where descriptions include both the concepts of "failing state" and "nuclear power" in the same sentence (nuclear North Korea is a partial exception). Pakistan is also not the only state that feels it is beleaguered and even that it faces a threat to its very existence; Israel comes quickly to mind as a state that experiences similar concerns.

It is the combination of and synergy among these factors that makes Pakistan stand out. Each of the major contributors to its claim to uniqueness—a high level of military participation in politics; a shaky, potentially failing status; and external and internal threats—exist elsewhere; in Pakistan they exist side-by-side and interact with one another to make Pakistan an especially volatile state. That they exist in a state that has the world's sixth largest population and straddles two of the most volatile, geopolitically critical parts of the world—the Persian Gulf/Southwest Asia and the Indian subcontinent—elevates their importance in the world and to American foreign policy.

Internally, the equation begins with the paramount position of the military in Pakistan and the military's ties to Islam. As noted at earlier in the chapter, the military has always played an important, arguably overweening, role in Pakistani political life, and it is fair to characterize that relationship by saying the military either is in power (the president is usually a military figure whose primary backing is from an element of the armed forces, normally the army) or is not far from power, casting a furtive eye toward the political scene and ready to reassert its authority if it feels doing so is necessary. The military, however, stands in competition with civilian elements, currently symbolized by Pakistan's legal profession, which seeks both to democratize and secularize the society. The attempt to create a secular political state ruled democratically by civilians has considerable resonance within the population because, as

Jones asserts, "Most Pakistanis do not want to live in a theocracy; they want their country to be moderate, tolerant, and stable." The tension arises because a key pillar of the military's internal appeal has been its alliance with and claim to Islamic support, combined with a not-undeserved reputation that civilian rulers have had over the years for corruption and ineffectiveness.

The contemporary scene is exemplary. The current civilian regime headed by Asif Ali Zardari (the widower of assassinated President Benazir Bhutto) succeeded the military rule of President (and General) Pervez Musharraf. Musharraf came into power in 2001 and retained control until 2007, when Bhutto was assassinated by a suicide terrorist as she returned to the country following a long exile. Part of the national reaction was to question the adequacy of the military's protection of Bhutto, and partially in reaction, factions loyal to Zardari gained a majority in the Pakistani parliament and threatened impeachment of Musharraf. He resigned the presidency in 2008, making way for the elevation of Zardari that year. The Zardari administration has since its inception been accused of official corruption, and the military remains in the wings, ready to resume control if it deems it necessary.

Haqqani, in his seminal *Pakistan between Mosque and the Military*, has detailed the military's ties to Islam most completely. He argues that there has been an uneasy alliance throughout Pakistani history between the professional military and Islamic elements in society that reflects their shared conservatism and that has generally been arrayed against democratizing elements, which are both more liberal and secular. Lacking any strong political traditions at national birth, the question of governance has always been tenuous and has largely been dominated by the military. The military's strength is derived in no small measure by Pakistan's self-image as a national security state surrounded by numerous enemies, and especially a much larger and stronger hostile India, against which vigil must be constant. Writing in 2007 in *Current History*, Haqqani describes "the perception among Pakistan's national security elite that the country is surrounded by enemies determined to dismember it. . . . Until that sense of siege is gone, it will be difficult to strengthen civilian institutions in Pakistan." Moreover, he maintains, "Pakistan's successive [military] rulers have allowed the degradation of the essential attributes of statehood."

This rivalry and its consequences coalesce to produce a venomous political situation that has existed throughout the Pakistani experience and that continues to the present. In his 2005 book, Haqqani summarizes the situation: "Pakistan is far from developing a consistent system of government, with persisting polarization among three intersecting fault lines: between civilians and the military, among various ethnic and provincial groups, and between Islamists and secularists." All three of these factors, along with a weak economy and educational system, coalesce to form the backdrop against which to assess whether—or the extent to which—Pakistan should be thought of the as the world's only current nuclear-armed failing state.

Fortunately for Pakistan and the rest of the world, no one claims that Pakistan has yet become a failed state—a country incapable of governing itself. Rather, the current author has distinguished levels of failure, from total state failure (e.g., Somalia) to various levels of approach to that status, notably "failing" and "failure-prone" states. With a ranking at the bottom of the top 10 of states on the *Foreign Policy* index, Pakistan is generally placed somewhere on the border between failing and failure prone. Three factors illustrate this status and its dangers: demographics, refugees and displaced persons, and its status as a "rentier" economy.

Some of Pakistan's problems are demographic difficulties that plague much of the Middle East: a rapidly growing, youthful population and the general lack of educational and employment opportunities to produce a satisfied, hopeful, and positive population. Cohen summarized the situation in 2004, and his depictions largely hold true today. "In the long run," he wrote, "the lack of economic activity, the booming birth rate (2.7 children per woman in 2009, according to *CIA World Factbook* figures), the youth bulge (an excessive concentration of people in their teens or younger), intensive urbanization, and a hostile regional environment could leave Pakistan with a large, young, and ill-educated population that has few prospects for economic advancement and could be politically mobilized." The educational situation is exemplary: Pakistan spent 2.6 percent of its GDP on education in 2006 (the most recent figures reported by the CIA), which ranked it 155th among the world's countries. Since most government funds are spent on defense, it is hard to imagine how much more can be diverted to education or other nonmilitary priorities. As noted, over half the population is illiterate, and the "school life expectancy" (how far the average student progresses in school) is seven years. At the micro level, the result is many young people entering the workforce educationally prepared for only the most rudimentary jobs; at the macro level, this depressed situation means that the country is gradually losing its educated elite, which cannot find appropriate employment; this loss in turn leaves Pakistan progressively behind countries like India in the pursuit of advanced industry and service professions. In 2008, the unemployment rate in Pakistan was 146th in the world.

This turmoil is increased by international religious terrorism and the refugee and internal displacement problems associated with it. The *World Almanac and Book of Facts*'s 2011 edition, for instance, cites the U.S. Committee on Refugees and Immigrants's *World Refugee Survey 2010* that there are 1,775,600 external refugees in Pakistan, mostly displaced Pashtuns from Afghanistan who have fled across the Durand Line into the frontier provinces, where they interact with both Afghan and Pakistani Taliban. Patrick Duplat, reporting in the *Huffington Post* in October 2009, says there are as many as 700,000 internally displaced persons (IDPs) in the country, principally in South Waziristan, largely the result of Pakistani Army activity in places like the Swat Valley and Bruner district to displace Taliban and Al Qaeda elements as part of Pakistan's commitment to aid the United States in its efforts in Afghanistan.

Pakistan's involvement with the United States, which is a conscious part of Pakistan's national security strategy as discussed in the next section, adds a third dimension to the problem: Pakistan's emergence as a "rentier economy."

The basic meaning of this designation is that Pakistan, like other rentier states, derives a significant part of its national income from foreign sources. The term was originally derived from the practice of deriving income from selling ("collecting rents on") the exploitation of natural resources like petroleum as a source of government income and was originally applied to Middle East and other oil producers. The concept has been extended to incorporate income derived from the provision of services for foreign providers. In the case of Pakistan, this means the provision of foreign assistance, mostly from the United States, in return for Pakistani participation in antiterrorist activities. When governments become dependent on these rents for regular operations rather than on taxes from indigenous sources, the state attains rentier status. Shaikh describes the situation as it applies to Pakistan: "Political scientists generally use the term 'rentier state' to describe states that finance more than 40 percent of their expenditures through 'revenue accrued from abroad.' Recently, the term has also come to refer to any state that hires out its services to the highest bidder. Pakistan qualifies neatly on both counts." In an Autumn 2008 *Washington Quarterly* article, Tellis reports that 57 percent of American aid has been to support antiterrorist activities, 18 percent for military procurement (mostly of American equipment), and 25 percent for economic activities. The accumulation of these dynamics leads Shaikh to depict the Pakistani economic trajectory as a "perilous voyage" in the title of his article, and the voyage could become even more dangerous in light of anti-Pakistan sentiment in the United States in the wake of the circumstances surrounding the bin Laden assassination.

Internal and external threats and conflicts exacerbate and feed into the shaky circumstances of the Pakistani state. The external threat posed by India dictates a high level of expenditure on defense, which means very limited resources are available for internal developmental purposes. Internal instability is made worse by regional differences, the turbulent relationship between the military and civilian institutions and their impact on the Pakistani polity, and economic difficulties that retard solutions to societal maladies. Internal and external aspects of instability collide in that Pakistan's concern with affecting the situation in Afghanistan largely caused it to help create (through the ISI) the Taliban, but as Afghan Taliban have become increasingly numerous in Pakistan's remote areas, they have helped strengthen and make more militant homegrown Pakistani Taliban who are unhappy with the government as well. Collaboration with the United States often makes this whole situation worse. Not only are the Americans major contributors to Pakistan's rentier status, but the actions they take against Al Qaeda and Taliban militants in Pakistan (such as drone aircraft attacks) inflame anti-American and antigovernment passions, both as violations of Pakistani sovereignty and because of "collateral damage" associated with them (casualties to uninvolved civilians who happen to be proximate to and are killed in the attacks).

ISI involvement with terrorism particularly roils the environment. As the aggregate of various intelligence assets within the country, the ISI has become a virtually autonomous player in Pakistani politics, not clearly controlled by either the military or the civilian leadership. It is famous for playing a "double game" wherein it trains and sustains terrorist groups and activities against Kashmir and India (it denies this latter) and at the same time formally cooperates with the United States in efforts to quell Taliban penetration of Afghanistan and to destroy Al Qaeda. Since the terrorist "pool" within the country is intermixed, the result is a double game that is viewed as increasingly an act of duplicity in the West.

All these factors are particularly accentuated by Pakistan's status as a nuclear power. The destabilization of a country the size of Pakistan and with its strategic location would be an international concern in any circumstances, but they gain added urgency because of the hundred or so nuclear weapons Pakistan possesses. Indeed, Pakistan is the poster child for one of the true horror scenarios that opponents of nuclear weapons proliferation often paint: the prospect that a nuclear state could destabilize to the point of being taken over by irresponsible elements who might not exercise maximum restraint in using or sharing those weapons. The nuclear minuet between India and Pakistan is arguably a secondary concern for an India more concerned with Chinese weapons, but differences like those associated with Kashmir always raise the prospects of renewed violence on the subcontinent.

What differentiates those prospects since 1998 are that both sides are nuclear armed, and thus, by definition, any future conflict between them is a potential nuclear war. That sobering fact may eventually lead the two countries to conclude they must settle their differences peacefully to avert Armageddon, but it also may not. Of possibly even greater concern—and a worry voiced as recently as the 2009 fighting in the Swat Valley—is the possibility that a nuclear weapon from the Pakistani arsenal might fall into the hands of a terrorist organization that might use it against the United States or some other Western target country.

The instability and nuclear weapons connection is even more pernicious because of connections between the two. As Allison pointed out in 2010, "Over the past eight years, as its stability and authority have become increasingly uncertain, the Pakistani government has tripled its arsenal of nuclear weapons and nuclear weapons material." That combination alone is enough to elevate Pakistan on the radar of American foreign policy concerns.

U.S.–PAKISTANI RELATIONS

Given the size, fragility, and geostrategic importance of Pakistan, some analysts have wondered publicly why Pakistan does not have a higher priority in American foreign policy, particularly in the conflict-riddled part of the world in which it is located. At the same time, the record of apparent Pakistani duplicity in the terrorism arena and sharp disagreement between the two countries in other areas leads some analysts to wonder if those relations should not be curtailed. Recent U.S. foreign policy initiatives toward Pakistan have tended to derive from actions the United States would like Pakistan to take to assist the American effort in Afghanistan, some of which have arguably negative effects both on internal Pakistani politics and on relations between the two countries. Many observers (including the late Richard Holbrooke) have argued that the United States may have its priorities inverted: that the situation in Pakistan is much more important to the United States (and the world at large) than what may happen in neighboring, and much smaller, Afghanistan. As a result, it is arguable that actions in Afghanistan should be measured in terms of their effects on Pakistan, not the other way around.

Historical and Domestic Interests

Relations between the two countries are long-standing and at least episodically quite close. This has, according to Haqqani (2005), been a quite conscious part of Pakistani policy since independence. The reason is fairly simple: "The United States was seen as the source of funding for a country that inherited only 17 percent of British India's revenue sources in 1947." According to the LOC country study, this has meant that "the economy is heavily dependent on bilateral and multilateral aid." Among the providers of that aid, the United States has always been seen a primary source that could be nurtured through policy positions such as fierce anticommunism, participation in American military arrangements like the Central Treaty Organization (CENTO), and actions such as facilitating the American approach to China in 1971. These Pakistani initiatives have often been successful and can be seen as examples of why the Pakistanis are trying hard to cooperate with American efforts along the Afghan–Pakistan (AfPak) frontier. This cooperation has, however not always worked, as Jones points out: "Pakistan's efforts to ingratiate itself with the United States have never produced long-lasting dividends."

Apparent U.S. inconstancy reflects the essentially asymmetrical nature of the relationship between the two countries. The United States, and principally American assistance, is very important to Pakistan, and that importance is continual. American interest in Pakistan, however, is more episodic and functional than it is basic and enduring. There are times, such as with regard to the Afghanistan War, in which the United States can benefit from a close relationship with Pakistan, but there are also periods when Islamabad is not central to American concerns in the world, when American interest and attention declines. The result is a greater dependence and sensitivity to American concerns by the Pakistanis than is always reciprocated. As Haqqani (in *Current History*) puts it, "Pakistan's military has historically been willing to adjust its priorities to fit within the parameters of immediate US global concerns. The purpose has been to ensure the flow of military and economic assistance from the United States."

The United States is thus critical to Pakistani foreign policy, and as long as the United States defines a prominent physical role in the region as part of its vital interests, Pakistan seems destined to remain a central object in U.S. foreign policy as well. American interest in Pakistan, on the other hand, can be thought of in two dimensions: interest in domestic dynamics in Pakistan that might affect Pakistan's stability and place in the region and world, and Pakistan's participation in the geopolitics of the region.

The United States has not had a long or sustained interest in internal affairs in Pakistan. The United States, of course, would prefer the emergence of a stable democracy in the country and has nurtured relations with prodemocratic figures like the late Benazir Bhutto, who was partially educated in the United States, but it has also been willing to work closely with Pakistan's military leaders—unless they became too oppressive and thus embarrassing to the United States. Similarly, the United States would prefer to see a more prosperous Pakistan on the grounds that such an outcome would further promote democratic growth, but it has never been willing to devote large aid commitments to that enterprise (most bilateral aid to Pakistan has been military).

Two things could, and arguably are, changing that assessment. One is evidence of internal destabilization in Pakistan as reflected in its presence on the failed state list. An important aspect of this unraveling of the Pakistani polity has been increased antigovernment militancy in the remote provinces of Pakistan—especially along the frontier with Afghanistan—accompanied by acts against the center of the country. These take on additional meaning in light of Pakistan's possession of nuclear weapons and the possibility that Pakistan's government might fall into the hands of a regime less inhibited from employing those weapons or one that might let some fall into the hands of terrorists. American concern with these dynamics is basically on hold, however, as long as the Americans are more clearly focused on neighboring Afghanistan, a fixation that tends to make the United States look upon Pakistan mostly in terms of its strategic contribution to American goals regionally.

Strategic Relations

The nature of the strategic relationship can be seen by borrowing, but rotating, the set of relationships found in Figure 5.1 regarding to India to make it focus on the United States and Pakistan, as Figure 6.1 does. The most notable change is the rotation of the matrix (Pakistan moves from a lateral to the top position) and the substitution of Afghanistan for China. The removal of China is not because China has been an insignificant player in the region or even in U.S.–Pakistani relations. China has been, after all, Pakistan's most steadfast supporter in its competition with India (possibly demonstrating the truth of the old saying that "the enemy of my enemy is my friend"). As the LOC study summarizes it, "China has perhaps been Pakistan's most consistent ally because of shared antipathies to other countries, such as India and Russia." Additionally, the United States took advantage of the China–Pakistan link to aid in its initial approach to reestablishing relations with China in 1972.

The removal of China from the figure is thus not a matter of suggesting that China is not an important factor in the relations depicted in the area, but rather it reflects at least the transient importance of Afghanistan in U.S.–Pakistani

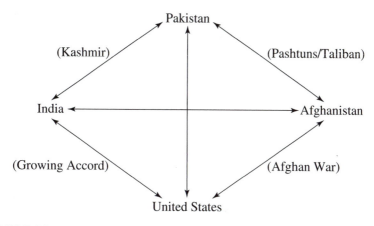

FIGURE 6.1

U.S.–Pakistani Strategic Relations

relations. Indo–Chinese relations are the key regional dynamic of southern Asia (as argued in Chapter 5), and Sino-Pakistani friendship is both a lever for Pakistan in its competition with India and a source of importance in its relations with the United States. China is not, however, a major player in the Afghanistan war that has been the geopolitical centerpiece of U.S. southwestern Asian policy, thus justifying the substitution from an American vantage point.

With these modifications in mind, the relationship is portrayed in Figure 6.1. There are, as the preceding discussion has indicated, two major flashpoints around which the strategic relationship currently revolves: Kashmir and Afghanistan. Each has a somewhat different focus. The Kashmir crisis has always been primarily an Indo-Pakistani conflict, in which the American interest is mostly in helping to keep it below the threshold of a major conflict that would affect the region (and possibly beyond) and that would affect negatively U.S. interests in access to both countries. The outcome in the Afghanistan War, on the other hand, has been defined as a primary U.S. interest (Chapter 8) in which Pakistani interests are more indirect: helping the Americans enough to keep the flow of aid coming, countering Indian (and Russian) influence in post-war Afghanistan, and dealing with the Pashtuns on both sides of the border.

Particularly within a Pakistani context, the two issues are connected because, as Rubin and Rashid point out, "the Pakistani government has turned the FATA into a staging ground for militants who can be used to conduct asymmetric warfare in both Afghanistan and Kashmir." Moreover, the Pakistani ISI has been implicated in nefarious actions on both fronts. Riedel provides an example of this, asserting "The ISI also used Afghanistan as a base for training Kashmiri terrorists." Moreover, the Musharraf government drew a comparison between the two situations that was arguably self-serving. As Haqqani (2007) summarizes it, "Musharraf's government continued to make a distinction between 'terrorists' (a term applied to Al Qaeda members, mainly of foreign origin) and 'freedom fighters' (the official preferred label for Kashmiri militants)."

The Kashmir situation has already been described in Chapter 5 and thus is a discussion that does not need to be reiterated here. In the context of American–Pakistani relations, however, it is primarily important because of the impact of Kashmir on Pakistan and its perception of the world. For the Pakistanis, Kashmir is the most visible of the existential threats that it faces from India. In turn, this concern creates a focus on possible military conflict with the Indians that makes necessary, at least in the minds of the Pakistanis, large expenditures on defense that might otherwise be devoted to other, internal priorities. This emphasis, however, has the positive side effect, according to the LOC study, that "opposition to India is often a greater source of social cohesion than either Islam or Urdu." As the United States has moved closer to India and become more committed to a non-Taliban outcome in Afghanistan, this has even helped contribute to greater strategic paranoia in Islamabad because, as Rubin and Rashid report, "The Pakistani security establishment believes that it faces a U.S.-Indian-Afghan alliance and a separate Iranian-Russian alliance."

Keeping the Kashmir conflict below the threshold of armed violence between the two subcontinent states is also important because of the conceivable nuclear connection. Since both countries publicly tested and acknowledged their nuclear weapons status, they have, after all, come to blows, and Kashmir was the cause. The so-called Kargil War of 1999 was not a major conflict. It erupted over a conflict over the so-called Kargil Ridge along the line of control, and in fighting between May 8 and July 4 of that year, 524 Indian and 696 Pakistani military personnel were killed. The world, however, held its collective breath over the possibility that it might have somehow been transformed into something far worse. The 2001 attack on the Indian parliament and the 2006 Mumbai terrorist attack (for which India blames Pakistan-trained terrorists) have kept relations tense.

The outcome of the Afghan War is also part of this strategic calculus and reflects a concern that is seldom raised specifically in American discussions of preferred outcomes to that war. Historically, India and Pakistan have been involved in Afghan politics because each favors a different kind of Afghan balance of power. Because of the Pashtun connection on both sides of the Durand Line, the Pakistanis favor a pro-Pashtun solution on the grounds that an Afghanistan ruled by the Pashtuns is more likely to be friendly to Pakistan than a government ruled by others. The Indians, on the other hand, prefer a diametrically opposed situation. During the civil war between 1996 and 2001 in Afghanistan, the Indians favored the Northern Alliance, a coalition dominated by non-Pashtun groups like the Tajiks, over the Pashtun Taliban on the grounds that such a government would be friendlier to India than a Pashtun/Taliban-dominated regime. During the pre-American phase of Afghanistan's struggle, the Northern Alliance "had been supported by India, Iran, and Russia," according to Rubin and Rashid, adding to the geopolitical intrigues of the conflict. What kind of government eventually prevails in Afghanistan will thus obviously have implications for both the Indians and the Pakistanis, and while this concern is and should not be more important to the United States than the question of what kind of government the Afghans themselves prefer, it is clearly part of the regional geopolitical calculus that seldom enters American public discussions of preferred outcomes. If, however, Pakistan is really more important to the United States than Afghanistan, as suggested earlier in this section, possibly it should be.

American and Pakistani interests in Afghanistan come into operational conflict. From an American military standpoint, one of the major barriers to success against the Taliban is the Taliban's ability to slip freely across the Durand Line that serves as the international boundary between Afghanistan and Pakistan. The Pashtuns live on either side of this boundary, which was created at least partially to divide the Pashtun "nation" into two different political jurisdictions, is not recognized by natives on either side and has traditionally been extremely porous and unregulated by either country. Being able to move freely across the frontier, however, creates a Pakistani safe haven for the Taliban into which the Americans cannot enter without violating Pakistani sovereignty and worsening a major breach between Islamabad and Washington already raw because of U.S. drone intrusions into Pakistan in pursuit of Al Qaeda and Taliban targets. The Pakistani people are especially sensitive to any hints of the violation of their territory by the Americans in pursuit of American Afghan interests, and thus any initiatives that even conceivably involve American infringement on Pakistani soil are roundly condemned politically in Pakistan and add fodder to the recruitment efforts among Pakistanis to oppose the Americans in the guise of either the Taliban or Al Qaeda.

The disagreement that emerges from the American incursion into Pakistan to kill Usama bin Laden in May 2011 illustrates these tensions. On one hand, Americans find it incredible that bin Laden could have hidden openly in his Abbottabad compound surrounded by active-duty and retired Pakistani military personnel for over five years without being noticed. The failure to share information or suspicions struck many Americans as evidence of Pakistani duplicity in their antiterrorist commitment at best and as a sign of being in league with the terrorists at worst. Those who argue the Pakistanis must have known about bin Laden's presence but did not share this intelligence with the United States conclude that Pakistan is an unreliable ally that does not deserve continuing American support. The Pakistanis do not enter into this discussion directly beyond denying they knew of bin Laden's whereabouts. Rather, they express what has been an ongoing dismay over American violation of sovereign Pakistani territory by the American raiders.

The brouhaha reflects the convoluted and delicate politics of Pakistan and U.S.–Pakistani relations. While it strains credulity to maintain no Pakistani officials knew of bin Laden's presence, it is not hard to imagine that knowledge was compartmentalized and not broadly shared within the Pakistani government. As part of its "double game," for instance, it is easy to imagine that the ISI knew of bin Laden's sanctuary but withheld that information from civilian authorities it holds in disdain (the case is more complex and ambiguous about knowledge by the military). U.S. retribution against Pakistan in the form of withdrawing assistance would likely affect the civilian regime most, and this is the sector the United States hopes to nurture and which was least likely to have been culpable. Protestations about violations of sovereignty are mostly sops to Pakistani public opinion, which has become heavily anti-American in recent years.

The American solution to this delicate, complex situation is to demand that the Pakistanis attempt to seal the border or at least to make traversing it more difficult for the Taliban, as well as becoming more diligent in the pursuit of terrorists (both of which reduce the need for direct American action on Pakistani soil). Because of its dependence on the United States for military assistance and as a partner in its geopolitical struggle with India, the Pakistani government cannot simply dismiss these demands out of hand, but neither can it enthusiastically or effectively honor them. For one thing, the government, mostly through the ISI, has been a prime sponsor of the Taliban, with which it has considerable interconnections that is does not really want to sever. Moreover, Riedel argues of their sponsorship and continued relationship with the Taliban, "Pakistan's army and the ISI have created a monster that, at best, they only partially control, and that has come increasingly to see Pakistan's government as the enemy as much as a benefactor." In recent years, there has been some overt political violence directed against Pakistan from the remote provinces along the frontier, and the Pakistanis are thus reluctant to take actions that might lead to greater political destabilization of the country. Since the Taliban and Al Qaeda have some common bonds, all this plays into the double game as well.

Beyond the political dynamics of turning on a movement it helped spawn, the Pakistani armed forces are, unfortunately, neither enthused nor well equipped for major actions in the frontier provinces. First, the Pakistani armed forces are configured for European-style heavy warfare on the relatively flat plains along the Indo-Pakistani border in the Punjab, and they have neither the equipment nor the training for the mountainous terrain or asymmetrical tactics employed by the Taliban. As a result, their forays into these venues have not been startling tactical successes. Moreover, the Pakistani military leadership is and always has been focused primarily on the military threat posed by India and is reluctant to see its resources diverted to other priorities in which it has less interest and which it considers less important.

Beyond these military considerations is a fundamental political conflict within Pakistan as well. Part of the de facto bargain that the government in Islamabad has historically had with the NWFP, the FATA, and other remote parts of Pakistan principally along its borders with Afghanistan is that the government grants essential autonomy from the central government in return for those territories not demanding resources or disturbing the politics of the Punjabi-controlled parts of the country. Joining the United States in its efforts to close down the cross-border flow (or suppress Al Qaeda wholeheartedly) requires the central government to establish an increased presence and assertion of authority in areas that would abrogate those de facto arrangements. Such change would create almost certainly adverse reactions in the affected areas, including civil violence the government does not need—given its basically fragile state—and which it is not especially well equipped to counter. Yet the United States' insistence that the Pakistanis assert control over these areas deemed vital to American interests could have the unanticipated consequence of further destabilizing Pakistan, which is also clearly not in America's interests.

The result of all these Afghan imperatives is a standoff between the two countries that has not proven easy to resolve. At least arguably, the fulcrum of disagreement is the balance between American interests in Afghanistan and Pakistan. The United States would, of course, prefer to pursue policies that would leave both countries strong, stable, and solidly in the column of countries that resist the influence of Islamic religious terrorism, but at the operational level, doing so is problematic at best and fundamentally incompatible at worst. It may come down to an American determination of, if it cannot have a favorable outcome in both Afghanistan and Pakistan, in which of the two and toward which goal it would prefer to concentrate its efforts.

U.S. OPTIONS

Unlike American policy considerations with many other countries, U.S.–Pakistani relations occur without a major influence of American domestic politics in one direction or the other. The historical ties between the two countries only go back a little more than 60 years since the founding of Pakistan, and they have never been intimate, limiting the extent to which there is any ingrained American interest in the disposition—there is, in other words, no "Pakistan lobby" to be confronted when policy changes are contemplated. Moreover, there is not the kind or quality of Pakistani expatriate community in the United States that there is for a country like India, furthering limiting any domestic political considerations about dealing with the country. This also means, of course, that Pakistan does not have many champions of its interests in the United States. Domestic politics are thus not a major consideration in making policy toward Pakistan. Pakistan is one of those places where the "experts" are fairly free to fashion policy with little concern for the political fallout their advocacy might produce.

One of the results of this has been that the United States has never developed, in the words of former U.S. ambassador Ryan Crocker, "a long-term, strategic commitment in the country." The reason for this situation, on which most observers concur, is that the United States has never had the kind of ongoing, inherent interests in Pakistan to require it to develop such an approach. One of the fallouts of this situation has been to frustrate Pakistan's achievement of a steady, constant flow of American resources as part of its strategic approach to the world. In Jones' words noted earlier, "Pakistan's efforts to ingratiate itself with the United States" have not succeeded in creating a long-term, stable strategic relationship.

Pakistan appears more prominent in current American policy than it often is because of the Pakistani implications of American efforts in Afghanistan and against Al Qaeda, but will these have a lasting, positive impact on those relations? There are at least two reasons to believe they will not. The first is historical and has been asserted: the United States becomes interested in Pakistan when it needs something from that country, and when that transient need passes, interest wanes. Currently, the United States has an interest in Pakistani activism in sealing its border to the Taliban and rooting out Al Qaeda, but will that interest transcend the end of American involvement in Afghanistan or the end of the war against terror (admittedly a more distant prospect)? Historical precedent suggests it will not. The second is the fact that American demands appear to be not very sensitive to Pakistan's own situation and may be demands with which the Pakistanis can comply only by acting in self-destructive ways that are also not in America's best interests. Until the United States formulates and articulates a comprehensive strategy for the region that is sensitive to the needs and realities of all regional states, it is hard to imagine how a country like Pakistan can be an enthusiastic partner of the United States.

These factors affect the options the United States has toward Pakistan. What is currently being asked of Pakistan is to act in ways that rather clearly have two important, negative potential consequences. One of these is an impact on Pakistan's role in global opposition to international religious terrorism. If Pakistan acts aggressively along its side of the Durand Line, one possible consequence could be to stimulate internal opposition, including opposition from groups with terrorist predilections, against itself. Admitting that Pakistan is itself at least partially responsible for creating this situation, that kind of outcome does not serve American, much less Pakistani, interests, and the Pakistanis know it. As Haqqani (2007) argues, "Given Pakistan's position as a critical ally in the war against terrorism, neither the United States nor other Western nations are likely to apply serious pressure" on the government. The other negative is the perils associated with Pakistan's nuclear weapons and the danger that destabilization could loosen the government's control of the arsenal. Allison states the prospect starkly: "If Pakistan were to lose control of even one nuclear weapon that was ultimately used by terrorists, that [event] would change the world."

These dire possibilities are, of course, tied to the delicate internal situation in which Pakistan exists—its status as a potential failed state. Pakistan emerges from any detailed analysis as a place that is inherently more important than it is given credit for being and as a place that needs to be dealt with on its own terms rather than as an instrument for achieving other goals. Until such a debate occurs and is applied directly to the dialogue between the United States and Pakistan, it is hard to see how either side can formulate or execute mutually beneficial options toward the other.

CONCLUSIONS

The United States and Pakistan find themselves in a quandary of sorts, and one that has been accentuated by the circumstances surrounding the assassination of bin Laden on Pakistani soil. These long-time but still distant partners are currently locked in an arrangement focusing on Pakistan's neighbor Afghanistan, a state in which they have quite different interests but in which they are officially tied to an apparently common outcome (realizable or not). Because the United States is the dominant partner in this arrangement and because of Pakistani dependence on the United States for military assistance, the Pakistanis have had to sublimate their own interests to those of the United States. Washington's improving relations with India and Pakistan's fear that resistance to American desires will push the United States closer to New Delhi and further from Islamabad help impel Pakistan down a path that it would almost surely not want to travel in the absence of American pressure. Among the potential consequences that obeisance to the United States may create is further destabilization of the fragile political situation in Pakistan, a possibility that should concern the United States as much as, if not far more than, its hopes in Afghanistan.

The result is indeed a quandary for both sides. The Pakistanis are, to some degree, trapped in their slippery history of having created a Taliban monster for Afghanistan that has become a potential threat to them as well, with one jaw of the trap the pursuit of their interest in a weak, pro-Pakistani Afghanistan and the other jaw support for American efforts to destroy the very instrument they have chosen to further their own, contradictory goals in Afghanistan. The result has been tepid support for American policy that is, by and large, opposed by the Pakistanis because it encourages American forays into Pakistan in support of destroying the Taliban and Al Qaeda. The dilemma is illustrated by reports that the Pakistanis provide intelligence information to the Americans about potential Taliban and Al Qaeda targets within the remote areas of the frontier area, and after these reports are acted upon by the United States in terms of air attacks, the Pakistani government feels the need to condemn those attacks to assuage its own population. It is an important dilemma for a Pakistani government whose political base is shaky anyway; the fact that the situation is partly of Pakistan's own making does not remove American actions as a catalyst of negative reactions within Pakistan. The fact that the United States found out about and acted on information about bin Laden without Pakistani assistance or knowledge is a variant of this pattern; since there were no Pakistani "fingerprints" on cooperation, they have felt freer to criticize it than in more typical collaborations.

Pakistan and Pakistani–American relations have difficulties and challenges beyond Afghanistan, of course, but the current impasse in Afghanistan illustrates the convoluted, contradictory nature of relations and the apparent inability of the United States to come directly to grips with its policy and the consequences of that policy with a nuclear-armed state that has the world's sixth largest population and that continues to demonstrate some of the characteristics of a failed state. American policy makers acknowledge that Pakistan is in trouble and that its difficulties could become far more important to the United States than almost anywhere in the Islamic Middle East. Yet, until (or unless) they do, American attention is riveted elsewhere, with Pakistan viewed as a supporting actor, not the central character of regional foreign policy.

As the spate of antigovernment actions that began in Tunisia in January 2011 and spread quickly to Egypt and around the Islamic world demonstrated, resistance to ongoing governance in that part of the world is not impossible; the hold that governments have is tenuous; and American friends may be as vulnerable as anyone else. When the United States has tied its star to autocrats whose credentials were limited to support of the United States and opposition to fundamentalist Islamists, the very real risk for the United States is ending up on the wrong side of the history of those countries once their convulsions conclude. Pakistan eluded direct involvement in the round of 2011 revolutions, but their shadow hung ominously over the scene, and Pakistan may not be so lucky the next time around. Whether the United States will be part of the problem or the solution as this dynamic unfolds is uncertain, and it may ultimately boil down to a question of whether the United States decides that Pakistan is important enough in itself to be assigned a Pakistan-based policy that both supports American and Pakistani interests. If the United States really thinks Pakistan is as important as Washington often says it is, such a reorientation would seem both necessary and foresighted.

STUDY/DISCUSSION QUESTIONS

1. How has the Pakistani experience surrounding the partition of the Asian subcontinent been distinctive? What ongoing problems arose from that experience? Elaborate.
2. Describe the "idea of Pakistan." What problems have been associated with the implementation of that idea?
3. What makes Pakistan a unique state? Discuss the individual factors that comprise that uniqueness.
4. Why is Pakistan important to the United States? Discuss this importance in regional geopolitical terms, including Kashmir and Afghanistan as prominent parts of the equation.
5. Why is Afghanistan such an important symbol and lightning rod of U.S.–Pakistan relations? How does this issue illustrate the basic tensions in that relationship?
6. The text suggests that U.S.–Pakistani relations are asymmetrical in nature. What does that assertion mean? How does this dynamic of the relationship condition the ability of the two countries to influence one another?
7. What is the "double game" that Pakistan has been accused of playing with the United States? Relate the American operation to eliminate Usama bin Laden to this dynamic.
8. In your view, does the United States undervalue Pakistan as a regional actor and thus underemphasize U.S.–Pakistan relations? What is more important to the United States in the long run, a pro-American Afghanistan or a stable Pakistan? Are these goals compatible with one another? If not, which one is more important to the United States? What are the implications of your assessment for U.S.–Pakistan relations?

READING/RESEARCH MATERIALS

Allison, Graham. "Nuclear Disorder: Surveying Atomic Threats." *Foreign Affairs* 89, 1 (January/February 2010), 74–85.

Birdsall, Nancy, Wren Elhai, and Molly Kinder. "Pakistan's Political Crisis: The Limits of U.S. Leverage." *Foreign Policy* (online), January 23, 2011.

Cohen, Stephen Philip. *The Idea of Pakistan.* Washington, DC: Brookings Institution Press, 2004.

————. "Shooting for a Century: The India-Pakistan Conundrum." *Current History* 110, 735 (April 2011), 162–164.

Crocker, Ryan. "Pakistan Is Not America's Enemy." *Wall Street Journal* (online), October 12, 2010.

Duplat, Patrick. "Pakistan: Inconvenient Truths." *Huffington Post* (online). October 29, 2009.

"Failed States." Crisis Watch Workshop. London, March 2006. http://www .crisisstates/download.drc/failedstate.pdf.

"The Failed State Index." *Foreign Policy* (July/August 2008), 64–73.

"The Failed State Index: FAQ and Methodology." *Foreign Policy* (online), July 2009. http://foreignpolicy.com/articles/2009/06/22/2009_failed_state_index_faq_ methodo . . .

Fair, C. Christina. "Pakistan's Security-Governance Challenge." *Current History* 110, 735 (April 2011), 136–142.

Haqqani, Husain. *Pakistan between Mosque and Military.* Washington, DC: Carnegie Endowment for International Peace Press, 2005.

————. "Pakistan and the Islamists." *Current History* 106, 699 (April 2007), 147–152.

Helman, Gerald B., and Steven B. Ratner. "Saving Failed States." *Foreign Policy* 89 (Winter 1992/1993), 3–20.

Hussein, Zahid. *Frontline Pakistan: The Struggle with Militant Islam.* New York: Columbia University Press, 2007.

Jones, Owen Barnett. *Pakistan: Eye of the Storm.* New Haven, CT: Yale University Press, 2002.

Khan, M. Asghar. *We've Learned Nothing from History: Pakistan: Politics and Military Power.* Oxford, UK: Oxford University Press, 2005.

Library of Congress. *Pakistan: A Country Profile.* Washington, DC: Library of Congress, 2007.

Riedel, Bruce. "Pakistan: The Critical Battleground." *Current History* 107, 712 (November 2008), 355–361.

Rubin, Barnett R., and Ahmed Rashid. "From Great Game to Great Bargain: Ending Chaos in Afghanistan and Pakistan." *Foreign Affairs* 87, 6 (November/December 2008), 30–42.

Shaikh, Farzana. "Pakistan's Perilous Voyage." *Current History* 107, 712 (November 2008), 362–368.

Snow, Donald M. *Cases in International Relations* (fifth edition). New York: Pearson Longman, 2012, especially Chapter 15.

Tellis, Ashley J. "The Merits of Dehyphenization: Explaining U.S. Success in Engaging India and Pakistan." *Washington Quarterly* 32, 4 (Autumn 2009), 21–42.

————. "Pakistan's Record on Terrorism: Conflicted Goals, Compromised Performance." *Washington Quarterly* 31, 2 (April 2008), 7–32.

The Legacies of 9/11

The signature international event and foreign policy imperative of the early twenty-first century was an act of violence—the terrorist attacks of September 11, 2011 against U.S. targets in New York and Washington, D.C. The policy responses to them, both domestically and in terms of foreign policy direction and mandate, overwhelmed all other areas of concern. Among most enduring long-term effects of those attacks has been a lasting, consuming relationship between the United States and two countries, Iraq and Afghanistan. Both are countries with which the United States historically has had minor relations, but events and dynamics arising from the American reaction to September 11 impelled the United States to undertake major, long-term military actions that dominated American foreign policy for the decade of the 2000s and beyond. The paths to, reasons for, and endings of these wars have not been identical, and indeed, the ultimate outcome of each remains in some dispute as events unfold. In Afghanistan, the United States initially intervened in an internal war in late 2001 because the Afghan government harbored and refused to surrender to American authority the terrorists who had planned and executed the terrorist attacks, and American participation continues despite the virtual departure of Al Qaeda from the country (CIA estimates in 2011, for instance, suggested there were probably less than 100 Al Qaeda operatives active in the country); Afghanistan is now the longest war in American history. Iraq vies with Vietnam as the second longest war in the American experience, depending on how one defines active combat status. The Iraq War is different, however: rather than intervening in an ongoing conflict, the United States started the war there by its invasion of Iraq and remained in occupation for over eight-and-a-half years, an involvement now winding down (the last U.S. combat forces left Iraq at the end of 2011).

The two wars have created similar relationships with the United States, and the fact of a long American occupation of each has defined relations in the 2000s and will cast a shadow over U.S. foreign policy toward each in the 2010s and probably beyond. The American occupation of Iraq was the more encompassing, since the United States overthrew the existing government in 2003 when it invaded and only slowly returned power over time. The fact that the United States was an invading power will affect the future of U.S.–Iraqi relations and help to define the major postoccupation conditions in Iraq and in the region, as well as American relations with the country. Internally, Iraq must resolve somehow the triangular rivalry among its largest population segments, the Shia and Sunni Arabs and the Kurds. Internationally, it must define its relationship with Iran and thus the rest of the oil-producing Middle East.

The situation in Afghanistan is both similar and different. One source of similarity is the fact of occupation and its aftermath, and the greatest internal problems facing postoccupation Afghanistan is how to reconcile historically rival ethnic and tribal groups, a problem that has never been satisfactorily accomplished in Afghan history. The outcome of the internal struggle (essentially the outcome of the civil war between the Karzai government and the Taliban) will in turn affect the primary international problem posed by Afghanistan, which is the status of Al Qaeda after the Americans and their allies depart.

The contrasts and similarities extend to other dimensions of foreign policy concern. Although the United States managed to cobble together a "coalition of the willing" to assist it in Iraq and managed to gain some support (*not* including the authorization to employ military force) through United Nations Security Council Resolutions (UNSCRs) undermining Iraqi leader Saddam Hussein, the Iraq War was, and still remains, effectively an American operation justified as an application of the Bush doctrine, in which unilateralism (defined as acting without international approval when such action is deemed necessary on national security grounds) is a central tenet. Because the Al Qaeda attacks were planned and directed from Afghan bases protected by the Afghan Taliban government, there was an overwhelming international consensus behind military action there, exemplified by UNSCRs and eventually implemented by the NATO-run International Security Advisory Force (ISAF). In both cases, international support has gradually eroded as the long occupations of each country continued without decisive results.

The domestic political reaction to each has followed a pattern as well. At the outset, there was considerable, if differing, support for each. Because of the Al Qaeda connection, military action in Afghanistan was overwhelmingly supported with virtually no dissent as the opening salvo of the war against terror, and that support remained steadfast even after the United States failed in its primary mission of dismantling Al Qaeda in late 2001. As the Afghanistan conflict moved toward its status as the country's longest war, the American aversion to long (and particularly to indecisive) wars and the ambiguity of both American objectives and accomplishments acted to erode support. Initial high levels of support (although mixed with some dissent born of suspicion regarding claims against Iraq and the feasibility of the mission) about invading Iraq eroded more quickly as the rationales for the invasion proved to be increasingly suspect and the unpopularity of the occupation among Iraqis was manifested in a mounting Iraqi demand that it be ended.

U.S. relations with these two countries is thus unique in the recent American experience, with the United States having to construct a foreign policy toward countries that it has physically occupied against their apparent will and in which it has few historic interests. U.S. occupations are not unique: the United States occupied its former World War II enemies and several Latin American states, but these were places where the U.S. had clear interests before and after those occupations. The postoccupation status of neither Iraq or Afghanistan in American policy is so clear, and it is entirely possible that the reaction to a decade (the 2000s) of war as the primary dynamic of foreign policy will be replaced by an era in which other, less violent and geopolitical priorities may become more prominent, as many foreign policy analysts have predicted and championed.

Iraq: Making the Best of the Aftermath of a Controversial War and Occupation

PREVIEW

The United States and Iraq have undergone traumatic changes in their relationship across time. Prior to 1979, their relations were basically nonexistent, but they gradually broadened and intensified in the quarter-century afterward, culminating in the American invasion, conquest, and occupation of Iraq between 2003 and 2011. That period made Iraq a virtual colony of the United States, and the United States has struggled with how to try to create an Iraq that lacks the conditions that led the Bush administration to take the drastic step of war in 2003. Iraq, however, remains a complex, difficult place with which to deal, and the withdrawal of American forces leaves unanswered important questions about Iraq's future status as a country and as a participant in the international politics of the Middle East. The United States has limited leverage over how postoccupation Iraq evolves on both domestic and international levels.

A 1980s fast food commercial featured an older lady holding up the hamburger from a competing chain and asking in a clearly invidious tone, "Where's the beef?" Someone who looked at the relationship between Iraq and the United States across the sweep of American history might similarly ask, "What's the beef?" suggesting that it was incongruous that two such distant and disparate countries could come sufficiently into conflict for one to invade, conquer, and occupy the other for eight-and-a-half years in what amounts to a modern colonial relationship. And yet that is exactly what happened in 2003, when the United States declared war on Iraq.

Aside from being halfway around the world from one another, the two countries could scarcely be more different. Like a number of the other countries included in this survey, the roots of modern Iraq are ancient. Some argue that the roots of civilization date back to the earliest settlers of the "fertile crescent" between the Tigris and Euphrates Rivers (a part of contemporary Iraq), and the lands have been in contention ever since. While much of the time the area that is now Iraq has been the victim of its neighbors, it was also the site of Mesopotamia and the redoubt of Nebuchadnezzar II, who ruled in the sixth century BCE and is most famous for the hanging gardens of Babylon, an engineering feat he allegedly built to keep his young wife amused.

Iraq emerged as at least a nominally independent modern country in 1932, following centuries of Ottoman rule and a 12-year British mandate over the country granted by the League of Nations in 1920. The area has only occasionally been referred to as Iraq (from the Persian word *eraqh*, which means "the lowlands", according to Polk), and its territory and boundaries are almost entirely artificial (not unusually for Middle Eastern states) and arbitrary. As constructed from the ruins of the defeated Ottoman Empire at the end of World War I, the country contained at least three distinct ethnolinguistic groups that had been historically at odds with one another, and those three groups remain the focus of the difficulty of constructing a stable Iraqi state today.

For most of its history, the United States took no interest in or notice of Iraq. Indeed, the first formal contact noted by Polk occurred on the eve of World War II, when an American envoy counseled the rulers of Iraq to ensure British rather than German access to the budding oil industry of the country. American interest in the country did not resurface until well after World War II, when Iraq and its oil became an apparently important component in the Cold War competition with the Soviet Union. Even at that, American interests in the country were relatively minor, mostly concerned with trying to assure that American oil companies were not excluded from the Iraqi oil reserves. Indeed, as Polk describes it, "securing the flow of oil from the Middle East on acceptable terms has been a fundamental American government objective for half a century." Iraq became interesting to the United States because it possessed oil; otherwise, there is little reason to believe that an interest would have arisen.

The watershed for American interest in Iraq was 1979, a year which, as noted in Chapters 3, 6, and 8, was pivotal in defining continuing American involvement in the Persian Gulf region as a whole and a year of monumental importance in the Middle East generally. The events that would draw the United States deeply into the region's politics began with the overthrow of the shah of Iran and his gradual replacement with a militantly anti-American Islamic Republic of Iran. At the risk of some oversimplification, this event was important for two basic reasons. First and most importantly from an American vantage point, it meant that the United States no longer had a reliable, powerful ally in the region that could and would militarily enforce American (and other Western) access to Persian Gulf oil, a predicament that was directly related to the American decision to expand its permanent military presence in the region. Second, since revolutionary Iran was both Shiite and non-Arab, its emergence as a militant evangel of change was seen as an increasingly dire threat to the generally smaller, weaker oil-rich states of the Persian Gulf littoral, almost all of which had Sunni Arab majorities but relied on imported Shiite workforces to extract their fabulous wealth. Since those regimes rarely shared much of that wealth with their Shiite populations, these minorities were seen as a potential source of destabilization in the region, with revolutionary Iran acting as the catalyst for subversive activity. Although it possessed a population less than half that of Iran, neighboring Iraq, with a Shiite Arab majority but ruled by Sunni Arabs, seemed the logical counterweight and shield against Iranian expansionism in the Gulf, a dynamic embraced by the Americans as well as the Arab oil states the United States supported and on whose oil it depended.

Two other events occurred in the region in 1979 that would influence the future of U.S.–Iraqi relations directly or indirectly. Although hardly noted at the time, on July 16, 1979, an obscure (at least to the West) Iraqi Army colonel named Saddam Hussein emerged from one of Iraq's periodic governmental upheavals as the new Iraqi strongman. Employing methods that resonate through Iraqi history, Hussein gradually consolidated power until he was one of the most powerful, feared, and eventually hated leaders in a region not exactly known for endearing leaderships. Second, the Soviet Union invaded and occupied neighboring Afghanistan over Christmas 1979, thereby raising the salience of the whole region for the United States (see Chapter 8).

These were, it should be noted in passing, not the only important regional events of 1979. Of arguably equal importance to the overall region, Israel and Egypt followed up the Camp David meeting of 1978 by signing a peace treaty in 1979, a prominent part of the equation discussed in Part VI of the text. Radical Muslims attacked and seized the Grand Mosque in Pakistan, and Pakistani radicals attacked and burned the U.S. embassy in Islamabad, that same year. All these were seminal events, but in terms of U.S. policy toward Iraq, the political changes in Iran and Iraq provide the clearest link to U.S.–Iraqi policy evolution.

Emboldened by the apparent wreckage of the Iranian military by its revolution (e.g., most of its officer corps either fled the country or was jailed or executed), Saddam Hussein began a military campaign against Iran in 1980. In a harbinger of miscalculations to come in Iraq, Polk maintains that part of Hussein's calculation was that the Iranians were in such disarray that he could defeat them easily—apparently in three months or less—but that estimate (like a similar one made by U.S. Secretary of Defense Donald Rumsfeld in 2003) proved tragically overoptimistic. The war between Iraq and Iran dragged on for eight inconclusive years, during which champions of both sides ensured that neither country would be defeated decisively or could win decisively. During the war, the United States was one of the countries that helped keep the Iraqis going with military assistance, a practice that continued in the immediate years after the war ended. In 1988, the war ended as a stalemate but left behind a bitter heritage that continued long thereafter.

One aspect of the Iran–Iraq War's legacy was the use of weapons of mass destruction (WMDs) by Saddam Hussein against his own population, notably the 1988 use of chemical weapons against Iraqi Kurds in Halabja, an attack that left nearly 5,000 dead. The incident marked the first occasion since the Holocaust when such weapons were employed against a country's own civilian population (the Iraqis also used chemical weapons against the Iranians), and it established Saddam Hussein as a political leader who would indeed defy taboos against such weapons.

Of more immediate importance to the Iraqis themselves, the war virtually bankrupted the country. One of the enticing factors underlying Saddam's decision to attack Iran in the first place had been his conviction that his fellow Arab states would be grateful for his efforts and that their gratitude would extend to underwriting Iraq's military efforts. Among those countries that had responded initially were tiny Kuwait and Saudi Arabia, both of which lent Saddam Hussein substantial amounts of money, the disposition of which did not, however, live up to their expectations. As a result, when the war ended and Hussein beseeched them for more funds to rebuild Iraq and for extensions on or cancellations of loan obligations, they turned an increasingly deaf ear to those requests. As conditions worsened in Iraq itself and his former benefactors refused to intercede on his behalf, Hussein worried progressively about whether his regime could survive the aftermath of the war.

The result was a process that eventuated in the Persian Gulf War of 1990–1991, a clash that brought the United States and Iraq into direct conflict for the first time. The crisis centered on tiny, oil-rich Kuwait and its refusal to come to Hussein's aid. The Iraqi leader, in Polk's words, "first appealed to Arab brotherhood, next he pleaded, then he threatened, and finally he invaded" Kuwait. His rationales for the invasion included Kuwait's refusal to lighten Iraq's wartime debt, Kuwaiti collusion with other Organization of Petroleum Exporting Countries (OPEC) members in driving down the cost of crude oil that represented Iraq's only apparent pathway to economic solvency, Kuwaiti "poaching" of oil from the Rumallah oil fields through a process known as "slant drilling" (drilling for oil at an angle downward beneath a frontier into oil pools not under their territory), and the claim that Kuwait was indeed rightfully a part of Iraq (the part of Kuwait bordering on the Persian Gulf was referred to as the "nineteenth province" of Iraq by the Iraqi regime). This latter claim had more historical validity than it is generally accorded, as the British mandate separated territory that even most Kuwaitis conceded was rightfully Iraqi before the 1950s, when oil was discovered in the region and transformed Kuwait from a dusty Arab outpost to one of the world's richest countries.

The Iraqi army, hardened by its eight years of fighting Iran, had no difficulty conquering and occupying Kuwait, and in so doing, Hussein placed his armies directly across the frontier from the far richer and more significant prize in the region—Saudi Arabia. At that point, however, Saddam had made or would make two enormous mistakes that doomed his venture and began the road to the American invasion in 2003.

The first mistake was prior to his invasion and involved miscalculating the nature of the Western response to his actions, which in turn involved two sequential errors. One of these was his belief that the West would be indifferent to what, in geopolitical terms, amounted to little more than an internal adjustment of Arab boundaries that virtually everyone agreed had been arbitrarily and poorly drawn as the West exited the region physically in the interwar years. Further, there was some support for the Iraqi contention that Kuwait was really a part of Iraq anyway. The United States reinforced this belief by informing the Iraqis that it had little interest in Arab boundary disputes and their disposition, which Hussein took as giving him a green light in dealing with the Kuwaitis. This indifference disappeared as the United Nations rose in righteous indignation at the first cross-border invasion and occupation of a member state by another when the Iraqis moved into Kuwait, thereby triggering a United Nations response under Articles VI and VII of the UN Charter. At the same time, Saddam's actions aroused Western interests that required a forceful response. As Polk argues, "Saddam . . . put his hand on two things that the Great Powers would not tolerate: oil and money."

After the initial invasion, Hussein made another critical blunder that helped pave the way to his ultimate defeat. Once he had entered Kuwait, he had essentially three options about how to proceed. One option was simply to occupy and annex those areas along the Iraq–Kuwait border where Kuwait had been illegally poaching oil and along the coastline (notably Bubiyan Island) to establish greater Iraqi access to the Persian Gulf. Given general acknowledgement of Kuwaiti misdeeds and ambiguity about the border established in 1920, the international community would likely have acceded to his conquest with little more than sanctions. A second option, once the first had been discarded, would have been to drive south from Kuwait into Saudi Arabia, gaining control over the Saudi oil fields and refining industries. In the immediate wake of the invasion, before American and other forces were moved into position to thwart such a military action, he would likely have physically succeeded and placed his forces in an impregnable position, since they could have been dislodged only by attacking them in the oil fields and destroying those fields. In these circumstances, the Saudis might well have negotiated with Saddam, forgiving his debt and issuing additional credits in return for his withdrawal, an outcome the international community likely would also have accepted, if not embraced.

He chose the third option, which was to occupy and annex all of Kuwait. This decision was the only outcome that was virtually certain to elicit an international response, and it did. The annexation violated the UN Charter, guaranteeing a UN-sponsored opposition, and it also violated unwritten codes of behavior in the region, which maintained that the physical 1920 borders, while not immutable, could not be changed by force. As a result, a formidable coalition of 32 states led by the United States was assembled under the UN banner and imprimatur, in which Arab states, normally reluctant to endorse Western intrusion, became members. This coalition came together in the Saudi desert during the remainder of 1990, and starting in January 1991, it moved decisively to evict the Iraqis from Kuwait. This task was completed in April 1991, setting the stage for subsequent Iraqi international relations, especially with the United States.

IRAQ: A SKETCH

The 1990s was a traumatic decade for Iraq, especially in its increasingly hostile relations with the United States. In the immediate aftermath of the war, the Hussein regime had to deal with a two-sided insurrection against the regime that had begun while the war was still ongoing, and its handling of those uprisings helped cement its position as a rogue state in the region and world more generally. Part of the response was the imposition of crippling sanctions against the regime, and the pariah status with which the regime was increasingly saddled was further reinforced by actions it allegedly took and by accusations that it remained active in the WMD arena. All of these factors helped fuel the engine of a movement in the United States to take decisive action against Iraq.

The war and Iraq's defeat energized movements to overthrow the Hussein dictatorship from the two indigenous groups most disadvantaged by the regime's rule. In the north, the Kurds mounted one of their periodic attempts at separatism, generally directed at the dream of an independent Kurdish political entity called Kurdistan, which they had requested and been denied at the Versailles conference after World War I that had consigned them to the newly formed Iraqi state. In the southern part of the country, the Shiite Arabs, who predominate in the area and form the strong majority of Iraqi citizens, also rose in rebellion against their oppression by the Sunni Arab minority that dominated the Hussein regime. In the confused aftermath of the defeat and expulsion of Iraqi forces from Kuwait, Saddam Hussein unleashed his remaining forces in a brutal suppression of these two uprisings. By the time the international community took cognizance of and reacted to what he was doing, the revolutions in these two oil-rich parts of Iraq had essentially been put down.

The plight of the Iraqi Kurds first grabbed international attention as thousands fled across the border into Turkey, which was unequipped for and not disposed to deal with them. Many landed on the rugged mountainsides of southern Turkey, where they were discovered huddling tenuously and desperately by the emerging eyes of global television by outlets like Cable News Network (CNN), whose constant coverage made it impossible to ignore their fate. As their situation deteriorated, the savagery of Hussein's actions against them (including reports of renewed WMD use) was revealed as the reason they would not voluntarily return to Iraqi Kurdistan, a migration on which the Turks (who have their own Kurdish minority problem) insisted but which the Kurds viewed as tantamount to a death sentence. The impasse was ultimately resolved when the United States agreed to guarantee the protection of returning Kurds by creating an exclusion zone in Iraqi Kurdistan where Iraqi forces would not be allowed to operate. This arrangement, initially known as Operation Provide Comfort, was enforced by American military flights over sovereign Iraqi territory. This protection was later extended to the Shiites in the south as Operation Southern Watch (Provide Comfort was eventually renamed Northern Watch in 1997), and both operations were still in force when the U.S. invasion occurred in 2003. The operations also created the precedent for similar actions against Libya in 2011.

The Northern/Southern Watch precedents, justified and motivated by humanitarian concerns, had two longer-term, and mostly unanticipated, consequences that are often overlooked in later analyses. One of these was the precedent set, which was the implicit denial of Iraqi sovereignty by the operation and the implied notion that the United States and its partners (the British and French) had a "right" to interfere in what were Iraqi internal affairs. In addition, the action was legitimized by the United Nations, thus muting any lingering debates about the ongoing intrusion on Iraqi sovereignty. The commitment it created was also open ended. The Kurds and Shiites remained safe from Hussein's retribution for as long as the operations continued, but should they be terminated, there was the distinct possibility that the regime in Baghdad would return to its murderous ways. The only way in which these operations *could* safely be ended was through a change in regime in Iraq, and in fact it was the conquest of Iraq that terminated the mission.

The fact that Iraq had used chemical and biological weapons in the past also left the international community suspicious about Hussein's likely future behavior, and the result was UN Security Council Resolution 687, which imposed a sanctions regime on the Iraqis specifically aimed at preventing the reenergizing of their WMD capabilities and forcing upon the Iraqi regime inspection of its facilities to assure that no sanctioned behavior was occurring. This sanctions regime imposed considerable hardships on the Iraqi population, and Hussein's periodic resistance to the sanctions further enhanced his reputation as an international rogue (although subsequent evidence suggests that he did disband most of his WMD facilities during the 1990s). In addition, evidence of a purported assassination plot against former American President George H. W. Bush (who had led the American war effort in 1990–1991) during a visit to Kuwait in 1993 added to the villainy in which Hussein was viewed. While the truth of these latter accusations remains dubious, they added to the reputation of Hussein as a thoroughly reprehensible character for whom regime change seemed an appropriate solution.

All of these factors from the 1990s percolated through the ruminations of a group of international analysts who would gain power and influence in the American foreign policy community with the election of George W. Bush in 2000. Known collectively as the *neoconservatives* (or neo-cons), this group of foreign policy intellectuals had been in the vanguard of advocates who argued in 1991 that the United States should have toppled Hussein as the culminating act of the Persian Gulf War. Mostly consigned to the middle levels of the foreign and national security bureaucracy at the time, they were unable to convince the first President Bush to endorse a march into Baghdad, which the president opposed because of the chaos and civil resistance such an action would create. Forced out of the limelight by the election of Bill Clinton in

1992, the neo-cons repaired to lower-profile positions during the 1990s but never abandoned their dream of overthrowing the Iraqi dictator as the first step in what they called "regime change" that they hoped would sweep across the region. When George W. Bush entered the White House, the road was cleared for their return to power and the implementation of the dream denied them in 1991.

Iraq in the World

Prior to the Iraq–Iran War, very little international attention was paid to Iraq. For most of the post–World War II period, Iraq was an international backwater, mostly notable for its internal instabilities (a series of intrigues and governmental changes) that began with the assassination of King Faisal II in 1958 and the gradual accumulation of power of the Baathist Party, which preached a somewhat incoherent philosophy of "Arab socialism" but was not considered of particular importance to the United States. During this period of time, American interests in the Persian Gulf area were solidly, and virtually exclusively, focused on relations with Shah Reza Pahlevi's Iran, which both enforced security and stability in the region—meaning they kept the oil flowing—and provided the United States with a steady supply of petroleum energy. In those circumstances, the fact that the United States was excluded from access to the one tangible asset of Iraq, its vast petroleum reserves, was insignificant.

The events of 1979, to which allusion has already been made, changed that calculus for the United States and the rest of the region. The most momentous change at the time was the overthrow of the shah, which left the United States without a reliable, powerful ally in the area, but that was ultimately not the most important impact of the Iranian Revolution on the region and thus the United States. Essentially all of the oil-producing states other than Iran were Sunni Arab and had a long-standing distrust of the Persian Shiites of Iran. As long as the shah ruled and suppressed Shiite evangelism (through a process of secularization not unlike Turkey's which underlay much of the shah's rule), Iran was not an active problem, despite the fact that it was both considerably larger and more powerful than any of the other oil producers. When Iran became militantly, and evangelically, Shiite, the Arab Gulf states began to worry, with justification, whether Iran would try to export the Shia faith to the Sunni states, all of which had Shiite minorities (or in the case of Bahrain, a large majority) imported to work in the oil industry and generally exploited by the regimes.

This turn of events made Iraq suddenly important. Although its population is less than half that of Iran and its size is less than one-third that of Iran, Iraq had always been considered a counterweight to the Persians in the eyes of the Arab oil producers, and once the restraint of Iran's tight relationship with the United States was severed, that counterweight expanded in importance—a phenomenon noted by the United States, which was anxious both to compensate for the loss of its ally and to demonstrate sensitivity to the concerned states like Saudi Arabia on which it increasingly depended for oil.

Saddam Hussein, newly in power in 1979, recognized this change and seized upon it. When he assumed power, little was known publicly about the ruthlessness and savagery with which he would rule his country, but his willingness to take on Iran in the 1980 war was seen as evidence that Iraq could hopefully live up to its projected role as a balance of power against the Iranians. Hussein himself, it has been reported, hoped to gain personally from his country's war against the Persians in the form of his anointment as successor to Egypt's Gamal Abdul-Nasser as the acknowledged leader of the Arab people. Between 1980 and the invasion of Kuwait, the United States acquiesced in Hussein's actions, including the provision of assistance to his regime from the middle 1980s until the eve of the Kuwait invasion.

Iraq's role as a balancing power, combined with Hussein's 1980s pursuit of WMD as a way to enhance Iraqi power, catapulted it into a position of regional and world power it could not otherwise possibly have attained. Because Iraq became important to containing Iran, some of the more hideous aspects of the Saddam Hussein dictatorship were overlooked on the grounds that he seemed to represent a lesser evil than the regime headed by Ayatollah Ruhollah Khomeini in Iran, even when reports emerged in 1988 that the Iraqis had used chemical weapons against Iraqi Kurds. It also created the perception that Iraq was a key player in achieving stability in the region, a conviction that led some Americans—notably the neoconservatives—to conclude that if regime change in Iraq could have a democratic end result, Iraq could become a cornerstone of a more peaceful region. This conviction, in turn, provided much of the rationale for advocacy of invading Iraq in 2003. As will be argued later in the chapter, the invasion has had the ironic possible consequence of undercutting the geopolitical role of Iraq as a counterbalance to Iranian power in the region since Iran appears virtually certain to emerge as the dominant outside influence in postoccupation Iraq.

The Physical Setting

Iraq gains its significance in the Middle East as much by where it is as by what it is. The country is not especially large in physical size, with an area of 168,868 square miles that ranks it 58th among world states and about twice the size of Idaho. The country is physically divided into three basic regions, each of which has great significance in the evolution of the country discussed in the next section: a northern region that contains mountainous areas adjacent to both Iran and Turkey (Kurdistan), a central region that includes the plains around the capital of Baghdad, and a southern region that extends through the swampy lowlands to the Persian (or Arabian) Gulf. The country is strategically located within the region, sharing land borders with Iran, Jordan, Kuwait, Saudi Arabia, Syria, and Turkey.

The country is also unexceptional in terms of the size of its population, which, according to July 2010 estimates, stood at 29,671,605, making it the 40th most populous country in the world and placing it regionally in the middle ranks, smaller than neighbors Iran (at roughly 76.9 million) and Turkey

(77.8 million) but slightly larger than Saudi Arabia (25.7 million) and Syria (22.2 million) and considerably larger than Jordan (6.4 million) and Kuwait (2.8 million).

Location and the composition of its population make Iraq physically important. Geographically, Iraq is at the hub of a wagon wheel at the top of the Persian Gulf, with boundaries with all the important contestants in that region. Its borders with Turkey, Syria, and Iran are important, for instance, because Kurdistan radiates out from northern Iraq into all three of those countries, among all of which there is a significant (10–20 percent of the total population) Kurdish minority. The Kurds are a classic case of the so-called "stateless nation": an ethnic population—or nationality—that does not have its own sovereign state. Kurdish nationalism is alive in all the countries involved, creating a thorn in each country's side and a source of tension within Iraq. At the same time, Iraq has a long border with Iran that effectively separates the Persian Iranians from the Arab Sunnis of the Persian Gulf states, forming a buffer between these two historically feuding Islamic factions.

The composition of the Iraqi people reflects this latter distinction. Ethnically, the country has two major groups: the Arabs, who compose 75 to 80 percent of the population, and the Kurds, who make up 15 to 20 percent. Within the Arab majority, however, there is a strong Sunni–Shiite split, with roughly 60 to 65 percent of the total Arab population Shiite and 32 to 37 percent Sunni. This Shiite majority is important for several reasons. One is that in a fully representative democracy in Iraq, it forms an electoral majority when Iraqis vote along religious lines (as they tend to do). Thus, advocacy of democracy in the country is effectively support for Shiite rule. Second, traditionally the Sunni minority has ruled the Shiite majority, often tyrannically and cruelly. This means the Sunnis are reluctant to see the emergence of full democracy, certainly based on the one-man-one-vote principle, because such rule potentially leaves them vulnerable to retribution. Third, while the Iraqi Shiites and the Iranians share Shiism as their faith, the Iraqis are also Arab, which means they are also traditional opponents of the Persian Iranians. During the Iran–Iraq War, it was commonplace to speculate about where the Iraqi Shiites' loyalties lay: were they more Shiite or more Arab? In that case, they remained loyal to Iraq. Exactly how this split allegiance is resolved in postoccupation Iraq will go a long way toward settling the amount of influence Iran has in Iraq—and thus the degree of difficulty it poses for the Arab states.

One of the most interesting and controversial physical attributes of Iraq is its mineral—which is to say petroleum—base. Iraq is potentially one of the largest, and some accounts even suggest the largest, oil-producing powers based on known and extrapolated estimates of its reserves. These estimations are clouded by two factors. First, they are far in excess of actual production figures, which make Iraq currently a comparatively minor regional oil producer. This modest position, however, is partly the result of an Iraqi oil industry that has hardly scratched the surface in terms of exploitation and exploration, a second factor exacerbated by the long American occupation.

Using 2010 figures from the *CIA World Factbook*, Iraq is currently no more than a medium player in the world's petroleum equation. It produces 2.1 million bbl/day, which ranks it 12th among global producers. Most of that amount is shipped overseas; its internal consumption is 687,000 bbl/day (24th in the world), whereas it exports 1.91 bbl/day, 11th most in the world. These numbers are, of course, dwarfed by the production numbers for Middle East oil giants like Saudi Arabia and Iran, whose known, confirmed reserves are greater than those of Iraq.

Oil becomes an important part of Iraq's future for three reasons. The first is its production characteristics. In global terms, Iraq is one of the least developed sources of world oil, with only a small number of oil wells operating. As Holt pointed out in 2006, "A mere two thousand oil wells have been drilled across the entire country; in Texas alone there are more than a million." This means that exploitation of Iraqi oil is still in its infancy; a large amount of Iraqi oil is located not far beneath the surface, making it relatively cheap to extract (current estimates suggest about $2 a barrel), and it has low sulfur content, making it "sweet" oil that is inexpensive to refine. The result is that Iraqi oil is both cheap and valuable, making access to it a major international concern after in the post–American occupation era because, as Polk asserts, "Iraqi oil is the cheapest in the world to produce."

Second, Iraqi oil is plentiful. Current estimates of known reserves are pegged at 1.15 billion barrels, the fourth largest in the world after Saudi Arabia, Canada (most of whose reserves are in oil sand deposits difficult and expensive to exploit), and Iran. The fact that the Iraqi oil industry is comparatively underdeveloped extends to exploration, however, and some estimates suggest a more accurate figure may be closer to 200 billion barrels. Estimates for the countries with larger known reserves are based on more complete exploration data, meaning there is likely less reserve oil unaccounted for than in places like Iraq. Thus, Iraq's potential to rise among producers is probably greater than those countries currently ahead of it. It has even been suggested that Iraq may prove to have the world's largest reserves when all sources of reserves are included in measures of Iraqi petroleum.

Distribution of oil reserves is the third reason for oil's importance in the Iraqi equation. Historically, the oil industry of Iraq has centered on two regions: the largely Kurdish north in the shadows of the Zagros Mountains, and the swampy marshlands of southern Iraq. This distribution puts control of roughly half of known reserves under potential Kurdish control, if the disputed Kirkuk oil fields are included among Kurdish assets (a matter of serious dispute discussed later in the chapter), and under Shiite control of the southern oil fields. Postoccupation leases have already been let in the southern field to international interests, and the American oil companies were conspicuously absent among the participants in the agreements reached. Parallel contracts on petroleum from the Kurdish region have not yet been awarded, and both American petroleum companies and the U.S. government have a keen interest in how they are distributed.

The area of the country that has historically been excluded from oil pro-jections is the central part of the country, and notably the so-called "Sunni triangle" that includes Baghdad and is where a majority of Iraq's Sunni popu-lation resides and forms the majority. This fact has been a major underlying source of Sunni insistence that oil revenues be shared among all regions in the country, since the Sunnis are potentially beggared from this rich source of rev-enue otherwise, and the distribution of revenues from oil concessions has been and will likely continue to be a central part of the Iraqi political dialogue.

The prospects of expanded Iraqi oil reserves offer a tantalizing possibility in this latter regard. Polk, for instance, argues that "still undeveloped is a vast sea of oil" believed to be located under the Sunni Triangle that may "equal all of Saudi Arabia's fields." This claim is, of course, speculative and will likely not be confirmed or debunked until sometime after the end of the American occupation, when conditions become stable enough for exploration to be un-dertaken with some level of safety. If this claim has even partial validity, how-ever, it potentially changes the calculus of postoccupation Iraq.

Iraq as a Unique State

Iraq is and always has been a classic example of the so-called "artificial state," a sovereign political entity with little (if any) historical base that unites various and often antagonistic population elements under one political jurisdiction. Iraq clearly meets the criteria for such an entity, and Iraq's artificiality helps explain both the impact that the American invasion and occupation has had on the Iraqi political entity and what problems these divisions pose in crafting postoccupation realities, including both domestic and international aspects. Iraq's artificiality also calls into some question whether America's stated goals and aspirations when it decided to attack Iraq were realistic.

The divisions that plague Iraq today were present when the boundaries of what would become the independent state were drawn after World War I. The British were heavily involved in determining who and what territory should be part of the British mandate (which basically became Iraq) as the Ottoman Empire was being taken apart. A leading role fell to Colonial Secretary Winston Churchill, who repeatedly admitted his lack of expertise about the area. The southern and central parts of the country formed the core of the new entity, and the Kurdish north was tacked on after the postwar negotiators decided to deny Kurdish statehood for a Kurdistan that could have incorporated parts of Iraq, Iran, Syria, and Turkey.

The basic divisions that cleave Iraqis from one another and define the ar-tificiality of their state are by now familiar and have been introduced. Most Iraqis (those from the Shiite south and the Sunni middle) are Arabs, but they are deeply divided along both sectarian and politico-economic dimensions. The Shiites outnumber the Sunnis by about a three-to-one ratio, but historically the Sunni have controlled the country politically and economically. As Iraqi so-ciety developed after independence in 1932, the typical pattern was for Shiites to live in the rural areas, toiling effectively as tenant farmers for their Sunni overlords, who tended to reside in urban areas like Baghdad. Economic bondage has been reinforced by political control by differing Sunni factions, a pattern last represented by the reign of Saddam Hussein and effectively ended by the American conquest and occupation. This relationship created significant bitterness among the majority Shiites, and one of the great fears that Sunnis have is that a postoccupation majoritarian Iraqi political system will exert retributive discrimination against them. This fear was intensified by the nature of anti-Sunni violence in 2004 and has had, among other things, the result that a large number of Iraq's estimated two million external refugees are Sunni.

The Kurds are a separate, but by no means less difficult, problem. Like the Sunnis, they constitute about one-fifth of the population of Iraq and practice their own variant of Sunnism. Unlike other Iraqis, however, they are non-Arab and speak an Indo-European native language (the Arabs tend to be first-language Arabic speakers). Moreover, the basic loyalty of most Kurds is to an independent Kurdistan, as already noted. They remain part of the Iraqi state because they do not have the power to establish their own sovereign existence and because the idea of Kurdistan is also opposed by the governments of the other countries in which the Kurds are a minority since that Kurdish state would incorporate part of their territory as well. Within occupied Iraq, the Kurdish region has established a kind of de facto autonomy, including informal border crossing points manned by Kurdish *pesh merga* fighters. The disposition of postoccupation Iraq will have to take account somehow of Kurdish demands for substantial governmental and economic autonomy, notably over the question of the disposition of oil revenues in the Kurdish areas. Of particular concern will be the final status of Kirkuk, the unofficial capital of the northern oil industry and a city that has sizable Kurdish and Arab components.

The ethnic balance in Iraq has important international ramifications as well. Neighboring Sunni Arab states have historically viewed a Sunni-controlled Iraq as a bulwark and barrier to the spread of Persian-inspired and -directed Shiite expansionism, a status that is threatened by the possibility of a Shiite regime in Iraq that is close to and influenced by Iran. The Iranians, on the other hand, have spent considerable resources and energies courting their Shiite brethren in Iraq. Virtually all of the Shiite political leaders on the contemporary political scene in Baghdad have, at one time or another, been in exile in Iran, and the Iranians have invested monetarily in support of virtually all Shiite political factions in the country. This means that a Shiite government of postoccupation Iraq is potentially sympathetic to and capable of being influenced by the Islamic Republic of Iran. Such an outcome is abhorrent to the rulers of the oil-rich Sunni Arab states and would create a situation that basically violates the interests the United States has in Iraq's future role in the region.

U.S.–IRAQI RELATIONS

The relationship between the United States and Iraq, along with U.S.–Afghan relations, is distinctive among American relations in the world. The source of that distinction, of course, stems from the fact that Iraq was invaded, conquered, and has been occupied by the United States between 2003 and 2011, meaning the relationship since 2003 has not been between two governments representing sovereign states but instead between a conquering state and the more-or-less representative and legitimate political entity in the conquered state. Although the United States maintains—plausibly enough—that a large part of its intention all along has been to reinstate Iraq's sovereign status with an improved political system, the simple fact remains that the relationship has been, at its base, between a conqueror and its vassal. Americans can, and many do, deny the relationship described in this manner; Iraqis cannot avoid the distinction and its implied humiliation, which feeds their desire to be freed of American presence in the country.

American–Iraqi relations have changed radically across time. As already noted, there was a long period after World War II during which Iraq was of little concern to the United States, just another emerging independent state among many. That distance and disregard began to melt in 1979 and 1980 and accelerated through the 1980s and 1990s, culminating in the American invasion in 2003. Between 2003 and 2011, the relationship was defined by the occupation, including American efforts to help the Iraqis prepare themselves for a reassertion of their sovereign governance of the country. How that transition evolves will determine the future of Iraqi–American relations and, to a significant extent, how Americans evaluate the previous eight years of conflict and occupation.

This overview suggests that U.S.–Iraqi relations can usefully be organized into three distinct yet related phases that build upon one another. The first phase is the prewar phase leading up to 2003 and includes prominently the question of whether the war was justified by the events that led to it. The second phase encompasses the years of occupation, including some assessment of how effective that phase was and how it influenced the transition away from the American occupation. The third phase is the postoccupation period, which is only beginning and which forms the context for contemporary and future U.S.–Iraqi relations.

Pre-Invasion Relations

Relations between Iraq and the United States prior to the decision to invade Iraq, depose its leader, and transform its political system were largely a mirror of relations between the United States and Iran. During the period after the end of World War II those relations were generally cool and remote, as the United States placed its primary emphasis on Shah Reza Pahlevi and his White Revolution in Iran. Iraq, meanwhile, was a rapidly changing, unstable country which, along with other Arab states like Egypt and Syria, flirted with the idea of "Arab socialism" and had generally more favorable relations with the Soviet Union than it had with the Americans (American oil companies were, for instance, excluded from participating in the exploitation of Iraqi oil assets). Iran and Iraq were, of course, historical and sectarian rivals, and the United States closely aligned itself with the secularizing efforts of the Shah's

Shiite Iran against the Iraqis. As a result, U.S.–Iraqi relations for the first third of a century after World War II were decidedly minimal and distant.

That situation changed with the shah's replacement by a violently anti-American Shiite theocracy that declared the Islamic Republic of Iran and its militant hatred of the "Great Satan" in 1979, a sea change punctuated most dramatically by the occupation of the American embassy and hostage-holding of embassy personnel in Tehran for 444 days. When the newly seated Saddam Hussein declared war on the Persians under the banner of Arab unity, the United States moved from wary suspicion of the new Sunni strongman gradually to neutrality and eventually to support for Iraq in its efforts against Iran.

The events of 1979 and 1980 began a roller-coaster ride in U.S. relations with Iraq and, more specifically, Hussein. During the balance of the Iran–Iraq War, relations gradually warmed between the two countries, including the institution of American military and civilian assistance programs to help the Hussein regime in its battle with the more numerous Iranians. By the end of the war in 1988, relations between the two countries were warm, even cordial, despite some atrocities committed by the Hussein regime (such as the chemical attacks against the Iranians and his own Kurds) that would later be raised as parts of the case against Hussein.

The courtship of Saddam Hussein ended with his invasion, annexation, and intention to integrate Kuwait into Iraq in 1990. The United States, at Saudi invitation, led in the formation of the UN-sanctioned coalition that evicted Iraq from Kuwait and, in the process, established Iraq—and especially Hussein—atop the list of countries in need of "regime change," the phrase used by the neoconservatives who would become the champions and architects of the 2003 war.

As already noted, the Persian Gulf War did not leave all parties satisfied with its outcome. Particularly among the neoconservatives who had for some time opposed Hussein (Richard Perle and Paul D. Wolfowitz being prominent examples), the outcome represented an opportunity lost—had the war been taken into Iraq and on to Baghdad at the time, Hussein could have been swept from office and his regime erased. President George H. W. Bush demurred from an invasion that would sweep northward and engulf all of Iraq, largely on the dual assumptions that the Desert Storm coalition would dissolve if ordered into Iraq (which it most certainly would have) and that the action would trigger a long, difficult civil war against the invaders (a position with which his son George W. Bush originally agreed but later abandoned). The war did, however, result in sanctions by the UN against Iraq, as well as the American-led Operations Northern and Southern Watch, all of which reinforced the antipathy between the American and Iraqi regimes. These sanctions included demands that Iraq abandon its WMD programs, compliance with which was erratic.

The roots of the 2003 war lay in the period after the 1991 end of the Persian Gulf War. During the 1990s, the neoconservatives who were the chief champions of overthrowing Hussein left government but never lost their ardor during the two terms of Democratic President Clinton. Rather, they erected arguments in support of Iraqi regime change and actively engaged in the process of recruitment of a national leader who would raise the banner of their cause. They found their champion in George W. Bush.

The process by which the arguments for war grew during the 1990s are more detailed than are appropriate in this context and have been extensively chronicled elsewhere (the author's own version is found in *What After Iraq?*). By the time of the 2000 election that brought Bush to office, however, the determination to attack and displace Hussein was well developed among the cadre who would rise to power in the new administration. For them, the terrorist attacks of September 11, 2001, served as an enabling event, spurring the country to a determined militancy that could be channeled against the Iraqi government, despite scant evidence that Hussein or his regime was in any material way connected to or even supportive of the tragic events.

The justification for taking down the Hussein regime had two separate tracks. One of these tracks, which received the most publicity at the time, surrounded supposedly provocative actions by Hussein in the areas of WMD and congress with terrorists. As American demands grew against the Iraqi dictator, the public rationales (which served as a call to arms in the United States) concentrated on Iraq's supposed possession of stores of WMDs, complete with the veiled inference that the Iraqis were actively engaged in a renewed attempt to gain nuclear weapons. At the same time, allegations were raised that Hussein's regime had connections to Al Qaeda. The two concerns were linked by the awful prospect that Hussein's government might share WMDs—most frighteningly nuclear weapons—with terrorists, thereby heightening the fervor surrounding the "war on terror" and tying terrorism suppression and Iraqi regime change into one convenient package.

The stated reasons for going to war with Iraq have never included access to Iraqi oil, and participants in the decision process (notably Secretary of Defense Rumsfeld in his memoir) have consistently denied this was ever an objective or consideration. Whether access to that resource played into the American decision process remains a matter of contention, however, and one that can only be fully assessed as remaining leases on Iraqi oil—principally in Kurdistan—are negotiated.

The WMD and terrorism charges against the Hussein regime have never, of course, been substantiated. If anything, these assertions have been largely debunked by the absence of supporting evidence, leaving open the question of how they became so widely believed (Jervis offers a good summary analysis). It will be a matter for dispassionate historical analysis to determine if those who made them truly believed these arguments or saw them as a pretext for justifying regime change in Iraq. Certainly, to many supporters, including many of the neoconservatives who had favored conquest of Iraq over a decade earlier, the end of throwing out Hussein certainly justified the means of supporting questionable justifications. Their arguments prevailed, as the Congress approved resolutions in 2002 authorizing President Bush to take whatever actions he deemed necessary to sever Hussein's WMD programs and connections to terrorism. The stated purpose of the regime changers was to rid Iraq of the Hussein dictatorship and replace the Sunni-dominated autocracy with a model democracy that would be a beacon in the region, thereby reducing Middle Eastern tensions and thus making the security of Israel (arguably *the* major concern of the neoconservatives) stronger. Given the apparent falsity of the claims about WMD and terrorism, the success or failure of the war to meet its objectives must largely be measured against the criterion of democratization, although, as the United States has moved toward disengagement from Iraq, the standards for determining success have been relaxed somewhat.

The Occupation

The invasion of Iraq began on March 20, 2003. Despite some initial resistance by Iraqi armed forces, the invasion progressed with relatively few difficulties, as the Americans marched to, entered, and occupied Baghdad, thereby ending the reign of Saddam Hussein. It was a lightning affair that caused such euphoria in official circles in the United States that American Secretary Rumsfeld triumphantly proclaimed that within 129 days of the initial invasion date, American objectives would have been achieved, and all but a handful (about 6,000) of American troops would have been withdrawn from the country.

Had the Iraq War played out that way, both its conduct and subsequent U.S.–Iraqi relations would have been decidedly different than they turned out. Like the reasons for going to war in the first place, the failure to produce a quick, decisive, and positive outcome are attributable to numerous reasons, most of which are captured in some of the numerous analyses contained in the suggested readings. For present purposes, however, two can be isolated that bear on the current situation. The first is the question of whether the United States went into the Iraq War with reasonable, realistic purposes or whether the reasons were less than worthy or attainable. The second is whether the occupation itself was skillfully handled or whether it was inept to the point of making the entire experience worse than it otherwise would have been.

In retrospect, it has become commonplace to refer to the Iraq War as an unnecessary conflict. The charge is largely based in the inability of its champions to substantiate their charges against the regime (WMD and terrorism connections) and the gradual fading of the overarching goal of transformational change in the area (democratization). This latter change has occurred at least in part because the neoconservatives for whom the goal had been a shibboleth were largely replaced in the U.S. government after Bush left office, but also by the halting, uncertain steps of Iraqi politicians to overcome the difficult, and some would argue insurmountable, obstacles to its accomplishment. The result has been that expectations have been reduced. Emma Sky, a former Bush-era political advisor in Iraq (who served under U.S. commander General Ray Ordieno), referred to the goal for Iraq as "a nation at peace with itself, a participant in the global market of goods and ideas, and an ally against violent extremists (terrorists)." While these are valid goals, they are not as expansive as the justifications for going to war in the first place.

The other criticism, well developed in the literature, is that the United States handled the occupation poorly, in the process making matters worse and prolonging the experience. Part of this criticism centers on a virtual lack of preparation for occupying the country (planning for the so-called Phase IV—occupation—aspect was assigned almost exclusively to a middle level-office in the Pentagon headed by neoconservative Douglas Feith that excluded advice from other agencies), and was thus unprepared to manage the post-conflict environment and to prepare Iraq for restored sovereignty. Another criticism is that the United States took a number of avoidable missteps, such as disbanding the Iraqi army and the excesses associated with the Abu Ghraib prison, and that these helped foment opposition to the occupation that had risen to the arguable level of full-scale civil war among confessional groups and the American occupiers by 2004.

The road to American disengagement began in 2006. In that year, the Americans convinced a number of Sunni tribes that had been fighting the occupation instead to turn their militias against the terrorist organization Al Qaeda in Iraq. This "Awakening," as it is known, was financed by American payments to the converted Sunni militiamen, and it had the major impact of lowering violence directed at the American occupiers and thus settling down internal matters in Iraq. As the effects of the Awakening were taking hold, General David Petraeus led the so-called "surge" of 2007 that put an additional 30,000 American combat forces into the country. With both the surge and Awakening in operation, the level of violence in the country gradually has declined. In 2008, the United States signed a Status of Force Agreement (SOFA) and a Strategic Framework Agreement (SFA) with the provisional Iraqi government. The SOFA agreement specified the removal of American forces from Iraqi cities by June 30, 2009, and the removal of all U.S. combat forces from the country by the end of 2011, while the SFA outlines "the economic, cultural, diplomatic, and security components of 'long-term' bilateral ties, " according to Parker. On August 31, 2010 President Obama declared an official end to all American combat operations in the country. The war's toll for the United States at that time stood at over 4,400 American dead and almost 32,000 wounded as Operation Iraqi Freedom became Operation New Dawn.

Post-Occupation Relations

The shape and nature of the Iraqi polity and American relations is evolving as the post-American occupation period begins to unfold. The effects of war and occupation have been ambivalent for Iraq itself. The American intrusion certainly ended the brutal Saddam Hussein dictatorship, but it also effectively brought to an end a Sunni hegemony in the country that had been the basis of societal order, if not an order to which all, or even a majority, of Iraqis subscribed. The war also created enormous destruction in a country the infrastructure of which was already in stress, and the occupation period did little to restore or upgrade the living conditions and productive underpinning of the country. Whether or how much better nearly nine years of war and occupation left Iraqi is a debatable matter and depends on who one talks to.

The end of the occupation left Iraq with deep unresolved problems, and how they are worked out will determine both the future of relations between the two countries and how Americans view the worthiness of their Iraqi activism. The problems are complex and enduring—they existed before the American intrusion, and they were not "cured" by the American presence. Some of these are internal, notably how power will be distributed and regulated within a new, democratic Iraqi political system. Much of that evolution will be the revised relationship between the Sunnis and Shiite, but it will also have to come to grips with the continuing status of the Kurdish north in the country. Internationally, the great question is the orientation of the new Iraq in the regional order. Sunni-dominated Iraq was a bulwark against expanded, Persian-abetted Shiite expansionism in the Gulf Arab states from which so much of the world's oil flows. Whether it will remain so, or in the worst case become instead a virtual vassal of expansionist Iran is a question still to be answered.

The status of the new Iraqi government remains a work in progress. As Parker puts it, "Iraq is evolving from a state in crisis . . . to a sovereign nation," and Sky largely echoes that sentiment, referring to it as having gone "from being a failed state to being a fragile state." Looking at the political balance in the country, Serwer concludes that "Iraq's fledgling democracy . . . looks much like other parliamentary democracies whose electorates are fragmented." Multi-party democracies evolve that way because of a lack of consensus within the political system and are generally fairly unstable and indecisive, characteristics that the new Iraq will have to surmount. The short-term prospects for doing so are not entirely encouraging because, as Parker says, "Iraqi politics is halting, messy, and factionalized in ways that seem unlikely to change any time soon."

The basis of this division is the historic structure of Iraqi translated into a politically triangular relationship depicted in Figure 7.1. These three basic configurations currently vie for political control in the country. The Dawa is the party of Nouri al-Maliki, the current prime minister and is the leading component of the Iraqi National Alliance (INA), a coalition of Shiite parties that has an important competitor in the Sadrists, supporters of radical cleric Muktada al-Sadr, who returned from a self-imposed exile in Iran in 2009 and remains something of a wild card in Iraqi politics. The Iraqiya party is headed by Ayad Allawi, who was the original provisional prime minister appointed by the Americans and has the support of most of the Sunni minority. In 2010 elections held to determine leadership in the Iraqi parliament after independence, the Allawi Iraqiya Party won 91 seats to 89 for al-Maliki's 89, both short of a majority in the 325-seat legislative body and creating the need for a coalition. Sadr's followers form one source of movement toward a parliamentary majority, as do supporters of the Kurds in the KRG.

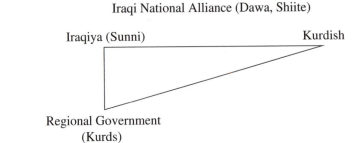

FIGURE 7.1
Iraqi Political Triangle

The problem is how to meld these strong and historically contentious factions into a coherent and stable working coalition, because, as Serwer points out, "no government can be formed without substantial Sunni, Shiite, and Kurdish participation." Different outsiders have interests in one outcome or another. Serwer, for instance, says that the United States would prefer an Allawi-led government, but would accept an Allawi-al-Maliki coalition in which power is somehow shared. Neighboring states have preferences reflecting their own confessional preferences. The Turks and most of the Sunni Arab states would prefer a government led by fellow Sunni Allawi, whereas Iran prefers a Shiite leadership, which effectively means current leader Maliki. The Kurds remain suspicious of any Arab leader who may become too powerful and use his power to reduce the autonomy of the Kurdish region. The current government, of course, is headed by Maliki, but Sky points out that "reconciliation among Iraq's ethnic and religious groups remains elusive, and what progress has been achieved so far could unravel."

Among the most contentious relationships to be worked out is the status of the Kurdish region, which the Kurds and many of their supporters refer to simply as Kurdistan. If the Kurds had their way, they would likely secede and form an independent Kurdish state, but that is unlikely to occur in the short run. Such a state would have claims to Kurdish areas of Iran, Syria, and Turkey, none of which is anxious to encourage or condone Kurdish separatism in their own jurisdictions. Kurdistan is thus, in Parker's observation, "surrounded by states hostile to its independence." The fall-back position for the Kurds is substantial autonomy within Iraq that poses minimal interference with Kurdish life. In the current situation, there is a de facto form of such an arrangement, whereby Kurdish militias (the *peshmerga*) effectively enforce a ban on physical interference with the KRG through devices such as border crossings that look for all intents and purposes like similar constructs dividing sovereign states. American forces have acted to smooth relations between Kurdish and Iraqi army units at these boundaries, and their removal will pose something of a test of the entire arrangement.

The Kurdish question becomes a vital matter largely because so much of Iraq's oil is located under territory that is part of Kurdistan. The Kurds insist on maintaining control of revenues from Kurdish oil fields for their own use and fear that the Iraqi government would deprive them of such revenue if they gained control of the region. This fear is particularly aimed at the Sunnis who, until or unless believed oil reserves in the Sunni Triangle are realized, feel they are the victims of an arrangement where the Kurds keep their oil money and the Shiites keep revenues from oil production in the Kurdish south.

This dispute is both territorial and international. Part of the oil legacy of the northern part of Iraq lies in the large oil reserves surrounding Kirkuk, a city and locality in which there is ethnic dispute between the Arabs and Kurds. The KRG claims the area as its own, and has insisted that Arabs settled in the region by Saddam Hussein be returned to their historical tribal lands, mostly in the Sunni Triangle region. As long as disagreement remains on the status of Kirkuk, "the disputes over territory and oil between the Kurdish Regional Government and the central government" will continue to be contentious and potentially explosive, according to Parker. Internationally, the disposition of oil leases for Kurdish oil is a major concern of oil producers, notably the United States since it was excluded from similar concessions in the Shiite south in 2009.

The major geopolitical concern surrounding full Iraqi independence is its future relationship with Iran and thus its continued existence as a barrier to spreading Iranian influence in the region and thus potentially over its oil. The United States has historically aligned itself with the Sunni Arab states on this issue because of its post-1979 animosity toward Tehran and its dependence on oil from the Sunni Arab states, and thus, "the most important question for the United States is whether the next Iraqi government will be heavily influenced by Iran," according to Serwer.

American actions to maintain Iraq as a bulwark have been decidedly ambivalent in effect. The United States has consistently opposed the breakup of Iraq into three states (Sunni, Shiite, and Kurdish states) largely on the grounds that the resulting countries would be too small and weak to stand up effectively to Iran (and a Shiite state might not want to). At the same time, the Iraq War may—probably inadvertently—have contributed to closer bonds between post-occupation Iraq and Iran. An Iraq based on a one-man/one-vote majoritarian system will be, as pointed out, Shiite politically, testing whether the Iraqi Shiites are more Shiite or Arab. Moreover, the United States action removed a staunchly anti-Iranian force represented by Hussein, and much of the inevitable anti-Americanism among some Iraqis resulting from occupation has been exploited by the Iranians. As noted, most Shiite factions have received physical exile and/or financial support from Iran. Some critics argue that Iran may come out of the war as the great regional winner, with far greater influence over the Iraqi regime than it had over its pre-war predecessor. The degree to which the United States may be capable of avoiding or moderating such an impact is largely a question of U.S. leverage in its post-occupation relations with Iraq.

U.S. OPTIONS

Inferred from the nature of the actions it has taken and its stated positions, the U.S. goals for Iraq are fairly clear: a non-antagonistic country that does not threaten the United States with WMD of terrorism, that is a democratizing force in the Middle East that will contribute to rather than threatening regional security, and that continues to provide a bulwark against the spread of hostile Iranian influence in the region. The United States has pursued these objectives vigorously throughout the 2000s, notably through the invasion, occupation, and intended transformation of Iraq. But the occupation has ended as a formal relationship, thereby altering the degree of American leverage to affect Iraq's future.

The invasion and occupation clearly has succeeded in sweeping away the old regime and the troubles it created: there is no WMD or terrorist threat emanating from Iraq. The question is whether such a threat ever actually existed and thus the extent to which American policy affected the situation. What is unambiguous, however, is that the United States critically altered the political landscape in Iraq with the removal of the Saddam Hussein regime and the dismantling of the governmental apparatus he constructed. The question that remains to be decided after the United States leaves is whether the eventual successor regime will be much of an improvement over that which it replaces.

If the United States has clear preferences about the kind of Iraq that evolves after its departure, the question is the extent to which it can affect that evolution. Iraq has been relatively tranquil (at least by local Iraqi standards) since the 2006 Awakening and the 2007 U.S. surge, but will the positive trends continue? The underlying cleavages within Iraqi society have by no means been eliminated, and as Sky points out, "what progress has been achieved so far could unravel." Part of the reason for tranquility may be the concerted desire of major parties like the Sunni and Shia not to provide the Americans an excuse to stay longer, which a deterioration of the situation might encourage. On the surface, getting rid of the American occupation is a goal most Iraqis share and can rally around, but what happens after the American displacement object is removed? One possibility is that growing cooperation will continue; at the other extreme, the truce may be only a temporary ceasefire that will evaporate after American final withdrawal the same way events unraveled in India following the British departure. The influence of colonial powers can wane very quickly after the blunt symbols of their rule are removed, and that may prove the case once the Americans have effectively left as well.

That American influence will decrease after the withdrawal is complete is certain. One of the aftereffects of the American military involvement is certainly going to be a domestic anti-intervention tendency for a time, and one impact of that phenomenon will certainly be that the United States will be in no domestic political position to reinsert itself if the situation deteriorates. As this author points out in *What After Iraq?* the situation is likely to resemble Vietnam after the American self-removal from that conflict: when the worst happened (the fall of the entire country to communist control), there was nothing the United States could do to alter the situation without unleashing an enormous domestic backlash. Should Iraq come apart, the same is almost certainly true, and the Iraqis are undoubtedly well aware of it. Iraqis whose vision of their future differs substantially from the vision the United States have only to wait for the American presence to disappear, since American leverage will disappear as well. It is not clear if there is much the United States can do to reverse negative outcomes.

Iraqis have substantial tasks with implications for the United States that will help vindicate or raise further questions about the wisdom of U.S. commitments there. Internally, the Iraqis still face monumental problems they have not yet addressed. The most central is the political fate of the major groups within the country: the Sunni-Shia balance and the Kurdish-Arab divides. Neither has been resolved, and if they cannot be, then political democracy could be the victim, and, as Polk speculated over five years ago, "the current period without a dictator may turn out to have been only an interval between this dictator and the next." Internationally, the major question is the relationship between Iran and Iraq in the future. That relationship is by no means predetermined, as Serwer suggests. On the one hand, "Tehran might still find itself surprised by the Iraqi nationalist tendencies of both Maliki and the Sadrists," He writes, adding that American "'success' in Baghdad may include a Shiite-dominated government relatively friendly to Tehran."

CONCLUSIONS

It was suggested earlier in the chapter that U.S.–Iraqi relations have been something of a roller coaster ride, beginning at a very small, nearly insignificant level and gradually ascending to the top of a very long, steep incline the beginning of the rise of which was events in 1979 and 1980, gradually moving upward through the Iran-Iraq War and the Persian Gulf War and peaking with the American invasion and occupation of 2003. With the beginning of the American withdrawal after the apparent success of the surge, the descent has begun, reaching full velocity with the final removal of all combat forces at the end of 2011. The questions that lie ahead include how long those relations will remain at the bottom of the hill and what kind of secondary hill, if any, will follow.

The immediate future is likely to be ambivalent. Sentiment in the United States began to turn against heavy American involvement in Iraq (as symbolized by the war and occupation) in the 2006 election and rose with the election of Barack Obama in 2008, at least partially propelled to office by his promise to end the war. Disengagement has proceeded without major domestic repercussions in the United States, while the Iraqis have clearly waited with some anticipation to see the last occupier depart.

What happens next? One possibility is that, Vietnam-style, the United States will simply turn its back on its long and costly effort, letting the Iraqi chips fall where they may. Certainly the most war-weary Americans feel that way, but the fact remains that Iraq is now tied to the United States in ways it never was before the Americans effectively "colonized" it in 2003. The United States unmade and has tried to remake Iraq, and it can hardly totally ignore the results of those efforts.

The other possibility, of course, is that the United States will remain engaged with the new Iraq, continuing to push for reconciliation of its various factions and hopeful it will be able to maintain some influence that includes access to Iraqi oil—at least in Kurdistan. At the same time, it retains a geopolitical interest in seeing that Iraq does not become intimately entwined with Iran, forming a second militant Shiite state in an area where most American interests are with the Sunni Arabs.

Two broad variables will help determine which possibility prevails. One of those is the preferences of the Iraqis themselves—can they reconcile? Will they prove to be more Arab or more Shiite? These questions predate and postdate the American presence, which temporarily snatched the balance of internal power away from the Sunnis and awarded it, de facto, to the Shiites by promoting Western-style democracy in the country. Who wins the battle internally will likely affect the international stance of the new Iraq. The second variable is how much Americans will care about what happens in Iraq, a question not unlike what the relationship is between other former colonies and colonizers. On that question, the jury remains decidedly out.

STUDY/DISCUSSION QUESTIONS

1. Characterize U.S.–Iraqi relations as they were changed by events beginning in 1979. What were relations like before then? What were the change events, and what were their effects? How did relations evolve between 1979 and 2003?

2. Link the American intervention in the 1990–1991 Persian Gulf War to the decision process leading to the decision to invade in 2003, including transcending issues and advocates.

3. What were the principal demographic and natural resource characteristics of Iraq which distinguish it in its region and the world? How do these contribute to Iraqi "uniqueness"?

4. Trace U.S.–Iraqi relations through the three phases identified in the text. How did each phase contribute to the issues that distinguish post-occupation U.S.–Iraqi relations?

5. What are the chief U.S. foreign policy interests in post-occupation Iraq? Elaborate.

6. What degree of leverage does the United States have in post-occupation Iraq to realize its interests there?

7. Based on likely post-occupation conditions and relations, should the United States have become as heavily involved in Iraq as it did? Why or why not?

READING/RESEARCH MATERIALS

Baker, James A. III, and Lee Hamilton (co-chairs). *The Iraq Study Group Report: A Way Forward—A New Approach* (authorized edition). New York: Vintage Books, 2006.

Chandrasekaran, Rajiv. *Imperial Life in the Emerald City: Inside Iraq's Green Zone.* New York: Alfred A. Knopf, 2007.

Diamond, Larry. *Squandered Victory: The American Occupation and the Bungled Effort to Bring Democracy to Iraq.* New York: Henry Holt and Company, 2005.

Dobbins, James. "Who Lost Iraq? Lessons from the Debacle." *Foreign Affairs* 86, 5 (September/October 2007), 61–74.

Franks, Tommy, with Malcolm McConnell. *American Soldier.* New York: Regan Books, 2004.

Goldberg, Jeffrey. "After Iraq." *The Atlantic* 301, 1 (January/February 2008), 68–79.

Gordon, Michael R. and General Bernard E. Trainor. *Cobra II: The Inside Story of the Invasion and Occupation of Iraq.* New York: Pantheon Books, 2006.

Isikoff, Michael, and David Corn. *Hubris: The Inside Story of Spin, Scandal, and the Selling of the Iraq War.* New York: Three Rivers Press, 2007.

Jervis, Robert. *Why Intelligence Fails: Lessons from the Iranian Revolution and the Iraq War.* Ithaca, NY: Cornell University Press, 2010.

Katzman, Kenneth. *Iraq: Politics, Elections, and Benchmarks.* Washington, DC: Congressional Research Service, January 2011.

Kristol, William, and Lawrence F. Kaplan. *The War over Iraq: Saddam's Tyranny and America's Mission.* New York: Encounter Books, 2003.

Kumins, Lawrence. "Iraqi Oil: Reserves, Production, and Potential Resources." *CRS Report to Congress.* Washington, DC: Congressional Research Service, April 13, 2005.

Lewis, Charles, and Mark Reading-Smith. *False Pretenses: Iraq: The Oil Card.* Washington, DC: Center for Public Integrity, 2008.

Mueller, John. "The Iraq Syndrome." *Foreign Affairs* 84, 6 (November/December 2006), 44–54.

Packer, George. *The Assassin's Gate: America in Iraq.* New York: Farrar, Straus, Giroux, 2005.

Parker, Sam. "Is Iraq Back?" *Current History* 108, 722 (December 2009), 429–431.

Polk, William R. *Understanding Iraq.* New York: Harper Perennials, 2006.

Pollack, Kenneth M. *The Threatening Storm: The Case for Invading Iraq* (A Council on Foreign Relations Book). New York: Random House, 2002.

Record, Jeffrey. *Dark Victory: America's Second War Against Iraq.* Annapolis, MD: Naval Institute Press, 2004.

Ricks, Thomas E. *Fiasco: The American Military Adventure in Iraq.* New York: Penguin Press, 2006.

———. *The Gamble: General David Petraeus and the American Military Adventure in Iraq, 2006–2008.* New York, Penguin Press, 2009.

Roraback, Amanda. *Iraq in a Nutshell:* Santa Monice, CA: Enison Publications, 2008.

Rumsfeld, Donald. *Known and Unknown: A Memoir.* New York: Sentinel HC, 2011.

Serwer. Daniel. "Iraq Struggles to Govern Itself." *Current History* 109, 731 (December 2010), 390–394.

Simon, Steven N. *After the Surge: The Case for U.S. Military Disengagement from Iraq.* New York: CRS 23, Council on Foreign Relations, 2007.

Sky, Emma. "Iraq, From Surge to Sovereignty." *Foreign Affairs* 90, 2 (March/April 2011), 117–127.

Snow, Donald M. *What After Iraq?* New York: Pearson Longman, 2009.

——, and Dennis M. Drew. *From Lexington to Desert Storm and Beyond: War and Politics in the American Experience* (3rd ed.). Armonk, NY: M E Sharpe, 2010.

Yingling, Lt. Col. Paul. "A Failure in Generalship." *Armed Forces Journal* (online), May 2007.

Afghanistan: Containing and Ending a Protracted Conflict

PREVIEW

The active American military involvement in Afghanistan is now the longest war in American history, and there is yet no predictable end in sight either for the internal conflict on which it is based or for the continuing American presence. Prior to that involvement, American relations with Afghanistan were minimal, but the Soviet invasion of 1979 and subsequent events increased the importance of Afghanistan to the United States. The American intervention was caused by the Afghan Taliban government providing sanctuary to Al Qaeda terrorists in 2001, and the removal of Al Qaeda and the prevention of its return remain major U.S. foreign policy objectives, an outcome that may be facilitated by the assassination of Usama bin Laden in Pakistan on May 2, 2011. The outcome of the war will be critical to the future nature of U.S.–Afghan relations.

Most of the comments made to introduce Iraq as a part of American foreign policy apply equally to Afghanistan. It is in the same part of the world as Iraq, separated from that country by Iran, and it is a place with which the United States has historically had very few, peripheral, and largely episodic relations. If someone had asked Americans 30 years ago to locate the country with which they believed the United States would engage in a war that would surpass the Vietnam conflict as the longest in U.S. history, hardly any would have chosen Afghanistan. And yet that is exactly what has happened and continues to unfold as the United States remains enmeshed in a military operation that began in 2001, the end of which is not clearly in evidence.

Akin to Iraq, Afghanistan has a long history that can be dated back at least three or four thousand years. For the most part, Afghanistan's location as a central Asian crossroads has made it a battleground, as successive conquerors have crossed it, generally headed for somewhere else. The armies of Alexander the Great, for instance, passed through both on their way to India and on their way back in retreat, and the Golden Horde of Genghis Khan battled through and temporarily subdued the ferocious tribesmen in their bleak, mountainous terrain on its way westward. Location has been the curse of the Afghans because it has brought so many foreign enemies into their lands, but that same landscape and the toughness of the people who endure it have made Afghanistan a prize seldom enjoyed long by its conquerors. Afghanistan has, for many centuries, indeed earned its reputation as the "graveyard of empires," a moniker which Jones used for the title of his 2009 book on the efforts of the most recent invader, the United States.

If Afghanistan's overall history is long, its history as an independent state is not. The country first emerged as an independent entity in something like its present form in 1747, but this was a status it would not enjoy in an unrestricted manner for long. Located as a sort of buffer between British India (the Raj) and the expanding Russian Empire, Afghanistan became the object of the "Great Game" between those two European colonial powers in the nineteenth century, and all or part of Afghanistan was attacked and sporadically occupied by the British during three wars between the British and the Afghans spanning the nineteenth (1839–1842 and 1878–1880) and twentieth (1919) centuries. The outcome of the first Anglo-Afghan War is particularly instructive: a British army of 16,000 entered Afghanistan and was slaughtered so thoroughly that only a single British soldier survived; the episode inspired Rudyard Kipling's famous concluding entreaty in his epic poem "The Young British Soldier," "Don't let your sons die on the Afghan plain."

The British finally withdrew after their third encounter, and Afghanistan was once again liberated for 80 largely tumultuous years of rule mostly by the country's largest tribal group, the Pashtun. That period began to end in the early 1970s, when a 1973 coup d'etat set in motion dynamics which would lead to the ascent to power of the military in 1978, which in turn led to the Soviet invasion and occupation that began on December 27, 1979, when Soviet special forces and KGB agents seized the presidential palace in Kabul. What followed was a bloody resistance that lasted for a decade and inflicted heavy losses on both the Soviets and the Afghans themselves. The Soviets finally withdrew their last troops on February 15, 1989, and within months the Soviet Union would begin to disintegrate, at least partially because of the Afghan debacle. The withdrawal left Afghanistan free once again but in a state of social and political chaos, as the years of Soviet occupation had destroyed much of the infrastructure of the country, including the political basis of rule there. After seven years, the Taliban, which had its birth in the resistance to Soviet rule and which emerged as a contestant for post-Soviet control, came to power, ushering in the events that would lead to American physical involvement.

Prior to the Soviet invasion and occupation, American interest in Afghanistan had been decidedly limited. As Jones puts it succinctly, "Afghanistan was mostly a backwater of U.S. foreign policy." During the 1950s, there had been some sporadic interest in providing developmental assistance to Afghanistan, but that interest was largely diverted as the Cold War deepened, and it only reemerged when the Soviet Union moved into Afghanistan and made it a potentially threatening addition to the communist world. As the American national security community sought to make sense of the Soviet move in the weeks and months after the invasion, geopolitically ominous interpretations began to emerge in the United States, the most dire of which was that the Soviets would use their position in southwest Afghanistan to launch an invasion south along the Iran–Pakistan border and thus gain control of the Persian Gulf littoral adjacent to the Straits of Hormuz. While such a military adventure was unlikely to be successful given the geography and climate involved (300 miles of bleak landscape with no infrastructure that was either a swampland or a mud flat depending on the time of year) did not deter such thinking. After 1979, the United States decided that it had an interest in what happened in Afghanistan, and that determination began the process leading to the current morass.

The first stage of American direct involvement in Afghanistan was in the form of providing assistance to the various groups opposing the Soviets. The resistance to the Soviet Union was classically Afghan, consisting of armed attacks by isolated, barely connected or coordinated Afghan tribal units against the Soviets. Known as *mujahidin* ("warriors of God"), these units harassed Soviet military forces whenever they forayed out into the vast, bleak Afghan countryside, inflicting enough damage and casualties to cause the Soviets progressively to be isolated in Afghan cities. The efforts of the *mujahidin* were assisted by the West, and notably by the Central Intelligence Agency, which provided both arms and financing for the rebellious forces. This aid included setting up training camps and other facilities and, most decisively in the long run, equipping the Afghans with Stinger anti-aircraft weapons that they used decisively against Soviet helicopters, the only way that the Soviets could move about the hostile countryside. The longer the insurgency lasted, the more Soviets losses mounted. The estimated losses for the Soviet Union were about 15,000 killed, whereas Jones (2009) reports that "when the Soviets withdrew in February 1989 . . . an estimated one million Afghans had been killed, and as many as three million were forced to leave their homes to avoid the bloodshed." The war effort became increasingly unpopular in the Soviet Union, until Mikhail Gorbachev, the leader who presided over the dissolution of the Soviet Union, finally threw in the towel and began to withdraw Soviet forces in 1986.

Beyond creating an American level of interest that had not previously existed, the war with the Soviets was important to American involvement in the country for another reason. Among the *mujahidin*, there were two distinct elements. The first were native Afghan tribesmen from the various tribal units around the country who came together in a loose coalition to resist the occupation, as had been the tradition for centuries in the country. Within the Pashtun groups that participated were the precursors of what would become, in the interim between the end of the occupation and their rise to power in 1996, the Taliban. The second group was foreign fighters (often known as "Afghanis" in their native countries) from other Islamic countries—especially Saudis and Egyptians, but others as well—who enlisted to join the *jihad* against the outsiders. Among this group was a young, wealthy Saudi named Usama bin Laden, who served as a recruiter and organizer of foreigners, ushering them into service at a reception center that he called Al Qaeda ("the Base"). The formal terrorist organization with that name would come into being sometime around 1988, and its tie to the Taliban was established because of the anti-Soviet resistance. In 1996, the Taliban achieved power in Afghanistan, and bin Laden and his followers were expelled from Sudan (at American insistence). When bin Laden searched for a new sanctuary, he naturally called upon his wartime colleagues, who agreed to allow them into Afghanistan.

The legacy of the Soviet occupation was traumatic to the country and helped form the context leading to direct American involvement in the country. Prior to the Soviet intrusion, Afghanistan had been ruled by a succession of authoritarian rulers (which has been the traditional form of Afghan governance) whose reign was generally limited geographically and in terms of how strong and directive the central government would be. Except for a brief period in 1929 when Tajik Habibullah Kalakani assumed control of the country, the ruler was essentially always Pashtun, and the character and tenor of Afghan power struggles (the "normal" form of politics) were over how strong the central government would be allowed to become. A coup in 1973 began the destabilization process, which culminated in 1978 when another coup brought communist Nur Muhammad Taraki to power. The following year, Hafbullah Amin overthrew Taraki and invited the Soviets to enter the country beginning on Christmas Eve 1979. The Soviets then killed Amin and replaced him with a more compliant Babrak Karmal.

The Soviet occupation destroyed the traditional context of Afghan politics but left it with little replacement. That traditional pattern is described by Barfield and is instructive regarding the political culture into which the United States has thrust itself: "Afghanistan had its own political traditions, in which elections played no part, and the virtues of majoritarian rule were not immediately obvious to the country's regional and ethnic minorities," he writes. There was, in other words, no democratic tradition that could form the basis of a post-Soviet state. The Soviet period had, in the estimation of Biddle, Christia, and Thier, "led to a fundamental breakdown of centralized authority and legitimacy. . . . The era of dynastic control of the state by Pashtun elites [was] thus now over."

The result was a tumultuous seven-year period between the fall of the Soviets and the rise of the Taliban. In 1992, for instance, Jones (2009) reports that "Afghan groups conducted Beirut-style street fighting in Kabul, destroying parts of the city." As governance descended into corruption-filled chaos, the Taliban gradually entered into the picture. This group, the core of which was (and to some extent still is) composed of fundamentalist religious students (*talibs*, which translates as students) recruited among Pashtun refugees in Pakistan and trained in the infamous *madrassas* (religious schools). The Taliban preached a return to Koranic virtue and honesty in government and gradually came to control increasing parts of the country. In September 1996 Kabul fell under Taliban control.

Taliban rule was, of course, notoriously harsh and, from an outside view, fanatical and even bizarre. The Taliban, for instance, greatly restricted the rights of women (they could neither attend schools nor appear in public without full-body coverage) and systematically sought to remove all semblances of Western influence through acts like closing down television and radio stations and destroying computers, precedents that are raised as harbingers today when the possibility of a return to Taliban sway is discussed. The Taliban, both because of its harshness and Pashtun roots, also engendered a counter-movement in the form of the so-called Northern Alliance, a coalition of largely non-Pashtun tribal units waging civil war against Taliban rule.

The United States had largely absented itself from this process. In 1992, the U.S. government ended arms shipments to the Afghan government and militia units. While prominently decrying the increasing radicalization of Afghan politics and the entrance of bin Laden and his group into Afghan sanctuary, it did not play any particular role in these unfolding events. That attitude changed radically and forcefully after the attacks of September 11, 2001.

AFGHANISTAN: A SKETCH

The American response to the 9/11 terrorist attacks focused almost immediately on Afghanistan. Concern about Al Qaeda sanctuaries and bases of operation in Afghanistan (some centered in training camps originally financed by the CIA as part of American support for the *mujahidin*) was mostly limited to antiterrorism advocates within the U.S. federal bureaucracy before the attacks, but Afghan-based Al Qaeda operations in places like the bombing of American embassies in Nairobi, Kenya, and Dar es Salaam, Tanzania, in 1998 had been organized and prepared for within the Taliban-protected terrorist enclaves in the country. When the Taliban refused to turn over control of its Al Qaeda "guests" to the American government, the U.S. government leaped into anti-Taliban action. On September 25, 2001, American CIA operatives entered the country (Operation Jawbreaker), and on October 7, military actions by U.S. special forces and Air Force bombers, acting in cooperation with Northern Alliance rebels, intervened into what had to that point been a reasonably conventional (certainly by Afghan standards) civil war, tilting the advantage to the non-Pashtun northerners who had, prior to that assistance, been enjoying moderate success at best. During November, the Northern Alliance captured numerous Afghan cities, and on December 5 and 7, the regional capital of Kandahar fell, effectively ending Taliban rule.

The stated purpose and major objective of American intervention, however, was not achieved. The rationale that emerged in the immediate wake of 9/11 did not center on the Taliban per se, but on the Taliban's refusal to turn over members of Al Qaeda for their complicity in the terrorist attacks. While Americans reviled Taliban rule (to the extent they were aware of it), there was no great sentiment in or out of government for the Taliban's overthrow, and had it acceded to the American demands, it is quite likely that the United States would not have become further involved and would have left the Taliban in power. It was Taliban noncooperation with the United States efforts to bring Al Qaeda to justice, not its existence, that brought the United States into opposition to it—and thus into the Afghan civil war and its aftermath.

The early anti-Taliban actions by the United States, in other words, were not motivated by any particular stake in internal governance in Afghanistan, but by the perceived need to remove a regime that blocked achievement of America's real objective, the capture or killing of bin Laden and his followers. That effort, of course, failed, as Al Qaeda personnel managed to avoid the dragnet set out for them in the Tora Bora mountains along the Afghan–Pakistan border and to reestablish themselves within the primitive, remote mountainous areas of Pakistan, out of the reach of the Pakistani government which, as noted in Chapter 6, had played a role in creating the Taliban. Al Qaeda remains in refuge there to this day, even though their leader, bin Laden, has been eliminated.

Afghanistan in the World

There were two diametrically opposed views of the situation in Afghanistan at the end of 2001, and both are still present in the contemporary environment. The first was that Afghanistan is a remote, obscure, very poor but marginal state whose position was, and is, tenuous at best and desperate at worst, and that Afghanistan is not central enough to anyone's interest to justify a continued, concerted effort to influence it one way or the other. Certainly, Afghanistan's status was miserable, and the post-Soviet turbulence of the 1990s had contributed mightily to that condition. Barfield, for instance, simply states that, "In the civil war that erupted in the 1990s, Afghanistan became a failed state." Miller makes the point even more emphatically: "In 1991, Afghanistan was the world's most failed state."

While this situation was regrettable, the question facing the international community, including the United States, was "so what?" The second view of the situation in Afghanistan had an answer to the question, which was that Al Qaeda must be denied returned access to Afghan territory to continue its murderous campaign. In the view of Biddle, Christia, and Thier, the United States had two interests in Afghanistan: "terrorists who wish to strike the United States and its allies not to use Afghanistan as their base, and . . . that insurgent groups not use Afghanistan's territory to destabilize its neighbors, especially Pakistan." The second of these geopolitical objectives was not immediately obvious at the time, but the first was. As the United States (and by reflection, its allies) reeled from the horror of the September 11 attacks and looked at forceful ways to wage what was becoming known as the "war on terror," the campaign in Afghanistan came to be seen as a central theater of that effort.

The rationale for a continued effort was thus based on an essentially negative purpose, the indirect assault on the Al Qaeda terrorists by punishing their sponsors and by attempting to assure they could not resume their terrorist campaign from Afghan soil. In this light, any opponent of the Taliban within the country was likely to be seen as a better bet than the Taliban had been. From the Northern Alliance coalition a new figure emerged in the late 2001–2002 period to fill the role of an alternative to the Taliban. Hamid Karzai came from a family of warlords from the Kandahar region, but he was also a Pashtun clan leader who had opposed the imposition of Taliban rule. An obviously westernized Afghan who had lived in the United States (members of his family still do) and spoke flawless American English, he seemed the solution to the Afghanistan situation based in the need to find and support a government that would impose an environment hostile to an Al Qaeda return. The gradual transference of the mission from a primarily Al Qaeda–destroying to a Karzai-supporting role also helped divert attention from the botched attempt to capture or kill bin Laden and his supporters.

The second view of Afghanistan prevailed, despite any real evidence that the world came to see Afghanistan itself in any different way than it had before. There was essentially no argument made that coming to the aid of the Afghan people was an inherent interest of the international community, although there was also no stated opposition to that outcome. Afghanistan in its own right was unimportant before the events that began to cascade in 1979, and the international perception remained that way. Rather, the reaction to the Al Qaeda problem was akin to the problem posed by the Soviet occupation: a negative to be removed because it upset the international order, not because of any inherent concern for the condition of Afghans bearing the Soviet yoke or providing reluctant hospitality to Al Qaeda guests. The second view, in other words, largely prevailed while not bothering to negate the original view. This failure to debunk original indifference would probably have been acceptable had the mission in Afghanistan been relatively short and decisive. Since it has turned out to be anything but that, the question of "so what?" has returned as a haunting challenge to the rationale for what increasingly appears to have become an open-ended, arguably endless commitment.

The period following the initial American military involvement in Afghanistan beginning on October 7, 2001, thus saw a distinct shift in the reasons for involvement in the first place. The first goal, attacking and destroying Al Qaeda, was a discrete, concrete objective and, given the horror that produced it, was an objective that had overwhelming American support. The failure of that mission, however, did not bring an end to the operation. Instead, it continued into 2002 and beyond, but it was well below the radar of most observers. Instead, growing Bush administration argumentation and preparation for war against Iraq cast an obscuring shadow over the transformation of the international activity away from the old mission to the expanded mission of rebuilding Afghanistan as an antiterrorist state. In the process, the United States, in President Obama's campaign rhetoric during the 2008 election campaign, "took its eye off the ball" in Afghanistan, and the result has been the country's longest war.

What may be the most telling characteristic of this gradual change in emphasis is that it was not apparently accompanied by any detailed examination or attempt better to understand Afghanistan than the rudimentary understanding available when the United States first cast an eye toward the country in 1979. Jones, for instance, maintains that "the central tragedy of the American experience in Afghanistan is the way its history was disregarded." As a result, he argues in a 2009 *Foreign Affairs* article, "Current international efforts are based on a fundamental misunderstanding of Afghanistan's culture and social structure." Afghanistan's historical reputation as the "graveyard of empires" suggests that it is not an easy country to invade and occupy, even with the most enlightened and beneficent of motives. Its culture and structure further suggest that it is highly resistant to change and that proposed reforms based on Western notions of reform and progress may encounter greater resistance than those seeking to implement them might expect. An understanding of the problems that arose from sliding from one role in Afghanistan to quite a different one can be seen by looking more intensively at the country itself and the sources of its uniqueness in the world.

The Physical Setting

Akin to Iraq, Afghanistan gains its importance more by where it is than anything else. Located as it is in the heart of central Asia, the U.S. State Department has described the country as a "land bridge" between significant civilizations, a country that is traversed in all directions. Its history of invasion and occupation illustrates this: Alexander the Great headed south through Afghanistan on its way to India, and the nineteenth century Great Game was largely about how to use Afghanistan either to facilitate or impede the expansion of the Russian Empire southward. Genghis Khan traversed Afghanistan from east to west as his invading forces moved toward Europe. The existence of a strong or weak Afghanistan is part of the current Indo-Pakistani conflict: a weak (or at least compliant) Afghanistan allows Pakistan to concentrate its military energies on the Indian front, whereas a strong or turbulent Afghanistan diverts that attention northward, away from India.

Afghanistan is the 41st largest country in the world in land area at 251,827 square miles, a size slightly smaller than Texas. It is a bleak landscape mostly consisting of mountains and high arid plains, only 12 percent of which is arable. It borders on six other countries, including China, Iran, Pakistan (with which it shares its longest border), Tajikistan, Turkmenistan, and Uzbekistan, the latter three all former members of the Soviet Union. It has always been a very poor land because its physical endowment is also minimal, consisting of some natural gas and a probably large number of untapped mineral ores, but it lacks any known sizable oil reserves and is not an oil producer. Its people have scratched a meager existence for themselves from this bleak landscape, diverted mostly by tribal warfare and periodic campaigns to expel foreign intruders. Most of the country is rural and isolated, and personal and political loyalties tend to gravitate toward the local level and include a strong suspicion of and an aversion to outsiders, including central governance.

Afghanistan's people are also diverse. Estimation of the population is an example of the problems facing the country: much of Afghanistan is so remote and hostile that historic censuses have been little more than estimates that did not include extensive canvassing in remote regions, and the estimates are further compromised by extensive out-migrations by population groups (notably Pashtuns from non-Pashtun-dominated areas to Pakistani areas with a Pashtun majority along their common border) and by a large number of internally displaced people (IDPs). The most recent, 2010 estimate is that there are slightly less than 30 million citizens of the country (40th largest in the world). A telling statistic about the Afghan population is the life expectancy of its citizens; at 45 years, it ranks 222nd in the world—yet another testimony to the harshness of life in this forbidding, war-torn land.

The country's people are ethnically diverse. This ethnicity is, however, complex, and while it goes beyond present purposes to discuss it in any detail, it is important to recognize this complexity, at least partially because the nuances it contains were fairly clearly unknown to Americans at the time of the initial American involvement in 2001 and arguably today. Barfield describes a basic distinction. "Ethnic groups in Afghanistan come in two flavors: tribal and non-tribal," he writes. "Tribes . . . define membership through the unilateral descent from a common ancestor, real or imagined. The Pashtuns are the best example of this." Non–tribally based ethnic groups lack this common sense; Barfield says the Tajiks are the primary example of nontribal ethnicity. Tribalism, where it exists, presents a strong sense of self-identification that can overcome competing sources of loyalty such as identification with a particular locale.

The Pashtuns are the largest ethnic group in the country and comprise about 42 percent of the current population. Like all elements of the Afghan population, they are composed of a diverse set of groups, consisting of numerous tribes and sub-tribes, but for a long time the Pashtuns have been the dominant population and political influence in Afghanistan. As Barfield summarizes their status, "Afghanistan could be equally classified not only as 'the land of the Afghans' but the 'land of the Pashtuns' as well." As a result, almost all of Afghanistan's leadership (including Karzai) has been Pashtuns, and it is difficult to imagine an Afghan government ruling effectively that does not have at least the tacit support of the Pashtuns. This latter observation is important when conjuring future Afghan political solutions.

Three additional points should be made about the Pashtuns. The first is that the Pashtun people, especially those from the rural areas where they are concentrated (largely members of the so-called Ghilzai clan) have been the recruitment ground of the Taliban. While by no means all Pashtuns are members of or sympathetic to the Taliban, virtually all Taliban are Pashtuns. Thus, campaigns against the Taliban are necessarily directed at the Pashtuns, and efforts to turn the Afghan people decisively against the Taliban must successfully convert susceptible Pashtuns away from the Taliban cause.

The second point is that, for some purposes, the Pashtuns join the Kurds as a "stateless nation." The Pashtuns form a plurality within Afghanistan, and they are also the second largest population group within Pakistan (at about 15 percent) and, as suggested in Chapter 6, there has always been sentiment for an independent Pashtunistan formed of territory on both sides of the Durand Line separating Afghanistan and Pakistan (a border regularly ignored by Pashtuns who consider it an illegitimate frontier the purpose of which is to divide their natural "nation"). It also explains why Pashtun members of the Taliban can move fairly freely across the frontier between the two countries, a source of frustration to American and allied attempts to destroy their existence.

A third point is the existence of a Pashtun creed of behavior, known as *Pashtunwali*. While Pashtuns differ significantly on a number of matters, they generally subscribe to what amounts to a code of honorable behavior. One of the major tenets of this code is hospitality—the idea that guests are to be nurtured and taken care of—an admonition that clearly was extended to the Al Qaeda "guests" of the Pashtun-dominated Taliban regime in 2001, when the United States and its allies demanded that Al Qaeda's leadership be turned over to them for punishment—the very abnegation of the Pashtun code of moral behavior.

The rest of the Afghan population is divided among other ethnic groups. The largest of these are the Tajiks, who form about 27 percent of the population and have been prominent in both the military and governance since 2001. The Hazara and Uzbeks each comprise about 9 percent of the population, and the remaining 13 percent of the population is divided among several other ethnic minorities such as Aimak, Turkmen, and Baloch. The country has two official languages—Pashto (the native tongue of the Pashtuns, spoken by about 35 percent of the people) and Dari, a language similar to Persian Farsi, spoken by about half of the population. The country is uniformly Islamic, with Sunnis in the majority with approximately a four-to-one advantage over Shiites.

If Afghanistan is ever to become a stable, viable state, it is generally agreed that it must provide a more positive experience for its population, and improvements in the Afghan economy are at the heart of needed improvements. The prospects could scarcely be bleaker. At an estimated $29.8 billion in total GDP (2010 figures from the *CIA World Factbook*), the economy is only the 110th largest in the world, and per capita GDP is roughly $1,000, ranking it 212th—virtually at the bottom of world rankings. The literacy rate in the country is at a dismal level of 28 percent, meaning there are few educated people around from whom to develop more sophisticated elements of the economy (which is currently concentrated in rudimentary forms of manufacture such as textiles), and opium is the largest agricultural crop in the country. Indeed, some estimates suggest that illicit drugs are the main source of economic activity and are a mainstay for supporting both the government and insurgents against it. The prestigious Corruption Perceptions Index (CPI) produced annually by Transparency International ranks Afghanistan at 176th in its ranking of the most corrupt in the world, ahead of only Myanmar and Somalia among the countries it ranks. The 2010 Failed State Index compiled annually in the July issue of *Foreign Policy* magazine rated Afghanistan as the sixth most failed state in 2010, and the performance and prospects of the economy contributed measurably to that grim evaluation.

Afghanistan as a Unique State

The isolated, harsh existence of the Afghans and their loyalties to tribes and other forms of ethnicity is one of the most distinctive aspects of Afghanistan and dealing with it. Most Afghans live in rural areas where they scratch out a meager existence and where they are insulated from outside interference, a condition which they prize greatly. They share a sense of autonomy and self-reliance that makes them suspicious of the influence of outsiders, which may mean almost anyone who is not a member of their extended family, village structure, sub-tribe, or tribal or regional group. As former Taliban leader Zaeef puts it, the identity of Afghans "lies with their tribe, their clan, their family, and their relatives." These feelings of narrow, exclusive identification have historically made the Afghans insular and hostile to anyone interfering in their existence, and this feeling can be especially strong toward central government. Indeed, one of the themes of Afghan history has been the attempt by central governmental sources in the major cities, especially Kabul, to extend their sway nationwide, with the hinterlands strongly objecting to that extension of authority. A strong central authority is, of course, one of the central tenets of the American effort to stabilize Afghanistan and raise the level of its performance as a state, but it runs directly in the face of a sizable tradition in rural Afghanistan (where the Taliban has the most influence and from which it does most of its recruiting). Moreover, an aspect of this insularity and suspiciousness extends to the more urban parts of the population, who are most closely associated with places like Kabul and Kandahar. To rural Afghans, association with the major cities is a sign of corruption and alienation. While Karzai, for instance, is an ethnic Pashtun, he is tainted in the view of many ordinary Afghans because he is a member of the urbanized, westernized elite (he is from Kandahar). The very fact of his sophistication (things like his fluency in English) makes him as unattractive to many Afghans as it historically made him popular with Americans.

One of the great evidences of the corrupting influence of central government in Afghanistan has always been literal corruption. While practices that are viewed in the West as corrupt are commonplace in many Eastern societies (paying tribute for services—bribery—for instance), the corruption of central governmental officials in Afghanistan has been endemic and monumental in its scale, effectively alienating many in the countryside and giving them yet another reason beyond their ingrained suspicion of outsiders for resisting the imposition of authority from Kabul. Thus, one of the difficulties that now face the American attempt to wrest authority in rural Afghanistan and pass it on to the government is that although people may be grateful for the removal of Taliban authority, they feel that bringing authorities from the central government in Kabul offers no real improvement in their ways of life. In the contemporary context, the implication of governmental officials at the highest levels in profiting from the illicit drug trade has tarnished their legitimacy. The stains of official corruption are deeply tied to the Karzai regime, and although there is little evidence that the president personally profits from the corrupt practices of those around him, members of his immediate family are widely suspected of notorious levels of malfeasance. This belief that the government is not much of an improvement over the insurgency quite obviously impedes efforts to create an anti-Taliban consensus in the Afghan countryside.

The negative feelings that Afghans hold toward outsiders generally are especially strong toward foreigners. If the centrifugal forces of Afghan society are the norm during periods of peace, the Afghans have shown a remarkable ability to unite when faced with outsiders trying to interfere with their country and their way of life. Collaboration with an apparent invader is never positively regarded anywhere (the Quisling phenomenon), but, as Barfield points out, it is especially deleterious in Afghanistan: "Nothing undermines the legitimacy of any Afghan government more than the charge it was beholden to foreign masters." Jones (2009) adds that this negative influence is particularly strong in the rural areas that are the primary field in which the current struggle with the Taliban is being waged. "Outsiders—especially foreign soldiers— have a limited ability to shape local politics," he argues.

The Afghans understand these influences to a degree that is not so clearly understood by the Americans who are attempting to aid them. Karzai, for instance, began arguing with the United States as early as 2010 that it should reduce its operational presence in the countryside because it creates as much animosity as it does good amongst Afghans who dislike the idea of the foreign occupation, and anti-American sentiment is magnified when American operations backfire and produce civilian casualties. Moreover, Karzai realizes that the greater his dependence on the Americans appears to be, the lower the level of legitimacy he has with the Afghan people. Conversely, he also must be aware that a withdrawal of U.S. and allied forces would leave the remaining native Afghan forces likely incapable of competing with the Taliban. The result is to leave Karzai between the proverbial rock (the need for American assistance to survive) and a hard place (the fact that an American presence partially undercuts his own legitimacy). It also leaves the United States in a potential lose-lose situation where both continuing the struggle and abandoning it could result in defeat for the forces it supports.

U.S.–AFGHAN RELATIONS

American relations with Afghanistan bear both resemblances and differences with Iraq. American interest in both countries was historically limited, and in both cases, it was at least an arguable tie to terrorism that raised those relations to a critical level in the twenty-first century. The war effort in Iraq was more consuming and intensive, but it is now fading into the background as the

United States increasingly moves into the postwar period of those relations. The Afghan situation stands in some contrast on the continuing influence of the war: it was, for most of its American conduct, a much lower-key, less intense experience, but it has also been much more protracted. While the end of American military involvement in Iraq is nearly complete, the Afghan commitment remains open ended.

This contrast suggests the means by which the discussion will proceed. In Iraq, the war phase is essentially history, and efforts can be (and were) focused more fully on dealing with postwar relations. In Afghanistan, the war itself remains the continuing focus of attention, in terms of the objectives of the fighting and how to achieve those objectives. The question of postwar relations with Afghanistan certainly enter into the calculation of objectives (e.g., what does the United States need to do to maximize the prospects of an Afghanistan that will honor U.S. interests after American forces leave), but that prospect is sufficiently far enough away to make such calculations more amorphous than in Iraq. Moreover, antiwar sentiment in the United States helped propel the Americans out of the Iraq war, and it remains to be seen if a similar impetus will be influential in U.S. relations with Afghanistan. In May 2011, a wild card entered into the entire calculation with the death of bin Laden and the uncertain impact of his demise on the Al Qaeda threat that has activated and forms so much of the basic rationale for American policy toward Afghanistan.

U.S. Policy in the Afghanistan War

American active military involvement in Afghanistan now spans over a decade, and that duration, had it been foreseen at the time the initial decisions were made, might have produced different American decisions. That evolution has largely been incremental and, in some important ways, has been guided by tactical assessments of situations more than from any clear and overriding sense of mission or clear idea of what the major objective—the end state of the conflict—should be or how to achieve it. When the United States sent military forces into Afghanistan a little less than a month after 9/11, the United States had one objective in mind; that has changed over time and, according to war apologist Michael O'Hanlon, become less focused. As he understates it, "Over the years, the U.S. mission has lost much of its clarity of purpose." In the process, it has also lost much of its support among the American people.

The American involvement can be thought of conceptually in two distinct but related phases. The first phase, born of the 9/11 experience, was the pursuit of the Al Qaeda terrorists who had trained and prepared their attack against the United States from Afghan sanctuaries. As noted, military action seemed necessitated by the Taliban regime's refusal on September 21, 2001, to turn over the Al Qaeda leadership to American control. At that time, Afghanistan was in the middle of a conventional civil war between the ruling Taliban and an insurgent movement of mostly non-Pashtun tribesmen known as the Northern Alliance. In late 2001 before the American involvement, that civil war was essentially a draw, with neither side having immediate prospects of success.

Because the United States determined that access to their major objective, destruction of Al Qaeda, was impeded by Taliban rule, it threw itself onto the side of its opponents in the Northern Alliance, a commitment that tipped the civil war in the rebels' favor.

What is important to emphasize is that support for an alternative to the Taliban was not, at the time, a primary U.S. foreign policy objective. Although the United States decried the excesses of the Taliban internally in much the same way that it did similar fundamentalist Islamic activities in neighboring Shiite Iran, that opposition in itself would not have propelled the United States into the anti-Taliban column. Rather, taking sides on the internal matter of who would govern Afghanistan was an instrumental decision seemingly dictated as a way to get to the real American objective, Al Qaeda. That *tactical* decision to help overthrow the Taliban, however, became the primary American *strategic* aim in the longer run, but it did so almost accidentally. The primary objective of the United States was not realized at the time, however, since Al Qaeda managed to escape from Afghanistan in late 2001, largely because planning for what became the Iraq War diverted American concentrated energies from the pursuit of the terrorists.

What is notable (and discussed in detail in Snow and Drew) is that the original political objective of the United States was clear, measurable, and popular, whereas the policies of the United States since then have possessed none of those characteristics. The objective of destroying Al Qaeda was certainly clear, and one could determine whether or not it had been achieved. Although the enemy was a nonstate actor and thus presented logistical problems of where and whom to attack, there was virtual unanimity of support for trying to attain the stated objective. When the United States failed to achieve that objective but forced Al Qaeda out of the country, it was certainly arguable that the American mission in Afghanistan was over, albeit without triumph.

The mission did not, of course, end at that point. In the process of pursuing the Al Qaeda terrorists, the United States (and its anti–Al Qaeda allies) had proven critical in overthrowing the Taliban regime in Afghanistan, an unintended if not unpleasant outcome. With the United States not certain of the status of any remaining Al Qaeda operatives in the country and desirous of not allowing them to return, the mission did not end, and Western presence continued. In the process, the purpose of involvement subtly switched to support of the new government, and when the Taliban returned in 2003 to resume the civil war with the roles reversed (the Taliban as the rebels, its opponents as the government), the role of U.S. and allied presence tacitly became support for the Karzai regime and opposition to the Taliban. The switch in objectives was gradual and incremental, and it did not unambiguously match any of the three supportive characteristics of the original objective.

The switch to governance and support of the new government of Afghanistan was gradual. Taliban rule in the country effectively ended on December 7, 2001, when Kandahar, the last major redoubt of Taliban strength, fell. Two weeks later, Hamid Karzai was sworn in as the head of an interim replacement government. The first outside peacekeepers arrived in January 2002 under a new United Nations mandate (the International Security Assistance Force, or ISAF), and in June 2002, a senior tribal meeting of leading Afghan leaders (a *loya jirga*) named Karzai head of state with a mandate to govern until 2004. Another *loya jirga* convened in January 2004 and approved a new constitution, and in November of that year, Karzai was elected to his first term as president of Afghanistan (he was reelected to a second term in October 2009).

As these political events proceeded, the military front evolved as well. The Taliban retreated to Pakistan after their overthrow, where they reorganized and prepared to return—with at least tacit support from the Pakistani government, as suggested in Chapter 6. They began to infiltrate and resume military operations in 2003, and their activities gradually widened as they enjoyed high levels of success, particularly in rural Pashtun areas, a level of success that continues to the present. As Blackwill put it in an early 2011 article, "The United States and its allies are not on course to defeat the Taliban militarily."

American and allied involvement has increased incrementally over time. The United States did not withdraw militarily after bin Laden and his supporters escaped Tora Bora, but remained and became part of the ISAF force entering the country. An initially small but gradual buildup of American forces occurred in the country, masked from general public view by the much greater attention focused on the higher-profile Iraq War. By 2003, there were, however, 10,000 American forces in Afghanistan participating in sporadic fighting against the Taliban. In 2006, ISAF formally became a NATO operation (the first mission of the alliance outside Europe), and in September 2008, the United States announced a "quick surge" of 4,500 U.S. forces on a mission presumably parallel in intent to the more highly publicized 2007 surge in Iraq. Shortly after entering office, the Obama administration announced an increase in American force levels of 17,000 troops, and in December 2009, it announced that an additional 30,000 troops would be sent to Afghanistan, bringing the total American troop commitment to over 100,000. The administration also announced that it would begin the gradual reduction of those forces by the end of July 2011, without specifying the extent of the draw down.

This increase in American commitment was done incrementally, but it had the net effect of creating a political objective that went well beyond the original definition of 2001. The United States tied itself to a "favorable" political outcome in Afghanistan internally. Officially, as the 2010 *National Security Strategy of the United States* puts it, the goal remains a "commitment to disrupt, dismantle, and defeat Al Qa'ida," and Afghanistan remains the leading theater of that effort: "The frontline of the fight is Afghanistan and Pakistan, where we are applying relentless pressure on Al Qa'ida, breaking the Taliban's momentum, and strengthening the security and capacity of our partners."

On the surface, more continuity appears in those statements than exists, and as a result, the post-2001 objective of the United States lacks the clarity, measurability, and popular support that it originally had. Part of this is because the thread tying the two objectives—Al Qaeda and the internal governance of Afghanistan—is tenuous. Then-American Director of Central Intelligence (DCI) Leon Panetta, for instance, opined in early 2011 that there are probably no more than 70 Al Qaeda operatives active in Afghanistan. If Al Qaeda is the objective of the mission, then American efforts should be directed where they are present—places like Pakistan, Yemen, and even parts of Africa—not in Afghanistan, which houses hardly any of the terrorists. In this circumstance, the objective is more closely tied to an outcome centered on the postwar Afghan political condition, an objective that is shrouded in ambiguity, questions of attainability, and the general indifference of much of the American public.

There are three central questions that surround the ongoing war, all of which affect U.S. postwar foreign policy toward Afghanistan. The first is what the U.S. objectives in the war are. Clearly, they involve an improved situation that is sustainable after the war ends, but what exactly is that situation? The second is how the United States can achieve whatever end it specifies: does the United States have a viable strategy for attaining whatever objectives it has? The third is how long will it take to bring the war to a "successful" conclusion, and more particularly, can the objectives be achieved within a time frame acceptable to the American people? None of these questions have answers that are obvious or universally agreed upon.

What exactly does the United States hope to achieve in this effort? It is an important question to answer because the objective is the standard against which Americans will naturally judge the worthiness of the effort. When the objective was the destruction of Al Qaeda, there was little question of worth, and that is at least partially why official justifications retain it as the primary standard. In fact, of course, the current war effort has relatively little to do with subduing terrorists who are barely present in the country where the war is being waged. The only connection to this objective is indirect: whoever prevails in the current Afghan civil conflict will be more or less amenable to letting the terrorists return. That indirect rationale, however, leads to two other questions: Is that an adequate justification for the effort being undertaken (is it worth the cost)? And are there other ways to accomplish the same goal?

If preventing the return of Al Qaeda is only an indirect objective, why is the United States continuing to prosecute the war there? The answers tend to be more modest. Christia and Semple, for instance, argue that the goal is "to provide security for ordinary Afghans," the absence of which "has most prevented large scale reconciliation in the country." O'Hanlon phrases much the same objective in more purely military terms, arguing it is "to protect the population while gradually training Afghan forces to assume that responsibility." Directing their comment specifically toward the latest American surge in the country, Christia and Semple maintain the goal must be to "demonstrably stem the insurgents' influence in Pashtun areas" so that "militants there will start to believe that they might stay alive if they realign with the government." These rationales suggest, then, that the real goal is to help build support for the third most corrupt government in the world, arguably a dubious objective.

The second question is whether the United States has a viable strategy to move toward achievement of the goal. Once again, the answer is not obvious, as 10 years of inconclusive fighting has demonstrated. Borrowing from the apparent success of the counterinsurgency (COIN) doctrine of which General David Petraeus (the former U.S. commander in Afghanistan and, since mid-2011, director of central intelligence) has been the leading advocate, the United States has attempted a military strategy designed to remove Taliban influence from the countryside and provide a shield behind which the Afghan government can establish its legitimate authority. The effectiveness of that strategy in the Afghan theater has not yet been demonstrated, however, for at least three reasons.

The first problem is the size of the force conducting the operation. COIN doctrine, as enunciated in the current American manual (*FM 3-24*) suggests the need for one counterinsurgent soldier for every 20 citizens in the affected country. This large number is necessary to maintain a permanent presence that can provide security for the population; lower numbers mean that although COIN forces may clear areas of the opposition, they cannot stay because they are needed to secure other areas. When they leave, the danger is that the Taliban will simply return and take vengeance on anyone who has cooperated with the liberating forces.

Given the total population of Afghanistan, implementation of the COIN guidelines would require a combined U.S./ISAF and effective Afghan force of 600,000, and the force is nowhere nearly that large. Foreign troops are at about 150,000 (about the same size as the Soviet force that was inadequate for the situation), and while the size of Afghan proportion of the force is increasing, its reliability is uncertain. Some apologists argue that there are parts of the country that do not require pacification and occupation, thereby lowering the force level needed to around 400,000. The current force is not that large, and it only approaches the required size by making some very optimistic assumptions about the quality of the Afghan forces employed (this argument is presented most fully by O'Hanlon). If one makes the assumption that Afghan forces will be either inadequate in size or quality for the mission, the only way to approach those numbers is by a substantial commitment of American forces over a long period. Blackwill questions this solution, arguing "to stay the counterinsurgency course . . . would not make sense because American interests in Afghanistan are not high enough to justify such an investment."

A second problem that has become increasingly apparent in the past year or so is that the continuing presence of American forces is not clearly desired by the Afghans themselves. The most obvious manifestation of this growing anti-Americanism has been the strong dissent that has accompanied situations in which American missions have inadvertently resulted in Afghan civilian casualties. Karzai began arguing in 2010 for a reduced American presence for this reason. To many, and especially rural, Afghans, the Americans must appear to be nothing but the latest iteration of unwanted foreign invaders and occupiers. The Karzai government (and for that matter the United States) also faces the double bind that the apparent reliance of Karzai on the Americans undermines his legitimacy—which is in short supply anyway—but that the removal of that presence would leave his government highly questionably capable of survival against the Taliban.

The third problem is that it is also not entirely clear that the Afghans who are "liberated" by COIN operations see the replacement of Taliban rule by the current government as a particularly attractive alternative. Polling data indicate that the Taliban are highly unpopular in the country, but so is the government, for reasons already raised. Badkhen, a journalist who has traveled extensively in the country and who visited northern Afghanistan (which is not the most hotly contested part of Afghanistan) in early 2011, reported that "the people, frustrated by unfulfilled promises of international aid and prosperity, wondered whether puritanical and cruel governance by the Islamist militia may be a better option than the anarchy, corruption, and abandonment" they currently face. This problem reflects the need for grass-roots support for the government, a problem Jones addresses in his 2009 *Foreign Affairs* article: "the Taliban and other insurgent groups have recognized the local nature of politics in Afghanistan and have developed a local strategy. . . . The Afghan government and U.S. and NATO forces, meanwhile, have largely been missing at the local level."

The current American objective may be questionably worthy and its execution problematical, but that is not the only challenge that continued involvement in the war must confront. The third major question raised in the continuing conduct of the war is how long it will last. It is an important question both because of the strain the ongoing effort creates for the United States in a budget-constrained environment and the patience of Americans toward the war. The three factors—worth, progress, and duration—are, of course, related: the U.S. government would have a much easier job selling a strategy of "staying the course" if everyone agreed the course was worth pursuing and that progress was being made. Neither is unambiguously the case, making the need for a "light at the end of the tunnel" more important than it might otherwise be.

Unfortunately, the prospects, even when viewed by apologists of the war, are not very clear. Rather, they echo a general refrain of a protracted ongoing commitment. Miller states the case in an article titled "Finish the Job" (in *Foreign Affairs*) in general terms: "The application of increased military resources and a coherent strategy will have an effect on the Afghan battlefield *if given enough time to succeed*" (emphasis added). O'Hanlon, a consistent champion of the American involvement, offers a parallel, limited, and similarly vague prospect: "A significant level of success—represented by an Afghan state that is able to control most of its territory and gradually improve the lives of its citizens [will require] *several more years of resolve*" (emphasis added). Blackwill, who opposes a continuation of the present strategy, adds a measure of specificity, maintaining the current strategy must be applied "for the next seven to ten years" to hope for success.

Positive answers to these questions about the U.S. involvement are not evident, and they affect the current debate over how long the United States should continue its long commitment to the Afghan War. If more negative interpretations are accepted, the worth of continued involvement—continued efforts that will result in no better or only a slightly better outcome than if the United States does not—appear less appealing and convincing. If, on the other hand, the result of American perseverance is a greatly improved prospect both for Afghanistan and the realization of American interests—such as the resistance to a returned terrorist presence—this would suggest greater support for "staying the course." In the absence of definitive evidence about which outcome is more or less likely, disagreement will continue. The unknown future potency of a bin Laden–less Al Qaeda only adds further ambiguity to the situation.

U.S. Relations with Postwar Afghanistan

Projecting what American foreign relations with Afghanistan will be like when the war (or at least the American portion of it) is over is clearly an exercise in speculation that goes well beyond the uncertain nature of even U.S.–Iraq relations after the American withdrawal. The major variable in the mix is the condition of postwar Afghanistan, and that is highly uncertain at this point, with very different patterns of relationship highly dependent on which outcome holds in the country. Of some predictive relevance will be how the United States deals with postoccupation Iraq, which may serve as a harbinger to general U.S. policy in the region and thus toward Afghanistan.

A traditional, decisive military ending is probably the least likely outcome to the war. Such an eventuality, where one side or the other is clearly overwhelmed on the battlefield and surrenders to the other, is simply not the nature of how contemporary asymmetrical war ends, and neither side seems capable of imposing such a solution. Even with the considerable level of outside assistance it has received, there is no danger that the current regime will crush the Taliban, and even if that unlikely outcome were to appear imminent, the Taliban would probably simply do what it did in 2001: sneak across the border into Pakistan, regroup, and wait for an opportunity to return. Likewise, the insurgents are unlikely to reprise 1996, when they brought down the regime by conquering the major cities, because of the existence or threat of outside intervention to prevent that outcome.

These two unlikely scenarios (a decisive Afghan government or Taliban victory), however, frame the range of possible outcomes. A return of something like Taliban control is still possible, and depending on how such a regime deals with the possible reestablishment of relations with an Al Qaeda without the leadership of bin Laden, the prospect could be more or less greatly opposed by the United States. If it is true that the major core interest in Afghanistan is, as Christia and Semple argue, "to prevent the Taliban's Al Qaeda allies from exploiting Afghanistan as a base for terrorist operations," Taliban assurances that it would not do so—combined with American threats that reestablishment of the bond would result in violent retaliation against Al Qaeda in Afghanistan—might remove a critical barrier to American objections to some level of Taliban participation in postwar governance. For this to become feasible, as Christia and Semple further point out, "Taliban commanders will have to demonstrate that they have broken with Al Qaeda." The difficulty of American embrace of such an outcome, however, is that it would appear a defeat of the American rationale for the war since the objective was broadened in 2001. These possible dynamics provide some negotiating positions for talks between the Afghan government, the Taliban, and the United States. Such discussions have been going on at low levels for some time and will likely continue. The death of bin Laden could move these talks in either direction. An Al Qaeda without its leader (and friend) could be easier for the Taliban to abandon, but depending on how those who have succeeded bin Laden act and what Al Qaeda's degree of desperation becomes, it could also draw the Taliban closer as the protector of its old ally.

The other extreme outcome is a victory for the current government. This scenario is also difficult to envision, and its occurrence would not necessarily meet all American objectives. There is little indication, for instance, that this is an outcome either that can be obtained or that the Afghan people want. As Jones (2010) argues, "there are far too few national security forces to protect the population, the police are legendary for their corruption and incompetence, and many rural communities do not want a strong national government." The triumph of the Karzai regime, put a slightly different way, would not be embraced by the entire Afghan population and would thus not be a particularly amenable environment for American interaction with a future Afghanistan.

In addition, the Karzai regime's apparent direction, aided and abetted by the Americans, runs counter to the American "dream" outcome of a strong, stable, and vibrant Afghanistan. Such an Afghan outcome is premised on a strong, stable, and democratic postwar Afghanistan, and that is unlikely for contradictory reasons. On one hand, Miller points out that "the greatest threat to long-term success in Afghanistan is . . . the Afghan government's endemic weakness and the international community's failure to address it." One reason that Afghan governments have traditionally been weak has been that the fractured, fractious population distrusts strong governments, which they fear will impinge on their personal independence and way of life. If democracy has a meaning to rural Afghans, it is autonomy for them from outside rule and interference with their daily lives, and this desire contradicts the appeal of a strong central government. As Jones puts it, "talk of democracy . . . [is] difficult to reconcile with just how little power was delegated to any institution not part of the central government." One of the reasons that counterinsurgency pacification programs aimed at wresting power from the Taliban in localities and handing that power over to Afghan authorities are resisted is that the people do not trust the government much more than they do the insurgents. Finally, it is not clear that the "power brokers" behind the current regime uniformly welcome a democratization of the country because, as Biddle, Christia, and Their point out, "A transparent electoral democracy would threaten their status, authority, and ability to profit from corruption and abuse."

The final possible outcome is that the war will end with something like a return to the pre-Soviet Afghanistan, a country with a nominal central government in Kabul but with effective control devolving back to the local level. While this outcome could hardly be considered a great success for American policy, it might be the best possible outcome and one around which some justification could be woven. If nominally westernizing forces dominate the Kabul government (Karzai sheds of some of his most corrupt associates, for instance) and are in control of a security force that can maintain minimal order, the United States could argue that it has improved the situation as it existed before 9/11, and as long as the government can maintain enough power to keep Al Qaeda from returning, it could be argued that the core interest has been realized as well. Moreover, such a solution would seem to reflect the will of at least a sizable number of Afghans.

The evolution of postoccupation Iraq will also have an influence on how the United States interacts with postwar Afghanistan. The parameters of that relationship are, of course, only beginning to take place as postoccupation Iraq adapts to life without the American military presence, and it is speculative what the outcome of the process of adjustment may be. Certainly, American influence will be diminished from its apex in the years immediately after the invasion, and the Iraqi regime is almost certainly going to distance itself as far as it can politically from the former occupiers. In the case of Iraq, this tendency will certainly be reinforced by Iran, which is also likely to provide an alternative source of some funding for the Iraqi regime while it rebuilds and gets its oil industry working to a point that it can provide a meaningful source of revenue for the regime in Baghdad. To the degree these efforts are successful, the Iraqis will be able to create more distance between them and the Americans.

Some of these same dynamics are likely in Afghanistan. The longer the Americans stay, the more they are likely to alienate greater parts of the population (a reality seemingly ignored by proponents of the war) and thus fuel a political necessity for Karzai or a successor to appear as independent of the United States as possible. This will be somewhat more difficult for the Afghans than the Iraqis, however, because Afghanistan has no equivalent source of outside assistance in the region like the Iraqis have in Iran. Both Pakistan and India have interests in their own, contradictory outcomes, but they have largely cancelled one another out in the past, acting as a source of discord, not reconciliation. This means that any recovery assistance that Afghanistan will need will almost have to come with some American input, thereby limiting somewhat the degree to which the postwar Afghan regime can cut the umbilical cord with the Americans.

There are two trump cards in this equation. The first is the degree to which the United States seeks to distance itself from Afghanistan after it physically leaves the country. If the Vietnam experience is any indication, the American public might well lose interest very quickly in what happens there once the United States has physically departed, and the degree to which Afghanistan will resemble Vietnam will be foreshadowed by how the public reacts to the end of the occupation of Iraq. What makes Afghanistan potentially different than either Vietnam or Iraq is the continuing shadow of Al Qaeda, and particularly any indications that the terrorist group may be attempting to return to its old Afghan sanctuaries.

The other trump card, of course, is Al Qaeda after bin Laden, a factor most prominent in determining both the pace and structure of American withdrawal from Afghanistan and in the nature and quality of U.S. relations with that country after the American portion of the war ends. A dramatically weakened—even vanishing—Al Qaeda very much simplifies the American perspective. An Afghanistan that has no Al Qaeda presence or influence allows the United States to proclaim its original mission accomplished and thus expedites removing the American presence. A postwar Afghanistan that does not allow whatever may be left of Al Qaeda to return—regardless of what the United States may think of that government otherwise—is a far easier place with which to deal as well.

U.S. OPTIONS

How much residual interest the United States retains in Afghanistan is thus largely dependent on two factors. The most obvious is the continuing duration and extent of American active military participation in the struggle over political control of the country. As long as there are large numbers of American troops on the ground affecting the military situation there, the United States will continue to exercise some influence over the decisions of the Karzai regime. At this point, Hamid Karzai and the United States are effectively stuck with one another in a relationship about which both have reservations. The United States has a legitimate concern over the rampant corruption that impedes the ability of the current regime to gain legitimacy and support necessary to win the "battle for the hearts and minds" of the Afghan people, and the heavy American footprint on the scene clearly concerns Karzai for essentially the same reason; that is, the occupation is increasingly resented, and Karzai gets part of the blame.

At this point, the question is not whether but when the United States will complete the process of military withdrawal begun during the second half of 2011. A substantial American force remains in place, and there will be political pressures in the United States both to reduce and to maintain, even strengthen, it. As O'Hanlon summarizes it, "Although an anxious Congress may push him [Obama] to withdraw, the fear of seeming weak on national security will probably pull at least as firmly in the other direction." A movement in either direction—toward accelerated withdrawal or committing to "stay the course"—will be politically controversial domestically in the United States and is unlikely until after the 2012 presidential election. By the time of Obama's reelection or defeat, the changed status of Al Qaeda will also likely be clearer and provide either opportunities or limitations on post–U.S. election options.

The ideal solution for the United States, of course, is a gradual (and accelerating) development of the Afghan security forces (army and police) to the point that responsibility for controlling or destroying the Taliban threat can be turned progressively over to them; Iraq is a precedent of sorts. Such an outcome would suit all political elements: the political right in the United States could claim success against the Taliban and Al Qaeda and pride at U.S. resolve, while the political left will be relieved as American military presence fades and disappears. This outcome would also likely minimize the bad taste the Afghans have for the Americans and thus reduce the inevitable reduction in influence the United States will incur when it is no longer physically present with military forces. How this evolution affects the ultimate fate of Al Qaeda is crucial to its desirability and acceptability by Americans. Once again, the evolution of postoccupation Iraq will offer some harbinger of things to come.

It is also possible, however, that the situation will not change for the better at an acceptable rate for either side. As indicated earlier, apologists for continuing U.S. participation in the war project a protracted continuing commitment—a projected duration of five to ten years is not unusual. Such projections are almost certainly unsustainable: they will pose an increasingly unpopular burden on U.S. financial health and recovery, they will be accompanied by a progressive NATO abandonment of the field (leaving the United States largely on its own along with the Afghans), and they offer a prospect the Afghans themselves increasingly do not want to face.

How much ability the United States has to influence future Afghan events will depend on the decisions that the United States makes about its continuing presence after the dust is settled from the 2012 elections in this country. The options are reduced effectively to two, and neither is without potential drawbacks. Continuing the effort may or may not result in the kind of dramatic improvement in the Afghan situation that will be necessary for proponents to maintain the potency of their advocacy. The very real prospect is that doing so will result in a virtually imperceptible change in the situation that will be increasingly difficult to sell in the United States. The other option is a rapid withdrawal. That option means leaving the Afghan government to its own devices in the civil war, which could be a death sentence for it. The question is whether by then the American public will care enough about what happens in Afghanistan to respond.

CONCLUSIONS

The history of the last 30 years or more has not been kind to the Afghan people. They have been in a state of some kind of war since 1979: a decade of resistance to the Soviet invasion and occupation, another decade between the Soviet withdrawal in 1989 and 2001 when internal elements have fought for control, and, since 2001, a civil war in which NATO and the United States have been in effective occupation of the country. All of this misfortune reflects the reality of Afghan history that goes back across time and causes Badkhen plaintively to reflect, "It seems impossible for things to get worse in a place that has been systematically brutalized by invasions and fratricides for thousands of years. But nothing is impossible."

The United States has come late to the Afghan landscape, but the continuing war there has thrust this country into the middle of the contemporary scene in this long-playing drama. The initial impulse of the United States—lashing out at the source from which the September 11 attacks originated—is hard to fault, but what followed is not so immune from reexamination. The United States did, in President Obama's apt term, "take its eye off the ball" after the initial anti–Al Qaeda response was supplanted by a greater concern with Iraq, and the result was a gradual drift into what has become a major commitment that probably would not have been authorized had its evolution been anticipated. Had President Bush gone before the American people and declared that he intended to commit the United States to a major intervention in Afghanistan for 10 years or more with an uncertain outcome, the move would almost certainly have been blocked. Not the least of the reasons for a negative response would have been that beyond ridding Afghanistan of Al Qaeda, the United States has no sustaining interests in the country that would justify such a commitment.

Al Qaeda no longer maintains a substantial presence in Afghanistan, but the United States does. The sustaining premise of American efforts is to create a situation in Afghanistan that is sufficiently stable that Al Qaeda will remain unwelcome and will thus not be allowed to return. The irony is that the major accomplishment of the campaign against Al Qaeda—killing bin Laden—did not occur on Afghan soil, nor was it obviously related to the American action in Afghanistan. Whether that is an adequate justification depends on whether the American effort can result in that outcome and, even if it can, whether that outcome is important enough to warrant the effort in blood and treasure that has been expended on the Afghan plain.

STUDY/DISCUSSION QUESTIONS

1. Discuss the broad contours of Afghan history, including the impact of geography on that history. How does this experience create Afghanistan's reputation as the "graveyard of empires"? How and why did the United States first become involved there?
2. What was the impact of the Soviet invasion on Afghanistan? How has the Soviet period helped to frame the current situation?
3. What is the role of 9/11 in U.S.–Afghan relations? How did it create two different objectives for the United States there? Why is this distinction relevant today?
4. Who are the Pashtuns? Why are they critical to Afghanistan and also to Pakistan? How do they contribute to Afghanistan's uniqueness? Include a discussion of Hamid Karzai and the Taliban in your answer.
5. What are the major issues, debates, disputes, and possible outcomes of American involvement in the Afghan war? Elaborate.
6. What are the ongoing American interests and objectives in Afghanistan? How do these interests and objectives affect how and when the United States can end its

involvement in the war? What conditions arising from the war's end will define postwar U.S.–Afghan relations?
7. What are the U.S. options for ending its part in the Afghan war? Which do you think is the best? Why?

READING/RESEARCH MATERIALS

Badkhen, Anna. "Spring in Afghanistan: Cold and Violent." *Foreign Policy* (online), March 9, 2011.

Barfield, Thomas. *Afghanistan: A Cultural and Political History.* Princeton, NJ: Princeton University Press, 2010.

Biddle, Stephen, Fotini Christia, and Alexander Thier. "Defining Success in Afghanistan: What Can the United States Accept?" *Foreign Affairs* 89, 4 (July/August 2010), 48–60.

Blackwill, Robert D. "Plan B in Afghanistan: Why a De Facto Partition Is the Least Bad Option." *Foreign Affairs* 90, 1 (January/February 2011), 42–50.

Christia, Fotini, and Michael Semple. "Flipping the Taliban: How to Win in Afghanistan." *Foreign Affairs* 88, 4 (July/August 2009), 34–45.

Coll, Steve. *Ghost Wars: The Secret History of the CIA, Afghanistan, and bin Laden from the Soviet Invasion to September 10, 2011.* New York: Penguin Books, 2004.

Crews, Robert D., and Amin Tarzi (eds.). *The Taliban and the Crisis of Afghanistan.* Cambridge, MA: Harvard University Press, 2008.

Ewans, Martin. *Afghanistan: A Short History of Its People and Politics.* New York: Harper Perennials, 2002.

Giustozzi, Antonio (ed.). *Decoding the Taliban: Insights from the Afghan Field.* New York: Columbia University Press, 2009.

———. *Empires of Mud.* New York: Columbia University Press, 2010.

Jalili, Ali A. "The Future of Afghanistan." *Parameters* XXXVI, 2 (Summer 2006), 4–14.

Jones, Seth G. *In the Graveyard of Empires: America's War in Afghanistan.* New York: W. W. Norton, 2009.

———. "It Takes the Villages: Bringing Change from Below in Afghanistan." *Foreign Affairs* 89, 3 (May/June 2010), 120–127.

Kaplan, Robert D. "Man versus Afghanistan." *The Atlantic* 305, 3 (April 2010), 60–71.

Miller, Paul D. "Finish the Job: How the War in Afghanistan Can Be Won." *Foreign Affairs* 90, 1 (January/February 2011), 51–65.

Mortenson, Greg, and David Oliver Relin. *Three Cups of Tea: One Man's Mission to Promote Peace One School at a Time.* New York: Penguin Books, 2006.

National Security Strategy of the United States. Washington, DC: The White House, May 2010.

Nevile, Leigh. *Special Operations Forces in Afghanistan.* New York: Osprey Publishing, 2008.

O'Hanlon, Michael. "Staying Power: The U.S. Mission in Afghanistan Beyond 2011." *Foreign Affairs* 89, 5 (September/October 2010), 63–79.

Rashid, Ahmed. *Descent into Chaos: The United States and the Disaster in Pakistan, Afghanistan, and Central Asia.* New York: Penguin Books, 2009.

———. *Taliban: Militant Islam, Oil and Fundamentalism in Central Asia* (2nd ed.). New Haven, CT: Yale University Press, 2010.

Rubin, Barnett E. "Saving Afghanistan." *Foreign Affairs* 86, 1 (January/February 2007), 57–78.

Snow, Donald M., and Dennis M. Drew. *From Lexington to Baghdad and Beyond: War and Politics in the American Experience.* Armonk, NY: M E Sharpe, 2009.

United States Army and U.S. Marine Corps. *Counterinsurgency Field Manual (U.S. Army Field Manual 3-24, Marine Corps Warfighting Publication 3-22.5).* Chicago: University of Chicago Press, 2007.

Zaeef, Abdul Salaam. *My Life with the Taliban.* New York: Columbia University Press, 2010.

Domestic Politics and Neighboring States

One of the great historic advantages the United States has had in its dealings with the rest of the world has been its physical isolation from outside influences for much of its development. From the beginning of the Republic in the eighteenth century until the early twentieth century, the United States was effectively an island state, separated and protected from the outside world by wide oceans that facilitated America fulfilling its "manifest destiny" in North America to build a new and powerful state on the continent. This cocoon was further reinforced by the existence of comparatively weak, docile countries—Canada and Mexico—sharing frontiers with the American republic.

Despite this geopolitical situation, the United States has not been able entirely to ignore the countries on its immediate periphery, and particularly those states and areas to its south. The United States and Canada share so many common historical and cultural similarities that relations between them have never been especially problematic, but the same is not true for the areas south of the U.S. border, sometimes collectively known simply as Latin America.

The overwhelming geopolitical fact of American relations with the countries to its south has been the sheer size and comparative power of the United States vis-à-vis its Latin counterparts. The "colossus of the North" has cast a long and, in some cases, less than totally benevolent shadow over those relations, and they continue to evolve in the twenty-first century.

The chapters in this part provide an overview of American policy with two of its neighbors, Mexico and Cuba. The two countries are dissimilar in size and physical proximity to the United States—Cuba a relatively small island 100 miles off the Florida coast, and Mexico a medium power that shares a nearly 2,000-mile land border with the United States. Part of the United States (the Southwest) was wrested from Mexico in the nineteenth century, and Cuban independence and compromises of that independence in which the United States was a defining factor mark the turn of the twentieth century. The result is a somewhat ambivalent legacy for current policy in both cases.

A single, but quite different, dynamic dominates American policy toward the two countries. Mexican–American relations have been defined in recent years overwhelmingly in terms of differences between them at their joint border. Although the border itself is a part of the policy disagreements the two neighbors have, it is also a symbol rather than the heart of those disagreements. The basic matters of contention between Mexico and the United States center on three issues: immigration and trade, illicit drugs, and American national security defined in terms of terrorism. Each has a border dimension: drugs and immigrants, as well as trade, transit the border; any solutions have a border dimension; and the fear that terrorists might enter the United States across the long frontier is a concern as well. Solutions, however, require getting beyond the border manifestation to deeper causes of these problems.

U.S. foreign policy with Cuba has been defined in terms of the breach of relations between them in 1959 when Fidel Castro came to power and transformed a Cuban island that had been a virtual dependency of the United States into a hostile communist state. The United States responded to this event by imposing a harsh, all-encompassing economic embargo on the island in an attempt to isolate it and bring down Cuban communism. That policy has not produced its intended result, and the embargo remains the central feature of the severed relations between the two countries.

Domestic American politics adds a distinctive aspect to attempts to change U.S.–Cuban relations, especially in a projected post-Castro era, and also to U.S. relations with Mexico. With the possible exception of relations with Israel (see Chapter 11), U.S. relations with its southern neighbors probably are more influenced—some would say distorted—by domestic factors within the United States than are American relations with any other countries in the world. One of the major reasons for including these two states in the list of cases is to explore the extent to which *domestic* politics acts as a determinant of *foreign* policy apart from the international environment that is the more "normal" incubator of foreign policy.

Domestic politics affects American foreign policy toward the two countries in quite different ways. The relationship with Mexico is quite complex in a causative sense. U.S.–Mexican disagreements may center on their joint border, but that boundary is a more symbolic than substantive part of differences that have a clear domestic base in the United States that radiates to and affects their foreign policy interactions. As Chapter 9 argues, much of the current disagreement centers on two issues often erroneously portrayed as border problems: illegal immigration and drugs. The immigration problem is part of the global phenomenon of economic migration from the developing to the developed world, and its controversial American application is fueled by the existence of menial, low-paying jobs in the United States that most Americans will not perform for the low wages illegal immigrants will accept. The flood of illegal immigration (and the demand for social services they create) is a border issue to the extent that immigrants do cross the border, but the reasons why they do are primarily the result of economic realities in the United States. Similarly, drugs transit the U.S.–Mexico frontier because of the large American market for them. The basic problem is the demand, not the transit. These two issues thus have domestic roots, but since each is extremely difficult to resolve (if they can be resolved), it has been politically expedient to treat them as border issues, thus making them into foreign policy rather than domestic concerns.

The domestic constituency that has elevated the border issue to prominence is diverse geographically (although more concentrated in the border states and states with large immigrant populations than elsewhere) and fairly homogenous ideologically (it is strongest among conservatives). The domestic sources of U.S. Cuban policy are much more specific, concentrated in the Cuban expatriate communities in south Florida and New Jersey, where Cubans fleeing the Castro revolution have taken up disproportionate residence. This anti-Castro minority within the United States is well organized and financed, highly vocal in its opposition to any change in current policy, and strategically concentrated in two electorally important states, and is thus capable of exerting an effective stranglehold over a U.S. policy toward Cuba that would likely be quite different in their absence. Whether this control exercised by the Cuban-American community will weaken as Cuba confronts the post-Castro era and the most virulent opponents of Castro policy age and die is a part of the political dynamic of the relationship.

Mexico: Reconciling Common Borders with Underlying Tensions

PREVIEW

Because they are joined along a nearly 2,000 mile boundary, there has been a long and intimate relationship between the United States and its southern neighbor. Both share a common historical, developmental past of colonial rule followed by independence, but their common boundary has been both a cause and symbol of differences between the two countries. In the contemporary environment, the pattern of border-caused or border-related issues continues as the dominant theme of interaction. The current foreign policy differences between the two have the sanctity of the border as their most obvious manifestation, but the border becomes important because it symbolizes other issues, notably illicit drug traffic and the social problems it creates, unauthorized (or "illegal") immigration and its impacts on both countries, and national security, notably terrorism. Each of these problems has significant domestic as well as foreign policy implications in each country, and the United States is constrained in its ability to influence the Mexican aspect of the problem as long as it still has a corresponding domestic problem—a difficulty faced by Mexico as well.

Relations between the United States and Mexico, like those with Canada, have always been special since they involve the interaction between this country and one of its closest neighbors, with whom it shares a 1,933-mile land border. The relationship has always been complex and frequently tinged with controversy, as it is today. Throughout most of the nearly two centuries that both have been independent countries, the crux of that relationship and its most problematic aspects have centered on the boundary between the two, although the border has often been used as much as a symbol as it has been the basis for disagreement. The substantive issues that have divided the United States and its southern neighbor have changed across time, but the boundary that separates them has always been a factor.

The boundary issue has had two major facets across time. The first, which was basically decided to Mexican disfavor, is where the border should be. That issue was contested mostly during the first half of the nineteenth century. It began with the American push westward across North America, centering on the physical extent of the largely unpopulated (except sparsely by indigenous American Indians) territory west of the Mississippi River. The major contention was how far to the west the Louisiana Purchase extended, and the disagreement came to focus on Texas. After Mexican independence was completed in 1821, the populating of and claim over Texas dominated relations between the two countries.

The boundary that essentially exists today was determined mostly through two related actions during the 1840s. In 1837, Texas had declared itself independent of Mexico and established the Texas Republic. Eight years later, the United States agreed to annex Texas to the Union as a state in 1845. Still undecided at that point was exactly where the southern and western border between Texas and Mexico lay, and that dispute spilled over into armed clashes in 1846, precipitating the Mexican War that ended with the Treaty of Guadalupe-Hidalgo in 1848. That treaty established the essential outlines of the permanent frontier between the two, amended slightly by the Gadsden Purchase of 1854 that added parts of New Mexico and Arizona to American territory. In the process of adjustment, Mexico lost approximately half the territory that it inherited from the Spanish Empire (essentially what Americans think of as the American Southwest and California). To this day, many Mexicans resent both this process and its outcome.

The other aspect of the boundary issue has been control of the boundary and the underlying motives or reasons for maintaining more or less strict control over what passes across the border in one direction or the other. As a more or less general principle, this aspect represents a fundamental ambivalence over the functions that international boundaries perform. One function is as a barrier or *line of control* (a term used in Chapters 5 and 6 with regard to Kashmir). From this vantage point, the major role of a border is to serve as a way to exclude undesirable people or things from national territory. This aspect is controversial because there is generally not a consensus around what is "desirable" and what is not, at least as regards some items. The second function is as a *gateway*, a mechanism to promote the flow of *desirable* people and things across that same boundary. Once again, there will always be disagreement about what movement should be encouraged and what should not.

Boundary issues become complicated because the intention of border regulation is to promote both functions: letting desirable things and people in while excluding undesirable things and people. As an example in the current

U.S.–Mexico context, the provisions of the North American Free Trade Agreement call for the removal of policy and physical barriers between the member states (the United States, Mexico, and Canada), the gateway function, and as measured in terms of trade flows the implementing policies have been largely successful. At the same time, the border is also intended to keep contraband items out of the country, most notably illicit drugs in the contemporary U.S.–Mexican relationship. The problem is, of course, that although the two categories are discrete in principle, they are not always so separable in practice (e.g., a truck crossing the border going north may contain both blue jeans sewn in Mexico and cocaine). The two functions are often very difficult to reconcile: establishing procedures to maximize the controlling function may impede the gateway function, and vice versa, a quandary discussed later in the chapter. The underlying point, however, is that the border per se is more a symbol of the underlying tension (e.g., commerce versus criminal activity) than the problem itself.

The issues surrounding penetration of the boundary as a matter of control today have long roots in history. One point of contention is movement of people across the border, and it has long been a matter of disagreement. The heart of the immigration question is whether, or to what extent, the United States seeks to restrict entrance of Mexican citizens onto U.S. soil. There has always been a flow across the border, and there still is. According to Nevins, for instance, there are 250 million "authorized crossings of the boundary annually each way." Most of these crossings involve commercial activities of some kind, such as Mexican workers who commute from Mexican homes to American jobs and then return daily. Only a highly publicized fraction of this number is controversial—the so-called "illegal immigrants"—concern about which dominates headlines.

The other aspect of border control is *what* crosses the frontier. Once again, the emphasis has been on illicit traffic crossing the border from Mexico to the United States—notably drugs but including ancillary problems like Mexican trucks using American highways—although that is a two-way street: the Mexican government complains about the reverse flow of "narcodollars" and American-supplied weapons going into Mexico. At the same time, the volume of desired, perfectly legal movement of goods and services is enormous: between 1993 and 2004 (roughly since the North American Free Trade Agreement or NAFTA entered force), "U.S.-Mexican trade more than tripled in value from 89.5 billion to $275.3 billion," again according to Nevins. The same control regime that encourages legal interchange is expected to restrict illicit exchange.

The extent and intensity of the debate about the border is accentuated because the U.S.–Mexico boundary is the longest territorial border between a member of the traditional most-developed world and the traditional developing world. It is not the only such frontier, of course, where countries of relatively different levels of development meet either physically or in proximity: Malaysia and Indonesia in Asia, the European Union and many North African countries, and the Republic of South Africa and both Zimbabwe and

Mozambique share some of the qualities of Mexican–U.S. interactions. The shared border between these two neighbors, however, is different than the others: the border is more intimate and extensive, and the historic disparities in wealth and standards of living are the most striking.

This economic development disparity comes into direct conflict at the border. As long as there is a disparity between the wealth of two adjoining countries (as is the case with less-developed Mexico and more highly developed United States), there will always be a pull across the border for the less advantaged to try to partake of the greater advantages of the more-developed country— economic migration. That same dynamic is certainly true in the countries of the EU, where immigrant from the less-wealthy adjacent areas such as North Africa and Turkey migrate to northern European sources of wealth and income. Increasingly strict lines of control may try to restrict that flow, but they will never succeed entirely as long as people are desperate enough or have high enough incentives to move and try to increase their personal well-being. Wealthy states may enact legislation and erect barriers to this immigrant flow, but until conditions improve adequately in the less-developed country that its citizens do not feel compelled or motivated to move from poverty to greater affluence, such efforts will always be at least partially unsuccessful.

The border issue has direct domestic political consequences in each country as well. Mexican–American relations have become particularly controversial in the past two decades because of the increased flow both of unauthorized immigrants and illicit drugs into the United States transiting across the long frontier between the two. While the roots of both of these problems are not boundary issues per se, they become border problems as they enter the sphere of foreign policy. The reasons there is a drug problem along the frontier, for instance, have little to do with the border itself, but arise from other dynamics such as the diversion of drug trafficking from South America through the Caribbean Sea to Central American transit routes. The problem is increased by the continuing demand for large amounts of drugs in the United States market—which in turn is attributable largely to other dynamics such as the "democratizing" development of cheaper drugs like crack cocaine and methamphetamine that have enlarged the customer base for increasing and apparently insatiable demands for these illicit substances (both of these problems are discussed in more detail later in the chapter). This becomes a border problem because interdiction of incoming supplies across the long frontier is one very public way to appear to attack the underlying problem and one that requires minimal personal sacrifice for the majority of Americans.

The various issues symbolized by the boundary are not, of course, the entirety of the long-standing relationship between the two countries, just the most dramatic manifestation of underlying dynamics that have a more durable place in the overall relationship. In one form or another, the problem of trafficking in illicit substances across the frontier goes back well over a century, from the post–Civil War period (morphine addiction among veterans) to bootleggers running alcohol across the border during Prohibition in the United States (1919–1933). Immigrants of one kind or another have been coming across the frontier for even longer: in a few isolated cases, there are even Indian tribes who live on opposite sides of the frontier and transit openly across it (a particular nightmare for U.S. line-of-control efforts). Of the myriad of arguments made about border control, the only one of reasonably recent vintage is the possible cross-border movement of terrorists into the United States from Mexico.

These issues need to be placed in context to afford a panoramic view of U.S.–Mexican relations. Compared to the other countries discussed in this volume, U.S.–Mexican relations are different in that they are between two adjacent countries which necessarily have very important interests in what happens in the other and in what actions they take toward one another. One can, for instance, debate whether very important, vital U.S. interests are engaged in a civil war in a place like Libya, but there would be no doubt that the outbreak of important civil disorder in Mexico would invoke the most important American concerns. Likewise, Mexico, as the smaller and more dependent power in the bilateral relations between the two North American countries, has a strong vested interest in what happens in the United States that impinges on it, as many things do.

Unraveling the sources of foreign policy disagreement centering on the border thus requires taking a step backward and looking at those relevant aspects of the Mexican situation and experience that underlie and influence those relations, which is the function of the next section.

MEXICO: A SKETCH

Mexico has a long, if uneven, history. The first artifacts of social life in what is now Mexico have been dated back to around 1500 BCE, and the first Indian civilizations were active in the country between 300 and 900 CE. The Toltec empire thrived in the area known as the Valley of Mexico in south-central Mexico from around that time until about 1200 CE. They were supplanted by the Aztecs, who built the capital city of Tenochtitlan (Mexico City) in the middle 1300s. The Aztecs controlled most of what is now Mexico when Hernando Cortes led the first Spanish mission to the country in 1521, slightly less than a century before English colonization of what became the United States began in the American colonies of Virginia (1607) and Massachusetts (1620).

For the better part of three centuries, North America was divided among European colonizers. The British and French each had their domains in what became the United States and Canada, with France losing its territories in Canada to the British in the Six Years War (1756–1763) and selling its remaining holdings (the Louisiana Purchase) to the young United States in 1803, a move that was the springboard for the first Mexican–American border conflict three decades later. Mexico, including both the present-day country and generous parts of the American Southwest (including California) and Florida, remained under Spanish colonial rule until 1810, when the Mexican struggle for independence began under the leadership of Miguel Hidalgo y Castillo; Mexican independence was finally achieved in 1821.

The colonial experience equipped the United States and Mexico differently for independence, prosperity, and development. During the nineteenth century the United States expanded inexorably across the North American continent, in 1846 going to war with Mexico and wresting most of Spanish or Mexican holdings north of the current boundary from the Mexicans. Despite the trauma of the four-year American civil war, the United States prospered while Mexico largely languished throughout the century. During the nineteenth century, for instance, estimates suggest that the Mexican economy actually shrunk slightly, whereas the American economy grew by about 1,300 percent.

The result was a gap between the two countries that has continued to the present. The United States burst into the twentieth century as one of the world's great economic powers and, by mid-century, its greatest military power, whereas Mexico found itself consigned to the ranks of the world's less developed countries. The Mexican revolution of 1910 led by Francisco Madero sought to free Mexico of the stagnant political, social, and economic system that the Mexicans had inherited from the Spanish period and that had served as a roadblock to effective development. After World War I, the resulting new government began to make reforms, including a new constitution that institutionalized its leaders in power under the banner of what became the Institutional Revolutionary Party (PRI), which ruled an effective single-party state until it lost the presidency to Vincente Fox and his National Action Party (PAN) in 2000 but which was unsuccessful in raising Mexico's economic standards and living conditions to anything approximating those of its northern neighbor.

The legacy of the past continues to plague the Mexican political system. The PRI became such a fixture in power that most semblance of political democratization was lost as a force, and the Mexican political and economic system was rife with corruption and favoritism that blocked reform and fostered an economic condition of stagnation that has made Mexican entrance into the twenty-first century as a significant power extremely difficult. While the PAN has made some progress during its two terms in office (the first six years under Fox and the last six years under Felipe Calderon), the future remains uncertain from the lens of 2012. Calderon cannot succeed himself because of a single-term provision of the Mexican constitution, and the struggle between the government and the corrupting impact of the drug cartels makes the prospects of future stability and progress problematic.

Mexico in the World

Mexico is one of a number of countries that occupies an internationally ambiguous place in the world order between the great mass of less-developed countries and the most-developed democracies in both economic and political terms. Mexico joins other non-European countries such as the so-called BRICS

(Brazil, Russia, India, China, and South Africa) powers that are aspirants to major power status but that lack enough of the developmental economic (e.g., infrastructure and wealth) or political (e.g., established, stable adherence to democratic norms) qualities of the developed powers to join their ranks. As a result, they all attempt to ameliorate their unfilled aspirations.

This ambiguity of status is evident in both the economic and political realms. The economic situation is illustrative and, for some purposes, most relevant. Partly because it is a relatively large country physically, Mexico has the twelfth largest economy among world countries as measured by gross domestic product (GDP at $1.56 trillion in 2010, according to estimates published in the *CIA World Factbook*). That figure is larger than the GDP of only one member (Canada) of the Group of Seven (G-7) economic superpowers, but leaves it behind other aspiring economic powers like the BRICS states. When gross GDP is converted to a per capita basis, however, the Mexican status falls to the middle range of states at $13,800 (84th in the world). The failure of economic growth to erase the poverty-sustaining condition of very large populations is, of course, common to other rapidly developing countries such as India and China, as pointed out in earlier chapters.

Mexico, like the other countries in its developmental class, aspires to reach the levels of economic prosperity of the most developed countries, but the structure of its economy acts as a drag on development. As Gonzalez (2011) documents, the bulk of Mexican industry (really its distinguishing characteristic) is its concentration in the assembly of products (e.g., automobiles) from non-Mexican parts for sale as finished products in the United States. This process involves a minimal Mexican value-added contribution to the end products that could aid the structural development of the economy. A second important source of Mexican commerce is the sale of petroleum—once again, largely to the United States—but declining Mexican reserves make that likely to be a declining industry as well. In addition, many Mexican communities depend on remittances from family members living in the United States to augment the meager income they have, and illegal residents in the United States whom some Americans wish to send home are included among the providers of this source of revenue. Beyond economic dependency on a non-Mexican source, this also suggests that a successful program of deporting unauthorized workers from the United States would have the unanticipated effect of making Mexicans poorer—when it is Mexican poverty that has impelled many to enter the U.S. illegally in the first place.

Institutionally, Mexico has a foot in both the developing and developed worlds as well. When the G-7 forum of international economic powers expanded itself and was largely replaced by the Group of Twenty (G-20) as the leading international economic forum for discussing common issues, Mexico was one of the 12 countries added to the new group (the European Union, technically a nonstate actor, rounded out the total to 20). Mexico is a member of the Organization of Economic Cooperation and Development (OECD) and the World Trade Organization (WTO), both of which are leading developed-world advocates of globalization, but it is also one of the charter members of the parallel Group of 20 developing countries that promote global equality through developmental assistance and wealth transfer from the most-developed to the developing countries. Mexico is certainly not unique in having a foot in each economic developmental "camp" (countries like Brazil and India have similar affiliations), but this pattern does highlight the position of Mexico on the border between the more and less affluent countries in the world.

Mexican political development is in a state of transition as well. The 1911 revolution that eventuated in the rise of a PRI-controlled country for over 80 years certainly contributed to transformation of elements of the Mexican economy and to social reform (unraveling parts of the old Spanish-based, stratified social system), but it did very little to promote democratic growth. Indeed, the PRI one-party state controlled politics in many ways either by suppressing or distorting the growth of democracy and by developing a system based on corruption, cronyism, and patronage at both the national and state and local levels. Gonzalez (2011) described the result in terms of a system of "dysfunctional democratic institutions," one of the most prominent manifestations of which was the appearance but not the reality of free elections, which were in fact controlled to ensure that the PRI always prevailed.

The watershed event in Mexican political change occurred in 2000, when the Mexican voting public rose and defeated the PRI in the presidential election, bringing to power Vincente Fox and his National Action Party (PAN). In the process, according to O'Neil, "the old model—dependent on PRI dominance—was truly broken." The Mexican constitution limits presidents to a single six-year term, but in 2006, the voters once again rejected the PRI, electing instead Felipe Calderon, whose term in office expires in 2012, when elections are scheduled for a successor. The outcome of that election is not entirely predictable because Mexico remains, in Gonzalez's 2011 words, in a state where "democracy is a relatively new game that the Mexicans are still learning to play." The outcome of the election will, however, say a great deal about the degree to which Mexican democratization is taking hold.

One of the central features of PAN's, and especially Calderon's, incumbency has been an attempt to take on and control the drug cartels, which are both a source of great instability within Mexico and a major irritant in Mexico's relations with the United States. One of the outcomes of the struggle to control the cartels, however, has been to insert those criminal enterprises more directly into the political life in Mexico than previously. Before 2000, criminal elements enjoyed a *modus vivendi* with the PRI, what O'Neil describes as a "patron-client relationship," that Calderon in particular has sought to break. This struggle has caused the cartels to increase political violence and support for government at the more local levels in opposition to Mexico City. As a consequence, Gonzalez (2009) argues, "Individual rights continue to be violated systematically at all three levels of government, but particularly at the state and municipal levels. It is not far-fetched to say that the average Mexican lives in fear both of criminals and political authorities." Until the political

situation can be stabilized and political democratization better institutionalized, Mexican claims to greater international status will remain incomplete.

The Physical Setting

In physical terms, Mexico occupies a similar global position to its political
and economic status. At 758,449 square miles, its land area is the 15th largest in the world, a size sometimes underestimated by observers because of its
geographic proximity to Canada and the United States, two of the world's
largest countries in area (second and third largest). The land area of Mexico
is about one-third that of each of its larger neighbors and is about three times
the size of the state of Texas. In addition to its long land border with the
United States, Mexico borders on Guatemala and Belize to the south. It is
generally an arid country, with arable land making up less than 13 percent of
its area, but with considerable reserves of minerals, including precious metals
(silver, copper, gold, lead, and zinc) as well as significant energy resources
(petroleum and natural gas).

At 113,724,226 (a July 2011 estimate), the population of Mexico is the
eleventh largest in the world. By comparison with its North American neighbors and partners in NAFTA, its population is about three-eighths that of
the United States and about three times that of Canada. The population is
divided among three distinct groups, the distinctions between which have
historically had more social implications rather than being a source of political unrest. The largest portion of the population is *mestizo* (Amerindian/
Spanish) at 60 percent, whereas 30 percent of the population is Amerindian
and the remaining 10 percent is classified as "white" (which generally means
Spanish). Historically, those of European background (or predominantly
Spanish stock) have occupied the higher ladders of Mexican society, whereas
Amerindians (predominantly of Indian background) have constituted the
bulk of the poorer peasant population. Unlike some of the developing countries covered elsewhere in this survey, there is very little religious division,
with 76.5 percent of the population being professed Roman Catholics and
the remainder largely professing Protestant denominations or no particular
faith. Spanish is the first language of well over 90 percent of the population.
As with many other indicators in the country, life expectancy, at 76.5 years,
ranks 73rd in the world.

It is the Mexican economy that provides many of the more interesting
glimpses into the dynamics of the country. As already noted, the structure
of the economy is closely tied to that of the United States. The United States
is, especially since the implementation of the NAFTA agreement in 1994, by
far the major trade partner with Mexico: among Mexican exports, 80.5 percent are to the United States (its second largest trade partner is Canada, at
3.6 percent of exports), and almost half (48.5 percent) of Mexican imports
come from the United States (China is second at 13.5 percent), according to
2010 data. This closeness also means that the Mexican economy is highly
dependent upon the United States. As Gonzalez (2011) describes it, "when

the US economy undergoes crises—such as the dot-com bust and the Great Recession—Mexico suffers." The downturn since 2008 has hit Mexico particularly hard. In 2009, for instance, Gonzalez reports that "Mexico experienced by far Latin America's biggest year-on-year decline in economic activity (6.5 percent)."

The close relationship between the American and Mexican economies also contributed to the structural problem identified earlier—a dependence on the assembly, rather than the manufacture, of goods and services for the U.S. economy. The dynamics of this structuring are clear. In order to avoid high U.S. trade barriers against some kinds of products, foreign manufacturers instead export parts not so highly covered by tariffs and other duties to Mexico, where Mexican workers assemble them into finished products that can then be shipped into the United States with the aid of disappearing trade barriers between the United States and its NAFTA partners. This practice also avoids the higher labor costs associated with sending parts directly to U.S. assembly plants making the same completed product. The final assembly of an increasing number of automobiles, including some with American name plates, occurs in Mexico as a result.

This arrangement provides employment for a number of Mexican workers and lowers the price of resulting goods in the American market, but it comes with prices as well. For one thing, moving assembly jobs from the United States riles U.S. workers, and especially unions, who see the practice (not entirely inaccurately) as job-stealing outsourcing, which becomes a part of union objections to NAFTA. At the same time, while assembly jobs do provide direct employment for Mexican workers, this form of industry does not radiate many benefits more generally into the population. If, for instance, automobile parts that are assembled in Mexico were also produced by Mexican workers in the country, the benefits would be far greater than they currently are, but in other than exceptional situations, that has not been the case.

There is a subtler, insidious impact on the overall Mexican place in the world that arises from the combination of Mexican dependency on the United States and its status as an assembler but not producer of some goods and services—trade diversion. Gonzalez (2011) describes its dynamics: "To enjoy free entry into the US market, a majority of textile inputs must come from US sources, but such inputs are considerably more expensive than equivalents from, say, Bangladesh or India." In this case, an "input" might be the denim cloth, cheaper to produce overseas than in the US, with which to manufacture jeans. He adds, "If Mexico were to purchase inputs from such countries, prices for its finished textile products might be internationally competitive—but such goods could not gain access to the US market free of charge." Mexico is thus left with the options of being internationally competitive but shut out of four-fifths of its existing market or of servicing that market by disadvantaging itself with the rest of the world—both options with drawbacks.

The other important aspect of the Mexican economy, which again links it particularly closely to the United States, has been in the petroleum industry.

Controlled by PEMEX, a state-run corporation, Mexican oil production is, at three million bbl/ day, the seventh largest of any country in the world, and the vast bulk of its 1.225 million bbl/day export (20th in the world) is to the United States. This steady flow from its southern neighbor does not greatly reduce U.S. dependence (at about 12 million barrels per day) on foreign oil, but it does provide a secure and steady non–Middle Eastern source—as long as it continues to flow. For Mexico, oil production and export have provided an important source both of foreign exchange and revenues to finance the government.

The oil industry, however, is becoming a two-edged sword for Mexico. Mexican reserves are limited—at 12.42 billion barrels of known reserves, it ranks 18th in the world—and production of the cheapest and most easily accessible sources is declining, meaning that petroleum as a source of economic well-being will also decline. This eventuality will weaken one area of U.S. dependence on Mexico, and it will have a negative impact on the government's ability to collect adequate revenues to operate unless it begins to widen a narrow tax base. As Gonzalez (2011) points out, "The [Mexican] federal government gathers very low revenue in proportion to GDP—around 12 to 15 percent, in contrast to an average of 30 percent in other OECD countries—and also has relied significantly on steeply declining oil rents."

The picture of Mexico that arises from an examination of its physical condition is one of overwhelming dependence on the United States—a situation that most Mexicans dislike but realize they can do little about. The simple fact is that Mexico is very dependent on the United States, but the reverse is not true. As example, the United States is overwhelmingly Mexico's largest trading partner, but Mexico is only the third largest partner for the United States. The emergence of Mexico as an independent major power is limited by this dependency on the "colossus of the North," but it is further compromised by unique internal circumstances in which drug traffickers are at or near the heart.

Mexico as a Unique State

The state of the Mexican political system is one of the country's most troubling problems. The process of democratization is, as already noted, an embryonic and uncertain enterprise, and one of its most obvious shortcomings has been a high level of graft and corruption that has permeated virtually every level of governance. This corruption is serious (Transparency International, for instance, ranks Mexico 98th of 178 countries in the world in its 2010 Corruption Perception Index) and impedes the further development of the country. As Gonzalez (2011) puts it, "Mexican public authorities and industrial leaders have to prove that the country is a safe, cost-effective, value-adding platform for the North American economic space." Political turmoil threatens demonstration of all those needed characteristics.

The problems of the Mexican political system are historical, and many of both their historical and contemporary roots are tied to the problem of drugs and the relationship between government officials and those who traffic in illicit narcotics. More specifically, the origins of the current dilemma facing Mexico go back into the early parts of the twentieth century, when two influences comingled. As O'Neil puts it, "the ties between the PRI and illegal traders began . . . during Prohibition. By the end of World War II, the relationship between the drug traffickers and the ruling party had solidified." This relationship between the ruling political party and criminal elements was synergistic. PRI members permeated the political structure of the country at all levels, were generally underpaid in their official duties, and were thus susceptible to corruption, an affliction that spread to the military and security or police forces as well. At the same time, those engaged in illicit substance trafficking needed protection from prosecution in order to maximize the profitability of their enterprises, and from this coincidence of interests an alliance was formed. Bonner summarizes it: "The Institutional Revolutionary Party . . . permitted these major drug cartels to increase their influence and control. This was partially due to entrenched corruption and the government's lack of accountability. But it was also the result of weak law enforcement agencies." The long period of PRI rule solidified its relationship with the drug lords and the status of the drug lords in political terms, and although seen as regrettable outside the country, was simply the Mexican way of doing political business.

Three phenomena of the 1990s and 2000s changed this dynamic and both started the process of democratization in Mexico and destabilized the country, the latter problem gaining the particular attention of American policy makers. The first was the impact of NAFTA. Beginning in 1994, the implementation of this free trade arrangement among the three major North American states both opened the political and economic system of Mexico to inspection and concern and made improved conditions for doing business in the country important. Moreover, the opening of Mexico meant that the gateway function of the boundary between the two states would become more important, thereby creating greater interest in the United States and Canada about the quality of their Mexican partner.

The second phenomenon was the impact of the U.S.-led "war on drugs" in Colombia during the 1980s and 1990s. That effort produced two notable results with an impact on Mexico. One was to destroy the large Colombian drug cartels, leaving an opening for cartels and new drug leadership to develop elsewhere. The other effect was to redirect the traditional transit routes of South American drugs headed for American soil. As O'Neil describes it, "In the 1980s and 1990s, the United States cracked down on drug transit through the Caribbean and Miami. As a result, more products started going through Mexico and over the U.S.-Mexico border." The impact of these developments was to strengthen Mexican criminal cartels by increasing their centrality in the lucrative trade of moving illicit drugs into the insatiable American market.

The third phenomenon was the 2000 presidential election that ended the uninterrupted rule of the PRI. Attributing the observation to O'Neil, Bonner maintains that "the end of one-party rule set in motion a seismic political shift that undermined the cartels' cozy relationship with the government and their ability to intimidate its officials." This process of breaking the link between drug interests and the government began under the regime of Fox, but it intensified as Calderon accelerated this process with his own war on the drug cartels, because in Gonzalez's (2009) words, Calderon maintained "the root cause of the problem is the drug cartels' extensive penetration of government agencies and the cooptation of government officials. . . . Only now [under Calderon] are we realizing the extent to which top Mexican authorities are in the pay of the drug lords." The shocking levels of violence along the Mexican–U.S. border and between Mexican authorities and the drug cartels has indeed increased enormously since Calderon's presidency began.

The outcome of the 2012 Mexican elections will have a strong impact on the direction this struggle between democratization and the criminal cartels takes. The Mexican population has grown very weary of the enormous levels of violence that they have been forced to endure in recent years and are likely to be attracted to candidates and parties that embrace a reduction in violence. As Gonzalez (2011) argues, "The top priority of whoever wins the presidency will be to reduce the insecurity and violence intensified by the war on drugs." This desire is not necessarily compatible with a continued adherence to democratic processes since it has been the attempt to open and democratize the political system that has exposed its corruption and connection to the drug cartels; a continued commitment to democracy may have the effect of increasing the desperation of the criminal elements in this light to protect their status within Mexican society. One route they may well adopt is to support, probably covertly, the return of their old political partners, the PRI, to power in the hopes that old relationships between them and the PRI could be resuscitated. As Gonzalez (2011) warns, "a PRI return to the presidency could further strengthen the position of dominant vested interests that grew powerful through economic concessions granted to them under PRI presidents."

The PRI leadership, of course, denies any such connection or intent, but the historical connection suggests that the possibility exists. The outcome will have a direct bearing on the United States as well. As Bonner summarizes the worst case scenario from an American perspective, "If the cartels win, these criminal enterprises will continue to operate outside the state and the rule of law, undermining Mexico's democracy. . . . If the drug cartels succeed, the United States will share a 2,000 mile border with a narcostate." An observation made by Rubio and Davidov in 2006, when Calderon was coming to power, summarizes the situation: "Mexico's success or failure will have a significant impact on the United States."

U.S.–MEXICAN RELATIONS

The general theme of this chapter is that relations between the United States and its southern neighbor are physically and especially psychologically concentrated along the border between them. The "border issue" is in many ways a way to disguise other issues that happen to be symbolized by that border, because movement across the border and how it has an impact on those other problems. As Andreas suggested in 2006, however, "Relations between the United States and Mexico begin and end at their shared, 1,933-mile border. Indeed, the degree of harmony or conflict in the relationship increasingly depends on how the border and border-controlled matters are politically managed."

This emphasis stands in contrast to the United States' other major land border with Canada. There is no "border issue" of note between Canada and the United States, nor is there any movement to find ways better to restrict access to American soil from Canada, which is a staple part of the concern with the border between the United States and Mexico. The reason is simple enough: Mexico and the United States have *other* issues that come into focus on transit across the border that are unimportant or certainly less important in U.S.–Canadian relations. The real drivers of the foreign relations between the United States and Mexico are currently (and in two cases historically) over three concerns that have little equivalent in relations between the United States and its northern neighbor. These are immigration and trade, drugs, and national security (categories borrowed from Payan), and each is a concern because breaches of the boundary enliven and worsen each problem—in both directions. These are not the only issues on which the two countries disagree. Shifter (2010), for instance, expands the list, arguing "the bilateral agenda is impressively broad, encompassing issues such as trade, immigration, drugs, human rights, and the environment." Two of these issues, human rights and the environment, can be subsumed for present purposes in other categories: human rights as part of the drug problem in Mexico and the environment as part of trade. The discussion can thus center on each of these three identified problems as the principal foci, including reference to the border implications of each, largely framed in gateway and line-of-control terms.

Immigration and Trade

The immigration issue has been the most visible source of conflict in the recent relationship, focusing politically on attempts by an increasing number of American states to impose restrictions upon and to stem and reverse the flow of unauthorized (or, more polemically and dramatically, illegal) immigrants in the United States. The domestic debate and impact of this issue, which extends to issues of trade, has been quite emotional and in some cases "nativist" in its rhetoric, which has driven it higher on the American political agenda than it might otherwise be. The issue also has a Mexican dimension, however, that is generally given less attention in American discussions of this aspect of bilateral foreign relations.

In some important ways, the immigration problem is nothing new, nor is it unique to U.S.–Mexican relations. Mexican laborers have been entering the United States on a temporary basis for over a century and have provided the labor backbone for areas like agricultural harvesting of seasonal crops. This *bracero* labor has always been controversial and has been the subject of regulatory legislation for some time, mostly concerned with assuring that migrant workers return south when their function is fulfilled (a narrower effort has examined the conditions under which they perform their labor). The presence of invited or uninvited economic migrants is also a problem—in some cases more so than it is in the United States—in parts of Europe like Germany that have a labor shortage.

The heart of the current issue is large-scale Mexican (and other Central American) immigration across the U.S.–Mexican border in numbers far greater than in the past and by people who do not clearly intend to return voluntarily to Mexico. As a border problem, it is largely framed in line-of-control terms: how the border can be better protected in order to impede that flow. It is an argument related to trade issues because emphasis on the line-of-control aspect of stanching the northward flow of people also has a direct impact on quite legal activities, including trade relations encouraged by the NAFTA agreement.

The dimensions of the immigration problem are enormous. According to the 2010 census, Hispanics, of whom Mexicans are the largest subgroup, now number almost 50 million out of a total of 308 million in the United States and constitute the largest minority group within the American population. This figure does not, of course, reflect the number of people who are in the country without official authorization (illegally) and who clearly avoid being counted because they fear being arrested if identified. O'Neil, however, suggests the dimensions, stating "the large Mexican and Mexican American populations living in the United States [is] estimated at 12 million and 28 million, respectively." The most common figure for illegal immigrants is usually around 12 million, although some guesses range as high as 20 million.

Why have so many Mexicans come illegally to the United States? Rozenthal offers one explanation: "Few of our American friends like to recognize these realities driving immigration: an increasingly globalized economy, the social and economic factors that attract people to join families and friends who have already settled in the United States, a constant shortage of labor for certain jobs, because Americans will not take them, and the growing demands for immigrants to enter the service sector." The concentration of the jobs that these immigrants are in what Koser refers to as "3D jobs: dirty, difficult, or dangerous," and they are generally jobs at the lower end of the pay scale within the United States. The motivation for the people who enter the country as *economic* immigrants (as opposed to *criminal* immigrants, represented by drug dealers) is economic betterment, the goal that motivates immigrants to move from the less to the more developed world generally. They also serve a useful socioeconomic function within the United States because they will work at reasonably low wages doing jobs Americans either will not do or would only do for much higher wages.

The impact of NAFTA, what this author has identified elsewhere as "NAFTA's dirty little secret," (Snow, *Cases*) is a unique part of this equation. NAFTA is by no means the only cause of the rise in unauthorized immigration from Mexico to the United States, but in 1994, when NAFTA took effect, the total number of such residents was estimated at about 4.2 million, and the flood came in the remainder of the 1990s and 2000s. What happened?

In some ways, the NAFTA impact was indirect and certainly unanticipated. Part of it was contextual. As Martin points out, "The economic situation in both countries in the 1990s—a boom in the United States, a very slow recovery from a 1994 bust in Mexico—led record numbers of Mexicans to enter the United States during the second half of the 1990s." The direct impact of NAFTA added to this situation. As trade barriers melted in both directions, Mexico found itself flooded with American corn, which was, and still is, subsidized by the American government, an exception to more general NAFTA free trade principles made necessary by domestic American politics (the U.S. agribusiness lobby). This subsidized corn was substantially cheaper than crops produced by peasant farmers in Mexico, who could not compete and were forced out of business. The problem was compounded by changes in Mexican banking regulations urged on the Mexican government by the United States that resulted in foreclosures on these small land holdings and converting these to larger, more economically efficient farms more akin to American agribusinesses. The result was a large, dispossessed, and unemployed population looking desperately for ways to survive economically.

Inevitably, some found their way northward in what one analyst calls an "inevitable consequence" of NAFTA. Krikorian summarizes: "The massive immigration growth of pressures was not a failure of NAFTA, but an inevitable consequence. Economic development, especially agricultural modernization, *always* sets people on the move, by consolidating small farms into larger, more productive operations." That this process was unanticipated added to the problem, in Krikorian's opinion: "The problem with NAFTA was that neither country did anything meaningful to make sure the excess Mexican peasantry moved to Mexico's cities, not to ours." In addition, the problem has direct policy implications for the United States, if it wishes to address seriously the immigrant problem. As Rubio and Davidov suggest, "Among the many good reasons for the United States to review and reduce farm subsidies, an especially compelling one is that these subsidies undercut small Mexican producers, which pushes them across the border to find work."

The result is a problem that works in both directions. There is among many Americans a need to "do something" about the excessive number of Mexicans illegally in the United States, and the most commonly prescribed "solutions" are to make penetration of the boundary more difficult (a line-of-control approach) and to identify, detain, and return as many of these unauthorized citizens as possible back to their homeland. The benefits of "getting tough" are that a reduced illegal population would lessen the burden these immigrants place on social services (schools, medical facilities, etc.) and hopefully send a deterring message to potential illegal entrants contemplating entry into the country.

These solutions, however, are not unassailable. The first objection is that unauthorized immigrants fulfill an economic function in the United States.

They are a cheap source of labor and will do jobs Americans are loathe to perform (the 3D jobs) at substantially lower wages than Americans in areas like construction, landscaping, and tourism industries. Despite professions to the contrary, most Americans would object to the higher costs they would have to pay if this source of labor disappeared. Whether plans to restrict entrance, capture, and deport offenders would work is also a problem. Regarding line-of-control functions, there is an irony here: as it becomes more difficult to enter the United States, Castaneda explains, "stiffened enforcement measures have not reduced illegal immigration but has raised the costs and risks of entering the United States and kept many immigrants in the underground economy," where among other things, they do not pay taxes for the services they consume. Instead, "professional smuggling services" thrive, according to Andreas (2009), and immigration becomes more hazardous and expensive for the immigrants. Moreover, the proposed solutions are expensive and possibly beyond the system's capacity. The federal government simply lacks the resources to find, round up, and deport over 10 million people, and efforts to increase border security are both very expensive and subject to countermeasures. Regarding the latter, former New Mexico governor Bill Richardson once put it, "If we build a ten-foot fence, someone will build an 11-foot ladder." Line-of-control solutions also run directly counter to the letter and spirit of NAFTA, which promotes globalization by encouraging the flow of goods and people across the border. As O'Neil points out, "Nearly one million people and $1 billion in trade cross the border every day." Increased efforts to control access to the United States can only hinder that process.

The problem is exacerbated by Mexico's lack of enormous enthusiasm for the American situation. No government can be pleased with the demonstrated desire of a slice of its population seeking to flee, but the situation has some advantages as well. For one thing, the remittances that illegal workers send back to families in Mexico are a not- insignificant amount for the Mexican economy. Figures are inevitably imprecise, but O'Neil suggests that the sum of these remittances is nearly $125 billion a year from legal and illegal immigrants back to Mexico, a figure roughly 8 percent of Mexican GDP. Moreover, immigration provides a safety valve for unemployed Mexican workers and thus reduces the need for government welfare from the Mexican government. As Castaneda argues, "Latin Americans see immigration as both a solution to their own high unemployment and low wages and to the huge demand for workers in the United States."

From a Mexican perspective, the American fervor over the immigration issue strikes them as at least slightly hypocritical. In their view, the real heart of the immigration problem is the availability of jobs for illegal immigrants, and as long as these jobs exist, there will be a flow across the border to fill them, a simple matter of supply and demand. Andreas (2006) concurs, suggesting the cure is "tighter requirements and tougher employer penalties" for hiring illegal immigrants. Some American analysts agree, but, Andreas concludes, "unless there is the political will to 'seal' the US workplace . . . popular calls to 'seal the border' are little more than distracting political theater."

The Mexicans also have other problems that arise from their connections with the United States. Higher on the list of Mexican concerns is the problem of drugs. Unlike immigration, which provides benefits to the Mexican political and economic system, the impact of drugs is uniformly negative for Mexico. Moreover, Mexicans tend to see the problem as largely American in its source: were it not for the apparently insatiable American market for illegal drugs, there would be no reason for a substantial Mexican drug industry with all of its deleterious impacts on the Mexico (Mexico itself does not have an unmanageable narcotics problem). Moreover, the ultimate solution to the immigration problem is increased prosperity in Mexico that will create enough jobs so that Mexicans no longer feel the need to migrate northward. NAFTA was supposed to create that situation but has not, and the United States has not given serious attention to what it can do to contribute to a more prosperous Mexico that would narrow the developmental gap between developing and aspiring Mexico and the highly developed United States. Until such a change occurs, it is arguable that movement across the border will simply be a continuing part of the broader phenomenon of developed world–developing world interactions.

The Drug Connection

The narcotics connection between the United States and Mexico greatly precedes the current crisis that both infects the Mexican government and creates conflict in the relations between the two countries. The relationship goes back, according to Gonzalez (2009), to the aftermath of the American Civil War, which created an opium and morphine market among wounded, suffering veterans, and was reinforced by the aftermath of the world wars. Cocaine demands date back into the nineteenth century as well, when cocaine "was sold commercially in the United States as a cure-all," and "Mexican seasonal migrant workers in the 1920s introduced to Americans the smoking of cannabis leaves." During the 1950s and 1960s, drug markets (principally cocaine and heroin) flourished in Hollywood and New York, and the introduction of so-called "crack" cocaine and synthetic drugs (like methamphetamine) reduced unit costs for narcotics and thereby widened demand to include more Americans. In all case, Mexican sources of supply have been available to meet increased American demands for illicit substances.

The problem intensified in the 1990s, largely because of the American "war on drugs" prosecuted by Presidents Reagan and George H. W. Bush in the 1980s and early 1990s. These efforts concentrated on the cocaine cartels located in Colombia, and by the middle 1990s had succeeded in destroying these cartels and their stranglehold on the Western Hemisphere drug production and distribution trade. In the process, the means of transferring drugs to the United States via the Caribbean Sea and in aircraft was largely disrupted, and the movement of drugs northward came to concentrate on overland shipment through Central America across Mexico and over (or under) the American border. The demise of the Colombian cartels also propelled Mexican narcotics trafficking cartels, which had previously been less important, into the prominent role they have come to play.

This movement of the drug trafficking center of gravity had the additional effect of making the drug business a much more lucrative trade. The drug cartels suddenly had enormous amounts of money with which to arm themselves and to spend compromising officials in Mexico to ignore their illegal activities. The result has been to corrupt the Mexican political system in potentially very dangerous ways and to create the lawlessness and increase the dangers along the boundary that are currently occurring.

Two statistical representations capture the magnitude and difficulty of the situation. According to Shifter (2007), "roughly 70 to 90 percent of the illegal drugs entering the United States" come across the Mexican–American frontier, and, according to O'Neil, although "estimates of illicit profits range widely, most believe some $15 to $25 billion heads across the U.S. border into the hands of Mexico's drug cartels every year." The pervasive intrusion of cartel activity, Bonner adds, is such that the cartels "have distribution arms in over 200 cities throughout the United States—from Sacramento to Charlotte." The problem of interdicting the flow of narcotics into the country is captured in a second statistic. Although narcotics are clearly not shipped this way, Andreas asserts that "the amount of cocaine necessary to satisfy US customers for one year can be transported in just nine of the thousands of large tractor-trailer trucks that cross the border every day." Given that drugs are normally transported in very small quantities, the process of interdiction becomes akin to finding a needle in a haystack. Given that problem, attempts to inspect and discover that flow "are more likely to impede legal rather than illegal trade," in Andreas' words (2009).

The drug trade, like the question of illegal immigration, comes to a focus as a border concern even though, like immigration, it is not at heart a border problem. The border is obviously part of the equation since it is the conduit through which drugs pass in one direction and the profits pass in the other, and it is politically easier to deal with drugs as a border issue than it is to get at root causes based in demand and profits. In the United States, the major recent response to the drug flow has been the so-called Merida Initiative with Mexico which, according to O'Neil, "called for supplying $1.4 billion worth of equipment, software, and technical assistance to Mexico's military, police, and judicial forces over three years." The initiative has been criticized in terms of the relatively slowness with which funds have been disbursed, but the amount is also paltry given the amount of drug profits that can be devoted to countering any improvements that result from these efforts.

The drug problem has become a source of foreign policy tension between the two countries, largely because they disagree about its causes and thus its solutions. Americans, including American officials, tend to view the drug flow in *supply side* terms, defining the heart of the problem as the volume of narcotics transiting the border and the solution as stemming that flow. Mexicans, and some Americans, disagree, maintaining the problem is akin to the immigration problem in terms of causes and thus incentives. In this view, the drug problem is largely a *demand side* problem: it is the appetite of Americans that make drugs a problem. As Shifter (2009) points out, "Many Mexicans resent unabated US demands for drugs," and believe that the only way to ultimately stem the problem is to reduce that demand, an approach the United States has acknowledged but has not systematically emphasized.

Moreover, the United States contributes substantially to the problem on the Mexican side of the border, and particularly the balance of physical power between the Mexican government and the drug cartels. Large amounts of cash are certainly a major element in this, but there is more. Gonzalez (2009) adds the flow of "chemical precursors" such as the ingredients from which methamphetamine is distilled to the list. More basically in terms of the deadly situation along the border, however, is the flow of easily obtainable American weapons into Mexico to arm the cartels. Part of this problem is the result of increasingly lax and permissive American gun laws that make it easier for anyone, including criminals, to buy weapons of increasing sophistication and deadliness on the open market. Certainly greed plays a part in the absence of an American response to this aspect of the problem, and it is somewhat ironic that Americans living in American states adjacent to the Mexican border complain about increasing violence while, according to Gonzalez, (2009) "some 90 percent of armaments confiscated from the cartels come from the more than 7,000 gun outlets situated on US soil within 50 miles of the Mexican border."

The drug problem is more than a drug or border issue, however, in American relations with Mexico. That trade has pernicious impacts on both sides of the border, and not all of these can be solved by closer supervision of whom and what crosses the boundary between the two countries. The levels of drug consumption in the United States is in fact the root cause of the entire issue, and it is a national problem that can only be solved by a national effort to reduce or eliminate the recourse to illicit narcotics in this country. Interdiction and reduction of supply coming across the border is only one alternative way to attack that problem, and like Prohibition, hardly anyone argues that attempts to choke off supply is sufficient in the face of continued, persistent demand. Dealing with drugs coming across the Mexican border may be one element in attacking the drug problem, but a part of a more comprehensive approach that prominently includes reducing demand.

The problem of drug trafficking—as opposed to consumption—is a much more pernicious problem in Mexico. The rise of the drug cartels occurred at roughly the same time that the rejection of PRI leadership by Mexican voters began what many hope was a real process of political democratization and stabilization of the Mexican polity. The effect of the rapid expansion of the drug cartels, whose interests were better served under PRI stewardship, has been to further corrupt and weaken fragile democratic development. The result has been an ironic, unwelcome twist described by O'Neil: "Democratization has tilted the balance of power from politicians to criminals." This growing imbalance in effective power, which Calderon has attempted to counteract, could end with a weaker Mexico that is in by far the worst interests of the United States. In the worst case, drug-based violence and corruption could seriously undermine political stability in Mexico, a problem that would dwarf all other sources of Mexican–American tensions.

National Security Problems

Since September 11, 2001, the added element of dealing with international terrorism has played a part in U.S. relations with virtually all countries, and Mexican–American relations are no exception. The rationale for this aspect of concern is much more a border problem than in the case of immigration and drugs, for which the border is a cover for other underlying dynamics. At the same time, American national security is ultimately and intimately affected by the state of stability in the Mexican polity, for which the state of the immigration and drug problems—and especially the latter—are closely interrelated.

The terrorist problem—to the extent it exists—between the two countries is almost entirely a border issue. Mexico itself is not the source of known terrorist threats against the United States, but Mexico is a possible transit route through which terrorists from other places might attempt to enter the United States. Canada is the other contiguous candidate for terrorist entry, but the two pose quite opposite concerns. In the Canadian case, restrictions on who enters Canada are quite stringent, making it difficult for terrorists to get into Canada and embark on their journey to the United States from Canada, but most of the U.S.–Canadian frontier is unguarded and open. Thus, any terrorists who can get into Canada can fairly easily leave Canada and enter the United States. By contrast, Mexico is less stringent in its screening entrants into the country, but passage from Mexico across the border into the United States is more difficult because of border restrictions put in place for other reasons and for which the terrorism threat is only an added incentive. The terrorist problem has not caused the United States to take stringent efforts to seal the U.S.–Canadian frontier from Lake Superior to Boundary Bay in Washington, and it is unlikely that major border reinforcement would occur along the U.S.–Mexican border were terrorists the only thing that the government sought to exclude.

Mexican internal stability as a national security problem for the United States has a longer history. Government repression and lack of responsiveness have long bred civil unrest in the country, and places like the Yucatan and the Chiapas region have harbored insurrectionary groups for a long time. During the Cold War, there was occasionally an expressed fear that Marxist groups might seize control of one of the revolutionary movements, succeed, and present the United States with a Cuban-style communist state on the southern border.

The danger of either a hostile or extremely unstable Mexican state has been the major national security problem facing the United States from the south, which was a major reason why the United States embraced the ascension of PAN Presidents Fox and Calderon and their attempts to democratize the country and to legitimize the political system.

The drug cartels present the clearest and more present danger to Mexican political stabilization. Mexico not only did not develop a strong sense of democratic participation under PRI rule, but the intermixture between the party and state meant that other aspects of the state have been underdeveloped as well. The Mexican state is particularly vulnerable in the areas of criminal justice, both in law enforcement and judicial institutions. These weak institutions have historically been corrupt and thus are vulnerable to the corrupting influences of the drug cartels, for which a state of disorder facilitates their illegal activities. As Brewer puts it, "Mexico's failure to overhaul the justice system is the dilemma. . . . Other critical concerns are police corruption, along with difficulties in sharing critical intelligence, both primary building blocks in the fight against organized crime." These weaknesses are vulnerable to exploitation by the drug cartels, as Shifter (2007) explains: "The astronomical revenues generated by the drug trade fuel the rampant corruption that eats away at already fragile institutions," and as a result, "the police are thoroughly corrupt, unreliable, and ill-equipped to handle increasingly violent traffickers."

Beyond the possible emergence of a failed Mexican state or a narcotics-controlled "narcostate" on the U.S.–Mexican border, this creates at least two corollary problems for the United States. One is that the violence that has consumed border towns and cities on the Mexican side of the frontier will spill more significantly onto the streets of municipalities on the U.S. side of the frontier, a fear that drives many Americans along the border to favor tighter sealing of the border and even greater relaxation of gun restrictions. The other potential problem is that worsening conditions in Mexico, featuring but not confined to cartel-caused violence, will cause more Mexicans to flee across the border into the United States to escape the dangers and uncertainties within Mexico. In the end, a destabilized Mexico would pose more fundamental threats to U.S. interests than immigration, drugs, or terrorists. For one thing, it could make each of those problems worse, for instance by causing more Mexicans to flee across the border. For another, it could cause even more anti-American elements in Mexico to gains power. For yet another, it could leave Mexico a seething, failed, even anarchical state.

U.S. OPTIONS

The 1,933-mile boundary between the United States and Mexico is a lightning rod for other problems affecting the relationship between the two neighbors. It is a not-improbable focus because the underlying differences and problems it symbolizes indeed all have a border component to them. Immigrants do indeed cross the border, as do illegal narcotics, and terrorists might seek to sneak across the same frontier in order to carry out their mayhem. At one level, an emphasis on border security (the boundary as line of control) is thus appropriate: if the border could indeed be sealed so that only the people and things the United States wanted to come across would be able to get through border security, the problems would be solved. Certainly the domestic American debate reflects this contention, and it is a large part of the way bilateral relations between the two countries are portrayed in the United States toward Mexico.

As has been argued, however, this American perspective clashes both with the Mexican concept of the problems and with aspects of reality, and the result is that American influence over Mexican actions are restricted. Mexicans argue that the question of the border masks the real source of the problems between the two countries: immigration as a developed world–developing world question of supply and demand for workers to do the 3D jobs Americans do not want to do, and the drug cartel problem as the consequence of American addiction to illegal narcotics. Sealing the border may make it harder (e.g., more expensive, more dangerous) for Mexicans to enter the United States illegally, but until the United States acts to attack the root of the problem in the United States (the existence of jobs and the willingness of American employers to hire illegal workers) and in Mexico (the enormous poverty that drives Mexicans to move to where the money and jobs are), there is little hope of surmounting the problem. Moreover, Mexicans have to take the tenor of the American debate as evidence that the Americans are not really serious about looking for solutions in which both countries can participate.

The drug problem is similar but even more serious. Americans decry the cartel violence across the border, but few blame American consumption habits or American arms merchants for causing or contributing to that violence. American purchase of drugs makes the cartels rich and allows them to purchase huge stores of arms from American arms merchants perched along the frontier and more than willing to supply the cartels with all the firepower they need to kill one another and outgun Mexican officials. Until the United States addresses these problems (in which it shows little interest), there is little about the effort for Mexico to take seriously. Indeed, it is an irony that American armament of the cartels is used to justify increased armament of Americans to protect them from the very arms the people they buy guns from have sold to Mexican criminal elements.

Currently, the United States has very limited leverage on Mexico over the basic issues that divide them. Treating the problem of the border as a discrete line-of-control problem rather than as a symptom of more important, underlying issues distorts the American approach, and Mexicans know it. At the same time, this fixation masks the fact that the border is also a gateway in American–Mexican trade, an aspect of the border that is sublimated by the line-of-control emphasis.

How can this situation be changed in a way that can lead to American–Mexican common approaches to their mutual problems (and all the issues indeed have both American and Mexican aspects)? One way is to treat them realistically for what they are. Until, for instance, the United States begins to enforce already existing laws on employing undocumented workers, there will continue to be a flood of illegal immigrants across the border to take jobs which are illegally offered to them by American employers who can get away with disobeying the law. Cutting off the source of illegal employment will address that problem, but as a matter of U.S.–Mexican relations it needs to be accompanied by compensating actions to address the vital remittances back to Mexico that underlie much of the reason for illegal immigration. The problem of who will do the 3D jobs illegal immigrants currently perform is the domestic side of the equation. The drug cartel problem has become so pervasive (not unlike the impact of organized crime in the United States in the era surrounding Prohibition) that it can only be handled by better management, not rhetorical flourish. As O'Neil suggests "The best the United States and Mexico can hope for in terms of security is get organized crime in Mexico to become a persistent but manageable law enforcement problem." The domestic side of this problem includes demand reduction and supply regulation, both domestic issues. At the same time, ways have to be found to create a balance between the gateway and line-of-control functions of the boundary, recognizing that zealous border sealing undermines efforts at economic integration. These are not dramatic approaches that will yield instant, problem-solving results, but they are the beginning of dialogue.

CONCLUSIONS

The relations between the United States and Mexico are very intimate, with only U.S.–Canadian relations serving as a parallel example. The relations between the United States and its northern neighbor have been uniformly more tranquil than those with Mexico, however, because the United States and Canada are both highly developed products of the British, rather than Spanish, imperial systems. Although Mexico and the United States are significantly different in developmental, linguistic, and cultural ways, they do share a long common frontier and much heritage of interchange between the two.

In many ways, the reason the United States and Mexico find themselves at odds is because their shared border represents the collision between the economically developed and developing worlds, a source of friction wherever it occurs globally. There is not a line-of-control issue with Canada because there are very few economic immigrants from developed Canada to the developed United States. The same economic motivation that causes Turks to migrate to Germany motivates many Mexicans when they come north to better their lives. A long land border that is difficult to seal makes issues like immigration and drugs easy to categorize in line-of-control terms, even if they are outward manifestations of other dynamics, and even when that concentration comes into conflict with contrary, gateway issues such as those attendant to the implementation of NAFTA.

The major political concentration on the border aspect of U.S.–Mexican relations has a further domestic basis in the United States. There are strong domestic bases to both the immigration and drug problems that American politicians in the current highly charged, partisan political atmosphere are loath to confront. The heart of illegal immigration, *why* Mexican laborers come to the United States, is jobs. Jobs are available in the United States that Americans do not want to perform (particularly at the low wages and absence of benefits for which illegal workers can be forced to work), and those jobs would cost more to fill if there were no illegal workers to fill them. Thus, Americans decry the problem of illegal immigrants while benefiting from lower costs of lawn care as a result and do not press hard for enforcement of laws in existence, a hypocrisy their elected officials are reluctant to point out to them for fear of electoral revenge. American subsidies of domestic corn production, it should be remembered, contributed to the illegal immigrant flow in the first place.

The drug problem is similar. There would be no Mexican drug cartel problem were it not for the lucrative American drug market. Attacking that problem is also not politically popular, at least partly because it is so difficult and its results so problematic. The American penal system is already overwhelmed by drug-related offenders, efforts to reduce demand (such as educating young Americans about the dangers of drugs) have had limited success, and alternatives like legalization and regulation of drugs in ways similar to laws on alcohol have limited public appeal. Blaming the problem on the border is a convenient way to evade the issue while appearing to address it.

Is the common border the basis of ongoing tensions between the United States and Mexico or simply a mask behind which to hide more fundamental and difficult difficulties between the two countries? A cursory view may suggest that the border is the heart of the problem; a closer look does not necessarily reinforce that view.

STUDY/DISCUSSION QUESTIONS

1. What has been the historical importance of the border as a U.S.–Mexico foreign policy issue? Contrast this with the U.S.–Canadian border. Use the two functions of borders to frame your answer. How is the border a domestic issue in each country?
2. Discuss the contrast between the United States and Mexico in developmental terms, including Mexican aspirations. How do these differences in perspective affect relations between them?
3. What are the unique political developmental problems of Mexico? How do these relate to drugs and relations with the United States historically and in the contemporary context?
4. Is the "border issue" the root cause of difficulties in U.S.–Mexican relations, or is it a manifestation of other problems with a border aspect? Explain.
5. What are the three major problems dividing the United States and Mexico identified in the text? Discuss each in terms of structure and content and their relationship to the border issue. Are there distinct domestic and foreign policy sources of solution?
6. How do the complex problems between the United States and Mexico and U.S. insistence on treating these as line-of-control border issues divide the two countries? Are there alternative ways to view these problems? If so, what are they?
7. The conclusion raises the possibility that the border issue is, in effect, a smoke screen obscuring more fundamental domestic sources of the problems dividing the two countries. Do you agree or disagree? Why?

READING/RESEARCH MATERIALS

Andreas, Peter. *Border Games: Policing the U.S.-Mexico Divide*. Ithaca, NY: Cornell University Press, 2009.

———. "Politics on Edge: Managing the U.S.-Mexico Border." *Current History* 105, 695 (February 2006), 64–68.

Beezley, William, and Michael Meyer (eds.). *The Oxford History of Mexico*. New York: Oxford University Press, 2010.

Bonner, Robert C. "The New Cocaine Cowboys: How to Defeat Mexico's Drug Cartels." *Foreign Affairs* 89, 4 (July/August 2010), 35–47.

Brewer. Jerry. "Fighting the U.S.-Mexico War on Drugs." *Mexidata.com*, October 10, 2005 (http://www.mexidata.info.id634.html).

Castaneda, Jorge G. "Latin America's Left Turn." *Foreign Affairs* 85, 3 (May/June 2006), 28–44.

Gonzalez, Francisco. "Drug Violence Isn't Mexico's Only Problem." *Current History* 110, 733 (February 2011), 68–74.

———. "Mexico's Drug Wars Get Brutal." *Current History* 108, 715 (February 2009), 72–76.

Hober, Stephen, Herbert S. Klein, Noel Maurer, and Kevin Middlebrook. *Mexico since 1980*. Cambridge, UK: Cambridge University Press, 2008.

Krauze, Enrique. "Furthering Democracy in Mexico." *Foreign Affairs* 85, 1 (January/February 2006), 54–65.

Krikorian, Mark. "Bordering on CAFTA: More Trade, Less Immigration." *National Review* (online). July 28, 2005.

Lowenthal, Abraham F. "Obama and the Americas: Promise, Disappointment, Opportunity." *Foreign Affairs* 89, 4 (July/August 2010), 110–124.

Nevins, Joseph. *Gatekeeper and Beyond: The War on "Illegals" and the Remaking of the U.S.-Mexico Boundary* (2nd ed.). New York: Routledge, 2010.

O'Neil, Shannon. "The Real War in Mexico: How Democracy Can Defeat the Drug Cartels." *Foreign Affairs* 88, 4 (July/August 2009), 63–77.

Pan, Esther. *Backgrounder: U.S.-Mexico Border Woes*. New York: Council on Foreign Relations, 2006.

Payan, Terry. *The Three U.S.-Mexican Border Wars: Drugs, Immigration, and National Security*. Westport, CT: Praeger Security International, 2006.

Rockenbach, Leslie J. *The Mexican-American Border: NAFTA and Global Linkages*. Abington, Oxford, UK: Routledge, 2001.

Rozenthal, Andres. "The Other Side of Immigration." *Current History* 106, 697 (February 2007), 89–90.

Rubio, Luis, and Jeffrey Davidov. "Mexico's Disputed Election." *Foreign Affairs* 85, 5 (September/October 2006), 76–86.

Shifter, Michael. "Latin America's Drug Problem." *Current History* 106, 697 (February 2007), 58–63.

———. "Obama and Latin America: New Beginnings, Old Frictions." *Current History* 109, 724 (February 2010), 67–73.

Snow, Donald M. *Cases in International Relations* (3rd ed.). New York: Pearson Longman, 2008.

CHAPTER 10

Cuba:
Balancing Domestic
and International
Interests

PREVIEW

United States relations with Cuba are distinctive among American interaction
with any country in the world. The two countries have not recognized the other
formally for over a half century, and there seems little likelihood that a major
change will occur in the near future. The major stumbling block from an American
viewpoint is the continued communist dictatorship on the island, symbolized by
Fidel Castro and those around him, whereas the Cubans chafe under a 50-year
embargo against them by the Americans. In terms of breaking the impasse, a
major obstacle to change is the militant Cuban expatriate community concentrated in Florida and New Jersey, which has had an unprecedented stranglehold
on U.S. policy toward Cuba and will not relinquish its position until the Castro
model is repudiated. The passing of Castro may offer the only hope for change,
but it is not clear that Castro's death will usher in major reform on the island.
Meanwhile, the two countries try to improve relations at the margins, and Latin
America continues to view the American position as anachronistic.

The relationship between the United States and Cuba is unlike the U.S.
relationship with any other country in the world. In one sense, it
does not exist. The United States does not have, and has not had, any
official relations *with* Cuba, an island country that lies only a little more
than 100 miles off its coast, for over a half century. The absence of relations
among states is certainly not unknown, as the Iran case illustrates; such close

neighbors ignoring one another, however, is highly unusual. As one observer summarizes the situation in a Council on Foreign Relations background note on Cuba, relations are "virtually nonexistent." The road to this situation is long, convoluted, and, in the view of many observers, counterproductive or even comic in its actions and implications. These aspects help create the nearly surreal perspective from which the two countries have viewed themselves since 1960. The result is that the United States and Cuba have policies *toward* one another but not with one another.

In 1959, the Cuban Revolution led by Fidel Castro managed to overthrow the incredibly corrupt, inept, and unpopular dictatorship of Fulgencio Batista, an action that was initially met with enthusiasm in many quarters of the United States. The new Castro regime, however, moved swiftly to reform the country, adopting socialist or communist programs, much to the surprise of many American observers who had enthusiastically watched the young Cuban revolutionary's progress against a government that included significant contributions to its support from the American mafia. When Castro nationalized large parts of the economy and expropriated private, including foreign, properties that included large holdings by Americans, the romance quickly soured. The United States broke relations with Cuba as large numbers of Cubans fled the island for sanctuary in south Florida, and in 1960 economic sanctions were imposed on Cuba in the form of an embargo that has remained in place ever since and which Erikson (2008) describes as "the most comprehensive, far-reaching, and long-lasting policy of its kind in the world."

The embargo has been the signature feature of U.S. policy toward Cuba since 1960. Embargos are primarily economic instruments that restrict, or in the Cuban case prohibit, any economic dealings with the state against which they are imposed. The purpose of these restrictions is to harm the economy of the target state in order to force that state to change policies the imposer opposes, thereby allowing the embargo to be relaxed (made less stringent) or rescinded (abandoned altogether). In the case of Cuba, the bases of the embargo are the economic and political communization of the island by Castro, and its removal would require that the Cuban government renounce communism and unravel the pattern of political and economic practices created by communism. What makes the embargo against Cuba so distinctive is that its prohibitions against economic interactions extend to virtually all forms of contact and interchange between the two countries.

The policy has also been intensely controversial, and criticism of it has mounted as time has gone by. After Cuba declared itself a communist state and entered into intimate relations with the Soviet Union, the basis of American policy was officially the "strategic menace" posed by Cuba's location at the mouth of the Caribbean Sea and thus the potential it might have as a threat to oceanic access to the Panama Canal. This rationale, of course, was reinforced and highlighted by the Soviet attempt to emplace offensive, nuclear-tipped missiles on Cuban soil in 1962, resulting in the tense Cuban Missile Crisis that led to those weapons being withdrawn. This basis for disagreement, however, largely evaporated with the end of the Cold War; although Cuba remains one of four avowed communist states (the others are China, Vietnam, and North Korea), it no longer possesses the military capability to menace anything off-shore, leaving Finan to conclude, "Viewing Cuba as a strategic menace to the United States requires a suspension of disbelief." Stripped of its strategic façade, a former aide to then Secretary of State Colin Powell, Larry Wilkerson (a retired U.S. Army colonel), typifies the U.S. stance as "the dumbest policy on the face of the earth" (quoted in Finan), mostly because it has failed to achieve its goals.

Negative assessments of U.S. policy are shared by most foreign countries, and a source of friction between the United States and many of its friends and allies (Canada is a notable example) arises from their negative attitudes to-ward the embargo, which many other countries ignore. This opposition to the U.S. policy has been problematic since the 1990s, when the United States attempted to force its extension onto other countries. At the same time, highly vocal anti-Castro Cuban-Americans are so intent on achieving the embargo's goals that they refuse to consider any relaxation of its restrictions.

The animosity between the two countries has additional bases, however. The United States and Cuba have long had a very ambivalent relationship with one another that goes back to the aftermath of the American Revolution. Before the American Civil War, there was interest, primarily in the American South, to annex the slave-holding island, and the United States became actively involved and helped tip the balance in favor of those who desired Cuban independence at the end of the nineteenth century. Once the Americans facilitated Cuban independence, they occupied the country (1899–1902) and only left after issuing a highly controversial unilateral statement of policy, the so-called Platt Amendment, that effectively circumscribed Cuban sover-eignty by declaring an American "right" to intervene on the island whenever it saw fit. As the twentieth century progressed, Americans took over own-ership of increasing aspects of the Cuban economy (sugar plantations and railroads, for instance), and particularly toward the end of the pre-Castro era, "elements of the American mob set up shop in Havana in the 1950s, taking over nightclubs, opening casinos, and building high-rise hotels," according to Moruzzi, that transformed Havana into a high-rolling gambling and prostitution cen-ter that offended many Cubans. American mobster Meyer Lansky, owner of one of the largest casinos, was a close associate of Batista, and one of the appeals of the young Cuban lawyer and revolutionary Castro was to purge the island of these unsavory influences. Numerous American attempts to over-throw or kill Castro (including some utilizing the dispossessed mafia) added to mutual animosity during the 1960s and 1970s.

One of the most notable results of Castro's consolidation of power was the exodus of a large part of the wealthier segments of Cuban society from the island to Florida, where they established a close, fanatically anti-Castro pres-ence that has dominated American foreign policy toward Cuba ever since. Although not numerically a large group within the American electorate, the exile community has wielded disproportionate influence over U.S. foreign pol-icy toward Cuba, as Sweig (2007) summarizes: "Cuba policy has long been dominated by wishful thinking even more disconnected from reality on the island. Thanks to the votes and campaign contributions of 1.5 million Cuban Americans who live in Florida and New Jersey, domestic politics has driven policymaking." The power of this interest group is enhanced because of its strategic location. Overwhelmingly, the exile community votes for Republican candidates. Democratic candidate Al Gore lost the 2000 presidential election to George W. Bush because he lost Florida by about 7,000 votes, and the Cuban community, still enraged by the Elian Gonzalez episode under President Clinton, was probably crucial, a lesson not lost on others. This level of influence is unprecedented, approached only by the strategic electoral positioning of American Jewish citizens and their support for Israel (see Chapter 11).

The domestic policy debate over Cuba has become dogmatic, partisan, and sclerotic. Essentially, there are two sides to the debate, each of which is firmly wedded to its interpretation and rejects the alternative as misguided, even heretical. One side, dominated by the Cuban exile community, categorically opposes the present system in Havana and will not accept any outcome to the present situation other than a complete repudiation and reversal of the policies and leadership that have ruled Cuba since the rise of Castro. To this group, only the demise of Castro, what is sometimes called "the biological solution," will start this change in motion, and it must end with a system entirely purged of the current regime and its economic and political structure and policies. Of the current leadership, Cardenas says "this regime consists of a dwindling cohort of dogmatic revolutionaries," indicating that they all must go before policy toward Cuba can change. The other side, while hardly pro-Castro, sees the current policy of isolation and demands for fundamental change as the precondition for changing that policy to be both foolish and counterproductive. This view is held by most Cuba observers within the academic and policy advising community, but it has never been able to bring about change in a policy that Shifter and Joyce describe as having "been stuck on autopilot for years."

The partisan aspect of the debate is that it increasingly has been expressed in opposing positions held by the two major American political parties. Generally speaking, the Republican Party has accepted and promoted the anti-Castro position of the exile community, which is one of its strongest electoral bases in Florida and New Jersey. This preference derives to some extent from the historically more evangelical anticommunism of the GOP during the Cold War and from the more conservative orientation of both the GOP and the exiles. It is not coincidental that the major legislation that enforces current policy was largely sponsored by conservative Republicans (discussed later in the chapter) and that the anti-Cuban position gained greatly during the George W. Bush administration. Regarding attempts to improve relations between the two countries under Bush, Sweig (2007) observes, "By the end of its first term, the Bush administration had upended virtually all initiatives, official and unofficial, for improving relations." The Democrats have been generally more conciliatory toward Cuba and the prospects of a gradual thaw in and expansion of ties with Cuba, but that position has been neither fundamental nor important enough to push forcefully in the face of strong partisan opposition. President Obama has made some very tentative first steps toward improved relations, but they remain buried in a long list of more pressing, largely domestic issues.

The sclerosis in the debate arises from the unchanging nature of the situation across time. While not all Cubans revere Castro, no major internal movements against him have materialized. Although part of the reason is that Cuba is, for some purposes, a police state that suppresses opposition, part of it also undoubtedly reflects support for the government, much of which is based in Castro's opposition to and independence from American domination. There were attempts initiated by the American government in the years shortly after Castro's rise to power either to overthrow or assassinate him, but when these efforts failed, the United States has reverted to the long-term policy of isolation of the island.

At the heart of the isolationist basis of the Cuban–American relationship is the economic embargo of Cuba imposed originally in 1960 and made permanent by President John F. Kennedy in 1962. The broad purpose of the embargo is to strangle the Cuban economy and thus to isolate Cuba economically from the rest of the world, in the process bringing pressure on the Cuban regime to reform itself (which means to institute full democracy and market economics), policies that require repudiation of the Castro revolution and its leader. Whether the embargo has succeeded and thus should be continued is, not surprisingly, a matter of partisan disagreement. Shifter refers to it as the "anachronistic embargo," suggesting that it no longer serves any useful purpose (if it ever did). The "proof" of this position is that even after 50 years, the embargo has not forced the kind of change on Cuba that it was designed to create. Sweig (2007) summarizes this position: "The upshot of a half century of hostility . . . is that Washington has virtually no leverage over events in Cuba." Supporters of the embargo disagree with this conclusion, clinging to the policy as essentially the only means to keep pressure on the Cubans, and claiming that it does have some salutary effects. Cardenas, for instance, argues that a Cuban decision in summer 2010 to lay off a half million government workers is testimony to "the significant role played by U.S. economic pressure in bringing that situation about."

The current Cuban–American impasse and differences about how (or whether) to improve relations does not, of course, exist in a vacuum. Rather, it can only be adequately examined within the context of Cuba's own background and development, including where and how Cuba fits in the world system; the geography, demographics, and economy of the island; and those aspects of the Cuban experience that distinguish it from other states.

CUBA: A SKETCH

Cuba has a long and very mixed history as a part of the new world discovered by Christopher Columbus. Columbus visited Cuba in 1492, where he found the island sparsely populated by native Indians (the Taino). The Spanish returned as settlers and colonizers in the early 1510s, and the Spanish quickly began to import African slaves to replace dwindling numbers of Indians in the workforce that grew up around Cuban plantations that cultivated sugar and later tobacco as primary crops. Cuba joined the American South as a major center of human chattel slavery during the ensuing centuries, a connection which, along with geographic proximity, created a bond and sense of future union between the island and at least the slave-holding part of the pre–Civil War United States. Spanish rule was interrupted when the British capture Havana in 1762, introducing abolitionist and other notions, but those influences were soon supplanted by a Spanish return.

In the years leading to the American Civil War, there was regional sentiment in the United States to annex Cuba and add it to the union as a slave-holding state. The strongest expression of this sentiment was the Ostend Manifesto (named after the Belgian city in which it was announced) of 1854, which offered a justification for purchasing Cuba from Spain and adding it to the union. The controversy of adding another slave-holding state kept these sentiments from being realized but established in the minds of some Americans a sense of kindred bond between the island and the mainland.

Cuban independence became an active issue after the American civil war. Between 1868 and 1878, the first Cuban war of independence was fought, and although unsuccessful, it did result in the abolition of slavery in 1879. More decisive was the second war of independence between 1895 and 1898. This movement was inconclusive until the United States intervened in retaliation for the controversial sinking of the USS *Maine* in Havana Harbor, which caused the United States to declare war on Spain. Among the upshots of the Spanish-American War were the divestiture of Spain's remaining empire, basically Puerto Rico, Cuba, and the Philippines. The United States occupied Cuba as a result and remained there until 1902, when it withdrew and Cuban independence was declared.

That independence was not, however, unconditional. In 1901, the U.S. government issued the infamous Platt Amendment, a policy statement that granted Cuban independence with "stipulations" (Suddath's term) and created two conditions relevant to understanding U.S.–Cuban relations today. One of these was, in Staten's words, to grant "the United States the right to intervene in Cuba for the 'preservation of Cuban independence,'" a direct infringement on Cuban sovereignty that lasted until it was rescinded in the 1934 as part of FDR's "good neighbor" policy toward Latin America. The other provision was to grant the United States perpetual rights to its naval base at Guantanamo Bay at the southeastern tip of the Cuban island guarding access to the Caribbean Sea. This arrangement can only be abrogated by mutual consent of the two countries, an action fervently advocated by the Cubans and equally adamantly resisted by the United States.

The United States remained an important player in Cuban economics and politics for a long period after that. The primary tool of this policy was economic penetration, as Americans bought and developed major parts of the Cuban economy and, as noted earlier, turned Havana into a "tropical paradise"

(Moruzzi's designation in the subtitle of his book) for rich American tourists and gamblers (it became a major destination for Americans during Prohibition from 1919 to 1933). It is not unfair to say that Cuba was one of America's playgrounds when an obscure young Cuban lawyer turned revolutionary swept down from the mountains and seized control of Cuba from the Batista regime in 1959.

Cuba in the World

Since the Cuban Revolution of 1959, Cuba has lived in a kind of international ambivalence. On one hand, it has been treated as a pariah state. The United States has tightly and progressively isolated Cuba with the embargo and has, with limited success, attempted to spread that isolation by cajoling or trying to coerce other countries to join its sanctions against the Cuban regime. At the same time, many other states in the region and the world have shown considerable sympathy for Cuba. This sympathy does not spring from any affinity with or approval of the political system installed and maintained by the Castro regime. Rather, it arises from one of two sources. Within the region, Cuba elicits some sympathy because its suffering is imposed by the United States, whose perceived imperialism toward the region causes these countries to oppose the American position. This theme of a beleaguered Cuba bullied by the Americans is particularly associated with Venezuela's Hugo Chavez, but it is shared throughout Latin America. Outside the region, there is criticism of the American embargo as unrealistic and inappropriate, a sentiment that also includes chafing at American attempts to persuade or coerce others into avoiding what might be profitable intercourse with the island country.

For its part, Cuba has attempted to break this isolation and to create a place in the world, first aligning itself with the communist bloc through its alliance with the Soviet Union, and since the end of the Cold War through close relations with other countries opposed to American policy, most notably Venezuela. The longer the embargo and an unchanging American policy stays in place, the more international disapproval grows and thus the more successful Cuba appears in its efforts to carve for itself a more normal position in the community of states.

The Cuban relationship with the Soviets was a mixed blessing. While it resulted in a counterbalance to American animosity, it also increased that animosity, allowing its opponents to add the charge of communist "stooge" to its other indictments of the Castro regime and to make it more difficult for those who sought an improvement in relations to make their case. The Cubans benefited from foreign assistance from the Soviets until the end of the Cold War, but as its collapse was imminent, "The Soviet Union withdrew its $4 billion annual subsidy, and the economy contracted by 35 percent overnight," according to Sweig (2007). For a perpetually shaky economy, this loss was particularly devastating, and it has only partially been replaced by other outside income. Shifter and Joyce, for instance, report that "Cuba receives an estimated $2 billion a year in oil and aid from Venezuela," and Sweig adds that "by 2002, total remittance inflows (from relatives in the United States) reached $1 billion, and nearly half of the Cuban population had access to dollars." The Cuban economy remains, at best, on a shaky foundation, despite these outside sources of income.

The longer it lasts, the more the embargo itself has had a dilatory impact on the U.S.–Cuban situation. The embargo has never been enthusiastically embraced by the international community, and opposition to its continuation has increased as time has gone by. This sentiment is particularly true in Latin America, where there is growing resistance by the leaders of Latin American states to excluding Cuba from regional meetings and arrangements like the Summit of the Americas. Part of this reaction is simply an extension of Latin American dislike for pressure from the "colossus of the North," and part of it reflects a feeling that the American policy is foolish and counterproductive. Opposition is, however, a point of agreement and accord. As Shifter (2010) puts it, "No issue unifies Latin America in its posture toward the United States as much as the decades-long US embargo against Cuba." Writing with Joyce, Shifter goes a step further, arguing that U.S. policy has "failed to force democratic reforms [in Cuba] . . . succeeding only in undermining US credibility throughout Latin America."

A variety of countries have developed an active interest in Cuba in recent years, at least implicitly in contempt of American policy. These include Venezuela and Brazil, but also nonregional states like Russia, Spain, China, Canada, and Israel, all of which "are investing in Cuban oil, minerals, tourism, infrastructure, agriculture, and biotech," according to Sweig (2010). This situation is vaguely reminiscent of parallel U.S. policy toward Vietnam for 20 years after the end of American involvement in the Vietnam War: standing on the sideline while other countries developed commercial relationships with the Vietnamese regime so that, by the time the United States ended its prohibitions on such interactions, much of the economic ground had already been claimed by other countries.

Cuba has, of course, sought to make the most of this situation, portraying itself as suffering in the shadow of the Goliath to the north as a defenseless David. This portrayal has only been partially successful, and Cuba remains a very poor, undeveloped country. Whether it can move itself away from its condition of dependency on the outside world depends, in some measure, on the resources it has available to it.

The Physical Setting

Cuba presents a profile that, if it were not in its particular geopolitical situation, would be almost entirely unexceptional. "The Pearl of the Antilles," as it is sometimes known by Cubans, is a moderately large island that extends at its longest points (northwest to southeast) for 759 miles and north to south for 135 miles, for a total of 42,803 square miles, slightly less than the size of Pennsylvania and the 105th largest country in area in the world. As an island, it has no true international borders except for the roughly 18-mile perimeter of the Guantanamo Bay naval facility. A little over one-quarter of the land (27.63 percent) is arable.

The Cuban population is stable at about 11 million, according to 2011 population estimates, 74th largest in the world. The country has a slight (–0.104 percent) negative population growth rate, due largely to out-migration, but at 77.7 years, it has a fairly long average life expectancy, due mainly to a comprehensive medical care system that is one of the best in the developing world. The population is not divided along ethnic lines; essentially everyone considers himself or herself to be Cuban and speaks Spanish, but the racial mix on the island is approximately 65 percent "white," with 25 percent of the population classified as "mulatto and mestizo" and the remaining 10 percent as "black." The literacy rate is 99.8 percent, comparable to that of the United States.

The Republic of Cuba (its formal title) is, of course, one of the few re-maining communist states in the world. Only the Communist Party is legal within the country, and the upper ranks of the party and the state's political apparatus are virtually interchangeable. In keeping with its ideology, virtu-ally all economic activity has been nationalized and private property expro-priated, which is a major source of contention between the Castro regime and the exile population, which came disproportionately from the landed, profes-sional classes that were most adversely affected by the imposition of com-munist political and socialist economic models on the country after 1960. Although Cuba had a long-standing tradition of communist activity prior to the Castro Revolution, at the time of the revolution's success, there was little suspicion in the outside world that Castro himself had communist leanings and would lead the country along a communist path once in power. Indeed, observers of the Castro movement during the 1950s tended to depict Castro in heroic terms as a liberator from the corrupt, venal rule of Batista. The late Herbert L. Matthews, a *New York Times* reporter who spent considerable time covering the progress of the revolution during the 1950s (see De Palma) was particularly influential in creating this image of Castro, and part of the meteoric process of disillusionment of Americans with Castro arose from the feeling of having been duped by the Cuban dictator regarding his inten-tions once in power.

Like almost all of the countries that adopted a communist system world-wide, the Achilles heel of Cuba is its economy. The Cuban economy is barely self-sufficient, requiring outside assistance from governmental sources and gifts from exiles to family remaining on the island to meet needs. The coun-try's GDP stands at $114.1 billion (2010 estimate), which is 67th in the world, and this figure translates into a per capita CDP of $9,900, 109th among world countries. The growth rate in the economy is modest at 1.5 percent (169th in the world). As a socialist state, the largest part of the population is listed in the "service" sector (about 72 percent). In order to stimulate economic activity and growth, the Cuban government has, in re-cent years, loosened prohibitions on private enterprise, allowing small pri-vate businesses to exist in limited areas such as restaurants. This relaxation is seen by proponents of change in Cuban policy as a hopeful sign of future accommodation between Cuba and the United States, but opponents of change see these as results of "the significant role played by U.S. economic pressure," in Cardenas' words.

One of the key elements in Cuban economic growth is opening the country progressively to the rest of the world, a dynamic the U.S. embargo seeks consciously to avoid. Cuba does, for instance, have some significant mineral resources that can be exploited. It has, according to Hanson in the CFR Background Note, the world's third largest deposits of nickel, which is one of the three largest exports of the country, along with sugar and tobacco. Cuba also has exportable quantities of cobalt, iron ore, chromium, copper, salt, and silica. One of the more intriguing possibilities lies in the area of potential petroleum deposits of the Cuban coast, where reserve levels are currently unknown. Current oil production is minimal at 48,340 bbl/day, and petroleum is one of Cuba's largest import items (almost all from Venezuela due to Chavez's relationship with the Cuban regime), along with food and machinery and equipment. Cuba's largest export partners are China at 26 percent of Cuban imports, followed by Canada at 20 percent and Spain at 7 percent. Venezuela is the largest source of imports (30 percent), followed by China (15 percent) and Spain (8.3 percent). The United States, essentially exclusively in the form of monetary remittances from private citizens, is listed as fourth at 6.8 percent of Cuban imports.

The end of restrictions on the island would, of course, aid economic development. The country has already attracted foreign investment from some countries, as noted, and other countries are in the queue to invest there. One of the major potential sources of outside economic stimulus is a revival of what was a thriving tourist trade before the Castro revolution; tourism is an economic mainstay of most of the Caribbean islands. Canada and the European Union have been particularly interested in pursuing this possibility but have been frustrated by the adamant quality of American efforts to restrict economic interactions with the island.

The picture of Cuba that emerges from analyzing the physical setting is one of circularity. Cuba has many of the trappings of a stable and prosperous political order (exemplary medical and educational systems, for instance), but it remains trapped in a communist political and economic ideology that makes it anathema to the United States—and especially the Cuban exile community—that seeks to destroy the regime through economic strangulation. Those attempts place strictures on the Cuban system that suppress development of a vibrant Cuban economy and that, ironically, reinforce the strength of the regime. As Haass points out, strictures both enfeeble the Cuban system and reinforce the resulting sense of siege on which the regime thrives: "The policy of trying to isolate Cuba also works—perversely enough—to bolster the Cuban regime," he writes. "The U.S. embargo provides Cuba's leaders with a convenient excuse."

The result is a chicken–egg problem. Outsiders, notably in the United States, demand that Cuba change before restrictions are lifted on the island, but the reforms that are necessary include the repudiation and replacement of the current regime with one professing and practicing a very different economic and political ideology. Cubans, and especially the regime, are not enthusiastic about acting to create their own self-destruction for an uncertain future, and presumably would be more willing to do so if they saw some of the personal benefits of change. Loosening the embargo might produce the demand for further reform, but current U.S. policy is committed to retaining current levels of pressure and misery as the *precondition* for loosening the restrictions that might create the demand for more change. Supporters of current U.S. policy, on the other hand, argue any loosening will only reward bad Cuban behavior and make the regime more secure; thus, only continuation of the misery is acceptable. The question thus remains of how the circle can be broken.

Cuba as a Unique State

Much of Cuba's unique status in the world is the result of the historic accident of being located just off the coast of one of the world's largest and most powerful states. This accident of geography has resulted in a relationship between the two entities that is highly asymmetrical, with Cuba being the object of much more American policy than it has initiated, and dependent on American attitudes and changing interests. Cuba, after all, was once considered as a potential American state, and although such sentiment has long since disappeared, Cuba remains a place of special interest to the United States and Americans, whether it wants to be or not. This intimacy has worked in both directions to affect the very special way in which the two countries view one another.

From the American vantage point, Cuba has been like a special step-child. Slavery created a bond with the antebellum southern United States, and Cuba was the major objective when the United States decided to engage in its "splendid little war" with Spain at the end of the nineteenth century. The outcome of that war left Cuba in the ambivalent position of having been liberated by a country that subsequently occupied it like a new colonizer for three years and then granted it titular sovereignty while reserving for itself the right to interfere—even abrogate—that sovereignty whenever it saw fit (a situation not unlike what the United States created in the Philippines, which it also freed from the Spanish and then occupied rather than granting it the independence the Philippines expected). Although official American political domination of Cuba faded—especially after the Platt Amendment was rescinded—it was replaced by a large and growing level of American economic penetration of Cuba.

During the first half of the twentieth century, it is probably not an overstatement to say that Cuba became an economic, if not political, colony of the United States. American individuals and corporations bought increasing shares of the sugar plantation basis of the Cuban economy and came to control other aspects of the Cuban infrastructure—at one point, for instance, Americans owned one-half of Cuba's railroads, the primary method by which the sugar cane crop was brought to market. The Americans also brought with them their darker side in the form of the mafia.

Penetration of Cuba by American organized crime (which is discussed in detail by Moruzzi) dates back to Prohibition in the United States, during which time Cuba served both as an embarkation point for illegal alcoholic beverages being smuggled into the United States and as an escape for thirsty American vacationers. This relationship expanded after the war when, in Moruzzi's words, "elements of the American mob set up shop in Havana during the 1950s, taking over nightclubs, opening casinos, and building high-rise hotels." This activity was especially concentrated in Havana, which became a mecca both for gambling and prostitution, among other things.

Although it is not given enormous coverage in standard depictions of U.S.–Cuban relations, the emergence of Havana as a mafia-dominated "sin city" was offensive to many Cubans and helped foment support for revolutionary change. Partly, this was because the mob operated in close harmony with the Batista government which, by allowing itself to be corrupted with mafia money and association, became seen as a partner of the offensive behavior in the country. This trend was particularly odious to Cuba's large Catholic majority (estimated at about 85 percent of the population before the revolution). The mafia-sponsored industry was so profitable and self-sustaining that its operators, according to Moruzzi, "had a tin ear when it came to Cuba's rapidly growing guerrilla movement in 1958." Foreign observers were shocked at the rapidity and ease with which the Castro forces moved down from the mountains and into Havana in 1958, as the government simply collapsed before them. This surprise extended to those Americans who were profiting greatly in Cuba—mostly at the expense of the Cuban people. Neither side would forgive or forget the treatment the other gave them.

The reaction by Cubans was swift after the revolution. Americans, conditioned by heroic, adulatory depictions of Castro and enchanted when the bearded leader visited the United States early on after his victory, were shocked when Castro began the communization of the island, jailing political opponents and not reinstituting promised political liberties, restructuring the economy, and most odiously from an American viewpoint, appropriating American-owned assets valued at over $1 billion (in 1960 dollars) without offering compensation for the losses. This process stimulated the emigration from the island of over 700,000 Cubans who would become the core of the anti-Castro exile community in the United States. The Eisenhower administration responded by severing diplomatic relations with Cuba and initiating the embargo that remains in place today.

The emotional roller coaster in U.S.–Cuban relations in the early Castro years is well exemplified by the Bay of Pigs incident of 1961, which also helped set the tone of those relations. Almost immediately after Castro gained power in 1959 and began his reforms, movements to overthrow his regime were hatched. The Central Intelligence Agency (CIA) became heavily invested in one such plot during the last days of the Eisenhower administration, and when John Kennedy entered office in 1961, he was presented with a planned invasion by Cuban expatriates supported, financed, and trained by the CIA that included American air support for the invaders. JFK tepidly endorsed the planned liberation of the island based on the CIA prediction that the invaders would be treated as liberating heroes. When the invaders reached the beaches at the Bay of Pigs, however, they were met and decimated by pro-Castro government forces. The incident left a sour taste in the mouths of all parties involved. Kennedy felt he had been duped by the CIA, the invaders felt they had been betrayed by half-hearted American support for their landing, and pro-Castro Cubans felt they were besieged by Americans intent on overthrowing their revolution. The net result was to help solidify ill-will between the parties.

Many Americans, and especially those who had done business in and profited from their relationship with Cuba, felt particularly betrayed by the actions of the new Cuban leadership, but their sense of "benevolence scorned," in Erikson's (2008) term, became a key element in what has been an unrelenting hatred for the Castro government that continues to drive American policy toward the island and that has led to some elements of policy that remain cornerstones of the American refusal to deal with Cuba. In the early years of Castro's rule, this sense of betrayal extended to the mafiosi who had been expelled along with the other Americans, and it resulted in some of the most bizarre shenanigans in American foreign policy history.

What is important and unique about this evolution is the intensity of negative emotions that underlay it in both directions. Castro rose to power in Cuba as a popular, populist leader, and part of the reason for his ascension was the venality of the Batista regime that he overthrew. Batista, in turn, was viewed by much of the Cuban population (rightly or wrongly) as little more than a corrupt American puppet and certainly as little more than a mafia marionette. The level and quality of American penetration and control of the Cuban economy only added to the grievances average Cubans had for the regime and thus indirectly toward the Americans. For many Cubans, the Castro revolution was the final act in the process of achieving real and total independence from the United States, and Castro's subsequent railing against the Americans resonated well with those Cubans who did not flee with the Americans. Many of those Cubans have become disillusioned with Castro's rule since, but they revere the sense of independence he created and are deeply suspicious of any American (or Cuban-American) initiatives that might result in the return of the dominant *gringos* to the Cuban shore.

U.S.–CUBAN RELATIONS

U.S. relations with and policy toward Cuba can be divided analytically into at least three distinct phases: relations before the Castro revolution, relations during the Castro rule, up to and including the present time, and post-Castro policy. Each of these has had (or will have) its unique aspects, and each subsequent era derives important characteristics from the experience of previous periods. Unlike U.S. relations with most other countries, those relations have not been dominated by specific policy issues, which have generally been subsidiary or derivative, but rather by basic questions about the nature and status of Cuba and its resultant ties with the United States.

Relations before Castro

American interest in Cuba goes back to the founding of the American republic. Indeed, the third U.S. president, Thomas Jefferson, showed an interest in acquiring Cuba as a potential addition to the union, and there were periodic reassertions of this interest in the years leading to the American Civil War. After that event, interest in formal annexation waned as the United States shifted its attention to the American West and elsewhere. Cuba remained on the radar, however, and the United States designated itself a patron of Cuban independence toward the end of the nineteenth century. The Spanish-American Act removed the Spanish yoke from Cuba, but it was replaced by a temporary American counterpart in terms of a series of occupations of Cuba before World War I and the odious Platt Amendment's Damoclean effect on Cuban sovereignty. During the first half of the twentieth century, United States influence was fueled by economic penetration and control, including corrupting influences such as the American mafia.

The historical theme that arises from this experience was a kind of paternalistic relationship between the two countries that was almost certainly far more revered in the United States than it was among Cubans. While Americans might look upon their interference in Cuba as beneficial and well-intended, Cubans undoubtedly viewed it as demeaning and corrupting as well. In this light, the Castro phenomenon was at least partially and indirectly anti-American: many of the ills that Castro sought to overcome and correct were practices such as the hedonism of mafia-controlled Havana night life, the official corruption partly brought on by the mob, and the control of Cuban agriculture by absentee Americans who left average Cubans as little more than sharecroppers on their own country's land. Castro's appeals to remove such influences were, if not directly and forthrightly, at least indirectly an assault on American influences. That Castro would exploit the latent anti-Americanism as a recurring theme to justify his continued nondemocratic rule should come as little surprise given these dynamics.

The Castro revolution was thus, in a very real sense, a rejection of American paternalism as the basis of U.S.–Cuban relations. The United States reacted to the traumatic changes that accompanied this rejection as benevolence scorned, and much of the vitriol against Cuba and Castro arises from this source. Fidel Castro is the overwhelming symbol of U.S.–Cuban relations. As long as Castro (and his vision of Cuba and how it deals with the United States) remains dominant in Cuba, current policies are likely to remain largely the same as they have been for over a half century, changing only at the margins. The precondition for change is the removal of Castro from the scene and a Cuban repudiation of the tenets of the Cuban leader's vision of the world—Castroism.

Relations with Castro's Cuba

At the very outset of the chapter, Cuban–American relations were described as essentially nonexistent, and that description clearly reflects how the two countries have viewed one another since Castro consolidated power in 1960 and began the communization of the island. Much of the program that Castro swiftly enacted blindsided Americans, who believed the Cuban leader to be a reforming liberator, an impression created and reinforced by stories and books about him as he conducted the campaign against the Batista regime, and the result was a sense of betrayal made worse by a sheepish recognition of having been hoodwinked.

The communist system that Castro began to impose upon Cuba was both generally and specifically offensive to the United States. At the strategic level, it established a communist foothold in the Western Hemisphere that violated American policy first honed in the Monroe Doctrine of 1823. More specifically, a communist state in the Caribbean posed three specific problems. First, it could be used as a naval base of operations to harass American commerce and U.S. naval access to the Panama Canal, a vital link in American maritime policy. Second, the island could (and for a time did) serve as a launching point by which Castro and his Soviet sponsors could attempt to spread their influence elsewhere into the hemisphere, notably into Central America. In either case, the result is to create a security interest toward Cuba that is described by Erikson (2007): "Stability, not democracy, is the watchword in the Pentagon and the Miami-based US Southern Command" toward Cuba.

Third, a communist presence so close to American soil directly threatened American security and resulted in arguably the most dangerous confrontation of the Cold War, the Cuban Missile Crisis of 1962. In that situation, the Soviet Union attempted secretly to emplace on Cuban soil nuclear-tipped missiles capable of destroying targets in large parts of the eastern United States. When American reconnaissance flights over the island revealed work on the missile sites and the United States demanded their dismantling and removal, an extraordinarily tense confrontation ensued for nearly two weeks, during which many observers believe the world came closer to catastrophic nuclear war than at any other time (see Allison and Zelikow or Kennedy and Schlesinger). The crisis ended when the Soviets relented and dismantled the silos, but the incident only added to the already abundant level of ill-will between the United States and Cuba.

The specific and personal impact came in the form of Cuban expropriation of American (and other foreign) property in Cuba. Government seizure of property is an accepted right and practice in international law, but international legal conventions insist that just compensation be provided for expropriated properties, which Castro refused to do. The Americans were simply kicked out by Castro. The expropriation was part of the general abolition of private property on the island, meaning that wealthy, land-owning Cubans were affected as well, and many of them reacted by fleeing the country, mostly for American exile, where they remain the core opposition to the Castro regime and its policies.

The net effect of the events initiated by the new Castro regime in 1960 was a complete and total rupture of relations between the United States and Cuba. Since that time, the two countries have had no diplomatic relations with one another, and the few contacts the two governments have are conducted informally at low levels through the good offices provided by third parties. Since 1960, the United States has rejected Cuba, and Cuba has reciprocated.

The U.S. policy goal toward Cuba since 1960 has been simple: the removal of Castro from power and the renunciation of the political and economic system that he imposed on the island. Over time, there have been two primary instruments by which that policy has been pursued. One has been a policy of physically removing the dictator physically through assassination, attempts at which were particularly frequent during the 1960s and 1970s and were, in some cases, comically ineffective. Those policies have given way to a kind of death watch over Castro's demise—the so-called "biological solution"—that was encouraged by Castro's debilitating illness in 2006, to which he has, to the chagrin of his most fervent detractors, refused to succumb. The other thrust has been the encompassing embargo, the purpose of which has been to strangle the regime into submission and to cause the Cuban people to rise in opposition to Castro and demand change in the direction of a democratic, market-based economic model.

Attempts physically to assassinate Castro were undertaken in the early years after the Cuban's rise to power. These centered around the CIA, and in some cases, the CIA joined forces with the American mafia (still smarting from having their own licentious assets seized by the communists) that make almost a comic history. Suddath, for instance, describes some of these early attempts organized under a program known as Operation Mongoose: "A years-long series of increasingly far-fetched attempts on Castro's life" were organized, she says. "Between 1961 and 1963, there were at least five plots to kill, maim, or humiliate the Cuban leader using everything from exploding seashells to shoes dusted with chemicals to make his beard fall out." When these attempts proved uniformly ineffective and reportedly spawned reprisals against American officials (Cuba was, for instance, identified in some accounts as a conspirator in the assassination of President Kennedy), these plans were ultimately dropped. The sheer fact that they were ever contemplated and in some cases engaged in does, however, speak to the fervor, even fanaticism, that surrounded opposition to Castro. Moreover, there is still some residual support for this kind of policy among the most firmly anti-Castro elements in the United States. As Sweig (2007) puts it, "For decades, a vocal minority of hard-line exiles—some of whom directly or indirectly advocated violence or terrorism to overthrow Castro—have had a lock on Washington's Cuba policy."

The heart of Cuban policy was the sanctions process designed to isolate the island from the outside world. The instrument for this policy was the comprehensive economic embargo of the island by the United States, a set of restrictions that the United States has gradually made tighter and more restrictive and which it has tried to convince or coerce other countries to adopt as well. Whether the embargo has been effective—and thus whether it should be continued—is a point of contention, and there is fundamental disagreement on whether loosening it should be an incentive to improve relations or a reward only bestowed after Cuba changed its policies to make them more compatible with the American (and Cuban-American exile) vision.

The intent of the embargo is to isolate Cuba from the outside world though restrictions that are primarily economic but also extend to other areas, such as communications and travel to the island country. Beyond sheer isolation from the outside world, the purpose is punitive: to enforce upon the Cuban people economic deprivation to the point that they will force the government to reverse the policies that are deemed objectionable. At the beginning, this purpose was largely framed in terms such as just compensation for those whose property was seized, but those claims, while still present, are less intense than the basic goal, which are the removal of Castro and the replacement of the communist government that has ruled since 1960.

Immigration policy has also played a special role in the U.S.–Cuban relationship. The politically active Cuban immigrant population in the United States is here and has achieved sanctuary as a result of flight from the island, and it has generally supported generous immigration policies for Cubans still on the island. The Cuban government has shown some ambivalence on this issue: the fact that some Cubans seek to leave is somewhat embarrassing, but those who do leave are generally opponents whose departure reduces opposition. The Cuban Adjustment Act of 1966 sought to regularize eligibility for immigration (preference for émigré family members and those fearing persecution, for instance) and annual quotas. The Mariel boat lifts of 1980, when 125,000 Cubans (including a large number of inmates from Cuban prisons) and 25,000 Haitians reached the United States, upset the orderliness of this process. In 1995, the Clinton administration and Cuba informally negotiated the "wet feet, dry feet" policy whereby Cubans fleeing for the United States would be returned if they were intercepted while still at sea but would be granted asylum and made eligible for permanent residence if they physically reached American soil. As the Elian Gonzales case (a young boy whom his Cuban father argued was abducted from Cuba and taken to the United States, later to be returned) demonstrated, however, this entire process remains a matter of some contention.

These policy goals are most strongly developed in regard to the provisions of the embargo. The nature and character of the policy is largely defined in legislation passed by the U.S. Congress and signed into law by the President Clinton during the 1990s. Two controversial laws, in fact, most strongly and symbolically represent the implementation of the embargo: the Cuban Democracy Act (CDA) of 1992 and the Cuban Liberty and Democratic Solidarity

Act of 1996, better known as the Helms-Burton Act because of its sponsors, Senator Jesse Helms (R-North Carolina) and Representative Dan Burton (R-Indiana). Each tightened the economic noose around Cuba's neck in the pursuit of democratization.

The CDA was sponsored by Representative Robert Torricelli, a Democrat from one of the two states with the largest Cuban exile populations, New Jersey. It had several provisions, including banning the foreign subsidiaries of American firms from trading with Cuba, greatly restricting or prohibiting travel by Americans with Cuba, outlawing the sending of remittances by Cuban exiles to family remaining in Cuba, and, according to Sweig (2007) barring "ships travelling from Cuban ports from docking in U.S. ports." Some of its provisions have been relaxed—notably on remittances and to a lesser extent on travel—but the basic elements remain in place. Helms-Burton widened these restrictions, banning foreign companies from ignoring the embargo by imposing sanctions on countries and foreign companies defying the embargo and by "allowing investors to be sued in U.S. courts," according to Sweig (2007).These provisions were enacted largely as the result of an incident that inflamed the political right in the United States, which supports Cuban sanctions. Helms-Burton was passed, as Suddath states, "in retaliation after Cuba shot down two U.S. civilian airplanes" (which were piloted by Cuban exiles and were almost certainly in violation of Cuban airspace). The act, despite this underlying motivation, created great opposition in a number of countries that did business with both the United States and Cuba on the grounds of infringement on sovereignty, but was justified on the grounds that such activities took advantage of profiting from Cuban exploitation of illegally expropriated American property in Cuba.

The continuation of the embargo is at the heart of the controversy over American foreign policy toward Cuba. Haass states succinctly the consensus among most critics by saying simply that "the American policy of isolating Cuba has failed." The evidence for this assertion, of course, is that even over 50 years after it was instituted, it has failed to move Cuba in the direction it is intended to create, which is self-obvious. Supporters of the policy, largely in the exile community, vehemently oppose either relaxing or rescinding the embargo on the grounds that the situation with the Castro regime would be even worse in the absence of the embargo, that doing so would effectively reward what they contend is the bad behavior of the Castro regime toward its own people, and that the removal would take away any incentive the Cuban regime has to reform.

The result is a quandary that is reflected in the American political system. Essentially, the question comes down to which side must make the first steps toward change, and what those changes must be. Those in the United States who oppose change argue that Cuba must change fundamentally before the United States can or should entertain change in its policies. As Shifter describes it, "Lifting the embargo remains politically unrealistic absent significant reform on Cuba's part, such as releasing political prisoners or holding free and fair elections. And there is no indication that Cuban president Raul

Castro intends to adopt any such changes any time soon." The alternative approach is a gradual relaxation of U.S. positions to try to induce concessions from the Cubans, but doing so requires change in the American laws regulating the relationship, as Haass explains: "Current law . . . requires that Cuba becomes a functioning democracy before sanctions can be lifted. But it is precisely engagement that is far more likely to reform Cuba." There is not enough support within Congress to rescind the laws that restrict U.S. latitude in approaching Cuba because those who insist that Cuba must reform first have sway in legislative terms. As a result, Cuba policy remains frozen in place until some dramatic change intervenes that will break the impasse between opponents and advocates of change. To this point, most of that hope has been concentrated on the "biological solution."

U.S.–Cuban Relations after Castro

Current U.S. policy toward Cuba—nonrecognition accompanied by an intentionally crippling, comprehensive economic boycott—and Cuban policy toward the United States—relentless, militant opposition and noncooperation as long as the embargo remains in effect—are at an obvious impasse that neither side is willing or politically able to break. In this circumstance, the prospects for change rest on change *within* each country that facilitates taking the first step to start what is hopefully a process leading to the restoration of relations between them. Domestic politics in each country provide the primary driver of any change that might allow this to happen, and the prospects are different in each country, thereby creating differential prospects for the future—Cuba after Castro.

The Americans, of course, want concessions to start in Cuba in the form of democratization, which Erikson (2007) describes as "the central rationale for the longstanding US embargo." Since Castro erected and has administered the nondemocratic regime for over a half century and the embargo has not produced (nor does it seem in any danger of producing) this desired outcome, the only hope is that a post-Castro government that comes to power after Castro's death may be more amenable to instituting the reforms on which Americans insist.

Supporters of and participants in the Cuban government have also looked at the future, and particularly the inevitability that Castro will exit the scene at some time. When Castro fell victim to the debilitating illness in 2006 that caused him to relinquish the formal reins of power, there was much hope in the exile community that change was in the wind and that turning power over to his 75-year-old brother Raul would prove to be no more than a placeholder arrangement that would only temporarily slow fundamental change. That Raul Castro remains firmly in power over five years later suggests, to the contrary, that the communist leadership within Cuba has foreseen this process and prepared for it. As Sweig (2007) describes it, "Ranging in age from their mid-40s through their 70s, they have been preparing for the transition to collective leadership for years." Moreover, Gonzalez and McCarthy reported several years ago that most observers believe Cuban supporters of democratization are "weak" and "largely shattered," making internal opposition prospects minimal.

This suggests that the death of Castro will not likely result in the collapse of the current Cuban system or create overwhelming pressure for short-term change. Whether the symbolic loss of Castro's leadership will set in motion processes that will eventually create change is speculative and uncertain, of course, but the prospects that change will be rapid and dramatic seem unlikely. This unpromising prospect is particularly discouraging to those who have taken refuge in the United States in hopes of a fundamentally new Cuba to which they can triumphantly return. As Erikson (2007) describes this dream, "Even after all these years, some Miami refugees envision a future in which they return to Cuba and recreate the lives they abandoned after Castro came to power."

The other possibility if the death of Castro does not induce change in Cuba is for American policy to change. There has always been sentiment, mostly from the American political left, that has argued that the embargo policy is bankrupt (because it has failed almost completely to bring about the changes it seeks to induce), that it is counterproductive (because it reinforces the Cuban regime's claim of being beleaguered and thus reinforces rather than weakens its control), and that it harms American interests in the Western Hemisphere (since it is opposed by virtually all hemispheric powers). All of these arguments, of course, fall on totally deaf ears within the exile community.

Faced with a Cuban political system that is unlikely to meet the most extreme demands of the exile community (policies that would lead to their losing power), there are two alternatives that Americans might pursue after the mantle of authority passes from Castro to his like-minded successors. One path is to continue the embargo as it now exists. Supporters of this alternative do not accept the notion that the embargo has been the failure that its opponents portray. Rather, they tend to argue that without the embargo, the situation would be even worse than it is now both in Cuba and in Cuban–American relations, an assertion that can neither be demonstrated nor empirically refuted. A loosening of the restrictions would, among advocates of the status quo, reward and reinforce the Castro model which, in many cases, led to their personal dispossession. Moreover, the comparatively bland Raul Castro does not project the charismatic image of his older brother, and proponents of keeping the restrictions hope support for the successor regime will wither as a result. There is some evidence that support for this position regarding incremental change is beginning to wane, as those who personally fled Cuba are dying off and their offspring hold less severe views of the Cuban system and less passionate hopes for returning to the island.

The other possibility is a policy of incremental reductions in the terms of the embargo. Allowing remittances from the United States to Cuba is one such initiative, and loosening travel bans to and from the island is another. Cuba favors this relaxation of restrictions, because the result would an increase both in tourist traffic and visits from Cuban-Americans to the island, both of whom would provide valuable sources of foreign exchange the regime desperately needs. This path of trying to open relations, according to Shifter, "has some congressional support, but some congressional opposition as well," the latter mostly coming from conservative Republicans. Opponents of lifting such restrictions, of course, forcefully voice their opposition. Cardenas captures this sentiment: "two critical escape hatches for the Cuban economy—U.S. tourist travel and the extension of trade credits—remain beyond the regime's reach, and thankfully so."

The Obama administration basically supports the gradual lifting of aspects of the embargo, but with politically based reservations. In April 2009, the then new administration announced four steps it would take to improve the atmosphere for reducing barriers between the two countries: lifting travel restrictions for family members to Cuba, allowing remittances to flow, opening telecommunications links between the mainland and the island, and expanding humanitarian donations to Cuba from American sources. Recognizing the importance of the exile community vote, however, Obama also renewed the embargo later in the same year. The Obama policy has, in Erikson's (2008) sympathetic terms, combined a "more diplomatic approach to Cuba coupled with remarkable stability in terms of the substantial aspects of U.S. policy."

U.S. OPTIONS

The political viability of an American initiative to reopen relations with Cuba hardly exists at all. The inordinate influence of the small but well-organized Cuban exile lobby concentrated in south Florida and New Jersey has made it politically difficult for any American administration to reach out to Cuba, and "the Cuban exile community reached new heights of political power" during the George W. Bush administration, according to Erikson (2008). While that influence may be on the wane, it is still likely to have its maximum effect during major (i.e., presidential) election years. Because the policy alternatives are so stark (the embargo or beginning to dismantle it), the options are mutually exclusive, making the possibility of political compromise on the American side more difficult in an overall political environment that has not shown itself conducive to compromise on matters far less contentious than Cuba policy.

There is a conceptual difficulty as well. The grave illness of Castro in 2006 created a kind of false euphoria in the policy community that Castro was near passing from the scene, opening the probability of change, but that judgment that has proven to have been premature. Unfortunately, both the exile community and more moderate Americans had different visions of such a changed environment. The exiles envisioned a collapse of Cuban communism that would allow their triumphal return and the rehabilitation of the island to something like its pre-Castro nature, whereas the American mainstream favored more gradual change that would lead to concessions and the gradual erosion of nondemocratic practices in Cuba. The Cuban government, however, clearly understood both of these two visions and rejected them—and especially the exile's preference—out of hand. Those who hoped for a radically reformed Castro-less Cuba have been frustrated on that score, and the resilience of the Cuban system with Fidel no longer in control cannot offer much solace for dramatic change once he actually does die.

The problem in moving Cuban–American relations has been exacerbated by basically sclerotic views and plans about how to bring the two closer together. Some of the problem, as Erikson (2007) argues, comes from the United States. "The vacuum of new ideas in Washington and Miami has paralyzed any efforts by the United States to facilitate political or economic change in Cuba," he writes. As noted earlier in the chapter, the Cubans themselves, caught in an economic quagmire, have taken tentative first steps such as closing down jobs in the public sector in hopes that jobs will blossom in the private sector and expanding rights of private ownership of small businesses. The two sides in the United States cannot agree on the meaning of these changes or their implications. The exile community views the concessions as evidence of the failure of the Cuban system as a result of the embargo and thus as further justification for keeping the restrictions in place. The more moderate wing of policy preference in the United States has not aggressively embraced the reforms as evidence of moderation of the regime and thus as an opening around which to widen improved ties.

As long as the impasse within the American policy community remains as wide as it has been for the past half century, the United States will, in the words of Sweig quoted at the beginning of the chapter, continue to have "virtually no leverage" over the process of change in Cuba. Current policy has not produced the overthrow of the Cuban political system, and it is hard to find evidence that it will accomplish this goal in the near or medium future. Rather, the policy helps ensure the continuation of a communist system that, ironically, its opponents argue is fatally flawed in any case, although continuing to punish Cuba through the embargo may provide some visceral pleasure to the exiles forced off the island. In the meantime, the policy only seems to serve as an irritant in U.S. policy with the rest of the hemisphere, all of which opposes the U.S. embargo.

CONCLUSIONS

As stated at the outset of the chapter, what is remarkable about U.S. relations with Cuba is the dramatic degree to which they are dictated by domestic political forces and considerations rather than the calculation of national interests in the world. The only geopolitical base of militant, across-the-board opposition to Castro's rule arose from his association with the Soviets that led to the Cuban missile crisis and an ongoing concern about secure access to the Panama Canal, but that rationale has largely evaporated with the end of the Cold War. Relations with Cuba may, as Erikson (2008) argued, "matter a great deal to the United States," but it is not because Cuba poses any particularly military challenge or threat. Rather, as Sweig (2010) states the case, "domestic politics and campaign contributions, not national interest or foreign policy considerations, still carry the day in Washington when it comes to Cuba."

There is some tentative movement in the American political scene in this regard. Finan, for instance, reports that "more than 50 percent of Americans—and in some years more than 60 percent—favor 'reestablishing US diplomatic relations with Cuba.'" That shift in opinion has not, however, been sufficient to create any groundswell that can counteract the pressures from the anti-Castro lobby, and Finan adds, "Neither the Democratic Party nor the Republican Party has advocated moving in this direction." During the first two years of the Obama administration, which professed a more conciliatory approach to Cuba, Lowenthal argues, "The White House's approach to Cuba was constrained both by pressure from Cuban Americans and by the procedures of the U.S. Senate (which allow a single member to block debate on policy matters such as relaxation of the embargo)." U.S.–Cuba policy thus remains a remarkable case study in the way that a small but strategically located (in two hotly contested electoral states) minority can dictate the nature and content of American foreign policy. The only other place where anything like this phenomenon is clear in American foreign policy is toward Israel, to which the discussion turns in Chapter 11.

STUDY/DISCUSSION QUESTIONS

1. How are U.S.–Cuban relations distinctive? Include in your discussion the impact of the revolution of 1959 in Cuba and factors arising from the historic relationship between the two countries.
2. How do U.S. domestic politics affect the debate over how the United States should deal with Cuba? Elaborate.
3. Discuss the historical relationship between Cuba and the United States. How might that history have made Cubans suspicious of U.S. intentions toward them? How has it affected Cuba's place in the world since 1959?
4. The economic embargo is the centerpiece of U.S. policy toward Cuba. In broad terms, what is it? Discuss the provisions of the embargo, its purposes and impact, and support for and opposition to it. How does the embargo contribute to Cuban uniqueness in the world?
5. The text divides Cuban–American relations into three periods. What are they? Why is the distinction meaningful? Discuss the dynamics of each period.
6. How much ability does the United States have to influence Cuba? Will this influence increase after the death of Fidel Castro? What are possible ways to increase that influence? Assess each.
7. Analyze U.S. policy toward Cuba. Should that policy basically remain the same as it has been for the past half century, or should it change? If the latter, how? Defend your position.

READING/ RESEARCH MATERIALS

Allison, Graham, and Philip Zelikow. *The Essence of Decision: Explaining the Cuban Missile Crisis* (2nd ed.). New York: Longman, 1999.

Azel, Jose. "Cuba's Pre-Existing Condition." *Foreign Policy* (online), October 4, 2010.

Carbonal, Nestor. "Think Again: Engaging Cuba." *Foreign Policy* (online), April 10, 2009.

Cardenas, Jose R. "Cuba Move Is a Victory for U.S. Policy." *Foreign Policy* (online), September 22, 2010.

De Palma, Anthony. *The Man Who Invented Fidel: Castro, Cuba, and Herbert L. Matthews of the New York Times.* New York: Public Affairs Press, 2006.

Dominguez, Esteban Morales. *U.S.–Cuba Relations: A Critical History.* Lexington, MA: Lexington Books, 2005.

Erikson, Daniel P. "After Fidel, Oh, Brother. . . . " *Current History* 106, 697 (February 2007), 91–94.

———. *The Cuba Wars: Fidel Castro, the United States, and the Next Revolution.* New York: Bloomsbury Press, 2008.

Finan, William W. Jr. "Has the Cuban Moment Arrived?" *Current History* 109, 715 (February 2009), 93–94.

Gonzalez, Edward, and Kevin F. McCarthy. *Cuba after Castro: Legacies, Challenges, and Impediments.* Santa Monica, CA: RAND Corporation, 2004.

Haass, Richard N. "Forget about Fidel." *Newsweek* (online), March 7, 2009.

Hanson, Stephanie. "Backgrounder: U.S.–Cuba Relations." *Council on Foreign Relations* (online), January 11, 2010.

Kennedy, Robert F., and Arthur Schlesinger Jr. *The Thirteen Days: A Memoir of the Cuban Missile Crisis.* New York: W. W. Norton, 1999.

Lattell, Brian. *After Fidel: Raul Castro and the Future of Cuba's Revolution.* New York: Palgrave Macmillan, 2007.

Lowenthal, Abraham. "Obama and the Americas: Promise, Disappointment, Opportunity." *Foreign Affairs* 89, 4 (July/August 2010), 110–124.

Moruzzi, Peter. *Havana Before Castro: When Cuba Was a Tropical Paradise.* Layton, UT: Gibbs Smith Publishers, 2005.

Schoultz, Lars. *That Infernal Little Cuban Republic: The United States and the Cuban Revolution.* Chapel Hill: University of North Carolina Press, 2011.

Shifter, Michael. "Obama and Latin America: New Beginnings, Old Frictions." *Current History* 109, 724 (February 2010), 67–73.

———, and Daniel Joyce. "No Longer Washington's Backyard." *Current History* 108, 715 (February 2009), 51–57.

Staten, Clifford L. *The History of Cuba.* New York: Palgrave Macmillan, 2005.

Suddath, Calire. "U.S.–Cuban Relations." *Time* (online), April 15, 2009.

Sweig, Julia. "Absent at the Creation." *New York Times* (online), October 1, 2010.

———. "Castro's Last Victory." *Foreign Affairs* 86, 1 (January/February 2007), 39–56.

———. *Cuba: What Everyone Needs to Know.* New York: Oxford University Press USA, 2009.

"U.S. Administration Announcement on U.S. Policy toward Cuba." Washington, DC: White House (Office of the Press Secretary), April 13, 2009.

Voss, Michael. "Obama Renews Cuba Trade Embargo." *BBC News* (online), September 15, 2009.

PART VI

Conflicting Interests in a Global Hot Spot

Dealing with regional rivals in particular parts of the world presents complex problems for the United States, as the studies of India and Pakistan in Part III sought to demonstrate. In the Indian and Pakistani cases, relations with both countries have traditionally been important but not central to the United States. The most basic interests of the United States do not come into play and thus into conflict with the two rivals, although one can make the case that American–Indian relations could reach the point of vitality as India emerges as a world power. As the convolutions of relations with those two countries demonstrate, the difficulties that confront the United States—or any other country—are difficult enough when moderate levels of interest are involved. Those difficulties are magnified when a particular country or countries has special significance to the United States.

The relationships between the United States and two of the principal antagonists in the long Arab–Israeli contest represent the special case where very high priority U.S. interests are associated with one or both countries in a regional conflict. The relationship the United States has with both Israel and Egypt represents this kind of situation on several dimensions. First, the relationship involves core American interests. The preservation of Israeli security has been and continues to be a fundamental part of American foreign policy, and although Egypt has historically not occupied the same order of priority as Israel, its evolution since the Arab Spring of 2011 could elevate it to a much higher place in the pantheon of American interests. Second, the interests of the United States have come into conflict over the two countries: American interests in Israeli security have often come into conflict with U.S. desires for peace and stability in the region that include access to Middle Eastern petroleum. Egypt, of course, is not an oil producer, but the same policy concerns that the oil producers have are shared by Egypt, making it an effective surrogate for this conflict of interests. Moreover, one manifestation of historic American responses to interests in the region has been to support antidemocratic regimes like that of former Egyptian president Hosni Mubarak, thereby creating a difficult legacy for the United States in its dealings with the post-Mubarak democracy movement in the country.

Third, U.S. domestic factors influence policy toward these countries to a degree not present in many other situations. The chief limiting influence here is the existence of a powerful pro-Israel lobbying effort in the United States rivaled only by the Cuban exile community discussed in the last chapter as a limiting influence on decision making. Many pro-Israel Americans chafe at the idea and even deny the existence of such an organized effort, but by whatever name, there is clearly an organized pro-Israel influence in the United States that exceeds similar sentiment in behalf of most other countries. Fourth, non-traditional international influences are clearly at play in each case and in their intersection. The Arab Spring has clearly heightened international interest in the evolution of political events in the Muslim Middle East, most dramatically in the case of Euro-American involvement in Libya, but elsewhere as well. Although the Egyptians have managed to keep out of the violent spotlight of the Arab Spring, they are the largest and most influential Islamic country to be transformed by those events. The international community is very interested in the evolution of Arab Spring–inspired politics in places like Egypt, just as it tends to concentrate on the fate of the Palestinians in Israel's occupied territories. Subnational groups are also important parts of the environment in each country toward which American policy must be crafted: the Muslim Brotherhood as a potential influence in Egypt and Palestinian extremist groups like Hamas in the Israeli-occupied territories.

The intricacies these kinds of factors introduce help frame the examination of each of the counties in this part. Chapter 11 explores U.S. policy toward Israel. It begins with the observation that Israel and its fate are one of the core interests of the United States but that the two countries are at odds about the best ways to guarantee the safety of Israel in a hostile region. The major point of contention is the fate of the Palestinians and the question of where, or whether, there should be a sovereign Palestinian state in the occupied territories of the West Bank and the Gaza Strip. Both Israel and the United States are divided internally on this question, and Israeli factions reluctant to see the creation of such a state are very active in the United States and are in conflict with the desires of the Obama administration. The chapter also looks at possible outcomes of the Palestinian question, raising questions about which outcomes remain viable and their impact on Israeli security, the central interest of each party, particularly in light of the remarkable visit of Israeli Prime Minister Benjamin Netanyahu to the United States in May 2011.

U.S. interests in Egypt have historically not been as central or as important as those with Israel, for at least two reasons. One is that, unlike Israel, Egypt's basic existence has never been a question within the region, and the other is that there is not the organized support and pressure within the United States for Egypt that exists for Israel. Prior to 1973, when the United States perceived that the Yom Kippur War might have escalated to the point of a potential direct confrontation with the Soviet Union, American relations with Egypt per se were not central. After 1973, the United States moved closer to

Egypt as a way to mute the prospects of future wars between Egypt and Israel. In the process, it became closely associated with and supportive of the long reign of Mubarak, who offered the United States a faithful ally who supported the peace process with Israel but whose regime was decidedly antidemocratic. The legacy of embracing Mubarak limits the U.S. ability to deal with the emergence of an Egyptian political process since Mubarak's removal and has become the central problem of U.S.–Egyptian relations.

The two cases also implicitly show the dynamic tensions involved in relations between the United States and two rivals. In dealing with Israel, for instance, the United States must take into account the ambivalence the Israelis feel about the Arab Spring. The Israelis cannot publicly condemn the overthrow of autocrat Mubarak, but they also fear that a new Egyptian regime might prove to be less willing to honor their peace treaty with Egypt that has now existed for over 30 years, a concern heightened in May 2011 when Egypt opened its border with Gaza over loud Israeli objections. Both the United States and Israel are aware that Egyptian public opinion is more anti-Israeli than the Mubarak regime was, and part of U.S. efforts in Egypt are necessarily aimed at trying to influence the successor to be both pro-American and at least not anti-Israeli. At the same time, a major component of anti-Israeli sentiment in Egypt (and elsewhere in the region) is based on perceptions of Israeli intransigence on the Palestinian state issue, and the United States reminds Israel that the American mission in the region would be greatly simplified by Israeli movement toward a peace accord with Palestine that creates a Palestinian state. Thus, Palestine acts as an intersection between American relations with both countries and as a point of contention with the individual governments.

Israel: Recognizing and Coping with Tensions with a Special Ally

PREVIEW

American foreign relations with Israel are closer, more intimate, and more intense than U.S. interactions with virtually any other country in the world. The roots of this closeness are historical, dating back to the formation of the Israeli state and even before, but, like U.S. relations with Cuba, they are also greatly amplified and affected by domestic American politics and particularly the very strong "Israeli lobby" in this country. The heart of American interests in Israel center on its existence and prosperity in the otherwise almost exclusively Islamic Middle East, and the core objective of American efforts has been to create and reinforce a secure peace between Israel and its neighbors. The major contemporary threat to that policy goal has been the status of Palestine, about which the Americans and Israelis come into conflict. That disagreement has centered in recent years on territory (the West Bank) claimed by Palestinians as the heart of an independent state and other related questions, such as the territorial disposition of Jerusalem and the so-called "right of return" of former Palestinian residents of Israel to lands lost when they fled emerging Israel in the late 1940s. The extent of disagreement between the two countries on this subject was heightened by the contentious May 2011 visit of Israeli Prime Minister Benjamin Netanyahu to the United States.

The United States has closer ties with Israel than with almost any other country in the world. There are numerous bases of this intimacy, with strong ethnic and domestic political roots and ramifications. At the same time there is, and for some time has been, a kind of dynamic tension between these two close allies that reflects different approaches to and solutions for the key element of that relationship: the security, even survival, of the Israeli state in a hostile politico-military environment. The disagreements are not about the fundamental interest that the two states share in assuring the continuing viability of the Jewish state, but rather about the best ways to assure that Israel survives and prospers in the world. Moreover, U.S. interest in Israel, while historically unshakable, competes with American interests toward Arab states that oppose Israel.

The basic parameters of this essentially friendly discord have domestic political roots in both countries, with the American internal debate largely a reflection of the internal debate within Israel. In its most public manifestations, this debate often appears more basic and vitriolic than is in fact the case. Essentially no one in either country questions the basic premise about whether Israeli security is an American interest and whether the United States is firmly committed to guaranteeing Israeli survival. That commitment may create some problems for the United States in its relations with other Middle Eastern states (see Chapter 12), but it is an unwavering commitment nonetheless. The policy question is *how best* to ensure that security.

The explicit American commitment to Israel goes back at least to the declaration of Israeli independence on May 14, 1948, when the United States and the Soviet Union cosponsored the successful resolution in the United Nations Security Council that approved the new Israeli state. On that momentous occasion, American president Harry S Truman declared, "I am Cyrus," a reference to the ancient Persian leader who had helped to create a Jewish state in the region 2,500 years earlier. Much of the basis of American support for the creation of the new Israeli state arose from revulsion tinged with guilt over the Holocaust and the failure of the United States and its World War II allies to prevent or attenuate that systematic attempt to eliminate the Jewish population of Europe. The two countries have been closely related to one another ever since.

The history of Israel since its independence has been difficult and violent. Israel has fought four major wars with its neighbors (including the Arab reaction to the establishment of Israel in 1948), and in each case a major issue in the war has been the continuing existence of Israel. The last of these conflicts occurred in 1973, in a war where the success of Israel was not assured in the early going and where the situation arguably escalated to near the point of a nuclear exchange with unknown, but potentially dire, international ramifications (see discussion in Chapter 12). The American desire to ensure peace between Israel and its neighbors since 1973 has been motivated in no small measure by the very deeply held determination to prevent similar perils in the future.

Israel's physical fight for survival is the context of the modern Israeli dilemma. Although establishing the new state of Israel had the overwhelming support of most of the developed world—and even the Soviet Union—this sentiment was not shared by most of Israel's Islamic neighbors. Whether the animosity that is felt toward Israel is based in religion (Judaism versus Islam), territory (conflicting claims to parts or all of Israel), sympathy for those former residents displaced by the creation of the Jewish state (the Palestinians), history (claims to ownership based in historical control), or some combination of these motivations, it is highly controversial and the source of endless disagreement. Much of the discord is indeed historical, as Benn concludes: "the political culture has been shaped by incessant digging in history, aimed at supporting the dueling narratives of the Palestine conflict."

Israel fought four wars with its Muslim neighbors in the quarter century after its independence was declared. The first was a direct reaction to that declaration, as a number of the neighboring states reacted by attacking Israel in what was an almost entirely piecemeal and uncoordinated manner; Israeli forces (largely based on the paramilitary infrastructure that had successfully resisted British mandatory occupation after World War II) repulsed these attacks, but the 1948 war left behind two important and ongoing legacies. First, it established in the minds of Israelis a sense of being beleaguered and a deep and sincere belief that they faced a truly existential threat to their existence from their mostly Arab opponents. That fear still dominates Israeli defense thinking. Second, Israel increased the size of its territory in the war, and, combined with the dynamics of the declaration of independence itself, the result was the flight of a large portion of the Palestinian Arab population from their former homes into the surrounding Islamic states, thereby creating the basis for the reassertion of Palestinian nationalism and the desire for a new Palestinian state.

Three wars ensued in short order. In 1956, the so-called Suez War occurred after the British and French seized the Suez Canal from Egypt (which nationalized its operations earlier that year) in league with Israel, which occupied the Sinai Peninsula as its part in the British–French action. The war was ended and territorial gains reversed largely as the result of joint American–Soviet opposition. The American stance was one of the few times the United States has overtly opposed the Israelis, as well as two of the bulwarks of its security policy, Britain and France. The outcome included the establishment of a United Nations peacekeeping force along the frontier separating Egypt and Israel (the United Nations Emergency Force, or UNEF) in Sinai to avoid future conflicts. When Egypt demanded the removal of UNEF from Egyptian soil in 1967, that barrier was removed (the Israelis had never accepted UN forces on its side of the frontier), as an apparent first step toward a second general offensive against Israel; the Israelis responded with a decisive preemptive attack that overwhelmed their opponents—notably the Egyptians, Jordanians, and Syrians—in less than a week in the Six Days War.

The major result of the 1967 war was Israeli occupation of territories from each of its principal adversaries: the Sinai Peninsula and the Gaza Strip from Egypt, the West Bank of the Jordan River from Jordan, and the Golan Heights from Syria. Israel justified (and continues to rationalize) these occupations on the strategic basis that they provide protection of Israel from future invasions. Although Sinai has been returned to Egypt by treaty agreement, as part of the U.S.-led Camp David accords, Israeli occupation of the other territories remains a major source of regional tension and, by extension, U.S. concern. The final conflict occurred in 1973, when Israel's opponents used one of Israel's high holidays to launch the Yom Kippur War to regain their lost lands and, depending on one's view, to accomplish the final destruction of the Jewish state. Israel prevailed in the long run, but the distinguishing military aspect of the war was that Israel suffered serious setbacks in its early conduct that caused Israel to activate the nuclear arsenal that it had clandestinely assembled.

The legacies of the 1967 and 1973 wars, each in their distinct way, largely define the contemporary strategic landscape and thus the basis of American policy concern. The principal vestige of the 1967 war was the dispute over occupied territories. This legacy has, of course, come to focus mostly on the West Bank, but to a lesser degree on the Gaza Strip, a narrow slice of territory that was also annexed from Egypt by Israel in 1967. As long as the territorial dispute remains contentious, the chances for meaningful peace and stabilization of the region (one of the primary American goals) remain problematic. The carry-over from the Yom Kippur War was the nuclear shadow that loomed during that crisis. When the possibility of an Israeli nuclear response to its possible destruction seemed real, the world, and notably the United States, was forced to contemplate the prospect of being drawn, in some unknowable way with frightening prospects, into a nuclear war over the Arab–Israeli situation. The steely determination of the Americans after the war was that it was intolerable for Middle Eastern politics to degenerate to this level again, and from that determination the aggressive pursuit of a peace settlement in the area that has been the major American strategic interest in the area was born. Its special implications for Egypt are discussed in the next chapter.

The two legacies are related to one another in the sense that a territorial settlement (the 1967 vestige) is linked to achieving the result demanded by the second legacy. While the Israelis do not reject these American priorities, they are not the same as their own, which center more explicitly on the question of Israeli survival that, at least in the minds of many Israelis, is the true basis of the Islamic challenge. Israel's safety and existence are important to the United States, many of whose experts see a peace agreement that serves both Israeli and American interests as the best way to ensure that goal. Many in Israel agree with the American assessment, but others do not. A sizable part of Israeli opinion is that the existential threat is so overriding that pursuit of a peace agreement with untrustworthy adversaries is too risky a path and that the Israel state must unilaterally guarantee its own survival in a hostile environment. Many Americans also agree with this Israeli assessment of the situation, creating the basis of partisan policy disagreements in each country.

The domestic political impact, and particularly the effective alliances between like-minded Israelis and Americans on the basic issues underlying U.S.–Israeli relations, is another source of distinction in assessing U.S. policy toward its closest Middle Eastern friend and ally. The domestic impact on Israel policy is distinctive in at least two ways. On one hand, it is on both sides of the issue divide over Israeli security. Israeli hard-liners who resist an American-supported peace settlement centering on the Palestinian state issue occupy the political right in Israel, and they have their counterparts in the United States. Historically, the hard-line Israeli position has been associated with the Likud Party and currently with the leadership of Israeli Prime Minister Benjamin Netanyahu and his allies, many drawn from the West Bank settler community. The American side of this position is most closely associated with the American–Israel Public Affairs Committee (AIPAC), one of the largest, wealthiest, and most influential lobbies in the United States.

The effective liaisons between the American and Israeli supporters of this position have been the American neoconservatives who were influential in Bush administration foreign policy. The large impact of this lobby and transoceanic collaboration is, according to Mearsheimer and Walt in their controversial critique, considerable: "The Israeli lobby has successfully convinced many Americans that American and Israeli interests are essentially identical. They are not." Some of the strain between the Netanyahu administration and the American Obama administration that became apparent in 2011 was caused by Obama's purge of the neoconservatives and rejection of their philosophy when the new Democratic administration came to power in 2009.

The "peace" position in American and Israeli arguments is also represented in both countries. The position that peace is the number one goal of Israel and that Israelis must aggressively pursue policy possibilities (most notably in the direction of some form of Palestinian statehood) is generally associated with the political left in Israel. Its leading current spokesperson is Tzipi Livni, the former Israeli foreign minister and leader of the Kadima Party, which leads the opposition in the Knesset. Its equivalent in the United States, which is of generally lesser power and influence than AIPAC, is the so-called J-Street lobby, consisting of Americans who reject the Israeli hard-line position and seek to counter the influence of AIPAC.

The domestic influencers of U.S. policy toward Israel are more powerful than their sheer numbers would suggest. Support for the two positions, but especially the Likud-based advocacy, comes primarily from American Jews, who are strategically located politically in the United States: New York, Florida, and California are particularly prominent and magnify the influence of an American Jewish population of about 3 percent of the overall population on the process. Their position is reinforced by socially conservative Americans who form part of the GOP electoral base and whom Mearsheimer and Walt refer to as the "Christian Zionists," generally conservative, evangelical American Christians who profess admiration for the determination of the Israelis. Israel's self-portrayal as a beleaguered David also resonates well with these religious conservatives (who are also generally Republicans) in the United States.

Lurking over the entire debate and often ignored or underemphasized in discussions of Israeli security is what one can call the Israeli "demographic time bomb." Although the numbers are changing and probably imprecisely measured in any case, the Jewish/non-Jewish (Islamic) population balance is perilous from an Israeli vantage point. The population of Israel (the country as measured before its 1967 territorial acquisitions) is solidly Jewish (about 76 percent of the population of around 7.3 million), with a significant Arab, Islamic minority (about 23 percent of the population). Within these borders, a Jewish majority is guaranteed for a long time, despite unfavorable demographic trends (the Arab population is growing faster than the Jewish population). Thus, it is possible and sustainable to speak of both a Jewish and democratic Israel existing into the future within these boundaries.

When the occupied territories are added to Israeli demographics, however, the balance and prospects change. While current numbers are not totally reliable, a single country comprised of pre-1967 Israel and the West Bank and Gaza (one possible outcome of the current dispute) would have roughly equal numbers of Jewish and Muslim citizens, with the Muslim population growth rate assuring that the majority will soon be (if it is not already) Muslim. In such a unit, the possibilities of a democratic and a Jewish state simultaneously are very remote. Those Israelis and their American supporters who oppose an independent Palestinian state generally downplay the significance of these demographic certainties, but they represent long-term trends that cannot be ignored indefinitely and that place parameters on the practical outcomes of disagreements between the United States and Israel.

ISRAEL: A SKETCH

Israel's position in its region and the world has no other direct, comprehensive comparisons. It is a very small country physically and in terms of population, but it is also among the most advanced countries in the world by most measures (economic, social, educational, etc.), and were it a larger country, it would almost certainly occupy a position in the upper ranks of world powers. As it is, it is virtually sui generis, a highly advanced society and state within a comparatively underdeveloped (if selectively very wealthy) part of the world.

The fact that Israel is also the world's only Jewish state also distinguishes it and leaves it alone in the world by some measures. More than half of world Jewry lives within the Israel (the second largest Jewish population lives in the United States), and thus a threat to Israel is also a threat to one of the world's oldest religions. Given the attempt by Nazi Germany to extinguish European Jewry (before World War II, the vast majority of Jews lived in some part of Europe, including the Soviet Union), the possible existential threat to adherents of Judaism is a concern unshared by adherents of most other world religions.

Israel also emerges from a long history that is both a legacy and a curse. Much of the Old Testament of the Bible is, in some ways, a history of the travails of the quest of the Jewish people to find a suitable homeland in a hostile environment where there is hardly any parcel of land over which there are not multiple claims to rightful possession, either historically or divinely inspired or justified. In the case of Israel, the lands which many Israelis believe are bequeathed to them by God also happen to be territories that have been inhabited by multiple others with religious or historical counterclaims. The injection of "God's will" as the basis of conflicting assertions and aspirations does nothing to moderate the heat and intensity of competing claims to the same resources, in this case the relatively small amount of land that Jews call Israel and the Arabs calls Palestine.

Israeli uniqueness creates a very different orientation toward the world and Israel's place in it than most other peoples possess. To many Israelis, the overriding lesson of their history, most dramatically underscored by the Holocaust, is that they exist in a very hostile world in which their very survival must depend on their personal actions. In this environment, Israel can ultimately only depend on itself to ensure its survival; when the Jews have allowed themselves to be reliant on the others for their well-being, that vulnerability has been punished. In the first half of the twentieth century, the result was almost their extinction. If Israelis have a sense of suspicion and even defiance of outside assistance for them and their pursuit of their interests, it is in no small measure the outgrowth of their reading of and response to the kind of world in which they believe they live. Outsiders often underestimate the extent to which this Israeli conviction drives Israeli independence from world conventions and entreaties about how they "ought" to act. To Israelis, what others view as paranoia is reality, and anyone who argues to the contrary is to be viewed with suspicion at best and with disdain and resistance at worst. The result is that Israel has a relatively small number of friends or unquestioned supporters in the world community, but it is a necessary price to be paid in the eyes of those who see Israel's survival as the major, driving influence on national life. This affects Israeli relations with the United States as much as it does their relations with other countries, but it gives U.S.–Israeli discussions about Israel and what it "should do" an edge that is not present in similar relations with other countries that do not see their physical survival in such problematical terms.

Israel in the World

What distinguishes Israel from the rest of the Middle East is that it is the only truly democratic state in the region. Some Israeli Palestinians dispute how meaningful their participation in the Israeli political system actually is, but nonetheless, Israel has a tradition and commitment to democratic rule that is unmatched elsewhere in the Middle East, and that fact is often used to help justify the affinity that the United States has for Israel as opposed to its Arab neighbors and why, among Middle Eastern states, Israel is the United States' natural ally. The democratic tradition in Israel goes back to the country's formation and has never been interrupted or seriously challenged.

Israel's open, democratic government stands in stark contrast to its possession of and rule over its adjacent occupied territories from the 1967 war. The territories it acquired from Egypt, the Sinai Peninsula and the Gaza Strip, are no longer administered as occupied territories, Sinai having been returned to Egypt as part of the Egyptian–Israeli peace in 1982 negotiated earlier by President Carter at Camp David, and effective rule of Gaza was ceded to the

Palestinian Authority in 2006. Israel, however, remains in control both of the Syrian Golan Heights and the West Bank. The Golan Heights are a low mountain range bordering on the Jordan River (and Israel's water supply) and northern Israel that had, prior to Israeli conquest, been used to shell Israeli citizens, and it remains firmly in Israeli hands. Most of its Syrian population has abandoned their homes for now, and there is not a major governance issue in this territory (beyond the question of the international legality of the continuing occupation). The West Bank, however, is a different and far more controversial matter.

The West Bank and its ultimate political disposition are at the heart of the controversy between Israel and the Palestinians, and it has proven to be a dispute that defies solution. From an Israeli vantage point, the West Bank, which it has occupied since 1967, serves two purposes. One is strategic: when the West Bank is in non-Israeli, hostile hands, it is like a spear sticking in the middle of the country. At its narrowest point, the western boundary of the West Bank is only a little over 10 miles from the Mediterranean Sea, and it was the danger that Israel might be cut in two by a hostile military thrust across this narrow strip of territory that motivated early Israeli defense thinking regarding this area. The occupation has removed that concern. The other function is part of the dream of a "Greater Israel" held by many on the Israeli right (including current Prime Minister Benjamin Netanyahu). This view, rooted in Zionism, holds that the territories of Judea and Samaria, which compose all or nearly all of the West Bank, are part of Israel's historical past and endowment, an integral element of what Van Creveld refers to as "the land of Israel as the place where the Jewish people was formed, lived, and created the only independent state it had ever possessed." In addition, the West Bank serves as a place for further Jewish settlement of new population, particularly Jews from outside Israel who immigrate to Israel. The Palestinian Arabs, on the other hand, see the West Bank and Gaza as the only reasonable site for an independent Palestinian state and reject the Greater Israel position on both philosophical and practical grounds. As long as the issue remains and festers, the result for Israel is a perpetual state of mobilization and military alert where, as Van Creveld describes it, Israelis live "in a country where almost everybody is a soldier on eleven months' annual leave," meaning essentially everyone is at least part of the military reserves of the country.

The West Bank issue becomes a point of enormous U.S.–Israeli concern because the United States is, for most purposes, Israel's closest and, in some cases only, reliable ally in what it views as an excessively hostile world. The relationship is, of course, asymmetrical: the continued support of the United States is far more vital to Israel and its security than the conditions in Israel are to the United States. While the two countries have enormous affinity for one another and commitment to one another's well-being, the simple fact is that there is very little the Israelis can do to threaten fundamentally the United States or its security (the possible exception being in the area of nuclear provocation focusing on Iran). The withholding or withdrawal of American support for Israel, on the other hand, could leave the Jewish state perilously vulnerable in an environment where its opponents might well take advantage of such a breach of support. Largely because of support from pro-Israeli organizations like AIPAC in the United States, this asymmetry does not translate into an American ability to force Israeli acquiescence to U.S. policy positions.

The Israelis understand the dynamics of this asymmetry thoroughly, and it colors how they view the American political scene and why they act so overtly to influence it. One of the frequent criticisms of the Israelis has been their frequent resort to unilateralism, especially in the form of defying international positions on matters the Israelis believe to pose basic threats to Israeli security, even existence. Many Israelis share the belief that only Israel can guarantee its own survival and that the Israeli state must ignore others when it believes its survival is at stake.

The result can be a kind of self-fulfilling prophecy. While the Israelis may have little concrete reason to question the American guarantee, it is always possible it could evaporate. This makes them exceedingly concerned to ensure that only highly pro-Israeli American politicians come to power (a function for their lobbying efforts) and to hedge against the consequences of change. In many ways, the May 2011 confrontation between Netanyahu and Obama was an act of preemption by the Israelis to ensure that pro-Israeli conservatives maintain control in the United States.

The Physical Setting

Israel stands in stark contrast to its Arab neighbors. The Islamic countries that surround and generally oppose Israel generally fall into two categories, distinguished by whether they possess energy resources as a source of wealth or not. Israel's contiguous neighbors are non–oil producers, and they vary in size and thus threat potential: Jordan (with a population of 6.4 million) and Lebanon (4.1 million) are smaller than Israel, whereas Egypt (80.5 million) and Syria (22.2 million) are both a good bit larger than Israel. All four are, however, considerably less wealthy and prosperous than the Israelis. All the oil-rich countries have well-developed financial sectors to handle their oil revenues but few other symbols of the general accoutrements of development.

Israel (measured by its pre-1967 borders) is physically a very small state. It has a land area of 5,822 square miles, which ranks in 153rd in the world and slightly larger than the state of New Jersey. The occupied territories, of which the West Bank is the most significant part, add to this territory if counted as part of Israel (which essentially no one in the international community does): the West Bank, for instance, is a little less than one-third the size of Israel and is slightly smaller than Delaware. The land on which Israel is located is not especially fruitful, with only 15.45 percent considered arable and with modest natural resources, listed in the *CIA World Factbook*, that include timber, potash, copper ore, and natural gas.

Israel's strength is its people. The population of Israel, according to 2010 estimates, stands at about 7.35 million, including over 400,000 in the occupied territories (about 300,000 in the West Bank proper, over 125,000 in Israeli suburbs of East Jerusalem, and another 19,000 on the Golan Heights). Israel has a modest population growth rate among its Jewish citizens but, as Della Pergola points out, "Immigration has been the main driver of population growth." The population of Israel itself is approximately three-quarters Jewish and one-quarter non-Jewish, with the vast majority of these Palestinian Arabs. This balance is reflected religiously, with three-quarters of the population at least nominally Jewish, about one-fourth Muslim, and the rest divided among other religions (about 2 percent are Christian, for instance). Hebrew and Arabic are spoken within the respective confessional communities, with English as the major accepted common language. The population is well educated, with a literacy rate of 97.1 percent, and the life expectancy for Israelis is about 81 years, 17th in the world. Palestinian advocates argue that these indicators are higher for Jews than non-Jews, an assertion the Israeli government disputes.

Israeli regional distinctiveness is also reflected in its economy. Although Israel is only the 153rd largest country in the world in area, its economy, at $217.1 billion, is the 51st largest in the world, and its per capita income, at $29,500, is 48th among world countries. The bulk of Israeli economic competitiveness is in the high technology area, including things like avionics and computer design. It has diverse import and export partnerships. The United States tops the list of both its imports and exports; on the import side, China is second, followed by a number of European Union states (Germany, Belgium, Italy, the United Kingdom, and the Netherlands). On the export side, Hong Kong and Belgium follow the United States, but Israel exports goods and services to a broad array of countries.

The inclusion of the West Bank muddies this essentially rosy picture. Even with considerable settlement in the area by Israelis, they remain a small minority of citizens in these territories. When the Israeli and Palestinian Arab populations of pre-1967 Israel and the West Bank and Gaza are added together, there is a rough balance between the Jewish and Muslim populations. Higher population growth rates within the Muslim population show that the combined territories will have an ongoing Muslim majority in a few years; estimates vary somewhat about exactly when this will occur, but there is no doubt that it will. The fact that Jewish growth comes largely from migration from the overseas Jewish populations is a limiting factor, since most non-Israeli Jews are in the United States and not considered prime emigration material. This factor is critical when one discusses the future of the West Bank.

Israel as a Unique State

The major characteristic that distinguishes Israel from other states in the world is its security position and its perception of and reaction to its security predicament. This Israeli predicament starts from Israel's perception of its physical place in the world. To borrow an old and time-worn cliché, Israel is "a Jewish state in an Arab sea." Physically, Israel is surrounded on three sides by Islamic states, and all of them (or in the case of Lebanon, elements within it) have voiced and acted upon hostile intentions toward Israel, as its military experience has demonstrated. The particularly poignant physical problem, in addition to the possibility of being cut in two by a push to the Mediterranean from the West Bank, is the problem of a two-front war: having to deal with a military thrust by Egypt from the west while Jordan, Syria, and possibly Iraq attack from the east. This threat has been attenuated by the peace treaties that Israel has signed with Egypt in 1979 and Jordan in 1994. As long as that peace holds, the "Arab sea" is a little less hostile, but things can change. This Israeli fear of change creates great interest in the evolution of the 2011 uprising that toppled long-time Egyptian dictator (but friend of Israel) Hosni Mubarak from office in Cairo.

The psychological aspect of Israeli isolation is perhaps even more daunting and problematical. Before the establishment of Israel over 60 years ago, the Jews had been a classic "stateless nation" for over a millennium, and they had, like so many others in their situation (the Kurds are an obvious parallel) not always been treated well by those who served as their hosts. In particular, much of world Jewry had taken refuge in Europe for the century before Israel came into being, and leaving themselves physically at the mercy of the various host governments of the continent had nearly resulted in their literal extinction. Regional hostility from their neighbors and the remembrance of the Holocaust underlie and add fuel to this fear and the perceived need that Israelis feel to protect themselves against a future exigency that threatens their very existence in the world. Outsiders do not fully appreciate the depth with which this feeling is held in the Israeli psyche and tend to underplay and underappreciate it as an influence on Israel and its policies toward the world.

The policy differences between the Obama administration and Israel over Iran illustrate the consequences of this Israeli worldview particularly clearly. Many Israelis, and particularly people within the ruling coalition, are absolutely convinced that the Iranian government is committed to possessing nuclear weapons *and* to using those weapons to destroy Israel. Non-Israelis, including those whose opinions prevail in the Obama administration, do not consider the latter Israeli perception to be likely, but it activates the enormous opposition to the Iranian nuclear program the Israelis hold. The American position is particularly troublesome to the current Israeli government because, as Hermann points out, "Netanyahu believes the United States to be Israel's best and perhaps only ally—in particular when it comes to the international effort to prevent Iran from becoming a nuclear power." Because they fear what a nuclear Iran will do to them, they favor extreme actions to negate the threat, notably military actions to destroy the Iranian program before it can reach fruition. Because they consider the problem as an existential threat that only they can personally negate, they are willing to contemplate and possibly to act unilaterally against the Iranians, even in the face of united outside opposition. From the mindset of those who support this policy, it is the only possible solution to an intolerable, life-threatening situation. Moreover, they have a difficult time understanding why others do not understand or appreciate why they feel the way they do. The depth and emotional content of the Israeli concern over Iran was highlighted by the October 2011 revelation of an apparent Iranian-sponsored plot to assassinate the Saudi ambassador in Washington and to attack both the Saudi and Israeli embassies there.

U.S.–ISRAELI RELATIONS

The security and existence of Israel is a cardinal principle of American foreign policy, and it is one that is not questioned anywhere within the mainstream American political spectrum. Discussions focusing on differences the two countries have on specific policy issues sometimes are interpreted as assaults on that bedrock principle, but such attacks are normally more symbolic than serious, and generally overwrought when they may be sincere. The United States accepts and guarantees the continuing existence of Israel and Israeli security. At the same time, the United States and Israel do disagree on some matters, and the best way to buttress and reinforce Israeli security is a prominent area where the allies diverge.

There are both general and specific areas on which the two countries disagree. The general disagreements tend to center on other U.S. interests in the region; more specifically, they tend to be associated with American access to petroleum energy supplies from the Persian Gulf littoral. More specific differences, on which there is partisan difference *within* the United States as well as *between* Israel and the United States, focus on the Palestinian question.

Competing U.S. Regional Interests

Israel's security does not represent the only American interest in the Middle East. Traditionally, the explicit guarantee of Israel's existence has been seen as existing beside, and sometimes competing with, other priorities the United States holds. The most obvious other interest is in continued, secure access to petroleum resources in quantities and at prices that support the economies of the United States and its principal allies, who also depend on this source. The other major competing interest is the promotion of peace, stability, and democracy in the region, a goal intended to promote both Israeli security and American access to oil.

The competing American interests can be conceptualized in triangular fashion, as is done in Figure 11.1. All three points of the triangle are related, if in complex and sometimes contradictory ways. The promotion of peace and stability in the region serves both of the other goals, because a tranquil Middle East may be less antagonistic toward Israel and also be less likely to threaten interruption of secure flows of petroleum to the West. Most of the time, access to petroleum and friendship with Israel are at odds, since the countries who possess the petroleum oppose Israel, and most particularly the continuing Israeli occupation of the West Bank.

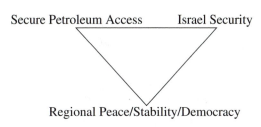

Secure Petroleum Access   Israel Security

Regional Peace/Stability/Democracy

FIGURE 11.1
U.S. Middle Eastern Interests

The existence of and tensions among these goals is disputed. The central, ongoing source of conflict has been the simultaneous support for Israel and quest for petroleum as American goals, but some argue this is a false dichotomy since the threat of Arab oil producers to withhold petroleum from the West is basically hollow. Their argument is that market forces are such that since petroleum is the lifeblood of the economies of the producers, they have to sell it somewhere, and that it will get into Western hands under the worst of conditions. Those most concerned with oil, on the other hand, argue that removing the cause of the potential threat in the form of Israeli intransigence on issues important to the producers—most notably, of course, the Palestinian question—would remove even the semblance of this problem.

The conjunction of competing policies comes over the promotion of peace, stability, and democracy in the region, which effectively means among Islamic states. Two points need to be made here. The first is that promoting peace and stability have been long-term American aspirations, and they are generally reinforcing: stable (which effectively means not militantly Islamist) regimes have long been seen as the instrument for promoting regional stability. U.S. support for the Egyptian and Jordanian regimes is evidence of this policy. The problem is that, in effect, this policy has had the effect of supporting *anti*democratic regimes. The addition of democracy promotion in the region largely under the Bush neoconservatives thus reversed part of that calculation and may, as the events of 2011 in the region demonstrate, have the effect of creating instability, at least during the process of democratization in various Middle Eastern states. The quandary for American policy makers is that, at least in the short run, democratization may lead to destabilization, a prospect explored in Chapter 12.

Second, a large part of the reason the United States has valued stability is that the nondemocratic regimes the policy has reinforced have been generally less threatening to Israeli security than other regimes in the region. As popular will is asserted across the region through some form of democratization (whether the resulting regimes are classically democratic or not), the possible outcome may be increased anti-Israeli sentiment, a challenge to that goal of American policy.

This set of prospects highlights U.S.–Israeli disagreement on the one major policy area on which the two countries conflict. In the current environment, anti-Israeli sentiment in the region—which threatens the achievement of all three U.S. foreign policy goals—centers on the Palestinian conflict. The fulcrum of this disagreement is the Israeli occupation and utilization of West Bank territories claimed by the Palestinians as part of the independent Palestinian state. The two sides are currently at great odds on this issue. Hermann states one side: "Israel's control over the occupied territories is in Netanyahu's view justified by two equally important arguments: the Jews' historical claim to the promised land and the constant existential threat that faces them." The current U.S. administration is committed to a two-state solution that includes a Palestinian state, putting the partners at odds on the West Bank question. Mearsheimer and Walt state the potential consequences of this situation. Referring explicitly to Jerusalem, an important part of the dispute, they argue that nonsettlement "makes it harder for the United States to address the other problems it faces in the Middle East." Regarding the prospects of continued Israeli resistance to American peace initiatives, they add ominously that the Israeli lobby "may be jeopardizing the long-term prospects of the Jewish state."

The Palestinian Question

All of the problems dividing Israel and the United States come to a focus over the disposition of Palestine and the consequent fate of the Palestinian people. As a territorial issue, the Palestinian question most directly applies to the parcels of land proposed to form an independent Palestinian state, the Gaza Strip and the West Bank. Both areas have been subject to Israeli occupation since 1967, a point of controversy within the region and the international community, both of which view the occupation as illegal (for this reason, the Israelis prefer to refer to the "administered," rather than the "occupied," territories). What happens to these areas (and especially the West Bank) has implications for Israeli security: the Israeli government argues it must maintain some level of control for strategic reasons already discussed, and the Palestinians and others argue that peace and stability are impossible as long as the current situation festers. An unresolved Palestinian problem irritates relations between the United States and the oil-producing countries, who argue that the United States continues to support the illegal occupation and its most glaring symbol, burgeoning Israeli settlements on the West Bank. Regional peace and stability are also affected, as an unresolved Palestinian situation promotes extremist movements in the region and leaves Palestine itself on the constant cusp of violence.

For all these reasons, the United States government has pressed the Israeli government to move forward in negotiations with the Palestinian Authority (PA), the body created by the Oslo Accords of 1993 that has been the formal starting point for negotiation of a Palestinian political entity. Successive Israeli governments have, with varying degrees of enthusiasm, pursued talks with the Palestinians, the objective of which was to create an independent Palestinian state, but these efforts have been more or less accommodating and, in some minds, sincere, as have Palestinian responses. Progress toward a final settlement seems no nearer than it did almost 20 years ago.

Israel is reluctant to complete an agreement because of the kinds of primordial fears it has for its existence, expressed particularly in terms of questioning the Palestinian commitment to honoring its right of existence. The United States insists that a peace agreement creating an independent Palestinian state is a necessary condition for regional peace; without such an agreement, proponents argue, peace is impossible. The Israelis counter than such an action alone is not sufficient (more has to accompany the action to solve the problem). Without guarantees that the creation of a Palestinian state will be accompanied by an honest renunciation of vows to destroy Israel, the Israelis are prone to argue the possible negative impacts: that a Palestinian state will be a sanctuary and launching pad for terrorists and that the loss of the West Bank would leave Israel dangerously vulnerable to destruction.

The result internally in Israel is a politically paralyzing disagreement over what to do about Palestine. The political right, represented most forcefully by Netanyahu, believes that, in Hermann's words, the existential threat "cannot be expected to disappear even if Israel signs a peace agreement with the Palestinians," a position that has popular support within the country: "two-thirds of Israeli Jews believe that the Palestinians in particular and the Arabs in general would destroy Israel if they could." On the other hand, Hermann also reports that "over 55 percent of the Israeli Jewish population . . . supports the 'two states for two peoples' formula," a position championed by the Livni-led Kadima.

The result has been an impasse that serves as the main divide in U.S.–Israeli relations and that flared dramatically in May 2011. The Palestine question actually encompasses four different, partially sequential aspects. The first is the nature of the Palestinian state. The second is the status of East Jerusalem, an area claimed by both the Israelis and the Palestinians as their capital. The third is the vexing and growing problem of permanent Israeli settlements on the West Bank, and the fourth is the Palestinians' so-called "right of return" to lands they abandoned within Israel at the time of Israeli independence in 1948.

The Status of Palestine

The two-state solution involves the creation of an independent Palestinian state encompassing the West Bank and the Gaza Strip. Conceptually, this idea has been the predominant goal of the peace process since the 1990s, and it is a position strongly endorsed by the Obama administration in the president's

May 19, 2011, speech at the U.S. Department of State days before Netanyahu arrived in Washington. The essence of the problems blocking a two-state solution (other than unease among some Israelis, possibly including Netanyahu, about whether they want the process to succeed) has boiled down to two basic conditions.

One problem has been the status of the new state as a sovereign entity, a matter that is manifested in different conceptions regarding security arrangements for Palestine. Given their concerns about a Palestinian state, the Israelis would prefer such an entity whose sovereignty is circumscribed in ways that would make Israelis less nervous about their own security. More particularly, the Israelis would prefer a Palestine that has no military forces and for which the Israeli Defense Force (IDF) is the Palestinians' source of security from external threats. In this construction, the PA would provide internal security for Palestine with an indigenous constabulary, but the IDF would serve as its "army," thereby assuring that threats to Israel could not emanate from Palestinian soil and that Israel could respond to terrorist activities on Palestinian soil. The result would be essentially a partially sovereign Palestinian state with a permanent Israeli garrison on its soil, an idea the Palestinians reject categorically. Netanyahu endorsed such a presence in his May 2011 visit to the United States.

The other problem is the physical dimensions of the Palestinian political entity. Palestinians, of course, argue that the Palestinian state should have borders congruent with the preoccupation, pre-1967 borders of Israel, a position the Israelis do not embrace and that Obama said should be the starting point for negotiations. The amount of the West Bank offered to the Palestinians has varied from 42 percent by Ariel Sharon (the amount of territory already administered by the PA at the time the offer was made) to 95 percent (Ehud Barak) or 97 percent (Ehud Olmert). None of the offers, however, has been accepted by successive representatives of the Palestinians (Yasir Arafat or Mohammad Abbas), generally for reasons associated with the other problems surrounding the Palestinian question. The resulting impasse has led one former AIPAC member, Henry Siegman, to declare a peace process "where Israeli governments pretend they are seeking a two-state solution, and the United States pretends to believe them" ("Can Obama Beat the Israeli Lobby?").

The Fate of Jerusalem

What to do about Jerusalem has been a problem that has plagued the peace process in the Middle East since the first Camp David meetings in 1978 conducted by U.S. President Jimmy Carter. In a 2000 op-ed piece in the *New York Times*, Carter explained the problem as it existed then and as it continues to exist: "We knew that Israel had declared sovereignty over the entire city but that the international community considered East Jerusalem to be legally part of the occupied West Bank. We realized that no Israeli leader could renounce Israel's position, and that it would be political suicide for

Sadat or any other Arab leader to surrender any of their peoples' claims regarding the Islamic and Christian holy places." Since that pronouncement was made, about 200,000 Israeli settlers have moved into homes in the disputed sections of East Jerusalem.

The Jerusalem question has two highly emotional aspects. One derives from the importance of the city in Judaism, Islam, and Christianity. Each has significant religious shrines within Jerusalem. Before 1967, when Jerusalem was controlled by Jordan, Israelis could not visit Jewish shrines in the city (e.g., the Wailing Wall), and after the occupation, Muslims have been restricted in their access to places like the Al Aqsa mosque. Thus, control of Jerusalem implies the ability to regulate and restrict who can visit what religiously important places. The other aspect derives from the fact that both Israel and Palestine claim East Jerusalem as their rightful capital. This overall issue is conceptually amenable to some form of partition, but since each side claims the entire city as its own on canonical and political grounds, progress toward settlement has remained elusive. An exacerbating factor is the continued building of additional residences for Israelis in the disputed areas; as late as 2011, the Israeli authorities continued approving building permits for constructing additional condominium complexes in East Jerusalem.

Israeli Settlements on the West Bank

By far the most controversial, explosive issue, and what has come to be the symbol of the Israeli–Palestinian crisis and U.S.–Israeli disagreement, is the question of permanent Israeli settlements on the West Bank. Jeffrey Goldberg, writing in *The Atlantic*, summarizes the negative dimensions of this controversy: "These settlements have undermined Israel's international legitimacy and demoralized moderate Palestinians. The settlements exist far outside the Israeli political consensus, and their presence will likely incite a third *intifada* (uprising). Yet the country seems unable to confront the settlements." The settlements divide Israelis as well, with moderates and leftists opposed and rightists (a group that includes much of the settler population itself) in support of the settlements.

The settlements are large and growing. Prior to 2000, the entire settler population was limited to a much smaller number of Israelis living in territories generally contiguous to the pre-1967 boundaries, including parts of East Jerusalem. That number has grown both in total numbers of settlers to between 250,000 and 400,000 (depending on how one accounts residents of disputed parts of Jerusalem) and is increasing. The reasons include the need for additional space to accommodate immigrants and, according to Della Pergola, because settlement "housing is significantly cheaper than within Israel's pre-1967 boundaries," thereby creating the ability for some Israelis to improve their quality of life. Moreover, although the majority of early settlements were on territory contiguous to or near pre-1967 Israel, they have gradually spread to include much of the West Bank.

In order to accommodate this physical increase in settler presence, the Israelis have felt the need to step up Israeli military presence on the West Bank to protect the new settlers, and the result has been stark. As Friedman puts it, "The West Bank is an ugly quilt of high walls, Israeli checkpoints, 'legal' and 'illegal' Jewish settlements, Arab villages, Jewish roads that only Jewish settlers use, Arab roads, and roadblocks." As the settlements spread, Palestinians increasingly despair of the idea that Israel will ever abandon them, leading, in Hermann's view, to "the spread of Islamic fundamentalism" in the area.

Many fear that possible outcomes to the peace process are being compromised as well. As Siegman puts it, "No government serious about a two-state solution to the conflict would have pursued, without letup, the theft and fragmentation of Palestinian lands, which even a child understands makes Palestinian statehood impossible." He adds, "What is astounding is that the international community, pretending to believe Israel's claim that it is the victim and its occupied subjects the aggressors, has allowed this devastating dispossession to continue" ("Palestine").

The growing web of West Bank settlements also prejudices the future movement toward a Palestinian state-based peace process in two ways. Within Israel, the growing number of West Bank settlers has become a potent force on the political right. The champion of this movement is Israeli Foreign Minister Avigdor Lieberman, whose Israel Beiteinu party holds the third largest bloc of seats in the current Knesset and is a vital member of the Netanyahu coalition, and whose support is almost entirely based on occupied-zone votes of settlers. Any policy initiative on the part of the Netanyahu government that threatens the settlements could thus also jeopardize the tenure of the regime. The more the settler community grows, the more support for the Lieberman faction is likely to grow as a political force in Israel.

The other negative impact on the peace process is the sheer inertial influence a growing settler population has on the possibility of a peace settlement. The current settler population is about 10 percent of the total population of the West Bank, for instance, and it is increasingly difficult to imagine how they would be dealt with should a fully independent Palestinian state (which they uniformly oppose) be declared. They would almost certainly not want to stay under, nor would their presence be favored by, a new Palestinian government, but would they abandon their homes and leave voluntarily? Since the answer to that question is almost certainly negative, they would have to be evicted with at least some Israeli complicity, a politically suicidal course for any Israeli government. Since the Palestinians understand this dynamic, they cannot avoid despairing at the durability and growth of the settlements as evidence the Israelis are not really serious about negotiating a Palestinian state. Kodmani summarizes the continuing settlement process as a series of "daily confidence destroying measures inflicted on Palestinians." Veteran U.S. Middle East negotiator Aaron David Miller adds, "The chances of a conflict ending agreement . . . appears to be slim and none."

The "Right of Return"

Simmering not far below the surface of these other problems is the so-called Palestinian "right of return." At the time of the declaration of Israeli independence and the ensuing war waged against it, much of the Palestinian population—upwards of 500,000—fled their homes in the new Israel, leaving behind most of their belongings. This population, which has grown to several million in the intervening years, asserts a right to return and to reclaim the property they abandoned, or in other words, a right to be repatriated. This desire (which, it might be added, is shared by displaced Syrian former residents of the Golan Heights) is fundamental and deeply held among the former residents and their offspring.

Israel denies that any right exists. The Israeli argument is basically that in the process of abandoning their property in 1948, the Palestinians also forfeited their continuing claim on that territory, almost all of which has been purchased by Israelis, who have lived on this land as their own for over 60 years now. Moreover, the Israelis could not physically accommodate the millions of Palestinians who might try to come back and reclaim lost property, to say nothing of the legal battles that would ensue and the massive dislocations of Israelis that would be a consequence (a shortage of attractive living space in pre-1967 Israel is, after all, one of the reasons for settlements in the occupied territories).

The result is an impasse, and the inability to resolve it has been a deal breaker in peace negotiations. The positions of the two sides are mutually exclusive and impossible to compromise, and both sides are adamant in holding those positions. No Palestinian leader can renounce the right to return in principle and survive politically, and it is almost certain that the 2000 peace plan hammered out with the assistance of President Clinton (and which would have given the Palestinians 95 percent of the West Bank) foundered on the implicit renunciation of the right to repatriation contained within it. Israel is equally adamant in rejecting the Palestinian position on the ground that to permit Palestinian return would create a nightmare in Israeli society that could even eventuate in a Palestinian majority in pre-1967 Israel. The only possible compromise is an agreement to allow *some*, but not all, Palestinians to return, but that meets equal levels of objection. The Israelis could only agree to numbers of returnees that would be much smaller than the PA could accept, and the PA understands that being put in the position of choosing who would and who would not be allowed to return is an unpalatable political choice. The right to return lurks not far beneath the surface as a deal breaker in any agreement.

U.S. OPTIONS

Despite all these barriers, it has been the consistent position of American administrations that Israel and Palestine must agree to a political settlement that will produce a stable peace in the region. Such a solution clearly serves all

American regional interests: it would ensure Israeli security, remove the animosity toward Israel that makes U.S. relations with the oil producers more problematic, and promote regional peace and stability, with salutary effects on the other two goals. The problem is that the current Israeli regime and its supporters in the United States disagree about whether a durable peace is possible or if any agreement would be reliable. This was the fundamental point of contention that came to the surface during the 2011 Netanyahu visit to Washington.

Israeli reluctance to move decisively toward a territorial settlement that includes a fully independent Palestine (the only form of Palestinian entity the Palestinians will accept) reflects their suspicions about the possibility and durability of such a peace. Many Israelis, including Netanyahu, believe that animosity between the Arabs and the Jews is so great that no possible agreement could overcome it. The gist of this position is that the Arabs are so intent on Israel's destruction that any agreement they might negotiate would only be viewed as a step toward annihilating Jewry and the state of Israel. One can deny or dispute this contention, but one cannot deny that it is deeply and honestly held by those who believe and are motivated by it. The American position is based on the premise that a durable peace between Israel and its neighbors is possible; many Israelis are not so sure or openly disbelieve this prospect. It is such a fundamental disagreement that it touches every aspect of organizing for and dealing with the future.

There are three possible outcomes to the present situation, and each has different implications for both Israel and the United States. The United States and Israel disagree about the desirability of the options and about the consequences of either embracing or rejecting one or the other. In essence, the disagreement can be framed as a dispute over who best knows what is in Israel's best interests and thus what policy positions are more or less to Israel's benefit. Americans like Obama believe that the absence of a durable peace agreement is more harmful to Israel in the long run than what they believe is an unsustainable status quo. This latter judgment is based in the demographic time bomb introduced earlier. Israelis represented by Netanyahu are more concerned with what they view as potentially existential consequences of change, and are more reluctant to take chances that might have disastrous results for them.

Israeli geographer Della Pergola presents the fundamental dilemma that faces Israel. "From the perspective of Israeli strategy," he writes, "the state faces a conundrum because it has three fundamental goals, but can only achieve two of the three at the same time. The three goals are to preserve the Israeli state's Jewish identity, democratic character, and territorial state." The demographics of growth in the Jewish and Palestinian populations make it impossible to serve all three goals, and Israel, which maintains the semblance of pursuing all three in current circumstances, is reluctant to choose among the options, each of which involves abandoning one of the three goals. Whether the option of maintaining the status quo is sustainable, however, is a debatable question. These three goals are presented in Figure 11.2.

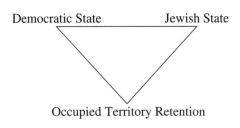

Occupied Territory Retention

FIGURE 11.2
Israeli Palestine Options

Della Pergola goes on to describe the consequences of adherence to each of the three Israeli goals he identifies. To pursue the first goal, "Israel can choose to apply a Jewish cultural identity to the whole territory and population, but in that case it cannot be a democracy," because non-Jews would both resist the process and would be in the majority. Second, "Israel can opt for the same territorial extension and apply to all residents the democratic principles of 'one man, one vote,' but it that case it cannot be a Jewish state," since the majority in "Greater Israel" would be non-Jewish. Finally, "Israel can choose to be a Jewish and democratic state, but in that case it will have to withdraw from significant parts of the territory and population." The Israeli government and its supporters do not directly deny or refute these conclusions, but neither do they embrace them. Each has a different effect upon the three possible outcomes: the two-state solution, a single Israeli–Palestinian state, or the status quo.

The Two-State Solution

The idea and nature of a two-state solution and conditions for creating it were the touchstones of the Obama–Netanyahu confrontation of May 2011. In his May 19 speech at the State Department (before Netanyahu's arrival) Obama declared that such a solution must be pursued using the pre-1967 boundaries as the starting point and proceeding with mutually agreed "land swaps." Progress is necessary, he argued, because the current status quo is "unsustainable"—unspoken reference to the demographic time bomb. While not rejecting the idea of a two-state solution, Netanyahu did reject using the pre-19678 border for negotiations as "indefensible"—proposing a boundary that would leave Israel unacceptably vulnerable. Since any alternative would begin from acceptance of some Israeli settlements as a point of reference (almost certainly including parts of East Jerusalem)—a position rejected by both the Obama administration and the Palestinians—the disagreement was joined.

A two-state solution solves several problems. It provides the stateless Palestinians with a homeland over which they can exercise sovereign control, which satisfies their demands. It ends the most troublesome part of the long Israeli occupation, thereby assuaging the international community's concern over the illegality of the occupation and thus muting somewhat criticism of Israel. It also relieves one of the major rallying cries of anti-Israeli sentiment among Islamic Middle Eastern states who have adopted the Palestinian cause as a prime basis for opposing Israel. It also removes the largest source of disagreement between the United States and Israel.

Despite these advantages, there has been little real progress toward the two-state solution. Most of the resistance comes from Israel and its ideological allies. One of the sources of their reluctance arises from the existential threat and the fear that a hostile Palestinian state would make that problem worse. The other major objection comes from the Greater Israel argument. Part of that argument is that areas of the West Bank are part of historic Israel and are thus rightly a part of the Jewish heritage. On a slightly less philosophical level, ceding the West Bank to the Palestinians leaves the dual practical difficulties of what to do with displaced Israeli settlers who either will not want to stay on ceded land or will have to be evicted, and the loss of living space for additional immigrants to Israel, a prime advantage of West Bank settlements. The security and Greater Israel arguments were prominently featured in Netanyahu's address to Congress on May 24, 2011.

The settlement problem may already have preempted the possibility of achieving a two-state outcome. Inhabitation by Israelis on the West Bank is now so extensive in terms of numbers and location that it is increasingly difficult to imagine how they all could be removed in the name of a Palestinian state. The attempt to do so was presaged in 2006 when the Israeli government suffered an enormous domestic backlash after it evicted less than 10,000 Israelis from Gaza settlements, and the problem would be increased 400-fold if all the West Bank and East Jerusalem settlements were returned to Palestine. In addition, the settlements are generally located on valuable land and have been financed from private sources: who will pay off the debts incurred in building them?

The Obama appeal for renewed negotiations arose from his sense of the increasing urgency of the situation. Although the Netanyahu government says it supports a two-state solution and blames the Palestinians for the lack of progress (positions the Israeli reiterated before Congress and in a speech to AIPAC and again before the United Nations in September 2011), the construction of new settlements—especially around Jerusalem—continues. The danger is of a fait accompli that leaves the two-state solution impossible to achieve.

If the two-state solution disappears, so too does one of Della Pergola's possible permutations of Israeli interests. The only way that Israel can remain both a democratic and a Jewish state is by maintaining a Jewish majority within Israel. The only way such a majority can be guaranteed is to reduce Israel back to something very close to its pre-1967 boundaries, possibly by making some small adjustments such as those suggested by Della Pergola and by Obama's land swaps. Doing so would guarantee a 75 to 80 percent Jewish Israel far into the future and thus allow for a truly democratic and

Jewish democratic state. Because of demographics, all other solutions deny that long-term possibility.

The One-State Solution

The other possible resolution that moves beyond the current impasse is a single Israeli–Palestinian state encompassing pre-1967 Israel, the West Bank, and Gaza. The advantage of such a solution from an Israeli vantage point is that it solves the settlements problem since the Israeli-owned settlements become part of the new entity. In this new entity, Israeli external security could presumably also be achieved since it would probably include a new permutation of the Israeli Defense Force.

No one seriously thinks such a solution would work, even though it may become the only possible outcome if a two-state solution is impossible. For one thing, the Palestinians would not accept it, feeling (probably quite rightly) that it would simply be a guise for continued Israeli domination and suppression: that they would be second-class citizens in the new entity. Thus, the creation of such an annexation could not be accomplished by plebiscite (the Palestinians would reject it) and would thus have to be imposed, thereby creating even greater resistance that would include the further scorn of the international community.

The most important problem such a solution creates is its impact on Israel and its goals. A single state would be roughly half Jewish and half Islamic, with demographic trends guaranteeing a Muslim majority within a matter of a few years. If such a state were to remain democratic, Jews would be in the voting minority, and the new state would cease being Jewish. The only way that Israelis could remain in power in such a state would be to impose a system of differential participation, where Jewish votes were weighted to be worth more than Palestinian votes. This possibility, which would allow the new state both to remain Jewish and within its expanded bounds, would no longer be democratic but instead would be a kind of "apartheid state," a designation that Jimmy Carter was highly vilified for suggesting several years ago but which is entirely accurate and descriptive.

Status Quo

Since there is noticeably little progress toward either of the two possible outcomes that alter the present state of affairs, maintenance of the status quo is the third solution. Given Israeli power and its general self-insulation from world criticism, this is a viable short-term strategy for Israel and one that, in the absence of any progress in peace negotiations, it is at least implicitly pursuing. The same may be true of the Palestinians, leading Miller to conclude that "the preponderance of blame surely rests with the locals' incapacity and unwillingness to get real and serious about what it would take to reach an agreement."

Neither side admits that it prefers the status quo to an agreement that would require both to compromise, and each blames the other—with arguable justification on both sides—for the impasse. The Palestinians, in any objective sense, need a peace settlement the worst in order to relieve the misery of many of their members, but the extremists among them want the West Bank *and* Israel back and will accept nothing less. Likewise, there are Israelis, including, Siegman would argue, the current government, "whose members oppose a two-state solution" ("Can Obama Beat the Israeli Lobby?"). Neither side can currently impose its extreme will; the status quo leaves the situation fluid for the future.

CONCLUSIONS

The United States and Israel are in fundamental agreement about the basis of their relationship, which is the continuing security and prosperity of Israel, but they disagree about the best ways to satisfy those ends. The public discord between Obama and Netanyahu dramatically frames that disagreement. Israel, faced with what it considers a basic existential threat, is very conservative in its approach to what it considers a very hostile global and regional environment and is consequently loath to take the kinds of chances that the United States believes could lead to a more secure Israel. At a fundamental level, there is a difference that centers on whether the United States or Israel knows what is best for Israeli security.

The current disagreement over a Palestinian peace settlement illustrates this difference in perspective. Americans like Obama who maintain that the two-state solution is the best avenue to Israel's long-term security are essentially arguing that accord with its neighbors will best preserve Israeli interests and survival by reducing the hostility of the environment in which Israel exists. Moreover, they argue that the current Israeli approach only adds further fuel to that animosity by denying rights to the Palestinians. Some Israelis agree with this assessment, but many do not and maintain that their condition is so perilous that they cannot afford to take the chances on which the Americans insist. American insistence, at the same time, is attenuated by the efforts of the Israeli lobby that argues against putting American pressure on Israel to change in ways that may meet perceived American, but not perceived Israeli, interests. The result has been the kind of Mexican standoff that became so obvious in May 2011.

The United States has leverage over Israel if it chooses to or can exercise it. The largest source of this is the very generous American economic and military assistance to Israel. The state of Israel receives more American aid than any other country in the world, gets that aid on highly favorable terms not made available to other states (most of it, for instance, is effectively in the form of grants, not loans), and the contribution is particularly striking when stated in per capita terms. American annual assistance to Israel, according to Mearsheimer and Walt, is nearly $500 per capita, whereas Egypt, also a large recipient, receives about $27 per capita.

The United States has never publicly threatened to withhold this aid in the face of Israeli intransigence, even defiance, of American positions. The reason for this is simple enough: the Israeli lobby. Those conservative elements in the United States, symbolized by AIPAC, have convinced the American public's representatives that Israeli and American interests across the board are so synonymous that threatening to punish Israel is not only anti-Israeli (whether that is its intent or not) but also anti-American. This position has enough political resonance within the United States from AIPAC-leaning American Jews and their conservative American Christian supporters to make opposition to the position of the current government politically hazardous. Much of Netanyahu's purpose in visiting Washington in May 2011 was to shore up support for his position, and he clearly won a tactical victory before Congress and AIPAC. The strategic question is whether that victory strengthens or weakens long-term Israeli prospects, a matter of legitimate disagreement between the two special allies.

The attempt by the Obama administration to put pressure on Netanyahu to push for a two-state solution represents the frustration and irony of dealing with Israel. By any objective measure, the power relationship between the two countries would seem to suggest that the United States should be able to get Israel to bend to its will, but that is clearly not the case. The very real limits on American influence over Israel are complex, tied as they are to Israeli survival and the enormous burden that responsibility entails. The merits of the disagreement between Obama and Netanyahu that became so publicly evident in late spring 2011 are in some ways less important than the very real veto that a foreign leader was able to exercise over a sitting American president at that time.

STUDY/DISCUSSION QUESTIONS

1. What is the basic nature of the U.S.–Israeli relationship? What factors make it unique in American foreign policy? Include Israel's impact on domestic American politics and the "demographic time bomb" in your answer.
2. What are the distinctive aspects of Israel's place in the world system? How does Israel's physical setting add to Israel's resulting unique position? Explain.
3. Describe the nature of the U.S. security guarantee to Israel. Place it in the context of other U.S. interests in the Middle East. Why does the U.S. position come into conflict with Israel's perception of its "existential threat"?
4. Why does the question of Palestine divide the United States and Israel? What are the four distinct aspects of that disagreement? Discuss each.
5. Why are the Israeli settlements in the occupied territories such a fundamental problem for Israel, the United States, and U.S.–Israeli relations? Elaborate.
6. What are the three possible outcomes of the Palestinian peace process? Discuss each in terms of its likelihood and desirability for Israel, the United States, and the Palestinians.
7. Can the three goals of Israeli policy toward Palestine be pursued simultaneously? Discuss the consequences of pursuing each pair of objectives. Which do you favor? Why?

READING/RESEARCH MATERIALS

Benn, Aluf. "Understanding History Won't Help Us Make Peace." *Foreign Policy* (January/February 2011), 70.

Carter, Jimmy. "A Jerusalem Settlement Everyone Can Live With." *New York Times* (online). August 6, 2000.

———. *Palestine: Peace Not Apartheid*. New York: Simon and Schuster, 2006.

Danin, Robert M. "A Third Way to Palestine: Fayyadism and Its Discontents." *Foreign Affairs* 90, 1 (January/February 2011), 94–109.

Della Pergola, Sergio. "Israel's Existential Predicament: Population, Territory, and Identity." *Current History* 109, 731 (December 2010), 383–389.

Eldar, Akiva. "Construction in West Bank Settlements Booming Despite Declared Freeze." *Naaretz.com* (online), January 1, 2010.

Friedman, Thomas L. "U.S. Must Shake Up Peace Process to Have Any Hope for Success." *New York Times* (online), June 7, 2008.

Gelb, Leslie H. "America Pressures Israel Plenty." *Foreign Policy* (January/February 2011), 71.

Goldberg, Jeffrey. "Unforgiven." *The Atlantic* 208, 4 (May/June 2008), 32–52.

Gorenberg, Gershom. "Think Again: Israel." *Foreign Policy* (May/June 2008), 26–32.

Haass, Richard N. "The New Middle East." *Foreign Affairs* 85, 6 (November/December 2006), 2–11.

Hermann, Tamar. "How the Peace Process Plays in Israel." *Current History* 109, 731 (December 2010), 363–369.

Kershner, Isabel. "Netanyahu Says Some Settlements to Stay in Israel." *New York Times* (online), January 25, 2010.

Khalidi, Rashid. "Palestine: Liberation Deferred." *The Nation* 286, 20 (March 20, 2008), 16–20.

Kodmani, Bassma. "Clearing the Air in the Middle East." *Current History* 107, 709 (May 2008), 201–206.

Makovsky, David. "How to Build a Fence." *Foreign Affairs* 85, 2 (March/April 2006), 50–64.

Mearsheimer, John J., and Stephen Walt. *The Israeli Lobby and U.S. Foreign Policy*. New York: Farrar, Straus, and Giroux, 2008.

Miller, Aaron David. "The Virtues of Folding." *Foreign Policy* (online), May 30, 2011.

Riedel, Bruce. "The Mideast after Iran Gets the Bomb." *Current History* 109, 731 (December 2010), 370–375.

Rubin, Barry. "Israel's New Strategy." *Foreign Affairs* 85, 4 (July/August 2006), 111–125.

Siegman, Henry. "Can Obama Beat the Israeli Lobby?" *The Nation* 292, 24 (June 13, 2011), 11–15.

———. "Tough Love for Israel." *The Nation* 286, 27 (May 5, 2008), 7–8.

Tiebel, Amy. "Netanyahu Stakes Claim to West Bank Settlement." *My Way* (online), January 24, 2010.

Van Creveld, Martin L. *The Land of Blood and Honey: The Rise of Modern Israel*. New York: Thomas Dunne Books, 2010.

Waxman, Dov. "Between Victory and Defeat: Israel after the War with Hizballah." *Washington Quarterly* 30, 1 (Winter 2006–2007), 27–42.

Egypt: Searching for Adjustments to the Consequences of the Arab Spring

PREVIEW

Prior to the spate of uprisings in Middle East countries popularly known as the Arab Spring of 2011, Egypt had occupied a tranquil place not very high on the American foreign policy agenda. As long as Egypt supported American goals in the region, the U.S. government largely ignored the malfeasance of its authoritarian political system. The popular uprising that toppled Egyptian President Hosni Mubarak has forced the United States to reassess and recalibrate its policy toward an Egypt that has become a much more uncertain international ally. How the Egyptian revolution evolves, what role the United States has in that evolution, and the consequences of that evolution for Egypt's part in the world and as a supporter or opponent of American foreign policy goals in the region are all matters of more urgent, but uncertain, concern. Debate over how to react to the Arab Spring in Egypt reflects a long dialogue in American foreign policy about whether the basis of policy should be the promotion of basic American values like democracy or serving more geopolitical interests.

Egypt is one of the oldest and most storied civilizations and countries in the world. Archaeologists have dated signs of organized human habitation in the fertile Nile Valley that forms the heart of Egypt to over 6,000 years ago, and the precursors of the fabled Land of the Pharaohs go back over 5,000 years. The heart of Egypt has been the Nile River valley, which early in human history made Egypt an agricultural supplier to many of the world's surrounding and competing powers of antiquity and formed the basis of the Pharaoh's empire that flourished into Biblical times.

The bases of Egyptian preeminence have simultaneously and enigmatically been a blessing and a curse. While the bounty of the Nile allowed Egypt to flourish, it also meant outsiders cast a frequently envious eye on Egypt, and in many cases, the result was invasion and conquest that haunted the country well into the twentieth century. As Marsot puts it, "Egyptians through the ages have had to cope with alien rulers or with rulers who were dominated by aliens so that a truly national government could be said to exist only after 1952." In 1952, the Egyptian Revolution brought Gamal Abdul Nasser, an obscure military officer who promised to restore Egypt to its rightful place among the states of the world, to power and established a sovereign state. Nasser's quest, under different leaders, has been ongoing for the past 60 years, and it is, at best, a process still underway.

The period immediately after 1952 seemed full of promise. Egypt was at the forefront of the decolonization process that swept through most of the Afro–Asian world in the 1950s and 1960s, and Nasser quickly gathered the reins as one of the leaders of the new self-anointed "neutralist bloc" (an oxymoron of sorts) of newly independent states. In those days, Egyptian leadership and prospects were spoken of in the same breath as those of China and India, and the expectation for the future was rosy. The apex of this ascent may have occurred in 1956, when the Nasser government nationalized operation of the Suez Canal, stood up to a joint British–French–Israeli attack (the so-called Suez War of 1956) to seize the canal, and with the not-inconsiderable assistance of the United States and the Soviet Union, managed to force the three invaders to reverse their action.

Things have gone downhill ever since. Nasser's dream of Egyptian leadership faltered over the ill-fated union with Syria to form the United Arab Republic (UAR) in 1958, a project intended to cement Nasser's leadership of the Arab world but that never achieved the integration it promised and that ended with Syrian withdrawal in 1961. In 1962, Nasser sent crack Egyptian troops into Yemen to influence the civil war there and failed, and in 1967, the Egyptian armed forces were decisively defeated by Israel in the Six Days War. When Nasser died in 1970, much of the promise of 1952 died with him.

The potential of the 1952 Revolution to change radically Egypt's place in the world was probably doomed to some extent from the beginning. The key for Egyptian renewal in the world was to transform the basis of a society and political system that had been dominated by foreigners for centuries, and this required the creation of a popular, participatory base that never emerged. As Marsot puts it, "the governments that came after 1952 were too insecure to adopt a truly representative government, and so opted for authoritarian repressive rule." Nasser was succeeded by Anwar Sadat, whose crowning achievement was to open the Middle Eastern peace process at Camp David with President Jimmy Carter and Israeli Prime Minister Menachem Begin in 1978. In 1981, however, Sadat was assassinated at a military parade by Islamic extremists partly motivated by his "treachery" at having entered into the relationship with Israel.

On the reviewing stand with Sadat when he was killed was General Hosni Mubarak, a decorated hero of both the 1967 and 1973 wars with Israel. Mubarak succeeded Sadat and remained in power for over 30 years, an exceedingly long time even by Egyptian standards. As Samer Shehata puts it, "Only a few pharaohs and Muhammad Ali (an Albanian who ruled Egypt for much of the first half of the nineteenth century) . . . have been in power longer than Hosni Mubarak." Like his predecessors, Mubarak oversaw the gradual slide of Egypt from its early postrevolutionary promise to its settling among the developing countries of the world. "In Egypt, society did not progress; in many fronts, it actually regressed," concludes Osman of the period between 1952 and the end of Mubarak's rule. By the end, Osman wrote in 2010, "Most Egyptians, after almost thirty years of Mubarak's rule, feel unimpressed or embittered, and even the Mubarak regime is increasingly in a political quandary."

Despite the gradual deterioration of life in Egypt, the revolution of 2011 in Egypt that began on January 25 caught virtually everyone off balance and unprepared, as did the dynamics of the Arab Spring in the other countries in which it has occurred. This was true of Middle East specialists as well as nonspecialists. As Gause puts it, the apparent stability of authoritarian regimes like Mubarak's "led some of us to underestimate the forces of change that were bubbling below, and at times above, the surface of Arab politics." The causes were numerous, are still evolving, and are discussed throughout the rest of the chapter. As Dina Shehata, points out, "The immediate trigger . . . was the Jasmine Revolution in Tunisia." Other factors included increasing corruption and economic exclusion, the alienation of youth, alleged fraudulence in the 2010 election, and questions within the elite about presidential succession, since presidential elections were scheduled in 2011 and Mubarak's physical fitness to stand for another term (he was 82 in 2011) was debatable at best. Each of these sources of discontent remains a concern for whoever eventually consolidates post-Mubarak power in the country. In the interim, however, Samer Shehata concludes that "next year, the country will celebrate Revolution Day on January 25" rather than the traditional observance on July 23, the date of the 1952 revolution.

What happens in Egypt is enormously important in the Middle East region. Ignatius enumerates why. "Egypt, in particular, is decisive. It has roughly 25 percent of the population of the Arab world, and it was for much of the 20th century the region's engine of modernization. If democracy succeeds in Egypt, other countries will follow." Standing as it does at the western end of the traditional Middle East as a pivot between Asia and Africa, Egypt can be a counterweight to the radicalization that is present in parts of the Persian Gulf region and is represented by regional rival and leadership aspirant Iran. It is that role that helped motivate the United States to back the conservative, authoritarian government of Mubarak. Much of the policy question facing the United States and others (including Israel) is whether post-Mubarak, hopefully democratic Egypt can remain a bulwark of moderation in the area, leading Ignatius further to conclude that "the success of democratic revolutions is absolutely in the interest of the United States." That outcome remains in doubt.

The United States thus has a particular interest in the march of events from its own standpoint, but it is an interest that must be put in context because, as Katulis reminds us about the revolutionary upheaval, "this is not about the US (nor should it be). This is about Egyptians empowering themselves." That rejoinder in mind, however, the ties between the two countries have become strong since diplomatic relations, which Egypt broke during the 1967 war, were restored in 1972 (after the Soviets were expelled). Samer Shehata catalogues those interests, each of which is potentially endangered if the Egyptian revolution of 2011 has an unfortunate outcome from an American point of view. "Egypt is a vital U.S. ally," Shehata writes. "American warships frequently pass through the Suez Canal, and U.S. military aircraft are routinely granted permission to fly over Egyptian territory. The Egyptian government maintains the terms of the Camp David peace treaty with Israel and as a consequence receives billions of dollars in annual U.S. economic and military assistance. . . . And Egypt's security and intelligence agencies have cooperated in the Bush administration's war on terror." In addition, Dunne writes, "Egypt is the most important friendly Arab country in which the Bush administration made an effort to promote democracy."

What is happening in Egypt has a further, symbolic importance in the general debate over foreign policy. Since the immediate post–World War II period, the prime direction of U.S. foreign policy has been to serve American geopolitical, "realist" values, and in the Middle East, that has usually translated into support for autocrats like Mubarak who promised stability and assistance to the United States in other areas like opposition to terrorism. This emphasis generally came at the expense of promoting democratic development in the area. During his single term in office between 1977 and 1981, President Carter sought to redirect U.S. policy toward the primary goal of promoting American values like democracy, which he argued ultimately better served U.S. interests. While Carter's views were rebuffed at the time as utopian, they are given new salience in the current environment.

The upheavals in the Muslim Middle East that began when a Tunisian street vendor, Mohammed Bouazizi, martyred himself in protest against an indignity inflicted upon him by a low-level Tunisian official, are still in their infancy. As of mid-2011 they had spread with varying success to a number of Middle Eastern countries, from Tunisia, Libya, and Egypt in Saharan Africa to Syria to the Arabian peninsula (Yemen and Bahrain), and there is no guarantee that they will not spread further nor about their outcomes where they have broken out and where they may yet break out. The process of revolutionary change is inherently unstable and unpredictable. While all revolutions may pass through certain predictable phases, such as those laid out in Crane Brinton's *Anatomy of a Revolution* three-quarters of a century ago (1938), each takes its own individual path. As Ignatius adds, those paths are neither linear nor necessarily tidy and attractive. "Although revolutions are always lovable in their infancy, they tend to become less so as they age," he writes.

The second Egyptian revolution is in such a state of evolution, and both its eventual direction and outcomes are in process, with ends that are not entirely predictable. The role of the United States in the specific Egyptian case or in the regional revolutionary process may or may not be critical or even important, but the outcomes will certainly have bilateral and regional consequences both for the United States and for collateral U.S. interests such as its support for Israel. The United States will be more than a casual observer of unfolding events in Egypt in particular for at least two reasons. One of these, as Dunne points out, is that "Egypt has been a close military and political ally for more than thirty years," and Egypt is a foothold in the Muslim Middle East the United States would hate to lose. At the same time, Ottoway reminds us that Egypt is important as a role model in the region. "Egypt has historically been a pioneer of political reform in the Arab world," and the United States would clearly like to see it evolve as a moderate regional influence.

The rest of this chapter will assess the prospects for Egypt and American foreign policy toward that country. Because the situation is in a state of flux that could last for years, the exercise cannot be a definitive description on either account but is rather an attempt to reduce the uncertainty and lay out some of the options and likelihoods associated both with Egypt's path internally and with the United States. To that end, the next section will deal specifically with factors affecting Egypt's internal evolution, followed by a discussion of U.S. policy interests, including underlying assumptions about the direction of that policy and what leverage the United States has to try to bring those interests to fruition.

EGYPT: A SKETCH

The central reality with which Egyptians, Americans, and other interested parties around the world must deal is the Arab Spring of 2011. Probably the most striking initial characteristic of the series of uprisings initiated by the Jasmine Revolution in Tunisia and sparked in Egypt by reaction to Tunisian events and the death of Khaled Said, "the blogger killed by Egyptian police and whose death initiated the uprising," according to Anderson, was how poorly they were anticipated. Writing in December 2008, for instance, Samer Shehata confidently predicted that "sustained nationwide protests are unlikely," that any problems were "more likely to erupt between forces within the regime than between the regime and its opposition," and that whoever succeeds Mubarak (whose health was questionable even at that early stage) "will not usher in democracy." These predictions were not unusual in the years leading up to the uprising and extended to the official realm in Washington where, according to Ferguson, "the administration . . . never once considered a scenario in which Mubarak faced a popular revolt."

At least part of the reason the signs of unrest and instability were overlooked was because outsiders, prominently including the United States, did not want to see them. By any internal measure, the Mubarak regime was certainly no exemplar, but its deficiencies tended to be overlooked because of the international role it played in the region. In particular, the Mubarak regime had developed close ties with the United States on the grounds of supporting the Israeli–Egyptian peace process (a position widely opposed within Egypt) and by opposing radical Islamist elements in the region through playing a prominent role in the U.S.-led "war on terror." Egypt's foreign policy was thus aligned with that of the United States, and the result was that the United States placed a blessing on the regime. As Nakleh describes this dynamic, "Policy makers have tended to bestow the 'moderate' moniker on pro-Western governments despite their autocratic nature. Equating authoritarian regimes with 'moderation' has resulted in a perception of hypocrisy and has helped drive the very radicalization the West has sought to counter." Lalami concurs in this assessment: "A pro-American dictator is not a guarantee of protection from extremism; more often than not, his tyranny creates the very radicalism he was supposed to stop." Thus, the fact that Mubarak supported U.S. foreign policy not only caused the Americans to ignore his weaknesses, it also contributed to them.

The crisis in Egypt that has been part of the Arab Spring had been boiling beneath the surface for some time, and it had increasingly come to center on Egypt's aging dictator. The crisis is reflected in Egypt's standing in the world system and also in physical aspects of Egyptian political life. In turn, the unfolding dynamics reflect the unique position of one of the world's oldest and proudest countries.

Egypt in the World

The roots of the current crisis through which Egypt is passing are by no means new. Egypt seemed full of promise to emerge to be a bedrock force for progress among developing-world states after the 1952 revolution that brought Nasser to power, but that promise has gradually dissipated. Nasser began the descent with his ill-advised union with Syria, his flirtation with the Soviet Union during the early 1960s, and the disastrous performance of the Egyptian military in the 1967 war. Nasser died before a revolution against him could arise, and his successor, Sadat, was felled by an assassin's bullet in 1981, while the jury was still out on Egypt's place in the world order.

The task of establishing Egypt's world role fell to Mubarak in 1981, and he remained in power until his resignation 30 years later in the face of popular ire. His legacy was mixed enough so that, at least in the West, the bankruptcy of his policies was not apparent or was overridden by the support he had in the United States as a result of his "moderate" foreign policy combined with a more general belief in the "persistence of undemocratic rulers" in the region, in Gause's term. In the end, however, the internal rot that set in and grew under Mubarak made Egypt a tinder box ready to ignite when change came to the region.

Despite his autocratic rule, Mubarak was a pivotal and positive figure in the region to the United States end especially to Israel. In particular, Mubarak embraced the peace process with Israel that Sadat had started and that had made Egypt a pariah among more militant Arab opponents of Israel. Those policies were never popular in Egypt itself—a source of future concern discussed later in the chapter—but could be maintained by what Goldstone refers to as a "sultanistic regime" like Egypt's that possessed great personal power and could impose its policies despite public will. These stances made Mubarak a favored world leader to the United States because, in Levy's colorful description, the Egyptian "became the cornerstone of an effort to maintain a farcical peace process that sustained Israel's occupation and settlement expansion . . . and that allowed the US to avoid making hard choices."

Mubarak further ingratiated himself to the United States first by his anti-communism and later by his outspoken opposition to Islamic religious terrorism and his willingness to assist the United States in dealing with the terrorist problem. Part of the cooperation between the two countries involved ties with Egypt's intelligence and security forces. The Egyptian security apparatus has a long history of human rights violations by its policing arms in the form of "torture and kill(ing) domestic opposition," according to a *Nation* editorial by Lalami, and some of these capabilities were apparently made available to American practitioners of the campaign against terror. A 2003 Congressional Research Service report to Congress even noted that "there is convincing evidence that the Egyptian police used torture to extract confessions and detain suspects without charge or trial." Anderson dismisses the national police as "in essence, a nationwide protection racket."

Egypt's opposition to Islamic extremism, however, created geopolitical sympathy with the United States and was, in Taleb and Blyth's description, "a trope that Mubarak repeated until his last moments." In this regard, when Mubarak attempted to save face by appointing an "interim government" before 2011 elections, his anointed successor was Omar Suleiman, a former military officer and head of the intelligence services who was tainted by this association and looked to Egyptians "like a behind-the-scenes compromise to replace Mubarak with Mubarak Lite," according to Lalami.

It was, however, Mubarak's domestic actions that formed the real basis of opposition to him. The simple fact is that living conditions in the country had deteriorated badly in the years leading up to 2011. Part of this deterioration was associated with the rise as heir apparent of Mubarak's son Gamal, a trained banker who worked for Bank of America and was described by Egyptian critic Ziad Aly (quoted in Dickey) as a "nerd." Tied heavily to big business in Egypt, Gamal Mubarak helped accelerate a process of wealth redistribution in the country that added to its economic woes as described by Dina Shehata. "The majority of the Egyptian population was increasingly marginalized, while a small minority prospered like never before . . . an unholy alliance between the ruling elite and the business elite." This was part of a more general downward spiral described by Anderson. "Hosni Mubarak's fumbling epitomized the protracted decline of his regime's efficacy," she wrote in 2011. "The government's deteriorating ability to provide basic services and seeming indifference to widespread unemployment and poverty alienated tens of millions of Egyptians."

Mubarak's personal contribution to and profit from this autocratic mess is a matter of some disagreement. A 2010 *Foreign Policy* rating of the 25 worst dictators in the world ranked him 15th, and study author Ayittey described him as "a senile and paranoid autocrat whose sole obsession is self-perpetuation in office." While there seems to be general agreement that the regime systematically engaged in "overt plunder" of Egyptian assets (Taleb and Blyth's description), the exact participation of Mubarak himself is unclear. Goldstone, for instance, alleges that "Mubarak and his family reportedly built up a fortune of between $40 billion and $70 billion, and 39 officials and businessmen close to Mubarak's son Gamal are alleged to have made fortunes averaging more than $1 billion each." On the other hand, an unnamed Western diplomat in Cairo is quoted by Dickey with a slightly less negative view. "Compared to other kleptocracies," the official argues, "I don't think the Mubaraks rank all that high. There has been corruption, but as far as I know, it has never been personally attached to the president or Mrs. Mubarak." Mubarak has repeatedly denied these allegations against him and maintains he did not personally profit from his service as president.

Despite his long stranglehold on Egyptian politics, there were some signs of discontent and possible fissures that might lead to change before January 2011. Mubarak was 82 years old as the election year of 2011 approached, and there had already been some discussions about the state of his physical and mental health that raised red flags about whether he would run or, if he did, whether he could survive yet another term in office. One view of that prognosis is stated by Ottoway: "It is clear that he cannot survive a new term in office even if he lives until the voting." Speculation about Mubarak in turn brought out one of the weaknesses in Goldstone's sultanistic regimes, which is a personalization of power and the failure to anoint who will follow. As Goldstone puts it, "The weaknesses of sultanistic regimes are magnified as the leader ages and the question of succession becomes more acute." The revolution assured that Mubarak will have little if any influence on the outcome of the succession process. As Samer Shehata puts it, "It is unlikely that Hosni Mubarak will be sorely missed. His accomplishments have been remarkably thin."

The Physical Setting

Egypt is a large, impressive, but very distinctive place. It has a land area of 366,682 square miles, about three times the state of New Mexico, which makes it the 30th largest country in the world. Most of that land area, which borders upon Libya to the west, the Sudan to the south, Israel and Gaza to the east, and the Mediterranean Sea to the north, is desert wasteland. What punctuates and makes the country distinctive and has served as the basis of Egyptian civilization is the Nile River valley running from its sources in Sudan to the sea.

Only 3 percent of Egyptian territory is arable, and essentially all of that productive land lies along the flood plain created by the Nile River. While the
country has some relatively small amounts of natural resources such as
petroleum and natural gas (primarily in areas developed on the Sinai Peninsula
by the Israelis during their occupation of that Egyptian territory) and some
minerals such as iron ore and manganese, it is the Nile River basin that made
Egypt the granary of the ancient world and which must support its contemporary population.

Egypt is also a very highly populated country, with a population estimated in July 2011 at slightly over 82 million, making it the 15th most populous country in the world and the most populous country in the Arab Middle
East (followed by Turkey and Iran). Among all countries with Muslim majorities, Egypt ranks third in number of people, following Indonesia and Pakistan
(India also has a larger Muslim population than Egypt but does not have a
Muslim majority). This fact alone makes Egypt a consequential place within
the region and forms some of the basis for friendship with it.

The Egyptian people, unlike so many other peoples in the region, are
remarkably homogeneous. The *CIA World Factbook* (2011) categorizes
98.6 percent of the population as ethnic Egyptian, and this group includes
both the roughly 90 percent that are Muslim (mostly Sunni) and the 9 percent
that are Coptic Christian (before the Arab invasion of Egypt in the seventh century, almost the entire population was Christian but converted—see Marsot for a
detailed discussion). Virtually the entire country speaks Arabic, although English
and French are spoken by large numbers of Egyptians.

The difficulties of Egypt begin to show when one examines the quality
of Egyptian life and politics. At 72.66 years, life expectancy in Egypt is only
123rd in the world, and the Egyptian literacy rate is only at about 71 percent
of the population. Moreover, at $6,200 per capita, Egypt ranks 137th in that
important measure of personal wealth and economic achievement. Politically,
the endemic corruption in the country is attested to by its 2010 rank of 98th
on the Corruption Perception Index, sandwiched between Burkino Faso and
Mexico on that dubious measure of believed governmental honesty. Likewise,
an inherently stable Egyptian society (at least in terms of composition) ranked
49th on the Failed State Index, not high enough to be of enormous concern
but still within the "warning" category created by those who compile that
index (the Fund for Peace and *Foreign Policy* magazine).

If one looks inside the demographics, some of the frustration that played
out in Tahrir Square becomes particularly evident. Like so much of the region
generally, Egypt has a significant "youth bulge," where "more than a third of
the population is between 15 and 29," according to Dina Shehata. Traditionally, one of the ways the Mubarak regime assuaged the youthful population
was through generous educational opportunities, including both a secondary and even collegiate education, but that strategy has backfired because the
economy has not grown adequately to provide meaningful employments for
those with educational credentials. Thus, Dina Shehata points out, "Youth
unemployment is highest among those with more education; in Egypt in 2006,

young people with a secondary education or more represented 95 percent of the unemployed in their age group." Goldstone adds that "in Egypt, college graduates are ten times more likely to have no job as those with only an elementary school education."

This affected group, of course, was at the forefront of the January uprising. As Anderson has observed, "urbane and cosmopolitan young people in the major cities organized the uprisings." One of the major characteristics of the demonstrators was their sophistication with modern electronic technologies that allowed word of the demonstrations to spread rapidly throughout the country. In some measure, this capability is tied to their education and exposure to Western technologies, meaning the Egyptian government indirectly and certainly inadvertently contributed to the nature of the movement with which it was confronted. Although it is too early to tell what direction the Arab Spring will eventually take in Egypt, this concentration of activity among relatively young and well-educated Egyptians probably means that they will likely be less vulnerable to the appeals of Islamic fundamentalists than less-educated Egyptians may prove to be.

These economic factors could bode poorly for the future evolution of the revolution. In an assessment in the June 13 and 20, 2011, edition of *Newsweek,* for instance, historian Niall Ferguson points out the economic conditions in the first half of 2011 have not only failed to improve but have further deteriorated. One cause is capital flight, which one Egyptian newspaper (*Al-Hayat*) estimated at $30 billion since January, and one consequences is the "employment is up," particularly among educated young adults who formed the revolution's core. Further deterioration of economic conditions could, as Ferguson puts it, result in "exasperation at the decline in living standards" with potentially negative effects on the trajectory of change.

At $500 billion, Egypt's 2010 GDP ranked 27th in the world, placing it on the fringe of the major developing countries but still considerably behind the BRICS grouping. Egyptian imports and exports are broadly distributed among a number of countries. In imports, for instance, the United States is Egypt's largest supplier with 10 percent of goods and services (presumably largely military) to Egypt. The United States is also the largest export partner for the Egypt, but with only 8 percent of Egyptian exports going to the United States. Egyptian oil production, at 680,000 bbl/day, ranks 29th, and its proven oil reserves of 4.3 billion barrels is 27th among world countries.

The physical, statistical profile of Egypt is thus not encouraging. The removal of the apparently kleptocratic Mubarak regime may eventually help to restore some sense of order to the economy and political system, but more will be necessary to establish some kind of orderly consensus. At the heart of the problem are those young Egyptians who filled Tahrir Square in Cairo; they are simultaneously the hope and the despair of the Egyptian future. They are the hope because they represent a currently underutilized asset of educated expertise; they are the despair because as long as they remain among the dispossessed and marginalized, they will pose a substantial barrier to stabilization of the country, especially if their perceived situation worsens. In order to harness their energies, there must be a considerable influx of opportunity-creating assistance, a quantity in short supply in a world environment of economic strain and constraint.

Egypt as a Unique State

As the world watches and seeks to anticipate and to influence the Arab Spring, much of its focus has to be on Egypt for all these reasons. It is not clear what kind of Egypt will emerge from the revolutionary process set in motion in January 2011, and its path may or may not be one that is emulated by other states undergoing their own distinctive versions of the uprisings. From an American standpoint, this outcome is important for four interrelated reasons. One is a concern over the kind of Egypt that emerges from the process. Will it be a more open and democratic Egypt? Or will it be a more militant, Islamic Egypt that might, at worst, be amenable to terrorist appeals? The second concern surrounds the new Egypt's stance toward Israel. Will a transformed Egypt maintain its comparatively close, cooperative relations under the peace treaty? Or will Egypt back away from commitments made by its former, discredited leaders and join other Muslim states in a more unified opposition to Israel? The third is how this new Egypt will view and interact with the United States. To the U.S. government, Egypt has been a "moderate," dependable ally generally supportive of American interests in the region. Since that relationship included the embrace of the overthrown dictatorship, will the Egyptians remain supporters of the United States? Or will Egypt distance itself from a United States that many consider as a source rather than a relieving influence on their misery? Fourth, Egypt is a test case for the ongoing U.S. policy debate about the relative emphasis on democratization and the effect of such advocacy. The fate of Egypt will have a strong effect on that debate.

These questions could be asked of any state in the region, and particularly of those that are not undergoing the kinds of revolutionary violence that has typified the Arab Spring. Not all of them share the profile of Egypt. They all share a history of despotic, authoritarian rule that has been the immediate object of their protestations, but none has moved as close to Israel as has Egypt, and most of them do not have the same history or support by the United States for their regimes. Nonetheless, how these questions are answered about the largest state in the region could have important consequences for how they are answered other places.

U.S.–EGYPTIAN RELATIONS

Egypt and the United States have had a mixed relationship since the Egyptians achieved their independence in 1952. During the rule of Nasser, the relationship was occasionally supportive (as in American support for Egypt when it was invaded in 1956), but the closeness of the United States to Israel and Egypt's refusal to commit to the Western side in the Cold War had the two countries at odds much of the time. Only after Nasser, the champion of neutralism, passed from the scene in 1970 did the possibility of positive relations emerge; the decisive tipping point came as a result of the 1973 armed conflict between Israel and its opponents led by Egypt.

The Yom Kippur War (so named because the initial attacks occurred on that Jewish religious holiday) was critical to American foreign policy in the region. Unlike the earlier conflicts, the Islamic states (principally Egypt, Syria, and Jordan) enjoyed initial success against the Israeli armed forces in 1973, and at one point, the situation became desperate enough that the Israelis reportedly activated their clandestine nuclear force as a last-ditch measure to avoid defeat and possible extinction. With reports swirling about that prospect and the Soviets threatening to come to the aid of their Egyptian allies after the military tide turned, the United States looked seriously at the possibility that these dynamics could have led to a nuclear confrontation that could have spread to a system-threatening confrontation with the Soviet Union—a nuclear World War III.

While it may never be clear exactly how close the world came to that catastrophe, it did convince the United States that it had to act to ensure that this dangerous episode would not be reprised in the future. To that end, the Nixon administration moved quickly to replace the expelled Soviets as the chief source of military and economic assistance to Egypt, thereby giving the United States leverage over the military machines of each of the major combatants. The purpose was to gain the ability to short-circuit any future crises before they could escalate to the level of the 1973 crisis. As this process was gradually put in place during the 1970, its chief beneficiary was Hosni Mubarak, who rose to power in 1981.

Although the United States benefited for a long time from its association with Mubarak, that association is now a burden on the United States because Egypt was a prime example of U.S. regional policy based on anticommunism but not the promotion of democracy. As Levy argues, "The truth is that administrations, Democratic and Republican, have provided cover, support, aid, and weapons for repressive Arab regimes, and with increasingly counterproductive results." This tradeoff seemed to make sense in the geopolitical environment of the Cold War, but it has had longer-term negative consequences. On one hand, Ottoway argues that "the war in Iraq . . . convinced many Arabs that democracy promotion was simply code for the overthrow of governments of regimes that Washington deemed hostile," rather than being a reflection of basic American foreign policy values. Instead, Hamid argues that "the United States remains a status quo power in a region undergoing radical change. Arabs across the region have been protesting an authoritarian order that the United States was, in their view, propagating."

The result has been a jaded view toward the United States and its role in their revolutionary process by many change-oriented Egyptians. Lalami, for instance, commenting on Obama's inspirational speech at Cairo University in 2009, counters that, "Year after year, [Egyptian students] have heard American presidents deliver hypocritical lectures on democracy while giving $1.3 billion in military aid to Mubarak, their torturer-in-chief." Moreover,

Dunne wrote in 2009, "the lack of U.S. consistency and follow-through from 2006 onward left Egyptian reform proponents (liberals as well as Islamists) exposed to government backlash, and angry at Washington for apparently abandoning them."

As the United States views what is happening currently in Egypt and both what that means for the United States and what the United States can realistically do to influence that process, it must be recognized that the American capability is compromised and limited by the role it played in bolstering the old regime. It is unlikely that the end result of the change process will be to anoint a new regime that is conceptually similar to that which it has replaced, although such an outcome is not impossible. There is instead a range of prospects with differing implications for American interests in the region. The policy preferences of the United States can usefully be organized in terms of the three questions raised about Egypt in the last section.

The Shape of a New Egypt

The most basic concern, and one that will help answer all three questions, is the kind of political order that will eventuate from the 2011 uprisings. The stated intent of the demonstrators in Cairo (where the action was concentrated) was clearly for the emergence of political democracy, a goal that the United States cannot dismiss out of hand and, as a general proposition, embraces as a central feature of its contemporary overall foreign policy stance in the world. Since there are several possibilities rather than a single democratic outcome that might emerge, however, the question is somewhat more complicated in the Egyptian case. While the earliest actions of the caretaker government that succeeded Mubarak was for an orderly process that could have stable democratic rule as its outcome, that result is by no means ensured. Indeed, as 2011 evolved, the Egyptian military seemed increasingly to solidify its control of the political process and to show reluctance to relinquish that control in its entirety to civilian political elements. Possible outcomes of the transition process include the "nightmare" scenario of seizure of the Middle East's largest country by radical Islamists who might, in the absolute worst case, be amenable to influence by terrorist organizations like Al Qaeda under the leadership of Egyptian expatriate Ayman al-Zawahiri.

The early months after Mubarak's ouster offered some hope for an orderly future. After the rejection of Suleiman as a caretaker, transitional power reverted to traditional sources, as Dina Shehata explained in mid-2011: "The military and the state bureaucracy are still in firm control of the country and in a position to dictate the course of the transition in the coming months." The military in particular has been important to a peaceful transition because of its monopoly on the instruments of coercive power (the Egyptian police establishment has not acted as a major force in the transition) and because it is one of the few trusted and respected institutions in the country. Samer Shehata summarizes the prevailing view on the military's position in the society: "The military is the most powerful and coherent institution in Egyptian society and, unlike any of the political parties, it enjoys a significant amount of legitimacy." In addition, the military is clearly a "citizen's force" in the sense that it could not be used, as foreign mercenaries have been in places like Libya and Bahrain, to attack the protesters, as was evident in the camaraderie between soldiers and demonstrators during the Cairo demonstrations. Opposition leaders who have emerged, such as former UN diplomat Mohammed Al Baradei, have generally been reasonably moderate and prodemocratic in their public policy advocacies.

The wild card in the equation is the Islamists and their chief spokesmen, the Muslim Brotherhood. Under the Mubarak regime, the Brotherhood was suppressed and its members occasionally jailed, but it also managed to run and elect candidates to parliament under different party labels than its own in the most recent elections leading up to the Arab Spring (it won 88 seats in 2005, for instance, to emerge as the largest opposition bloc). Any opening of Egyptian (or other Arab) societies thus "must include the Islamist parties and movements in those societies," as Nakleh points out. In Egypt, the Islamist tradition is clearly identified with the Brotherhood, which has been the prototype for similar political movements elsewhere in the region. As a result, what the Muslim Brotherhood does and how it is treated in Egypt will have symbolic importance for what transpires elsewhere in the region as well as in Egypt itself.

The question is what role the Brotherhood will play in the current transition and beyond. From an American standpoint, the problem is what Hamid calls "the Islamist dilemma—how can the United States promote democracy in the region without bringing the Islamists to power?" The Brotherhood cannot be ignored because, as Ferguson points out, they are "by far the best organized opposition force in the country." ("The Revolution Blows Up") The question is whether they are militantly committed to extreme Islamic causes, as Ferguson suggests, saying they are "wholly committed to the restoration of the caliphate and the strict application of sharia." The Brotherhood itself denies any such radical tendencies and quickly signaled that although they would participate in the electoral process that they had no intention either of seeking a parliamentary majority or of playing a formal role in any governing coalition. That the Brotherhood will be part of any democratic equation in postrevolutionary Egypt is a given; what role they do play remains a variable in that equation.

The worst-case scenario is the emergence of Al Qaeda and other terrorists as major forces in the country. The death of Usama bin Laden has greatly increased the uncertainty about his organization's fate and path, although his closest confidante and replacement is al-Zawahiri, who has opposed both Mubarak and democratic alternative forms of government. Bynam argues that the overthrow of Mubarak will hurt Al Qaeda efforts in Egypt for two reasons. First, "the repression Arab governments inflict on their citizens," a prime recruiting tool, is denied Al Qaeda by a popular, nonrepressive Egyptian regime. Second, Al Qaeda has consistently maintained that "secular democracy is as abhorrent as secular dictatorship" since neither is dedicated to the sectarian goal espoused by the terrorist organization. Moreover, the overhaul of the Egyptian political system is also likely to contain reforms that will further undercut Al Qaeda's appeal, because Egypt's security and intelligence apparatus probably created as many or more terrorists than it suppressed. The role of such agencies (which also suppressed and abused Egyptians) will almost certainly be curtailed or reduced in post-Mubarak Egypt. When added to the general disarray facing a post–bin Laden Al Qaeda, it is hard to imagine that the terrorist organization will benefit from the transition away from the Egyptian dictatorship.

Egypt and Israel

The Arab Spring makes Israel nervous, and to some extent, this nervousness is passed on to Israel's closest patron, the United States. The transition from the Mubarak dictatorship to some more uncertain future kind of regime is particularly upsetting to the Israelis, who had a close working relationship with the former strongman. Indeed, the key pillar to what is left of the Middle East peace process inaugurated at Camp David in 1978 is between Egypt and Israel, with the United States acting as mediator and guarantor of the results. From an Israeli vantage point, the overthrow of Mubarak has been a setback of sorts because of the long period of relatively close relations and collaboration between the two regimes. In essence, the positive relationship between democratic Israel and authoritarian Egypt has simplified the Israeli security problem detailed in the last chapter by neutralizing the largest and most threatening factor in that problem.

The problem, of course, is that Egyptian cooperation with Israel was never very popular among Egyptians. Their feelings could be ignored by a Mubarak government that operated outside public will, but now the repressive veil has been lifted and future Egyptian politicians must appeal to the desires of the voting population. Levy adds, "a political system more representative of Arab public will is likely to be less indulgent of Israel's harsh policy toward the Palestinians," an irritant that particularly catalyzes public opposition to Israel in Egypt and elsewhere.

A tantalizing view of the new Egyptian attitude may have occurred in May 2011, when Egypt opened its borders with the Gaza Strip in both directions. Intended to relieve the isolation of Gazans and to restore their access to the outside world, the move was vociferously opposed by Israel, which argued an open border will act as a conduit for Hamas terrorists and their supplies to attack Israel. The Egyptian interim government announced this action without apparent consultation with the Israelis.

Additionally, this concern also reinforces, in the minds of some primarily pro-Israeli observers, the fear they have of the rise of the Muslim Brotherhood. The reason is stated in forthright terms by Hamid: "Today's Egyptian and Libyan Brotherhoods refuse to recognize Israel's right to exist and call for the liberation of all of historic Palestine." The Egyptian Brotherhood denies this goal and its destructive implications, but the possibility that it lies somewhere behind their public statements is not easily dismissible and creates additional concern for the Egyptian political evolution.

Egypt and the United States

The United States has definite interests in how the Arab Spring plays out in Egypt. American interests in Egypt are not changed by the overthrow of Mubarak, but the challenges to achieving those interests have changed, and it is on how to channel those changes into ways that support American goals that the United States now focuses during the transition.

In his 2003 Congressional Research Service study, Mark stated four primary U.S. interests in Egypt, each of which remains a preference for the United States as the Arab Spring evolves. They are:

1. "To capitalize on Egypt's leadership role in the Arab world;
2. "To sustain Egypt's moderate voice in Arab councils;
3. "To maintain the Egyptian-Israeli peace treaty; and
4. "To oppose threats or aggression against regional friends."

These interests can be compared to overall U.S. foreign policy goals in the Middle East, as introduced in Chapter 11. The first three objectives are clearly most closely connected to the U.S. goal of protecting Israeli security since the Mubarak regime was a bulwark against radical influences on regional policy; the net effect is to suggest that the United States sees its interests best served by the emergence of a new Egyptian regime that has a foreign policy toward Israel that reflects the Mubarak policy. The problem is that the more democratic the new polity becomes and thus the more closely it reflects Egyptian public opinion, the more pressure there will be to adopt a more negative public stance toward Israel and the peace process. The fourth objective listed by Mark is aimed at a second U.S. regional objective, which is peace and stability in the region, and it could be argued that all the Egyptian objectives are also contributory to reducing tensions in the region, the better to assure the flow of petroleum to the West.

These basic objectives are not the only concerns the United States has with the evolution of its relationship with the new Egypt. Two other matters are of particular concern: the extent to which the United States can or should press its general foreign policy goal of democracy promotion in Egypt, and the ongoing contribution of Egypt to the American war on terror.

As already stated, the United States has been on the negative side of democracy promotion in Egypt by virtue of its historic relationship with the Mubarak regime, leaving the United States being seen as an obstacle rather than a facilitator of democratization and the American attempt to join in the prodemocracy chorus being perceived by some Egyptians as less than totally sincere. Nevertheless, Wittes argues in a 2008 book that the policy of promoting stability at the expense of democracy has been a mistake. The arguments she uses in support of her contention are that only democratization can guarantee long-term regional stabilization and that democratization is the only way to prevent the empowerment of radical elements in the region. With the status quo rejected by the Egyptian people, the United States has, belatedly, adopted the shibboleth of democracy promotion in Egypt and hopes that doing so will improve its standing among Egyptians and will not result in the rise of Islamist extremists to power.

This question is part of the broader strategic and philosophical debate about the appropriate general orientation of U.S. foreign policy. One group of advocates, who gained supremacy during the Cold War, argues the primacy of power relations and geopolitical interests as the overriding consideration, leading to support for and alignment with regimes acquiescent to American power interests, notably anticommunism during the Cold War and antiterrorism today. Geopolitical agreement effectively trumped regime quality when the two values conflicted, leaving the United States in support of various autocrats and dictators like Mubarak who were simultaneously pro-American (anticommunist/terrorist) but nondemocratic.

The other side of the argument is that U.S. policy toward the developing world—including places like Egypt—should be guided by a commitment to development, including democratization, on the premise that developed, democratic states will more stable and peaceful than their autocratic counterparts. This position has a long post–World War II history (as described in detail by Latham) but has fallen into disfavor because of its association with the dubious outcomes of so-called "nation-building" developmental efforts in places like Afghanistan. Figuring out which of these positions to follow—and how to follow them—will be an important element in the evolution of post-Mubarak policy toward Egypt.

The other, related concern for the United States is that the fall of a cooperative Mubarak regime may also have weakened the Egyptian–American link in suppressing terrorism, one of the main reasons for supporting Mubarak. Bynam explains the historical relationship: "U.S. counterterrorism officials have worked well with authoritarian leaders because their regimes have generally had a low bar for imprisonment and detention. The United States could send a suspect captured in Europe to Egypt and be assured he would be kept in jail." Sometimes the "services" rendered by the Egyptian authorities went beyond simple detention to alleged torture to extract information, but this is a practice more associated with the Bush than the Obama administration, meaning its loss may be less damaging than it would have been a few years ago. If this change is true, it is just as well, because Bynam further argues, "It is hard to imagine an Egyptian government . . . instructing its security services to work as closely with the CIA as Mubarak's forces did." The impact of the assassination of bin Laden on May 2, 2011, may further attenuate this situation if a result is a deterioration of the terrorist threat more generally.

U.S. OPTIONS

What the United States ultimately would like from the Arab Spring is a democratic Egypt that pursues foreign policies that affect the United States very much like those of its antidemocratic predecessor. The situation, however, is both enigmatic and unpredictable. For 30 years, the United States, with varying degrees of reluctance depending on the American president in office, supported an antidemocratic leadership in Egypt whose political values contradicted America's values, because that regime also was, in Ferguson's words, "a malleable ally" ("Wanted: A Grand Strategy") in foreign policy. Now that ally is gone, and a new Egyptian regime that may much better reflect basic American political values will come to power. Its leadership, however, is likely to be less "malleable," and public pressure may make it more anti-American as an extension of being more anti-Israeli. Thus the enigma is that the United States lived comfortably with an Egyptian regime that held contrary views about and means of internal governance but a compatible foreign policy, and it is now faced with a likely government that has compatible views on governance but with possibly very different foreign policy values.

What can the United States do to help move Egypt to a position that stems from democratic roots but that still supports U.S. foreign policy goals? The past limits the present in terms of influence because, as Goldstone puts it, "the United States and other Western nations have little credibility in the Middle East given their long support for sultanistic rulers." The Obama administration has made overtures to prodemocratic elements within the country (his 2009 speech to students at Cairo University is a prime example), but there is legacy of distrust that has built up over the years of close collaboration between the United States and nondemocratic rulers within the region, including Egypt. The question is what, if any, levers the United States has to turn an anti-American freedom movement into a pro-American movement that will not contradict American foreign policy goals in the region.

It is not an easy task, and the tools available are certainly limited. One can assume that a highly activist American policy posture toward Egypt would be counterproductive. Clearly, the use of military power would be inappropriate, and it is unlikely that American assistance to Egypt could be increased substantially given the current budgetary crisis now gripping American politics. It might be possible to "tweak" the package that currently goes to Egypt more toward economic assistance (which could be responsive to economic demands for job creation among the most revolution-prone elements in the society— out-of-work high school and college graduates), but the amounts available would be too small to make much of a dent. If the Egyptian postrevolutionary crisis continues, this could prove a crucial limitation.

Moreover, whatever amount was redirected would have to come from U.S. dollars now spent on the Egyptian military, which also entails risks. For one thing, a reduction of military assistance runs some risk of alienating the Egyptian military establishment, which has been among the staunchest supporters of U.S. policy and is one of the bedrocks of the transition process about which some of its members show some ambivalence, according to Martini and Taylor This would clearly not be a good time to alienate the Egyptian military. At the same time, most of the American military aid to Egypt is in the form of procurement-tied military equipment. What this means is that the dollars allocated to help the Egypt military are spent on American-made equipment, meaning the American economy is the beneficiary of much of this expense—an indirect form of economic stimulus. One can certainly quibble about whether such a stimulus helps the right segments of the American economy (e.g., the "military–industrial complex" of defense industries) but the withdrawal would have a negative impact on selected parts of the U.S. economy and be opposed on those grounds.

Policy options are further confined by the active interest that the Israeli lobby has in the situation in Egypt. Israel fears a popular backlash against itself from a democratic Egypt. Although it may have favored the continuation of the autocracy behind the scenes, it can neither embrace a new dictator nor publicly oppose democratization. One obvious approach for the Israelis would be to sit back and hope for the best—the evolution toward a democratic Egypt that becomes progressively less hostile toward Israel as the two domestic systems become more alike. The Israelis, however, are very reluctant to adopt such a passive approach given their view of the existential threat they face. An obvious way to reduce anti-Israeli sentiment among newly empowered Egyptians could be to enliven the peace process with the Palestinians, thereby reducing the emotional basis of anti-Israeli sentiment in Egypt. Such a motive, however, is unlikely to be persuasive by itself in terms of activating Israelis who otherwise believe a fundamental change in their policies toward the Palestinians is too risky unless more certain benefits are guaranteed.

American interests, as articulated by Mark, have not changed since the Arab Spring. The United States still wants a stable Egypt at peace with Israel that serves as a moderating influence on the region. What have changed are the environmental influences of the region—notably the change from an order based in Mubarak's authoritarian rule to a more uncertain future. Americans—and especially Israelis—will worry a great deal about the emergence of the worst case—a vibrantly militant Muslim Brotherhood trying to lead Egypt on an Iran-like path of Islamic purification and anti-Western fanaticism. This remains a concern that cannot be ignored, but the composition of the revolutionary support base appears heavily weighted toward more urbane, educated, and secularized parts of the population than the primarily rural, fundamentalist Shiite support base that propelled the Islamic fundamentalists to power in Iran. Islamic fundamentalism is always a possibility in Muslim societies, but in the case of Egypt, that prospect does not appear to be unduly great.

The constraints on policy toward Egypt also include a domestic element in the United States. As the 2012 presidential election approaches, there will almost certainly be less attention paid to nonemergency foreign policy problems (i.e., crises that cannot be avoided or deferred) and more attention to domestic issues that could affect the election itself. In the Egyptian case, this suggests that the administration is unlikely to engage in bold, activist policies toward Egypt unless it is forced to do so by unanticipated, traumatic events emanating from Egypt itself. Moreover, any dramatic policy initiatives would almost certainly be subject to a withering partisan criticism within the campaigning context. The very limited U.S. direct involvement in Libya is probably a pale harbinger in this regard. Although the Obama administration proposed and carried out a very limited role in the Libyan conflict, it was subject to criticism from both sides: from liberals who opposed any involvement at all and from conservatives (like John McCain) who argued the United States should do more. The administration is no doubt acutely cognizant of similar possibilities in Egypt, especially in the election campaign year of 2012. The only exception might be if matters were to turn decisively negative and Egypt were suddenly to pose an undeniable threat to Israel, in which case much of the opposition to activism would likely dissolve—or at least become much more restrained.

There are some ways in which the United States may be able to nudge Egypt in the directions the United States would like to see. One thing it can do is to remind the Israelis that they can be part of the problem or the solution in Egyptian political evolution. As Hamid correctly points out, "Anti-Israeli public opinion will remain a feature of Middle Eastern politics until a final and equitable peace treaty is struck." As detailed in Chapter 11, there are enormous barriers to reaching a settlement on the central irritant of Palestine that all sides could agree produces equity, but Israel could contribute to a lower temperature to the discussion by initiating some confidence-building actions like slowing or suspending growth in the West Bank settlements, a suggestion the Obama administration has certainly made to them in this and other contexts.

The most important direction in which the United States can encourage Egypt to move, however, is in its evolution toward a more peaceful, democratic base of society. Much of the key here is trying to encourage the growth of moderate influence through actions that will increase the satisfaction of the well-educated middle class in support of the evolving political order. As Ottoway points out, reformers in Egypt and elsewhere in the region "have been more interested in creating conditions for economic growth and good administration than in promoting democracy." If this remains true, then an alliance between the military and reformers may be possible, as both the military and civilians unite to remove "the long shadow of military rule," in Anderson's term, and move toward a secular democracy.

American ability convincingly to promote democracy in Egypt is, however, compromised by its past advocacy of nondemocratic alternatives on the basis of geopolitical compatibility with pro-American, antidemocratic alternatives. The United States has not completely broken away from its premising its policy toward regimes on their foreign policy rather than to democratic adherence, although it is probably moving in that direction. Until the United States adopts regime quality as its primary criterion for U.S. support, countries like Egypt will understandably view American promotion of democracy with a slightly jaundiced eye.

CONCLUSIONS

Because of the baggage the United States has accumulated in 30 years of association with the Mubarak regime, its ability to influence the course of Egyptian development in a useful direction is limited. The decision to promote order at the expense of democracy may have been—and probably was—justified by fears created by the possible escalation of the 1973 Yom Kippur War and the need to assure that Israeli–Egyptian animosities would not draw the major powers toward a possible nuclear war that could spread and engulf the globe, but times and circumstances have changed. Israel still has nuclear weapons, but the escalatory potential of any future standoff between Israel and its adversaries has decreased with the end of the Cold War. Israel and Egypt have now enjoyed nearly 40 years of continuous peace marred primarily by the failure to resolve the Palestinian situation. While Palestine roils regional stability, the threat to world peace from a possible escalation of the regional threat has decreased.

Although the United States has in effect voided the policy of promoting stability at the expense of democracy in the Egyptian case by withdrawing its support for Mubarak and applauding his retirement, 30 years of favoring stability over democracy cannot be removed immediately from the collective minds of the Egyptian people. A certain level of mistrust is the inevitable consequence of this legacy, and its effect is to make it more difficult for the United States to advocate forthrightly and forcefully the kinds of change in Egypt that would most benefit American foreign policy. Indeed, there are undoubtedly elements in the emerging Egyptian political spectrum who would seize upon American advocacy of any actions as a red flag of unwanted and suspicious American interference that could taint the idea, as well as any Egyptians who appeared to be aligning themselves too closely to an American-favored position or toward the United States generally. It may be, in these circumstances, that the best the United States can do is privately and quietly to encourage moderate political democratization in Egypt while recognizing that there is relatively little the United States can do actively to promote that outcome. "In the wake of such upheavals" as Egypt, Gause writes, "both academics and policymakers should approach the Arab world with humility about their ability to shape its future." A certain level of impotence may simply be the price the United States must pay for its legacy of past associations with opponents of its own political philosophy.

STUDY/DISCUSSION QUESTIONS

1. Discuss the evolution of modern Egypt since 1952. How does the Arab Spring of 2011 represent a major change in that experience? Why is this change important to the United States?
2. Describe Egypt's place in the contemporary world. How do its physical attributes contribute to that status? What is unique about Egypt?
3. How have Egyptian–American relations evolved since the first Egyptian Revolution of 1952? Emphasize the role of the Yom Kippur War and the relationship with the Mubarak regime that resulted from the American response to that experience.
4. The text argues that ongoing U.S.–Egyptian relations can be described along three dimensions. What are they? Discuss each and how they are related to one another and to overall American interests in the region.

5. How much leverage does the United States have to influence the evolution of post–Arab Spring Egypt and its policies toward the United States? Why is this situation the case? How have past relations between the two countries affected the American ability to exercise influence?
6. What do you think that American foreign policy toward Egypt should be as that country moves toward some form of democracy? More specifically, how should the United States treat the possible rise of Islamic fundamentalism and the Muslim Brotherhood in Egypt? Defend your position.

READING/RESEARCH MATERIALS

Anderson, Lisa. "Demystifying the Arab Spring." *Foreign Affairs* 90, 3 (May/June 2011), 2–7.

Ayittey, George B. N. "The Worst of the Worst." *Foreign Policy* (July/August 2010), 90–91.

Bellin, Eva. "Democratization and Its Discontents: Should America Push Political Reform in the Middle East?" *Foreign Affairs* 87, 4 (July/August 2008), 112–119.

Bradley, John R. *Inside Egypt: The Land of the Pharaohs on the Brink of a Revolution.* New York: Palgrave Macmillan, 2008.

Brinton, Crane. *The Anatomy of Revolution* (revised edition). New York: Vintage Press, 1965.

Bynam, Daniel. "Terrorism after the Revolutions: How Secular Uprisings Could Help (or Hurt) Jihadists." *Foreign Affairs* 90, 3 (May/June 2011), 49–54.

Dickey, Christopher. "The Tragedy of Mubarak." *Newsweek* (February 21, 2011), 18–23.

Doran, Michael Scott. "The Heirs of Nasser: Who Will Benefit from the Second Arab Revolution?" *Foreign Affairs* 90, 3 (May/June 2011), 17–25.

Dunne, Michele. "The Baby, the Bathwater, and the Freedom Agenda in the Middle East." *Washington Quarterly* 32, 1 (January 2009), 129–141.

Ferguson, Niall. "The Revolution Blows Up." *Newsweek* (June 13/20, 2011), 7–8.

——— "Wanted: A Grand Strategy for America." *Newsweek* (February 21, 2011), 2–3.

Gause, F. Gregory III. "Why Middle East Studies Missed the Arab Spring." *Foreign Affairs* 90, 4 (July/August 2011), 81–90.

Goldstone, Jack A. "Understanding the Revolutions of 2011: Weakness and Resilience in Middle East Autocracies." *Foreign Affairs* 90, 3 (May/June 2011), 8–16.

Hamid, Shadi. "The Rise of the Islamists: How Islamists Will Change Politics, and Vice Versa." *Foreign Affairs* 90, 3 (May/June 2011), 40–47.

Ignatius, David. "What Happens When the Arab Spring Turns to Summer? Ruminations on the Revolutions of 2011." *Foreign Policy* (online), April 22, 2011.

Katulis, Brian. "Time to Rethink U.S.-Egyptian Relations." *Foreign Policy* (online), January 28, 2011.

Lalami, Leila. "Winter of Discontent." *Nation* 292, 8 (February 21, 2011), 9–10.

Latham, Michael E. *The Right Kind of Revolution: Modernization, Development and U.S. Foreign Policy from the Cold War to the Present.* Ithaca, NY: Cornell University Press, 2011.

Mark, Clyde R. *Egyptian-United States Relations.* Washington, DC: Congressional Research Service (Issue Brief for Congress), 2003.

Marsot, Afaf El-Sayyid. *A History of Egypt: From the Arab Conquest to the Present* (2nd ed.). Cambridge, UK: Cambridge University Press, 2007.

Martini, Jeff, and Julie Taylor. "Commanding Democracy in Egypt." *Foreign Affairs* 90, 5 (September/October 2011), 127–137.

Nakleh, Emile. " 'Moderates' Redefined: How to Deal with Political Islam." *Current History* 108, 722 (December 2009), 402–409.

Osman, Tarek. *Egypt on the Brink: From Nasser to Mubarak.* New Haven, CT: Yale University Press, 2010.

Ottoway, Marina. "The Rise and Fall of Political Reform in the Arab World." *Current History* 109, 731 (December 2010), 376–382.

———, and Julia Choucairivioso (eds.). *Beyond the Façade: Political Reform in the Arab World.* Washington, DC: Carnegie Endowment for International Peace, 2008.

Shehata, Dina. "The Fall of the Pharaoh: How Hosni Mubarak's Reign Came to an End." *Foreign Affairs* 90, 3 (May/June 2011), 26–32.

Shehata, Samer. "After Mubarak, Mubarak?" *Current History* 107, 713 (December 2008), 418–424.

Taleb, Nassim Nicholas, and Mark Blyth. "The Black Swan of Cairo: How Suppressing Volatility Makes the World Less Predictable and More Dangerous." *Foreign Affairs* 90, 3 (May/June 2011), 33–39.

Wittes, Tamara Cofman. *Freedom's Unsteady March: America's Role in Building Arab Democracy.* Washington, DC: Brookings Institution Press, 2008.

INDEX